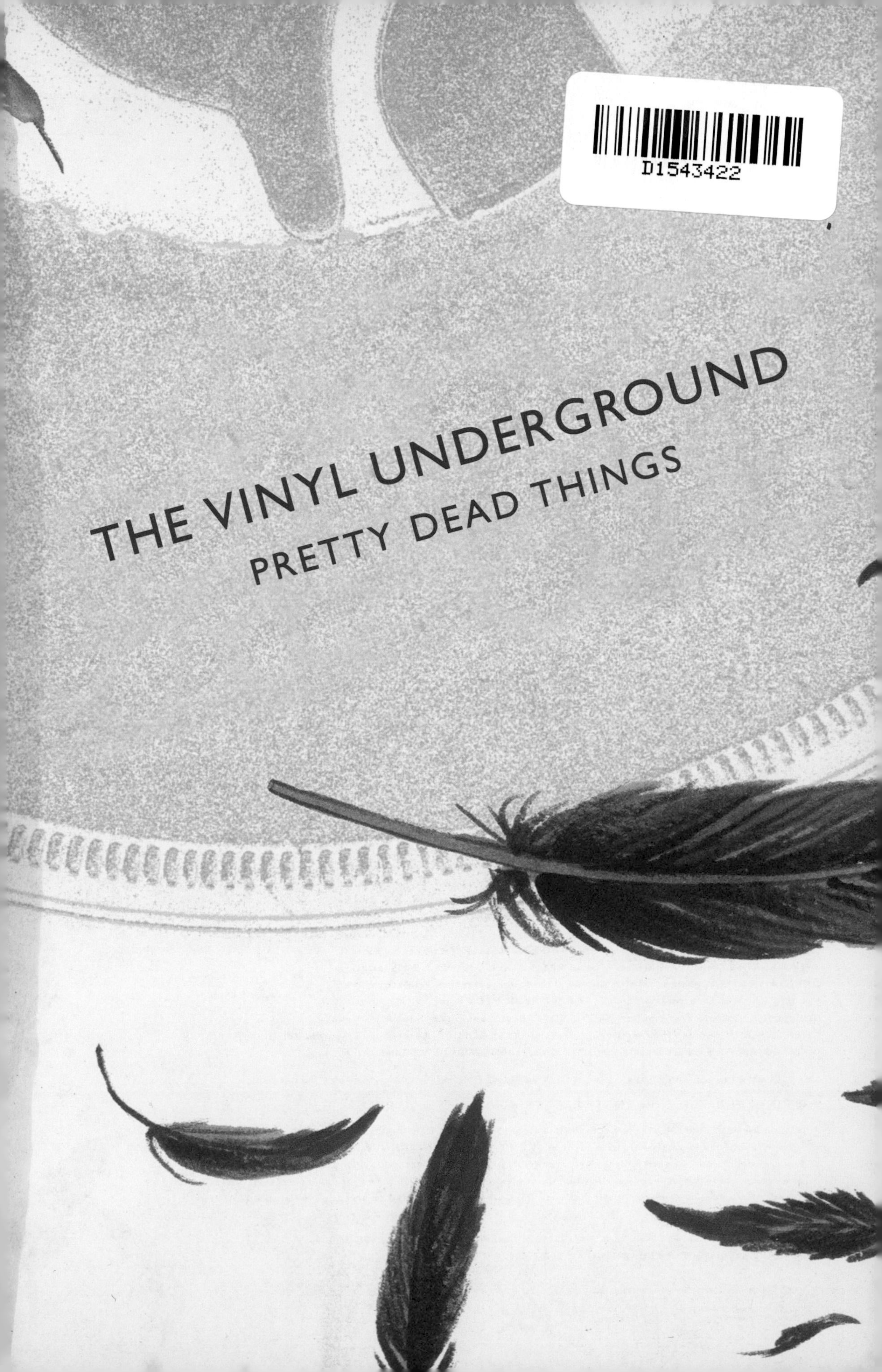
THE VINYL UNDERGROUND
PRETTY DEAD THINGS

KAREN BERGER Senior VP-Executive Editor   SHELLY BOND Editor-original series
ANGELA RUFINO Assistant Editor-original series   BOB HARRAS Editor-collected edition
ROBBIN BROSTERMAN Senior Art Director   PAUL LEVITZ President & Publisher
GEORG BREWER VP-Design & DC Direct Creative   RICHARD BRUNING Senior VP-Creative Director
PATRICK CALDON Executive VP-Finance & Operations   CHRIS CARAMALIS VP-Finance
JOHN CUNNINGHAM VP-Marketing   TERRI CUNNINGHAM VP-Managing Editor
AMY GENKINS Senior VP-Business & Legal Affairs   ALISON GILL VP-Manufacturing
DAVID HYDE VP-Publicity   HANK KANALZ VP-General Manager, WildStorm
JIM LEE Editorial Director-WildStorm   GREGORY NOVECK Senior VP-Creative Affairs
SUE POHJA VP-Book Trade Sales   STEVE ROTTERDAM Senior VP-Sales & Marketing
CHERYL RUBIN Senior VP-Brand Management   ALYSSE SOLL VP-Advertising & Custom Publishing
JEFF TROJAN VP-Business Development, DC Direct   BOB WAYNE VP-Sales

Cover illustration by Sean Phillips   Publication design by Amelia Grohman and Robbie Biederman

THE VINYL UNDERGROUND: PRETTY DEAD THINGS

DC Comics, 1700 Broadway, New York, NY 10019. A Warner Bros. Entertainment Company.
Printed in Canada. First Printing. ISBN 13: 978-1-4012-1977-2

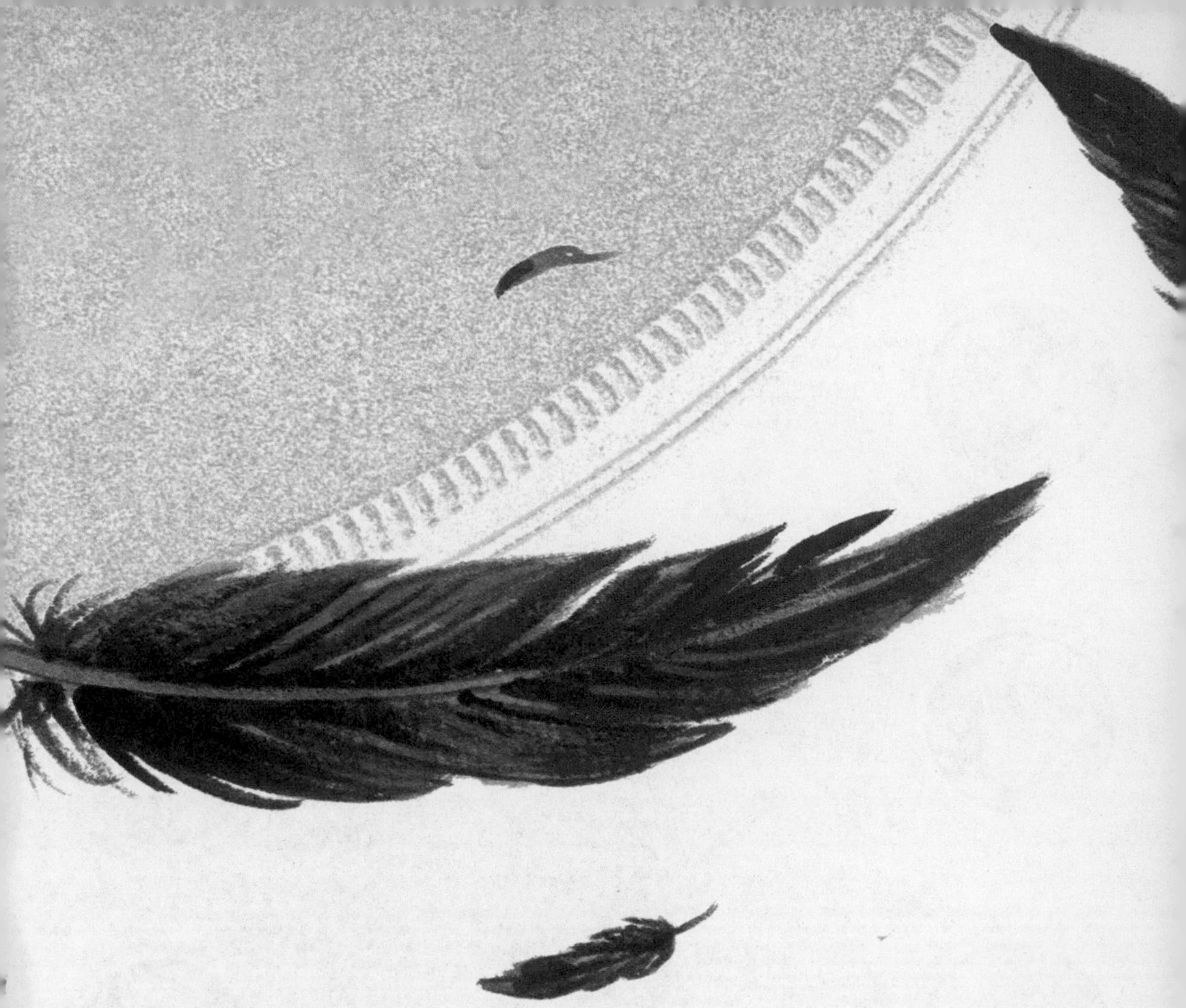

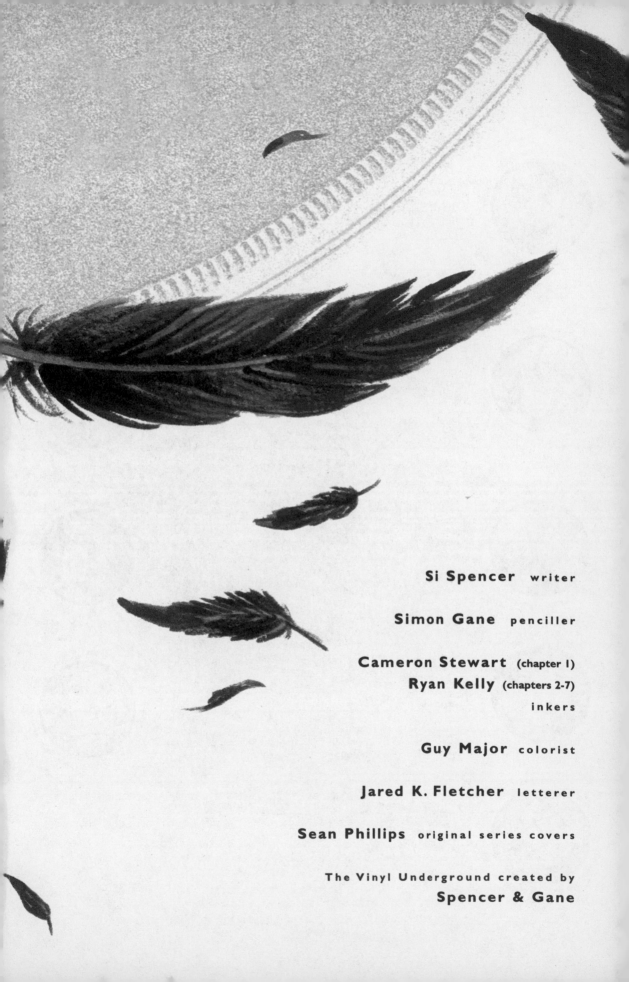

Si Spencer writer

Simon Gane penciller

Cameron Stewart (chapter 1)
Ryan Kelly (chapters 2-7)
inkers

Guy Major colorist

Jared K. Fletcher letterer

Sean Phillips original series covers

The Vinyl Underground created by
Spencer & Gane

WHO'S WHO IN THE VINYL UNDERGROUND:

MORRISON "MOZ" SHEPHERD
DJ, D-lister, and darling of the tabloids, Morrison was once London's premier wild child. Drink and drugs led to a stint in prison, from which he emerged clean and sober—and with a degree in criminology that he uses to crack occult crimes with his motley but glamorous crew, The Vinyl Underground.

CALLUM "PERV" O'CONNOR
Asthmatic psychic who recovered from child abuse by busting online predators—then got busted himself for stealing their money. Perv's seizure-like visions reveal each new case before it starts.

LEAH "JUICY LOU" HAYES
Mortuary worker by day, the Internet's only virgin porn star by night, nymphomaniac and pyromianiac round-the-clock. Leah uncovers the clues found in each corpse and serves as the group's muscle.

KIM "ABI" ABIOLA
Exiled African tribal princess—and Morrison's ex-fiancée—who makes London her adopted home. Abi's an honors grad with an encyclopedic knowledge of London's secret geography. Morrison cheated on her with half of London while she was pregnant. She did not keep the baby.

DETECTIVE SERGEANT CAULFIELD
Police officer who resents Morrison's ability to beat her to the culprit. She spies on Moz and his activities even as she uses his expertise to clear cases.

BOBBY "MR. CLEAN" SHEPHERD
Morrison's father—a famous footballer who got mixed up with the mob and died young in a tragic car accident.

SONIA RASMUSSEN SHEPHERD
Morrison's mother—a porn queen turned soap star who disappeared under mysterious circumstances after turning her son on to drugs.

TOMMY "THE TOOLBOX" McARDLE
One of London's original gangsters and a close friend of the Shepherd family, he's Morrison's connection to the underworld.

LANGLEY
Scumbag mobster acquaintance of Tommy, Bobby, and Sonia with whom he fathered a child before Sonia's disappearance. He was recently found hanged in his cell after a visit from…

…THE VINYL UNDERGROUND

You know they've been there if you receive a 45 piece of vinyl of the Northern Soul Variety.

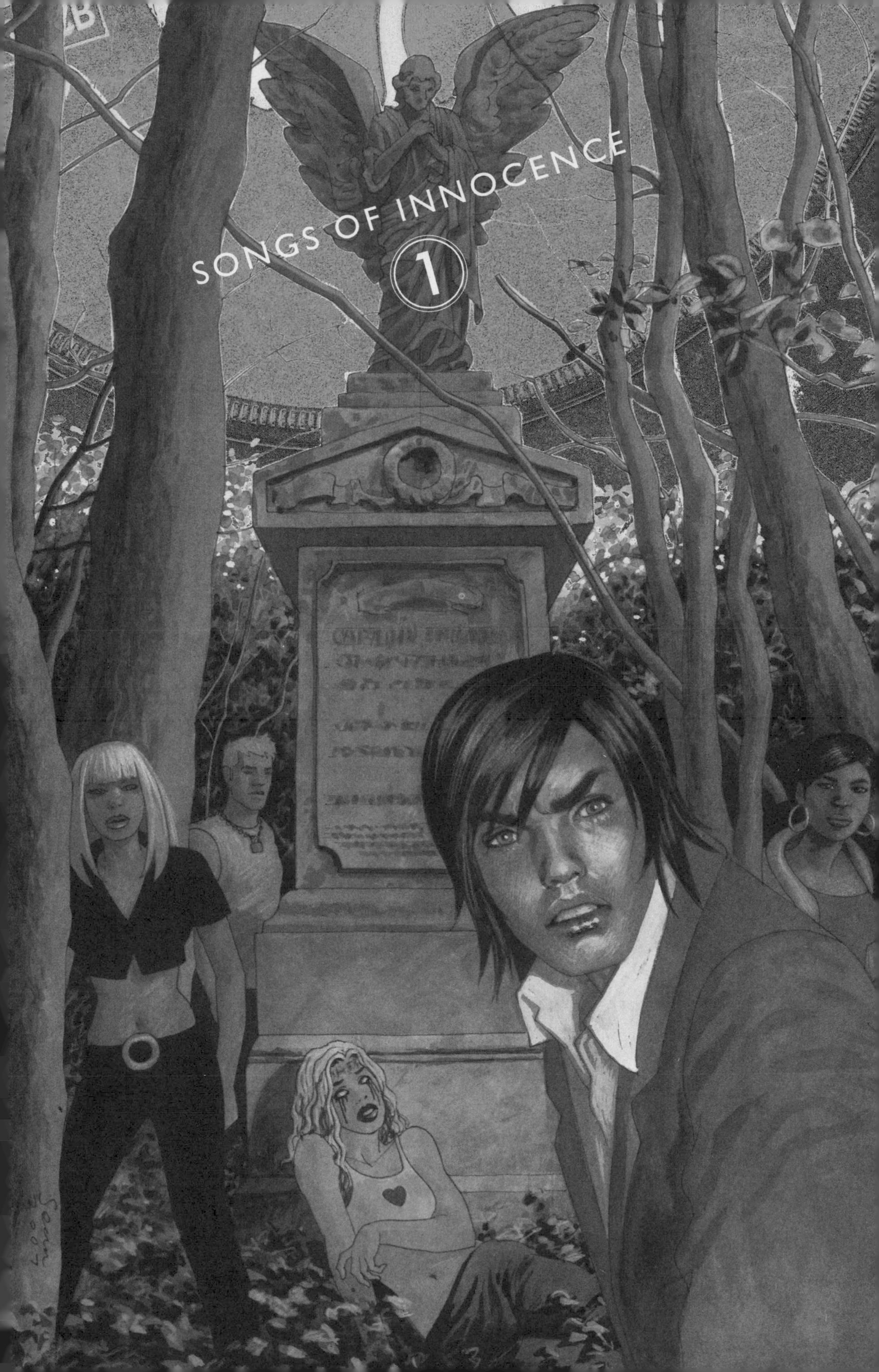
SONGS OF INNOCENCE
1

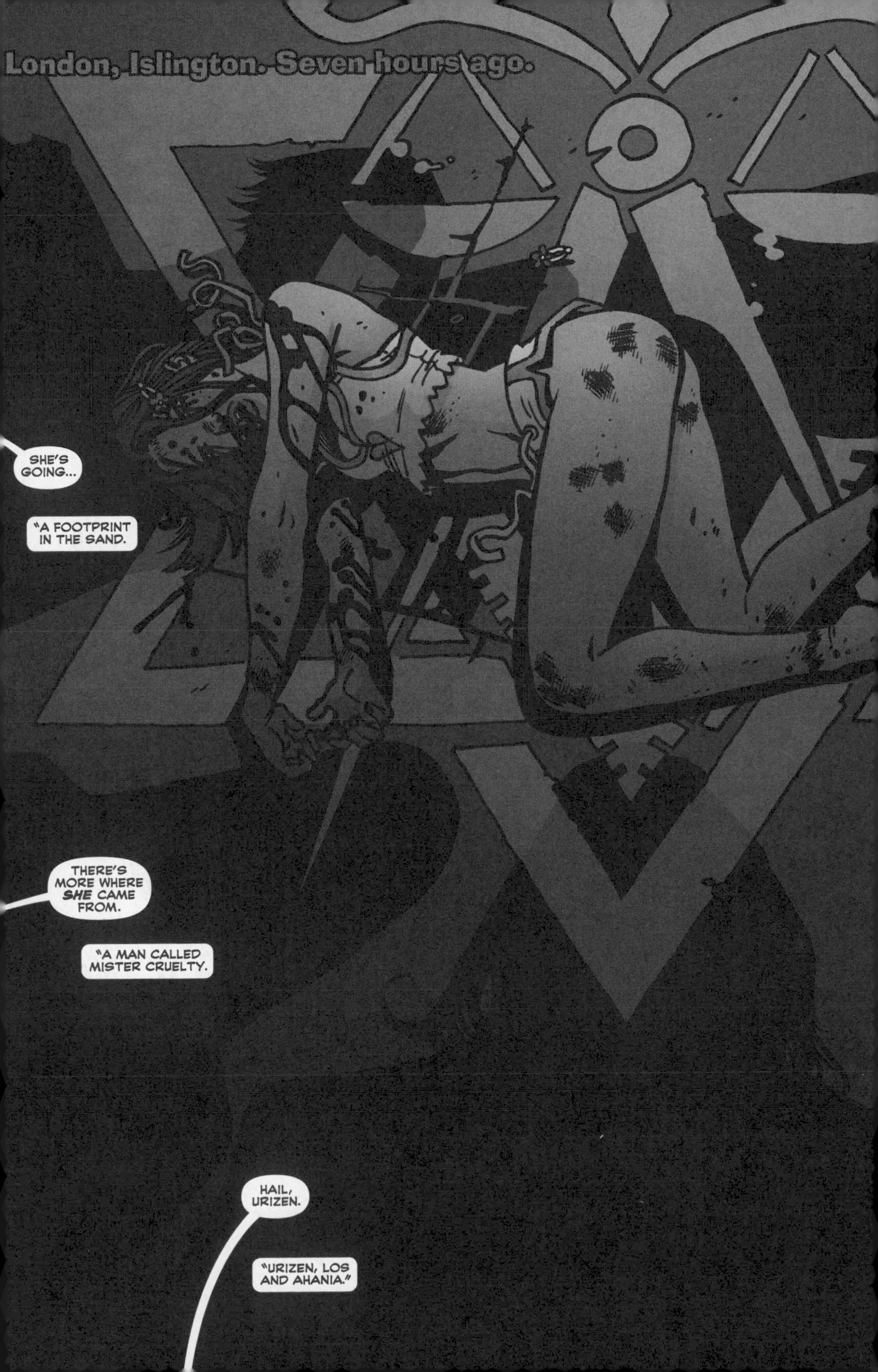
London, Islington. Seven hours ago.
SHE'S GOING...
"A FOOTPRINT IN THE SAND.
THERE'S MORE WHERE *SHE* CAME FROM.
"A MAN CALLED MISTER CRUELTY.
HAIL, URIZEN.
"URIZEN, LOS AND AHANIA."

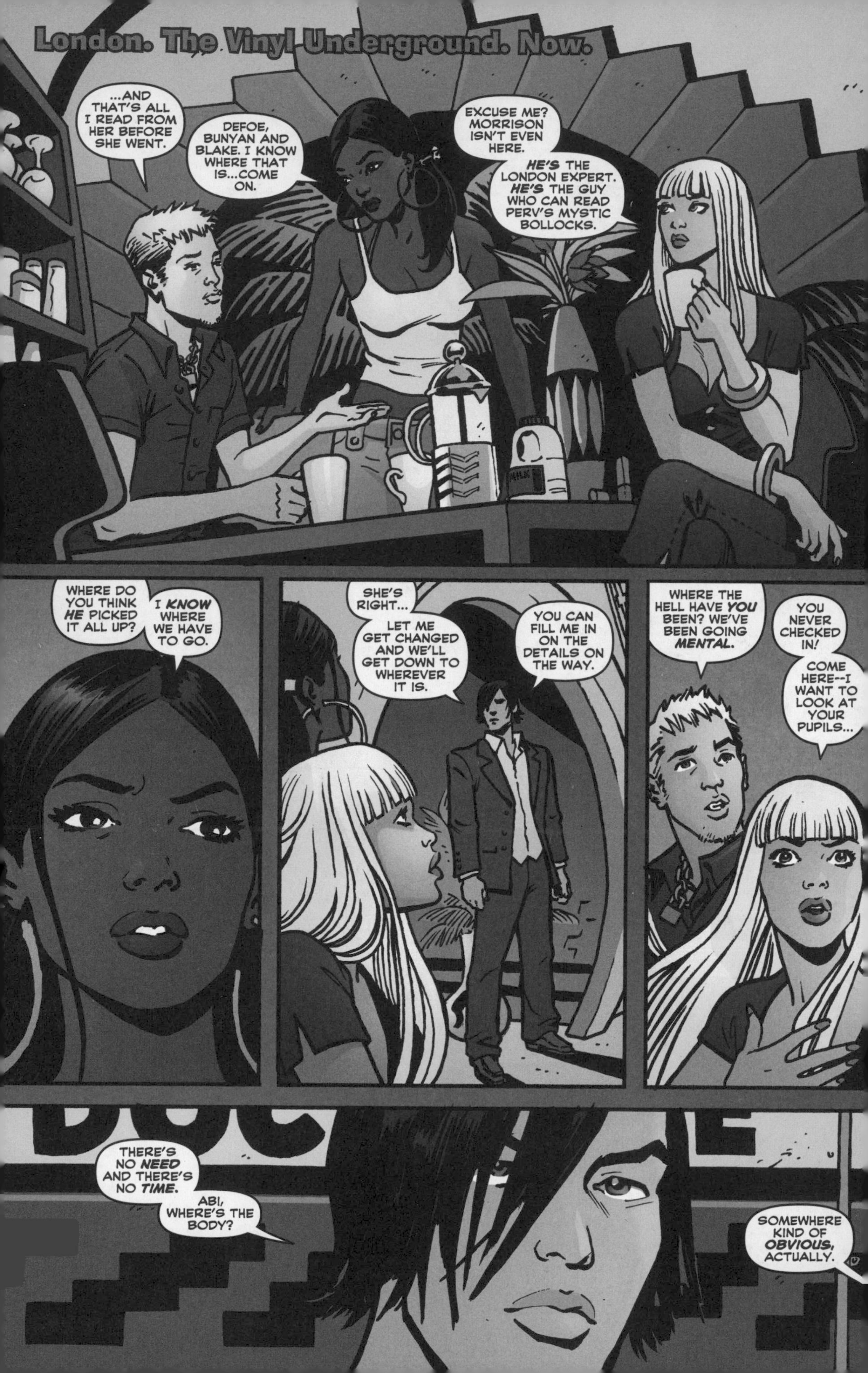
London. The Vinyl Underground. Now.
...AND THAT'S ALL I READ FROM HER BEFORE SHE WENT.
DEFOE, BUNYAN AND BLAKE. I KNOW WHERE THAT IS...COME ON.
EXCUSE ME? MORRISON ISN'T EVEN HERE.
HE'S THE LONDON EXPERT. HE'S THE GUY WHO CAN READ PERV'S MYSTIC BOLLOCKS.
WHERE DO YOU THINK HE PICKED IT ALL UP?
I KNOW WHERE WE HAVE TO GO.
SHE'S RIGHT...
LET ME GET CHANGED AND WE'LL GET DOWN TO WHEREVER IT IS.
YOU CAN FILL ME IN ON THE DETAILS ON THE WAY.
WHERE THE HELL HAVE YOU BEEN? WE'VE BEEN GOING MENTAL.
YOU NEVER CHECKED IN!
COME HERE--I WANT TO LOOK AT YOUR PUPILS...
THERE'S NO NEED AND THERE'S NO TIME.
ABI, WHERE'S THE BODY?
SOMEWHERE KIND OF OBVIOUS, ACTUALLY.

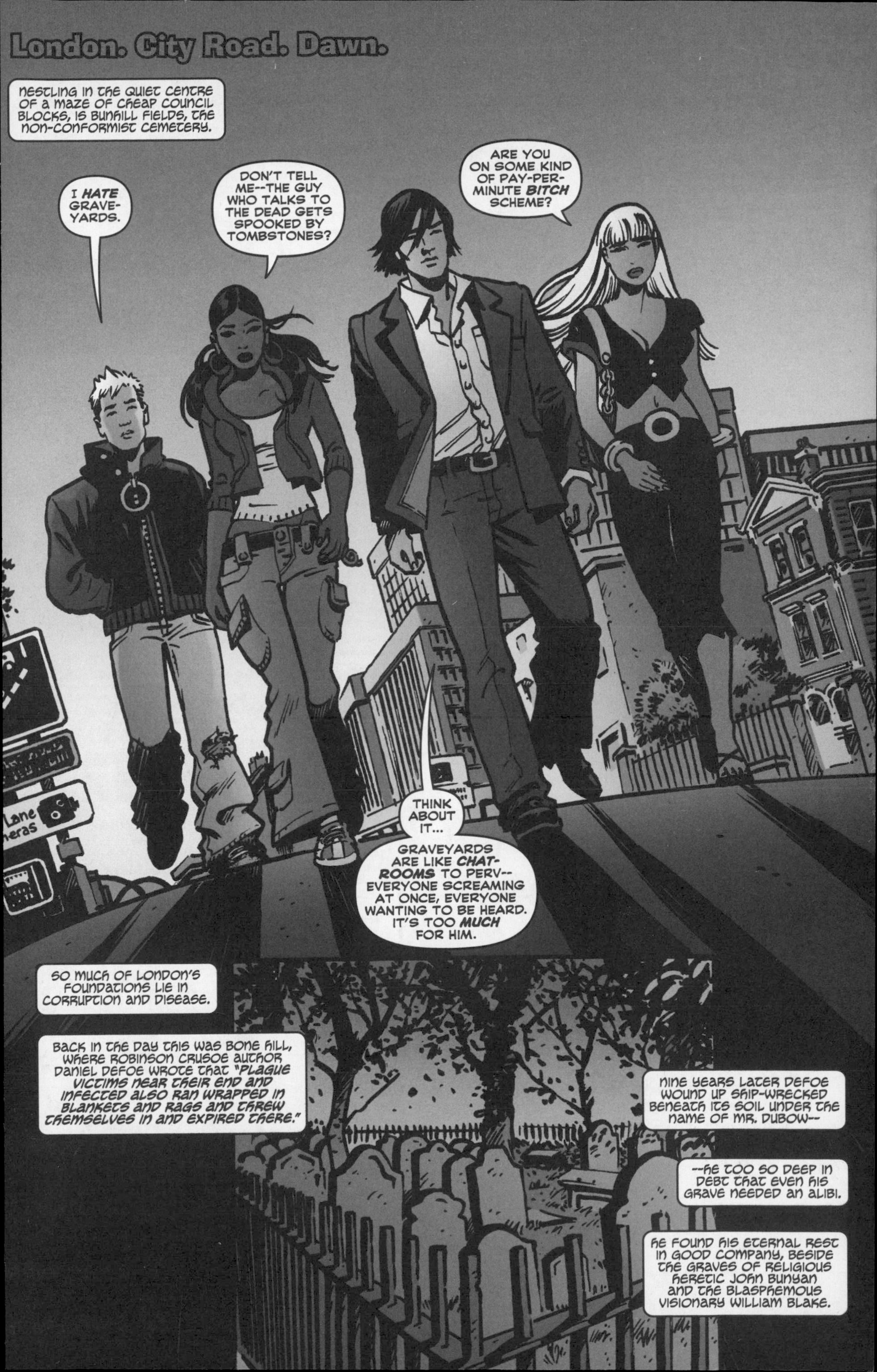
London. City Road. Dawn.
NESTLING IN THE QUIET CENTRE OF A MAZE OF CHEAP COUNCIL BLOCKS, IS BUNHILL FIELDS, THE NON-CONFORMIST CEMETERY.
I *HATE* GRAVE-YARDS.
DON'T TELL ME--THE GUY WHO TALKS TO THE DEAD GETS SPOOKED BY TOMBSTONES?
ARE YOU ON SOME KIND OF PAY-PER-MINUTE *BITCH* SCHEME?
THINK ABOUT IT...
GRAVEYARDS ARE LIKE *CHAT-ROOMS* TO PERV--EVERYONE SCREAMING AT ONCE, EVERYONE WANTING TO BE HEARD. IT'S TOO *MUCH* FOR HIM.
SO MUCH OF LONDON'S FOUNDATIONS LIE IN CORRUPTION AND DISEASE.
BACK IN THE DAY THIS WAS BONE HILL, WHERE ROBINSON CRUSOE AUTHOR DANIEL DEFOE WROTE THAT *"PLAGUE VICTIMS NEAR THEIR END AND INFECTED ALSO RAN WRAPPED IN BLANKETS AND RAGS AND THREW THEMSELVES IN AND EXPIRED THERE."*
NINE YEARS LATER DEFOE WOUND UP SHIP-WRECKED BENEATH ITS SOIL UNDER THE NAME OF MR. DUBOW--
--HE TOO SO DEEP IN DEBT THAT EVEN HIS GRAVE NEEDED AN ALIBI.
HE FOUND HIS ETERNAL REST IN GOOD COMPANY, BESIDE THE GRAVES OF RELIGIOUS HERETIC JOHN BUNYAN AND THE BLASPHEMOUS VISIONARY WILLIAM BLAKE.

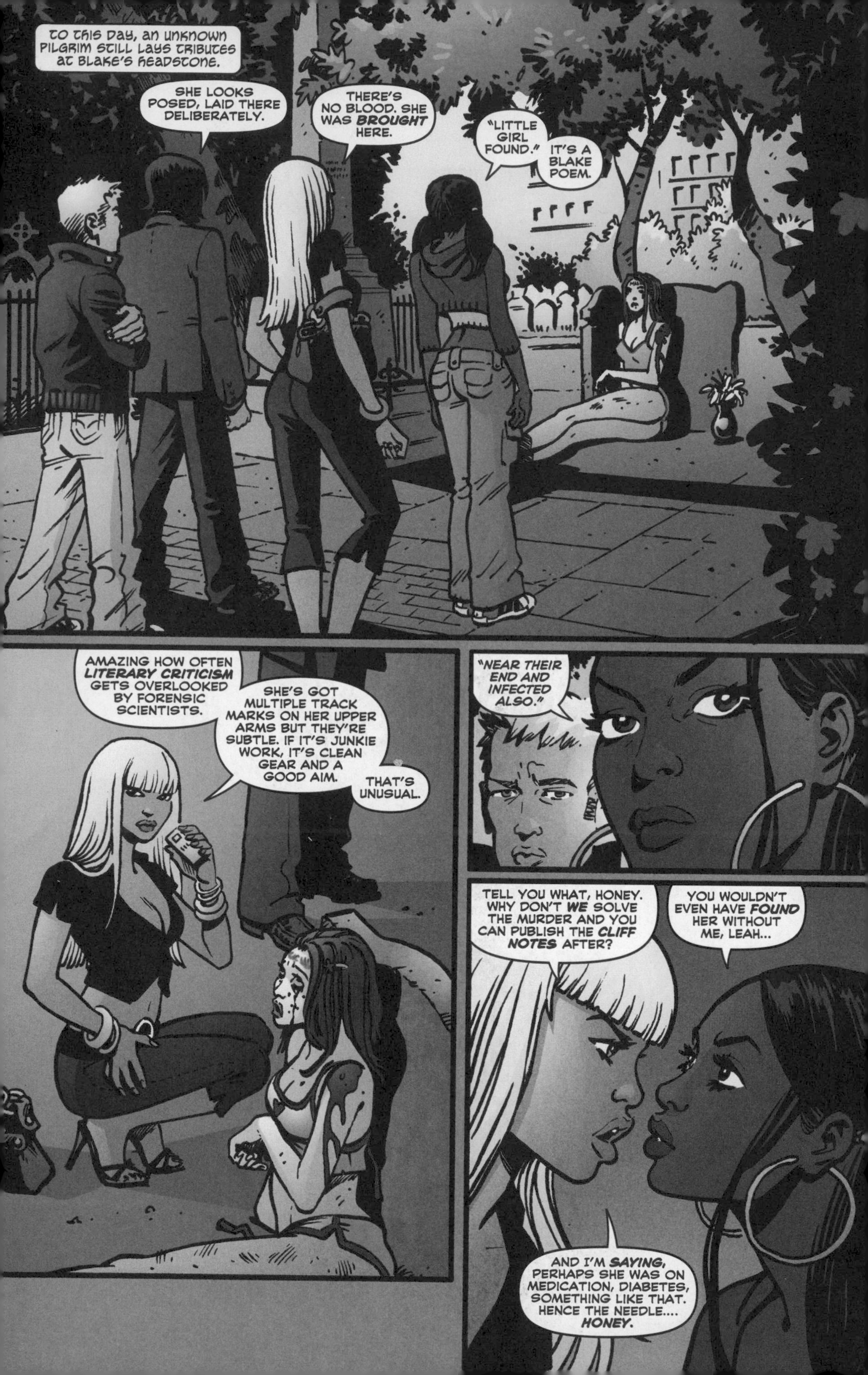
TO THIS DAY, AN UNKNOWN PILGRIM STILL LAYS TRIBUTES AT BLAKE'S HEADSTONE.
SHE LOOKS POSED, LAID THERE DELIBERATELY.
THERE'S NO BLOOD. SHE WAS BROUGHT HERE.
"LITTLE GIRL FOUND."
IT'S A BLAKE POEM.
AMAZING HOW OFTEN LITERARY CRITICISM GETS OVERLOOKED BY FORENSIC SCIENTISTS.
SHE'S GOT MULTIPLE TRACK MARKS ON HER UPPER ARMS BUT THEY'RE SUBTLE. IF IT'S JUNKIE WORK, IT'S CLEAN GEAR AND A GOOD AIM.
THAT'S UNUSUAL.
"NEAR THEIR END AND INFECTED ALSO."
TELL YOU WHAT, HONEY. WHY DON'T WE SOLVE THE MURDER AND YOU CAN PUBLISH THE CLIFF NOTES AFTER?
YOU WOULDN'T EVEN HAVE FOUND HER WITHOUT ME, LEAH...
AND I'M SAYING, PERHAPS SHE WAS ON MEDICATION, DIABETES, SOMETHING LIKE THAT. HENCE THE NEEDLE.... HONEY.

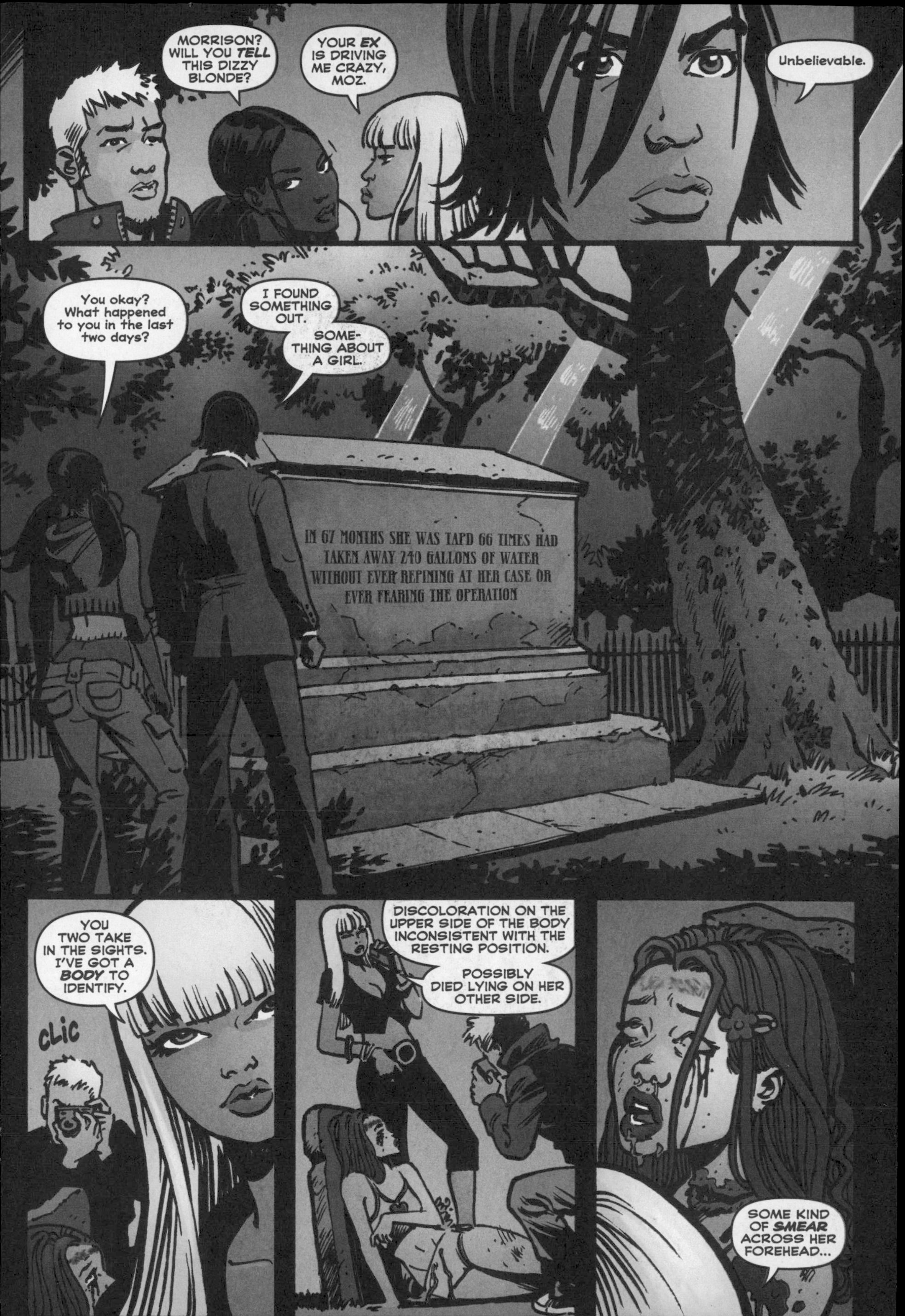
MORRISON? WILL YOU TELL THIS DIZZY BLONDE?
YOUR EX IS DRIVING ME CRAZY, MOZ.
Unbelievable.
You okay? What happened to you in the last two days?
I FOUND SOMETHING OUT.
SOME-THING ABOUT A GIRL.
IN 67 MONTHS SHE WAS TAPD 66 TIMES HAD TAKEN AWAY 240 GALLONS OF WATER WITHOUT EVER REPINING AT HER CASE OR EVER FEARING THE OPERATION
YOU TWO TAKE IN THE SIGHTS. I'VE GOT A BODY TO IDENTIFY.
CLIC
DISCOLORATION ON THE UPPER SIDE OF THE BODY INCONSISTENT WITH THE RESTING POSITION.
POSSIBLY DIED LYING ON HER OTHER SIDE.
SOME KIND OF SMEAR ACROSS HER FOREHEAD...

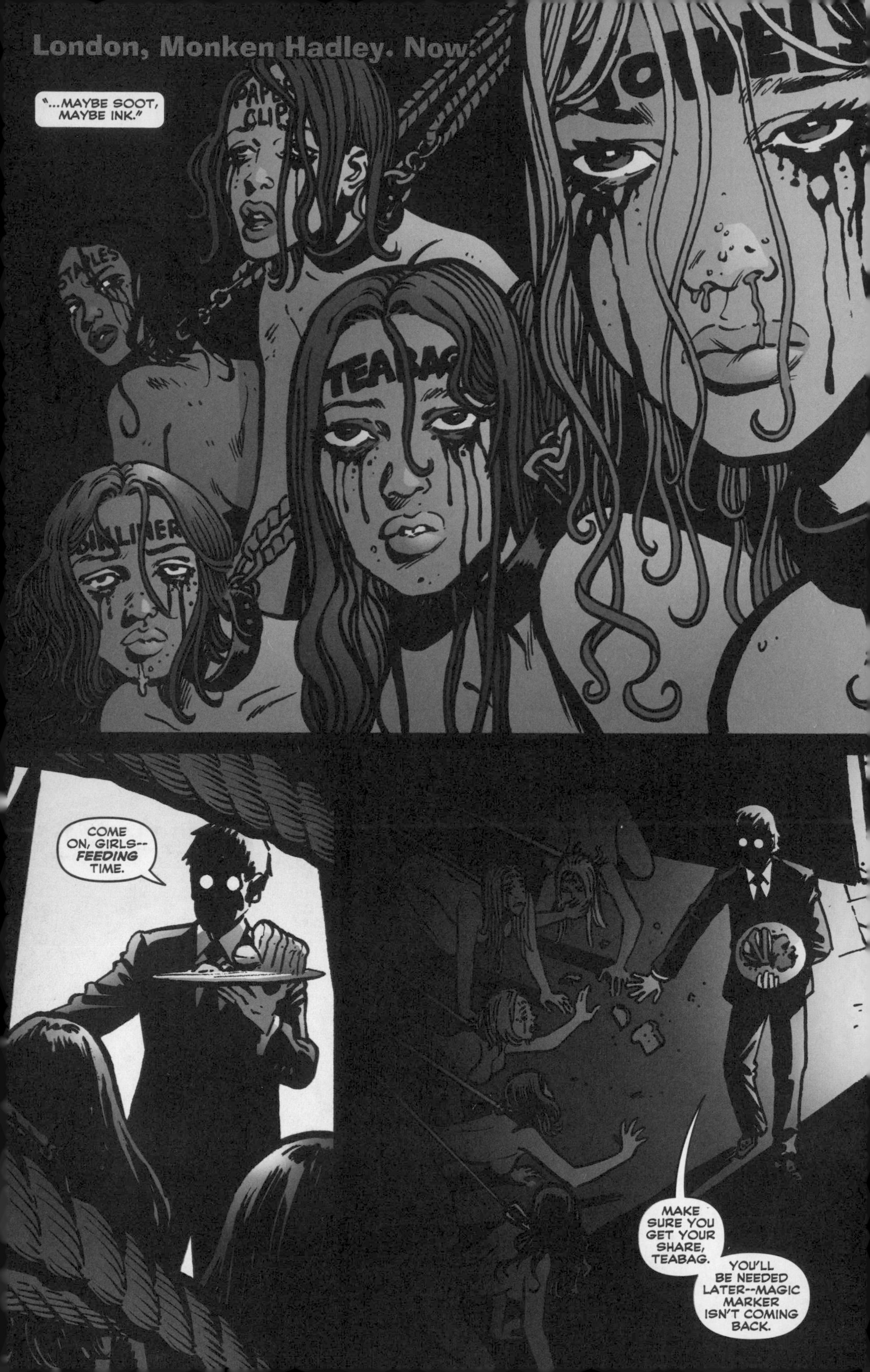
London, Monken Hadley. Now.
"...MAYBE SOOT, MAYBE INK."
STAPLES
COME ON, GIRLS-- FEEDING TIME.
MAKE SURE YOU GET YOUR SHARE, TEABAG.
YOU'LL BE NEEDED LATER--MAGIC MARKER ISN'T COMING BACK.

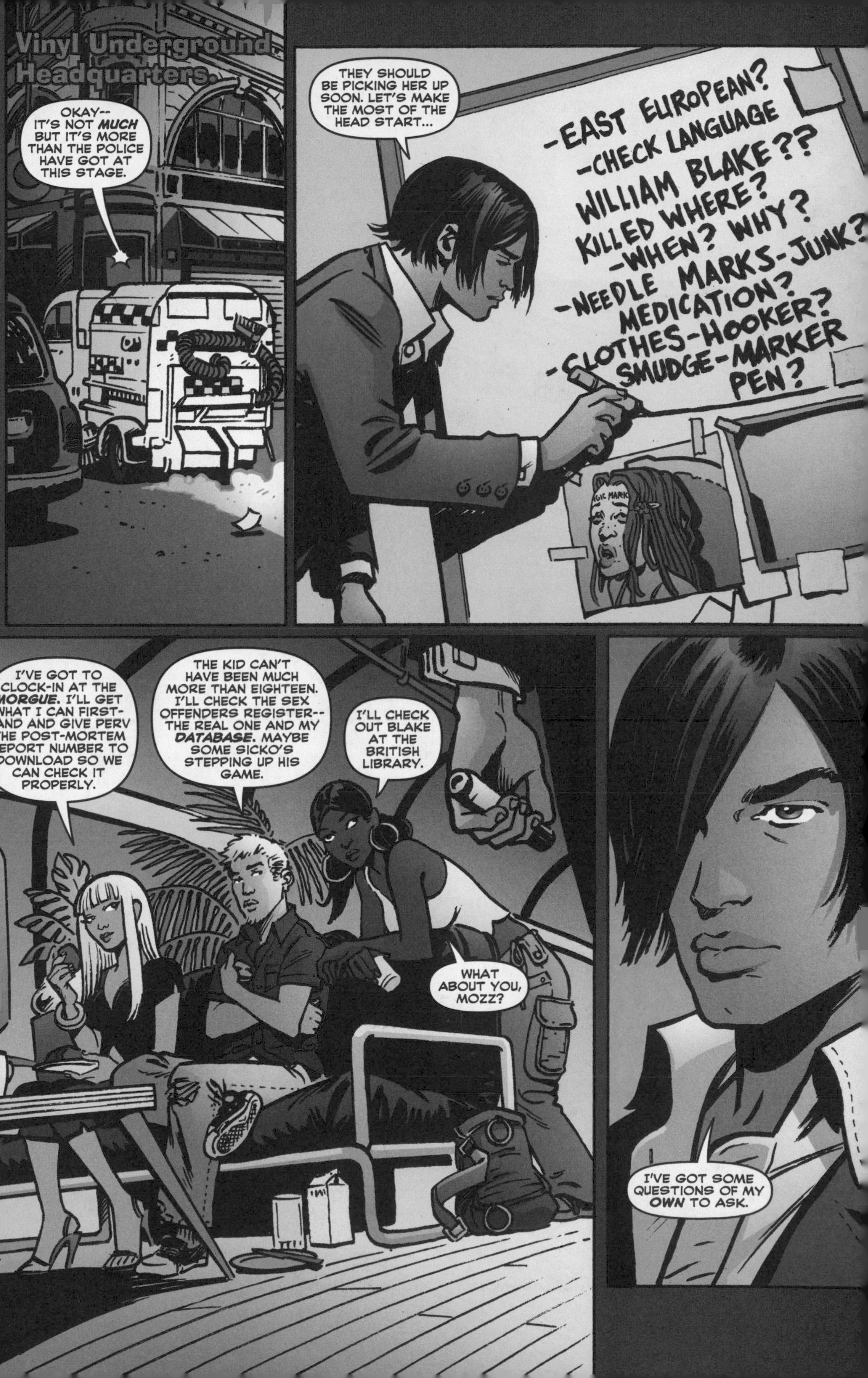
Vinyl Underground Headquarters.
OKAY-- IT'S NOT MUCH BUT IT'S MORE THAN THE POLICE HAVE GOT AT THIS STAGE.
THEY SHOULD BE PICKING HER UP SOON. LET'S MAKE THE MOST OF THE HEAD START...
-EAST EUROPEAN?
-CHECK LANGUAGE
WILLIAM BLAKE??
KILLED WHERE?
-WHEN? WHY?
-NEEDLE MARKS-JUNK?
MEDICATION?
-CLOTHES-HOOKER?
SMUDGE-MARKER PEN?
I'VE GOT TO CLOCK-IN AT THE MORGUE. I'LL GET WHAT I CAN FIRST-HAND AND GIVE PERV THE POST-MORTEM REPORT NUMBER TO DOWNLOAD SO WE CAN CHECK IT PROPERLY.
THE KID CAN'T HAVE BEEN MUCH MORE THAN EIGHTEEN. I'LL CHECK THE SEX OFFENDERS REGISTER-- THE REAL ONE AND MY DATABASE. MAYBE SOME SICKO'S STEPPING UP HIS GAME.
I'LL CHECK OUT BLAKE AT THE BRITISH LIBRARY.
WHAT ABOUT YOU, MOZZ?
I'VE GOT SOME QUESTIONS OF MY OWN TO ASK.

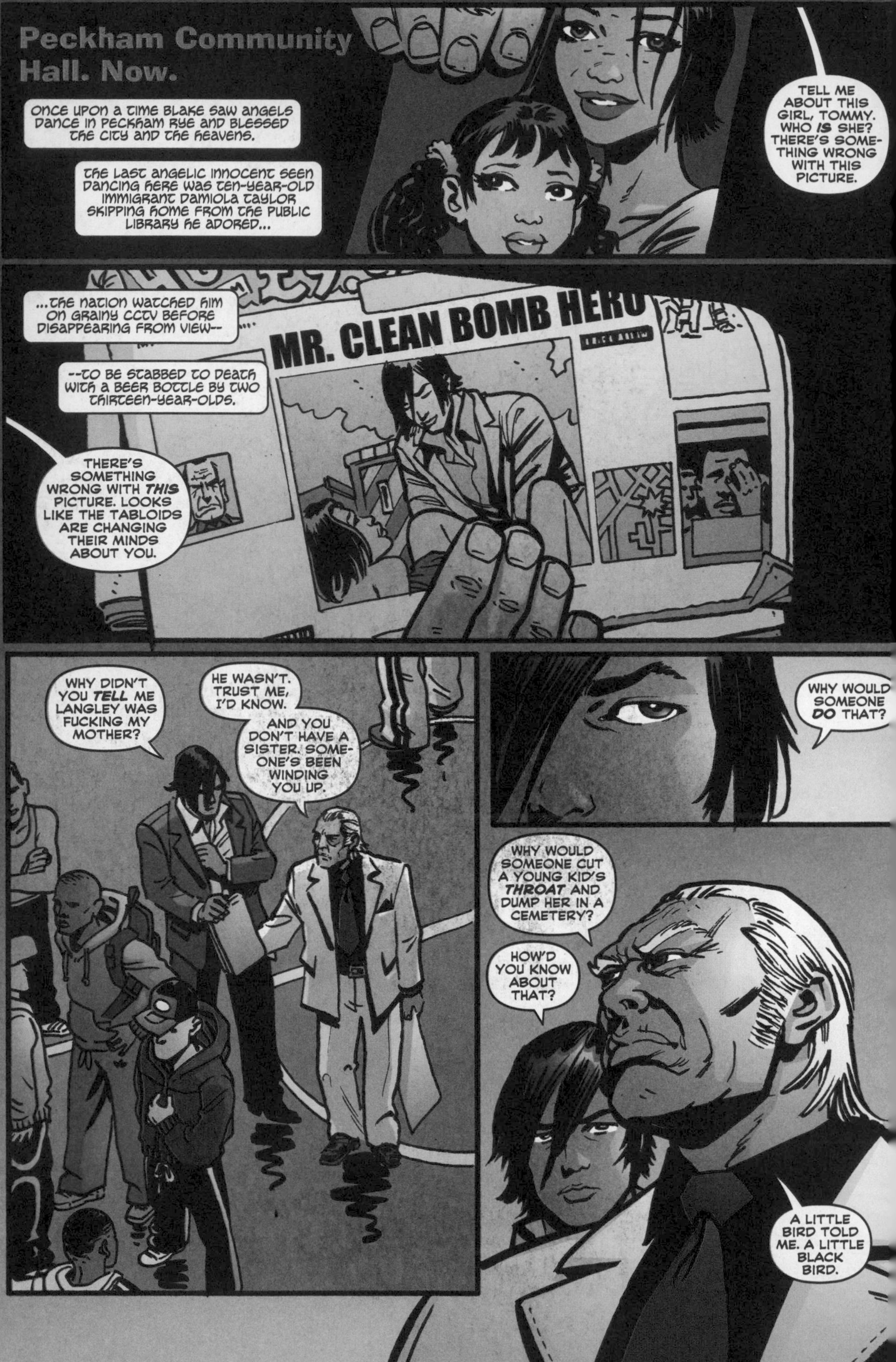
Peckham Community Hall. Now.
Once upon a time Blake saw angels dance in Peckham Rye and blessed the city and the heavens.
The last angelic innocent seen dancing here was ten-year-old immigrant Damiola Taylor skipping home from the public library he adored...
TELL ME ABOUT THIS GIRL, TOMMY. WHO IS SHE? THERE'S SOMETHING WRONG WITH THIS PICTURE.
...the nation watched him on grainy CCTV before disappearing from view--
--to be stabbed to death with a beer bottle by two thirteen-year-olds.
MR. CLEAN BOMB HERO
THERE'S SOMETHING WRONG WITH THIS PICTURE. LOOKS LIKE THE TABLOIDS ARE CHANGING THEIR MINDS ABOUT YOU.
WHY DIDN'T YOU TELL ME LANGLEY WAS FUCKING MY MOTHER?
HE WASN'T. TRUST ME, I'D KNOW.
AND YOU DON'T HAVE A SISTER. SOMEONE'S BEEN WINDING YOU UP.
WHY WOULD SOMEONE DO THAT?
WHY WOULD SOMEONE CUT A YOUNG KID'S THROAT AND DUMP HER IN A CEMETERY?
HOW'D YOU KNOW ABOUT THAT?
A LITTLE BIRD TOLD ME. A LITTLE BLACK BIRD.

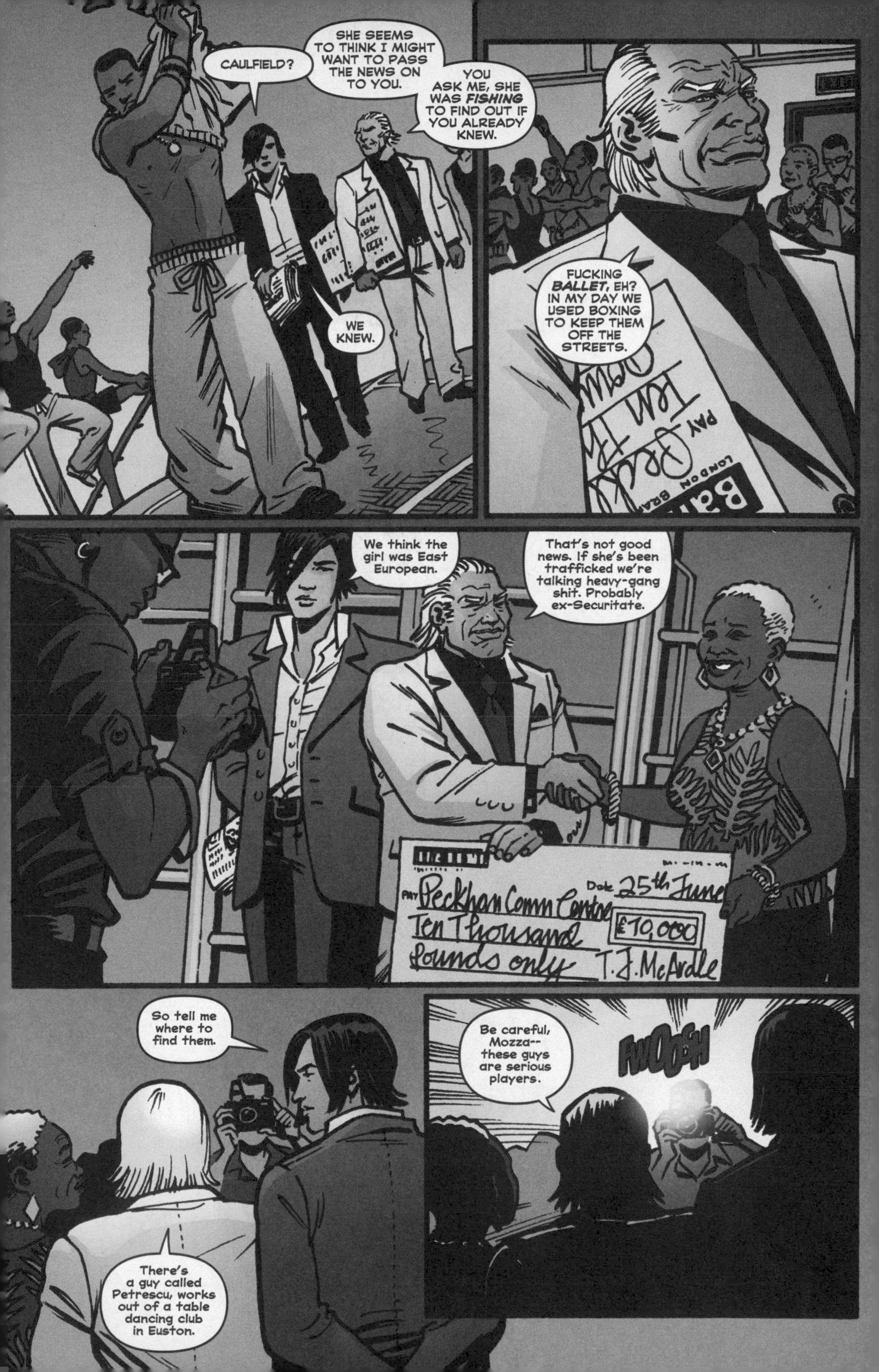
CAULFIELD?
SHE SEEMS TO THINK I MIGHT WANT TO PASS THE NEWS ON TO YOU.
YOU ASK ME, SHE WAS FISHING TO FIND OUT IF YOU ALREADY KNEW.
WE KNEW.
FUCKING BALLET, EH? IN MY DAY WE USED BOXING TO KEEP THEM OFF THE STREETS.
We think the girl was East European.
That's not good news. If she's been trafficked we're talking heavy-gang shit. Probably ex-Securitate.
Peckham Comm Centre
25th June
Ten Thousand Pounds only
£10,000
T.J. McArdle
So tell me where to find them.
There's a guy called Petrescu, works out of a table dancing club in Euston.
Be careful, Mozza-- these guys are serious players.
FWOOSH

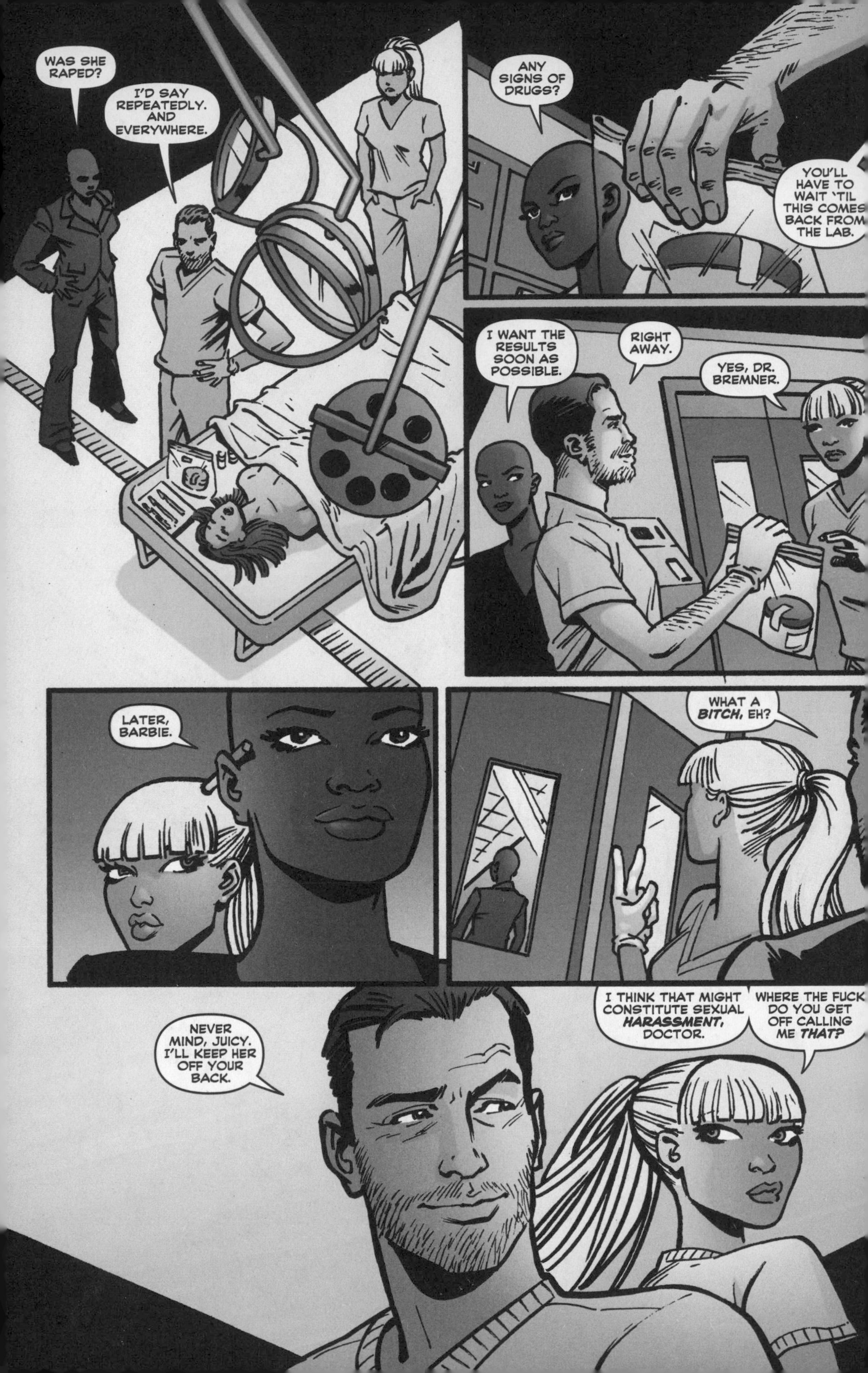
WAS SHE RAPED?
I'D SAY REPEATEDLY. AND EVERYWHERE.
ANY SIGNS OF DRUGS?
YOU'LL HAVE TO WAIT 'TIL THIS COMES BACK FROM THE LAB.
I WANT THE RESULTS SOON AS POSSIBLE.
RIGHT AWAY.
YES, DR. BREMNER.
LATER, BARBIE.
WHAT A *BITCH*, EH?
NEVER MIND, JUICY. I'LL KEEP HER OFF YOUR BACK.
I THINK THAT MIGHT CONSTITUTE SEXUAL *HARASSMENT*, DOCTOR.
WHERE THE FUCK DO YOU GET OFF CALLING ME *THAT?*

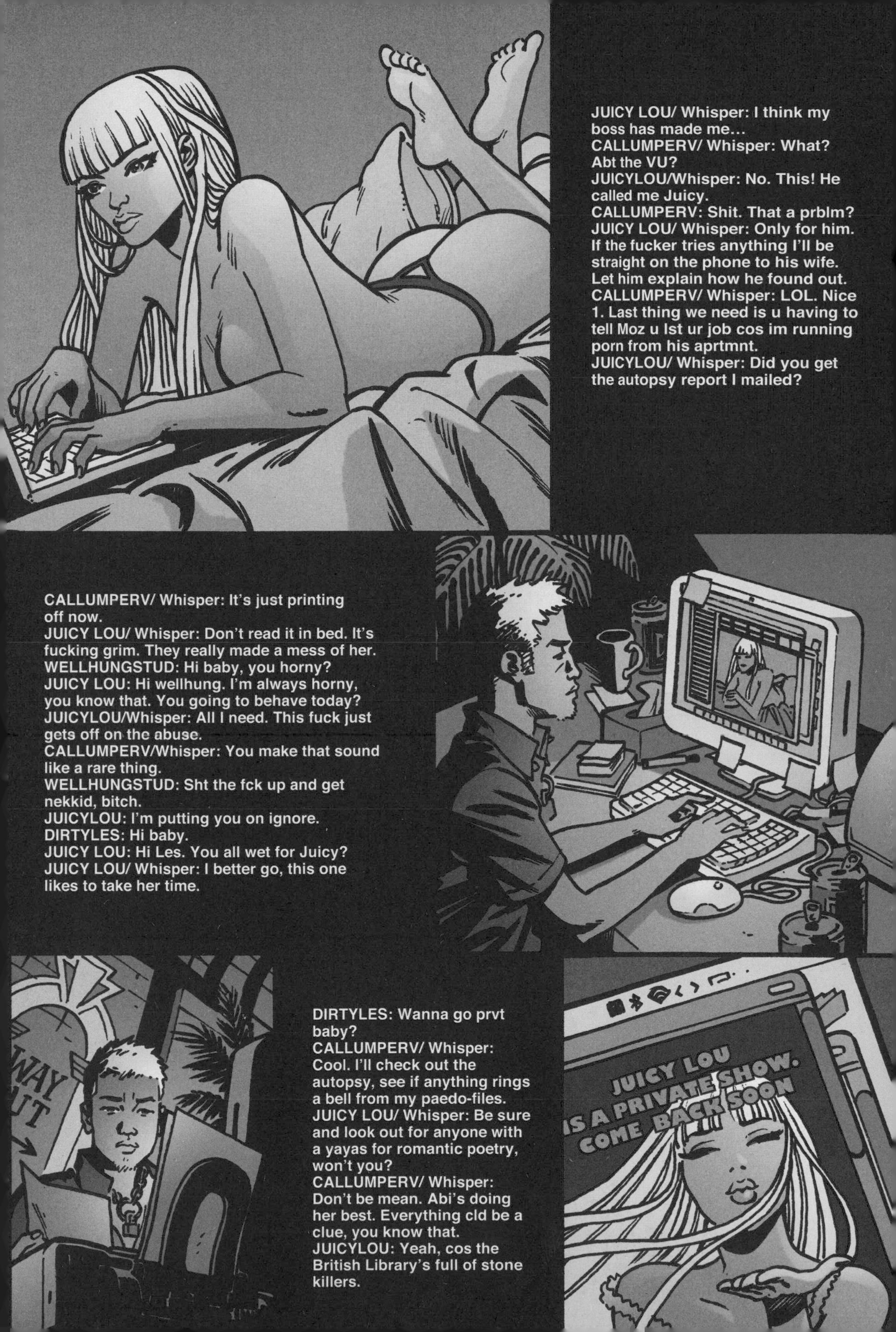
JUICY LOU/ Whisper: I think my boss has made me...
CALLUMPERV/ Whisper: What? Abt the VU?
JUICYLOU/Whisper: No. This! He called me Juicy.
CALLUMPERV: Shit. That a prblm?
JUICY LOU/ Whisper: Only for him. If the fucker tries anything I'll be straight on the phone to his wife. Let him explain how he found out.
CALLUMPERV/ Whisper: LOL. Nice 1. Last thing we need is u having to tell Moz u lst ur job cos im running porn from his aprtmnt.
JUICYLOU/ Whisper: Did you get the autopsy report I mailed?
CALLUMPERV/ Whisper: It's just printing off now.
JUICY LOU/ Whisper: Don't read it in bed. It's fucking grim. They really made a mess of her.
WELLHUNGSTUD: Hi baby, you horny?
JUICY LOU: Hi wellhung. I'm always horny, you know that. You going to behave today?
JUICYLOU/Whisper: All I need. This fuck just gets off on the abuse.
CALLUMPERV/Whisper: You make that sound like a rare thing.
WELLHUNGSTUD: Sht the fck up and get nekkid, bitch.
JUICYLOU: I'm putting you on ignore.
DIRTYLES: Hi baby.
JUICY LOU: Hi Les. You all wet for Juicy?
JUICY LOU/ Whisper: I better go, this one likes to take her time.
DIRTYLES: Wanna go prvt baby?
CALLUMPERV/ Whisper: Cool. I'll check out the autopsy, see if anything rings a bell from my paedo-files.
JUICY LOU/ Whisper: Be sure and look out for anyone with a yayas for romantic poetry, won't you?
CALLUMPERV/ Whisper: Don't be mean. Abi's doing her best. Everything cld be a clue, you know that.
JUICYLOU: Yeah, cos the British Library's full of stone killers.
JUICY LOU
IS A PRIVATE SHOW.
COME BACK SOON

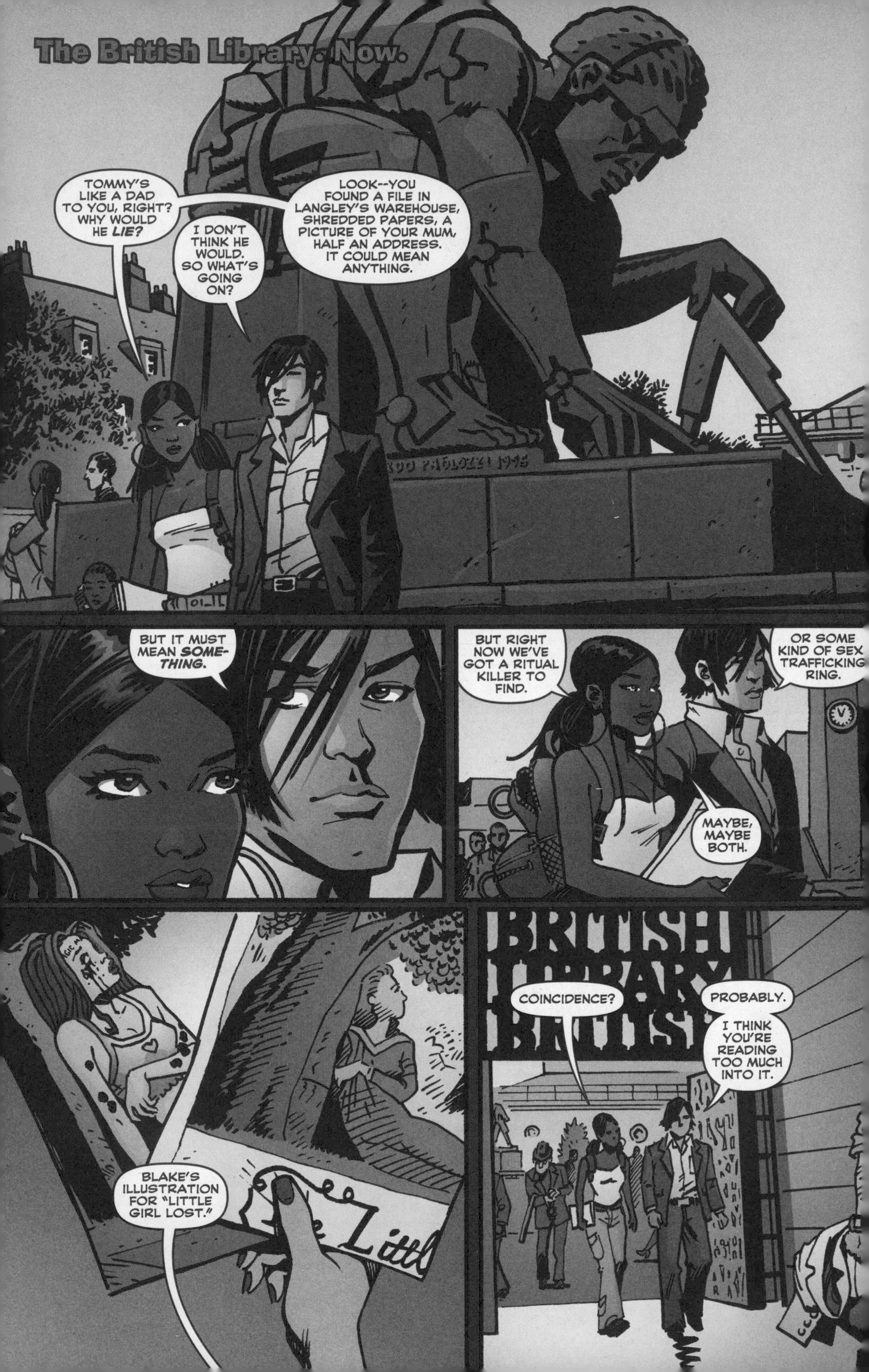
The British Library. Now.
TOMMY'S LIKE A DAD TO YOU, RIGHT? WHY WOULD HE LIE?
I DON'T THINK HE WOULD. SO WHAT'S GOING ON?
LOOK--YOU FOUND A FILE IN LANGLEY'S WAREHOUSE, SHREDDED PAPERS, A PICTURE OF YOUR MUM, HALF AN ADDRESS. IT COULD MEAN ANYTHING.
BUT IT MUST MEAN SOME-THING.
BUT RIGHT NOW WE'VE GOT A RITUAL KILLER TO FIND.
OR SOME KIND OF SEX TRAFFICKING RING.
MAYBE, MAYBE BOTH.
BLAKE'S ILLUSTRATION FOR "LITTLE GIRL LOST."
BRITISH LIBRARY
COINCIDENCE?
PROBABLY.
I THINK YOU'RE READING TOO MUCH INTO IT.

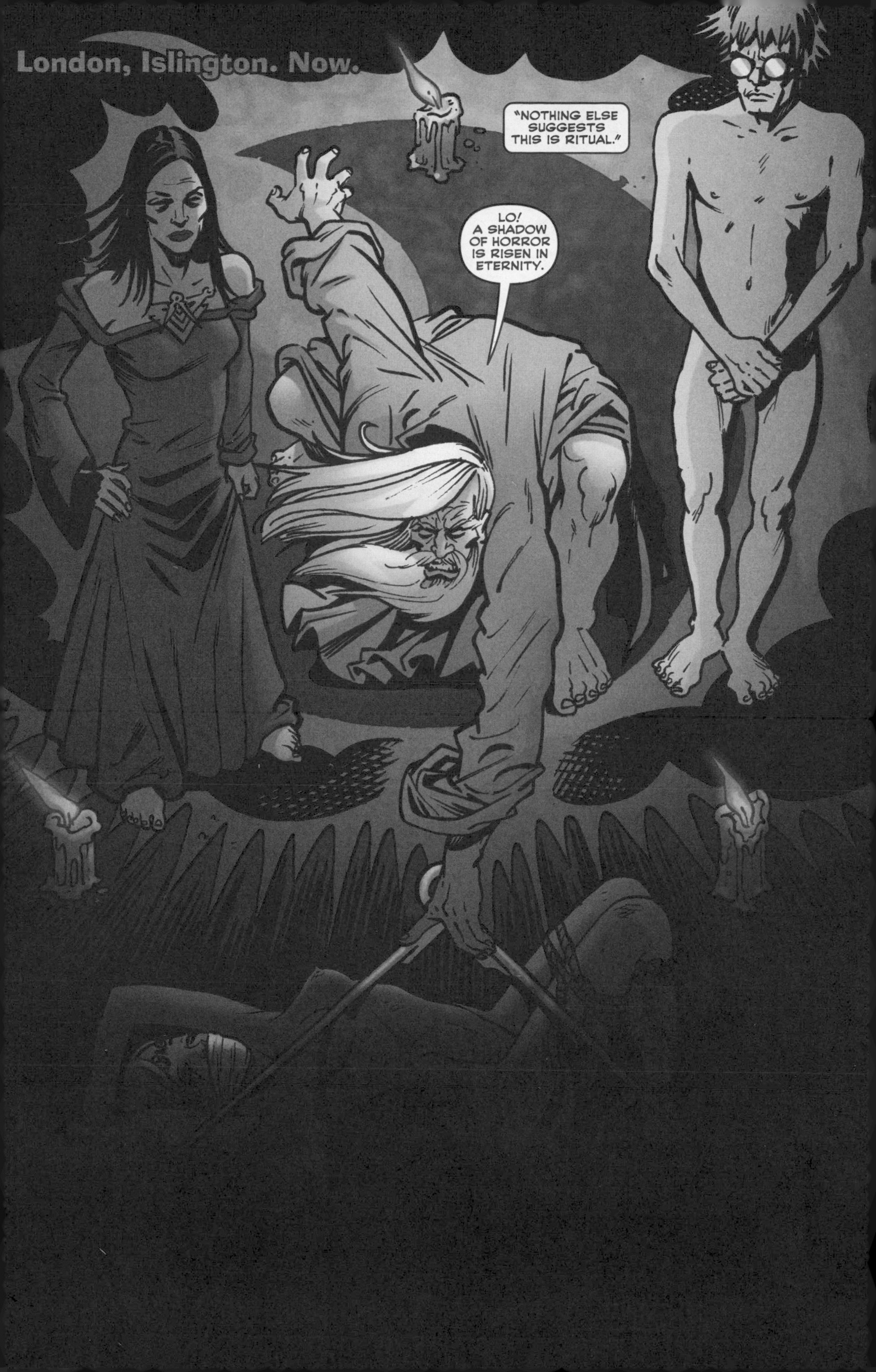
London, Islington. Now.
"NOTHING ELSE SUGGESTS THIS IS RITUAL."
LO! A SHADOW OF HORROR IS RISEN IN ETERNITY.

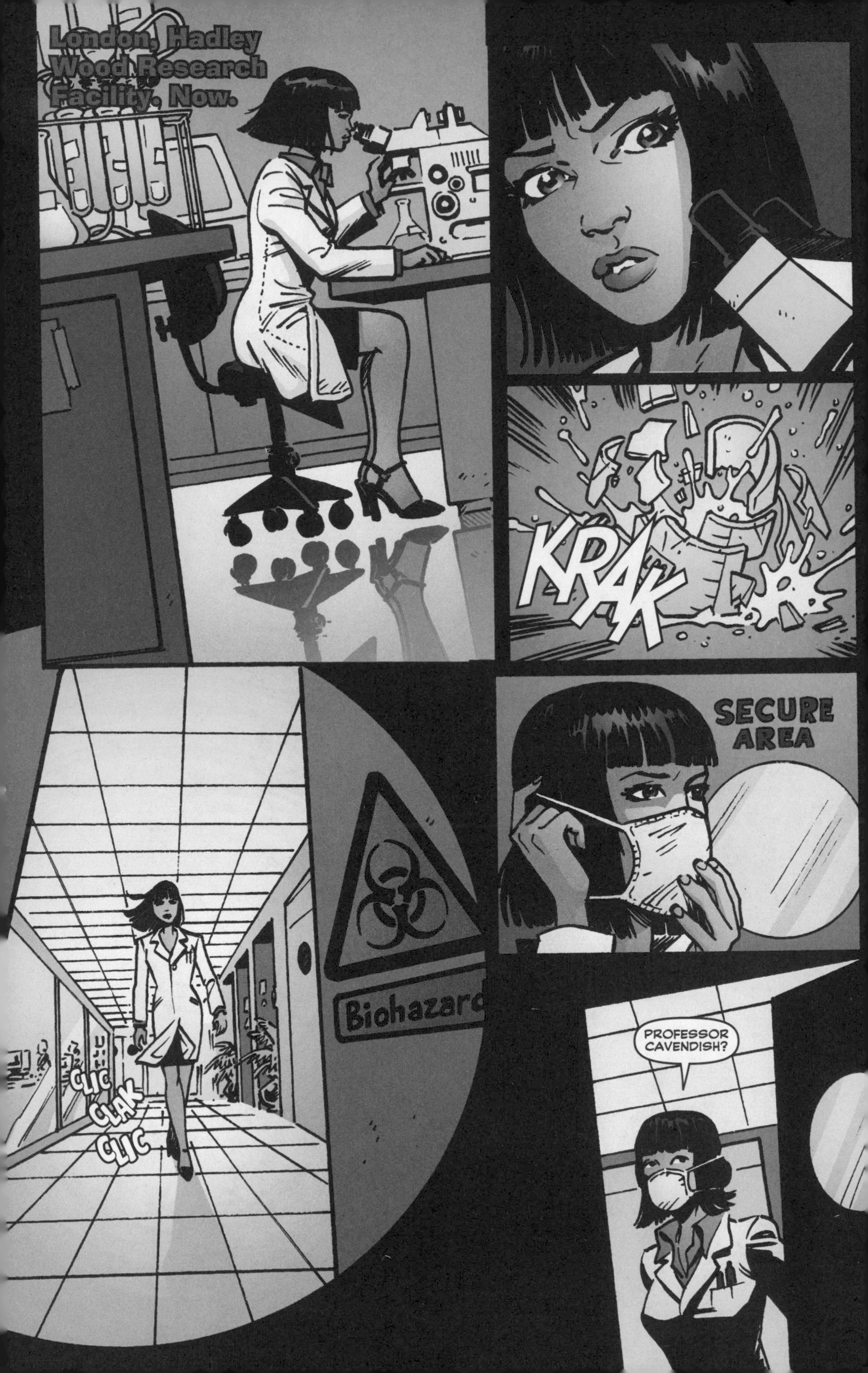
London, Hadley Wood Research Facility. Now.
KRAK
SECURE AREA
Biohazard
CLIC
CLAK
CLIC
PROFESSOR CAVENDISH?

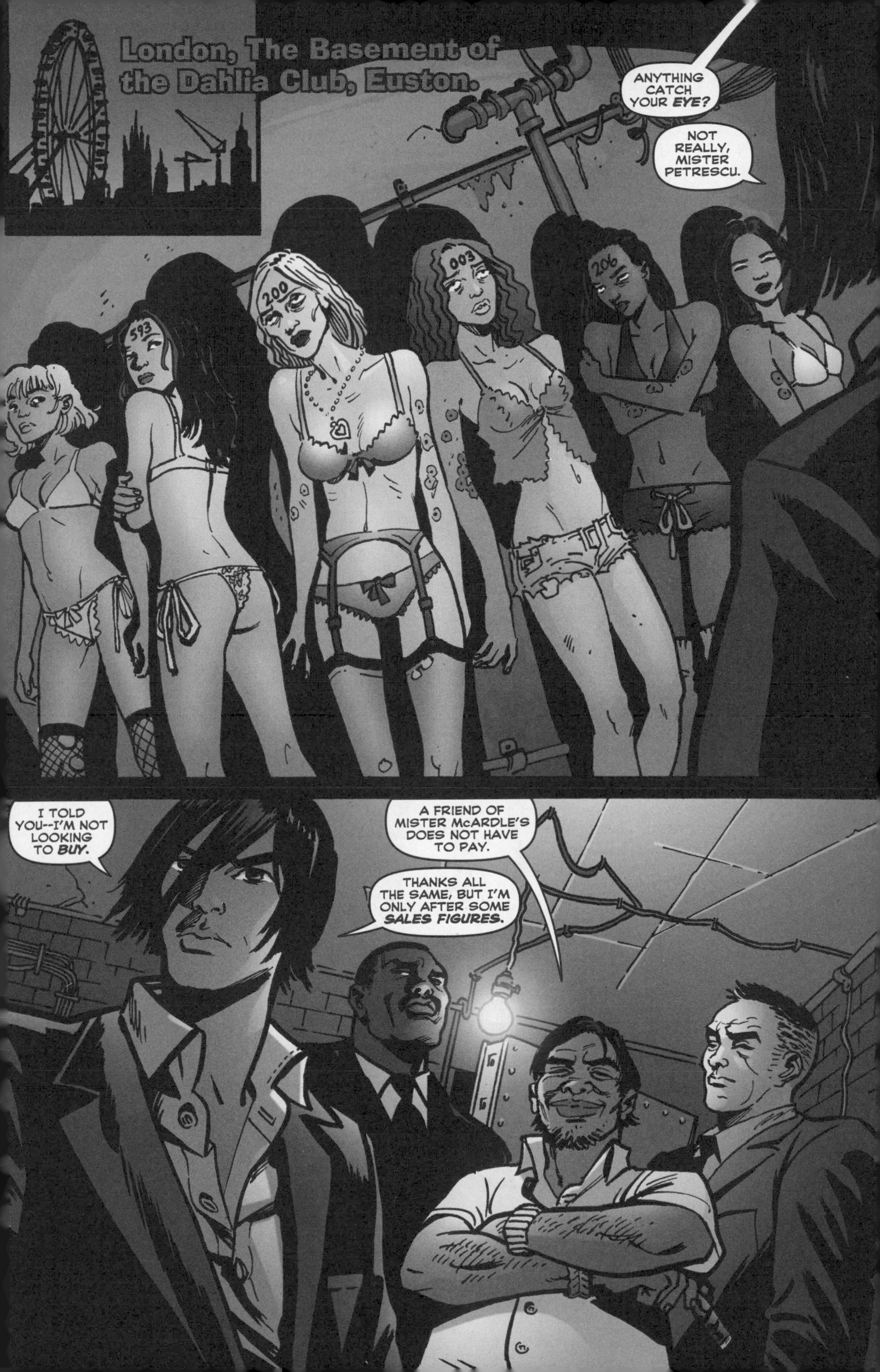
London, The Basement of the Dahlia Club, Euston.
ANYTHING CATCH YOUR *EYE?*
NOT REALLY, MISTER PETRESCU.
200
003
593
206
I TOLD YOU--I'M NOT LOOKING TO *BUY*.
A FRIEND OF MISTER McARDLE'S DOES NOT HAVE TO PAY.
THANKS ALL THE SAME, BUT I'M ONLY AFTER SOME *SALES FIGURES*.

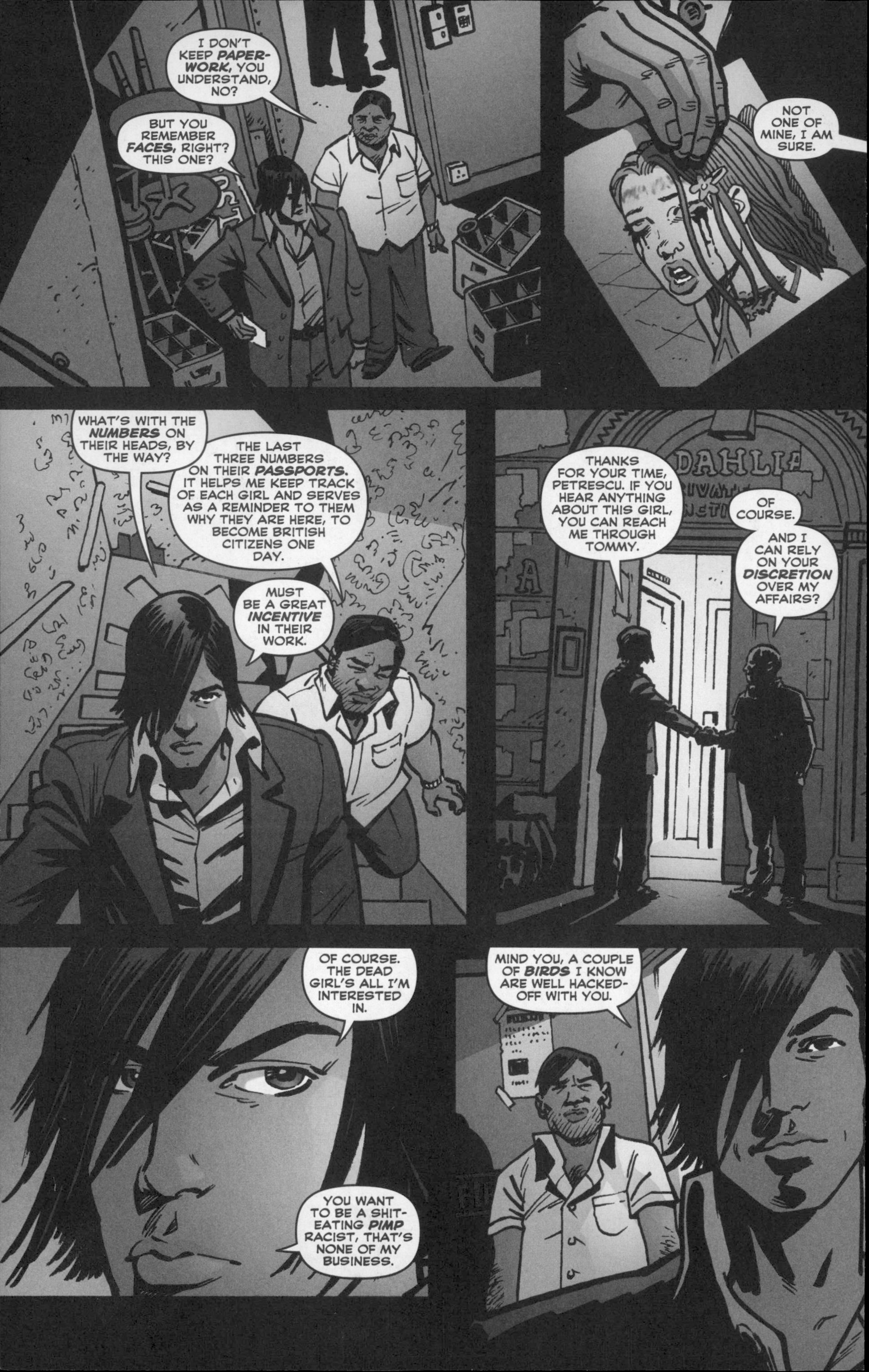

I DON'T KEEP PAPERWORK, YOU UNDERSTAND, NO?
BUT YOU REMEMBER FACES, RIGHT? THIS ONE?
NOT ONE OF MINE, I AM SURE.
WHAT'S WITH THE NUMBERS ON THEIR HEADS, BY THE WAY?
THE LAST THREE NUMBERS ON THEIR PASSPORTS. IT HELPS ME KEEP TRACK OF EACH GIRL AND SERVES AS A REMINDER TO THEM WHY THEY ARE HERE, TO BECOME BRITISH CITIZENS ONE DAY.
MUST BE A GREAT INCENTIVE IN THEIR WORK.
DAHLIA
THANKS FOR YOUR TIME, PETRESCU. IF YOU HEAR ANYTHING ABOUT THIS GIRL, YOU CAN REACH ME THROUGH TOMMY.
OF COURSE.
AND I CAN RELY ON YOUR DISCRETION OVER MY AFFAIRS?
OF COURSE. THE DEAD GIRL'S ALL I'M INTERESTED IN.
YOU WANT TO BE A SHIT-EATING PIMP RACIST, THAT'S NONE OF MY BUSINESS.
MIND YOU, A COUPLE OF BIRDS I KNOW ARE WELL HACKED-OFF WITH YOU.

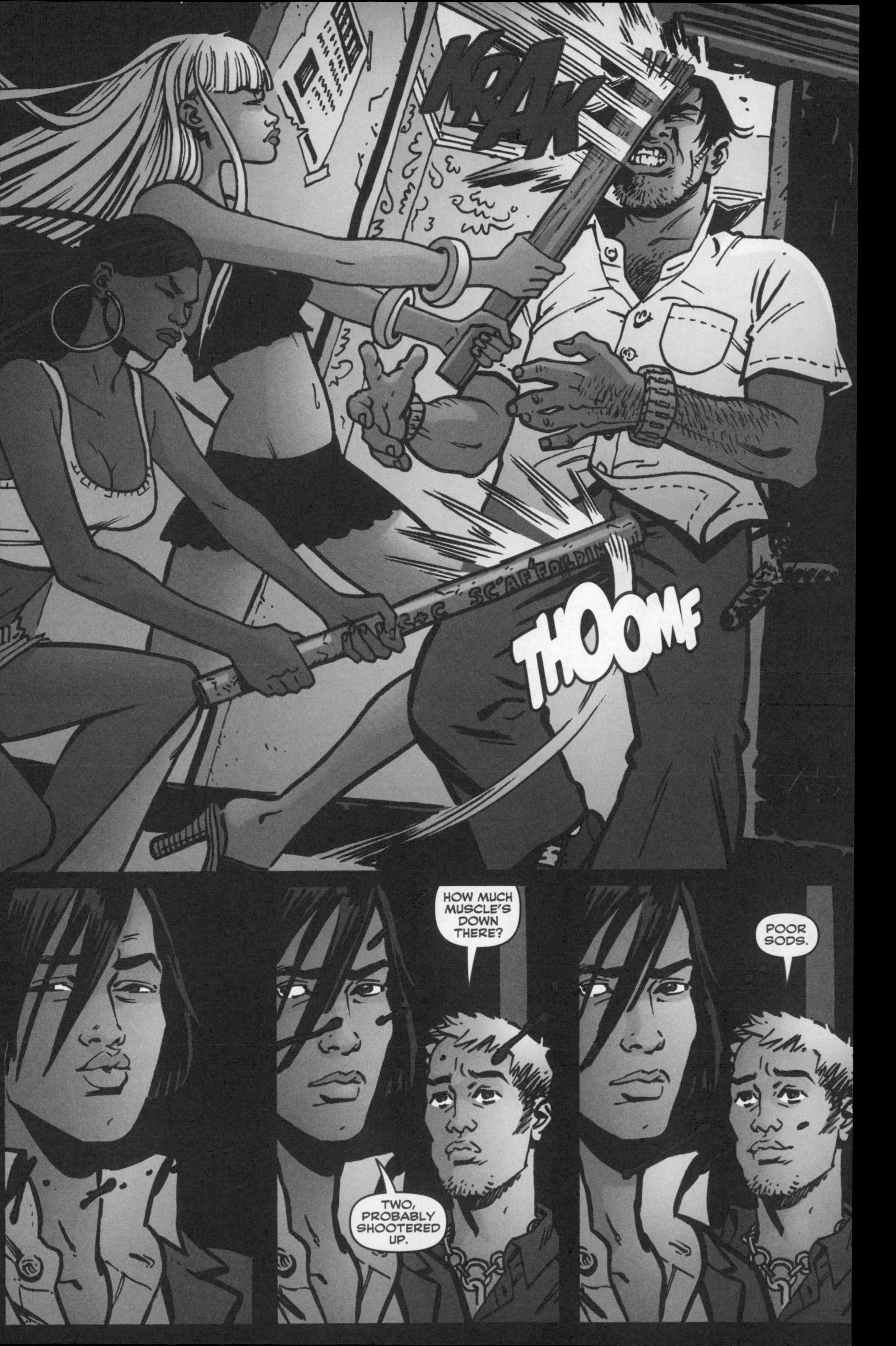
KRAK
THOOMF
HOW MUCH MUSCLE'S DOWN THERE?
TWO, PROBABLY SHOOTERED UP.
POOR SODS.

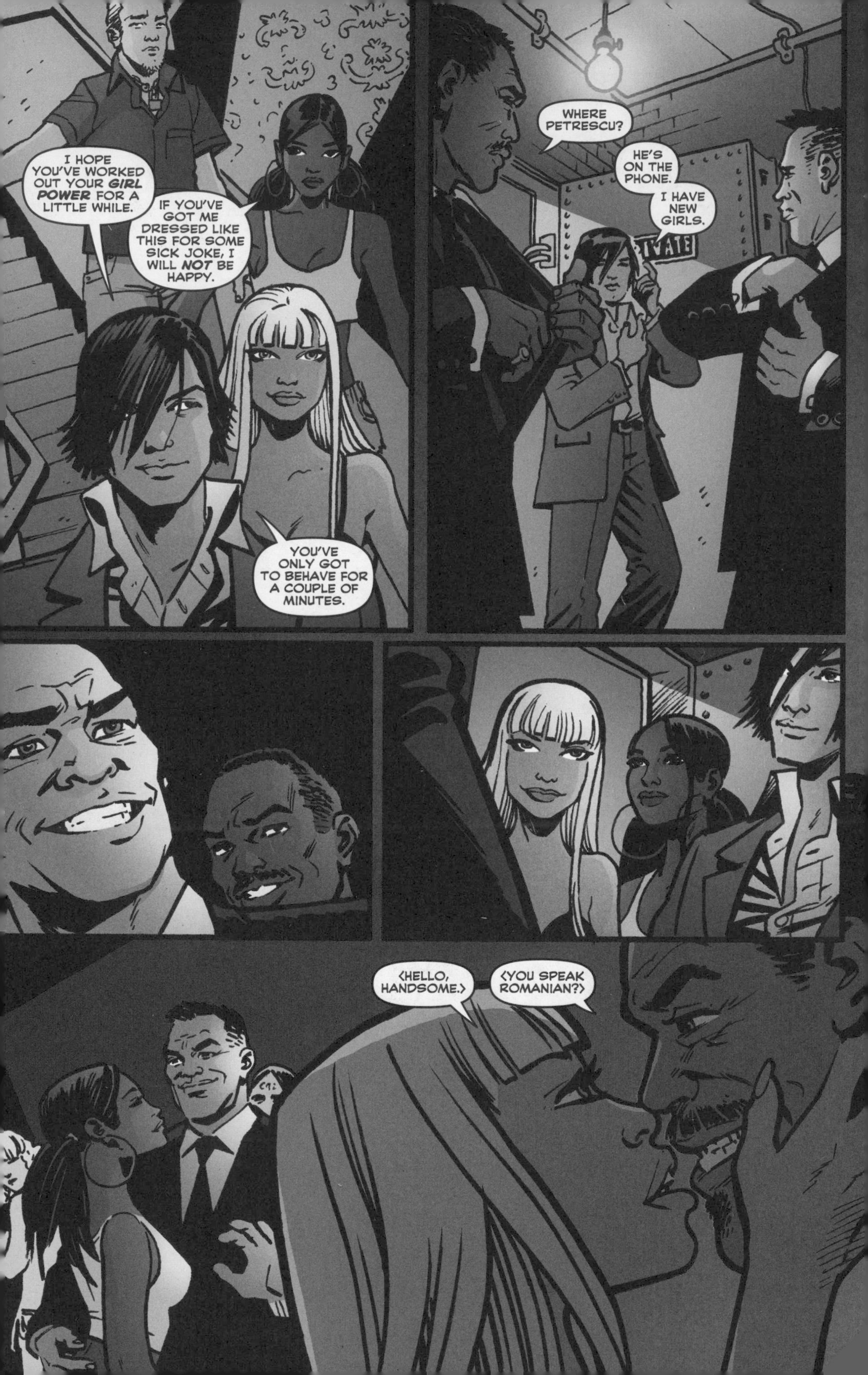
I HOPE YOU'VE WORKED OUT YOUR GIRL POWER FOR A LITTLE WHILE.
IF YOU'VE GOT ME DRESSED LIKE THIS FOR SOME SICK JOKE, I WILL NOT BE HAPPY.
YOU'VE ONLY GOT TO BEHAVE FOR A COUPLE OF MINUTES.
WHERE PETRESCU?
HE'S ON THE PHONE.
I HAVE NEW GIRLS.
<HELLO, HANDSOME.>
<YOU SPEAK ROMANIAN?>

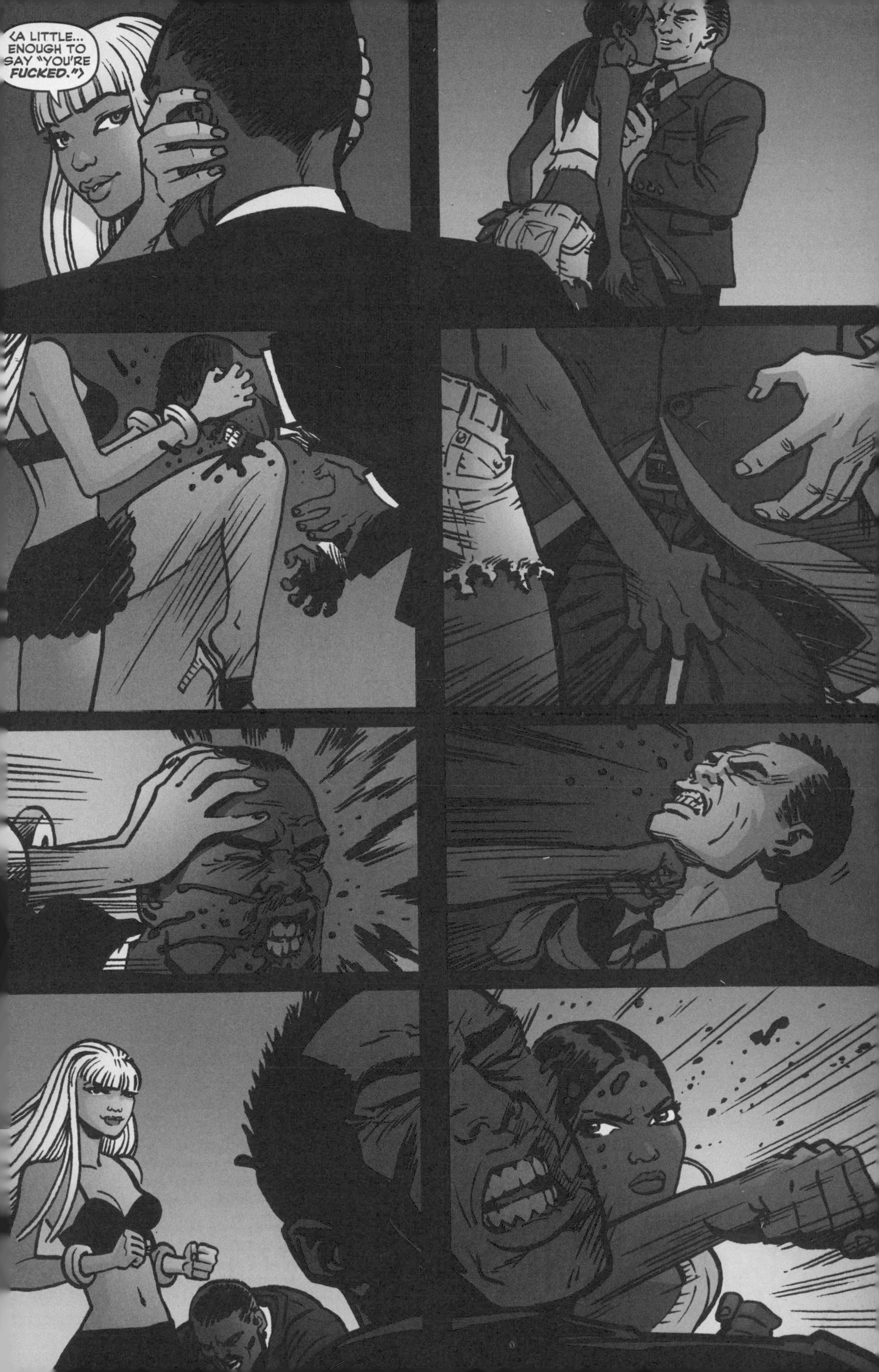
<A LITTLE... ENOUGH TO SAY "YOU'RE FUCKED.">

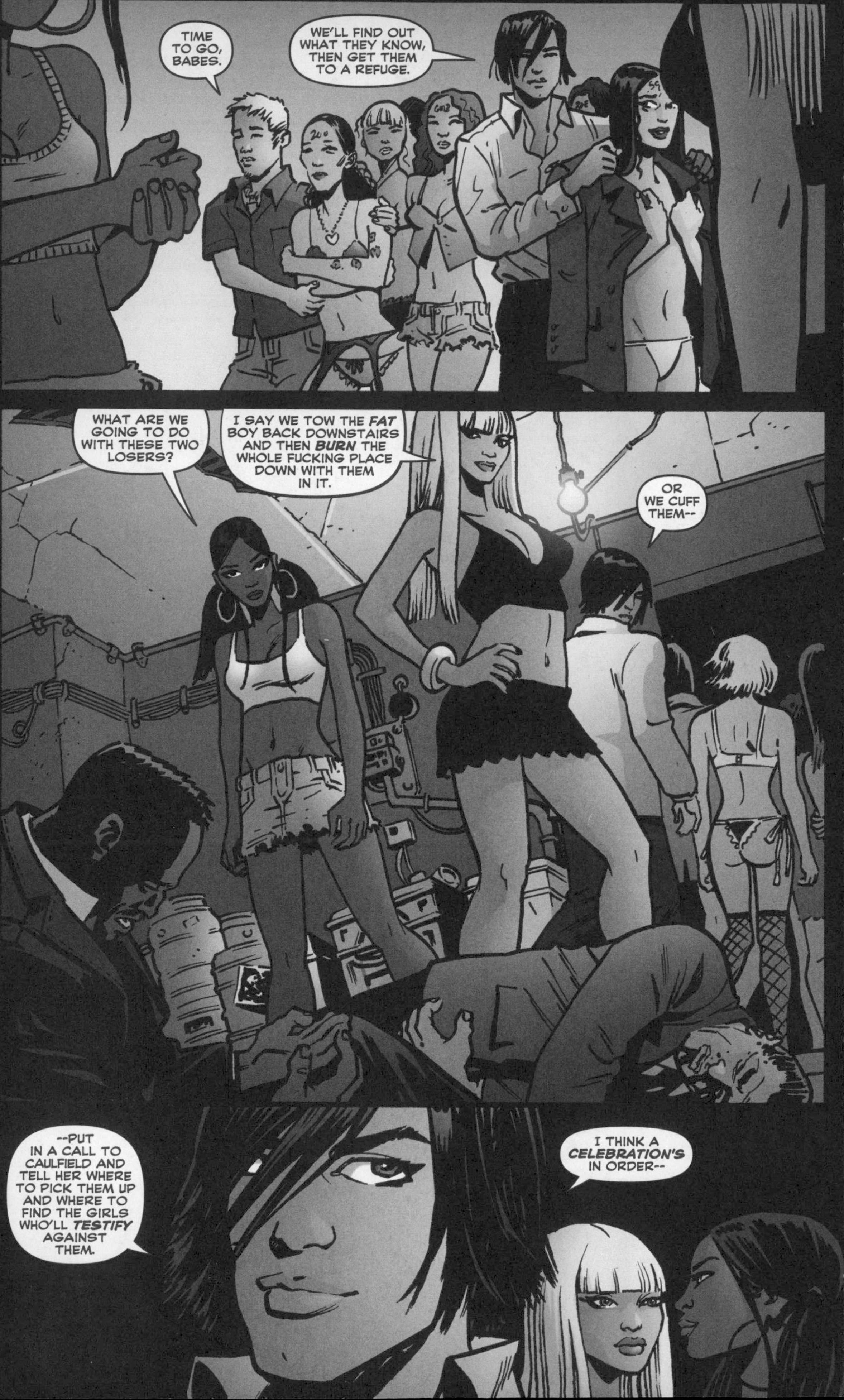
TIME TO GO, BABES.
WE'LL FIND OUT WHAT THEY KNOW, THEN GET THEM TO A REFUGE.
WHAT ARE WE GOING TO DO WITH THESE TWO LOSERS?
I SAY WE TOW THE *FAT* BOY BACK DOWNSTAIRS AND THEN *BURN* THE WHOLE FUCKING PLACE DOWN WITH THEM IN IT.
OR WE CUFF THEM--
--PUT IN A CALL TO CAULFIELD AND TELL HER WHERE TO PICK THEM UP AND WHERE TO FIND THE GIRLS WHO'LL *TESTIFY* AGAINST THEM.
I THINK A *CELEBRATION'S* IN ORDER--

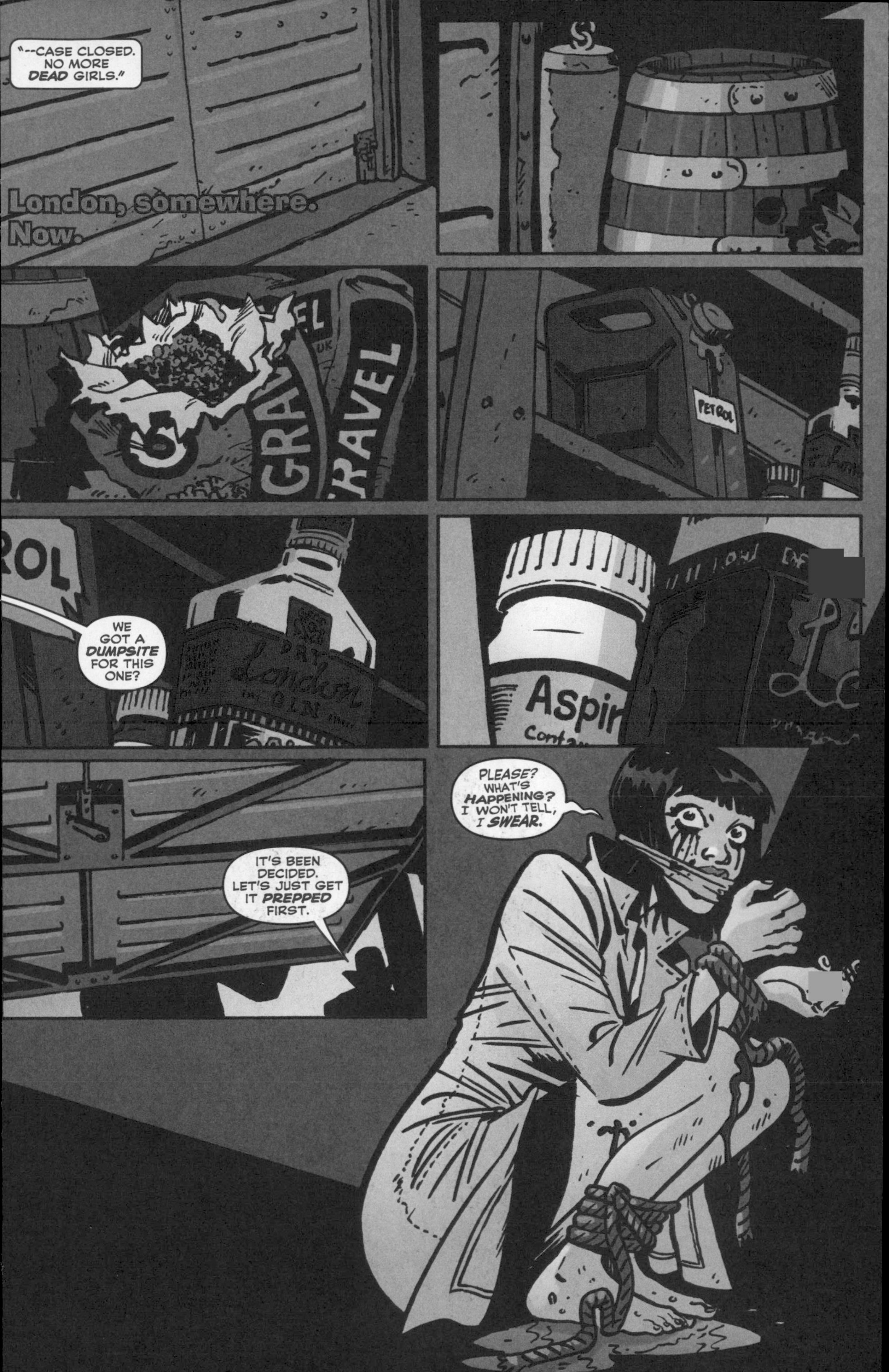
"--CASE CLOSED. NO MORE DEAD GIRLS."
London, somewhere. Now.
GRAVEL
GRAVEL
PETROL
WE GOT A DUMPSITE FOR THIS ONE?
London GIN
Aspir
PLEASE? WHAT'S HAPPENING? I WON'T TELL, I SWEAR.
IT'S BEEN DECIDED. LET'S JUST GET IT PREPPED FIRST.

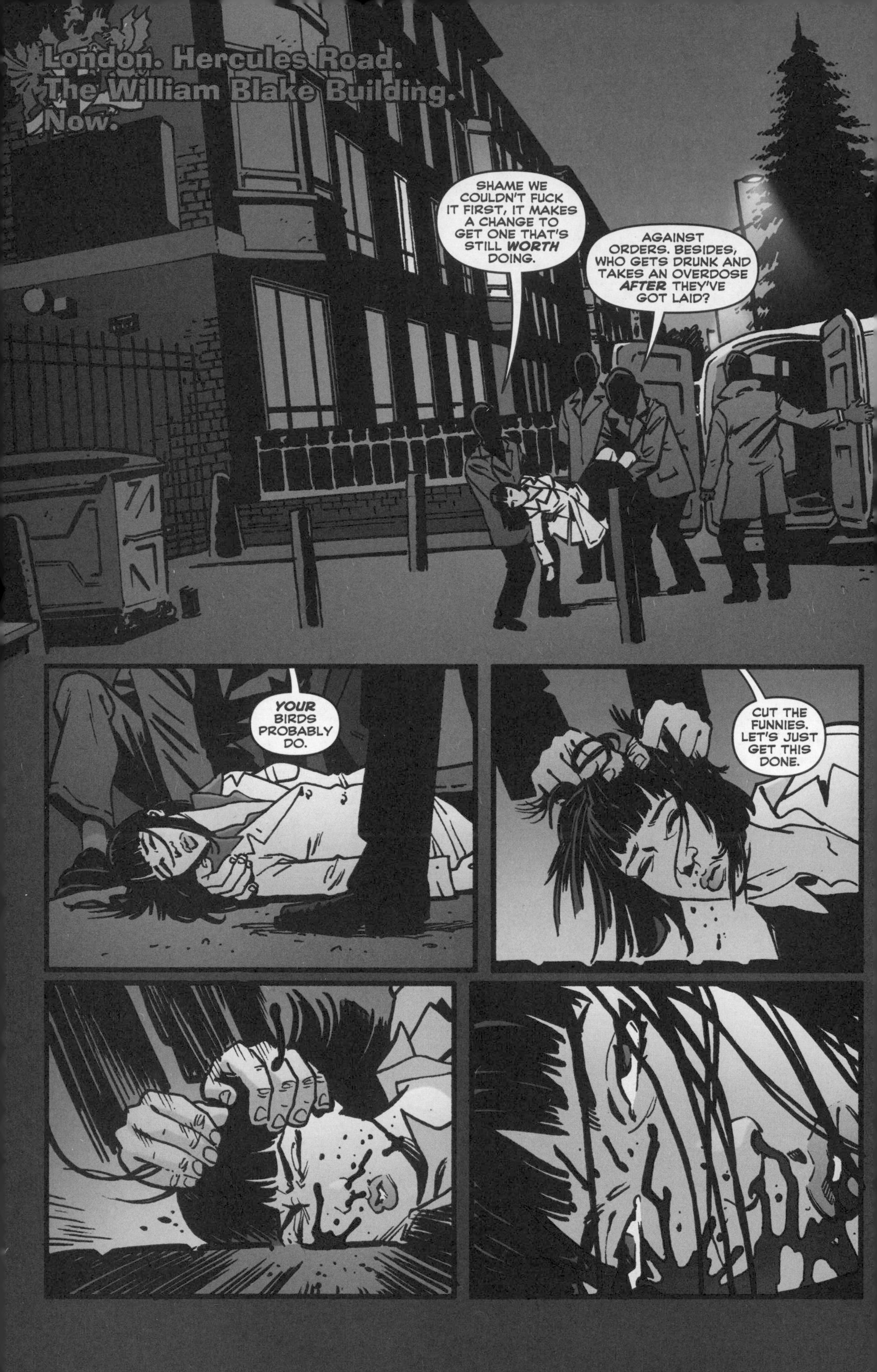
London. Hercules Road.
The William Blake Building.
Now.
SHAME WE COULDN'T FUCK IT FIRST, IT MAKES A CHANGE TO GET ONE THAT'S STILL WORTH DOING.
AGAINST ORDERS. BESIDES, WHO GETS DRUNK AND TAKES AN OVERDOSE AFTER THEY'VE GOT LAID?
YOUR BIRDS PROBABLY DO.
CUT THE FUNNIES. LET'S JUST GET THIS DONE.

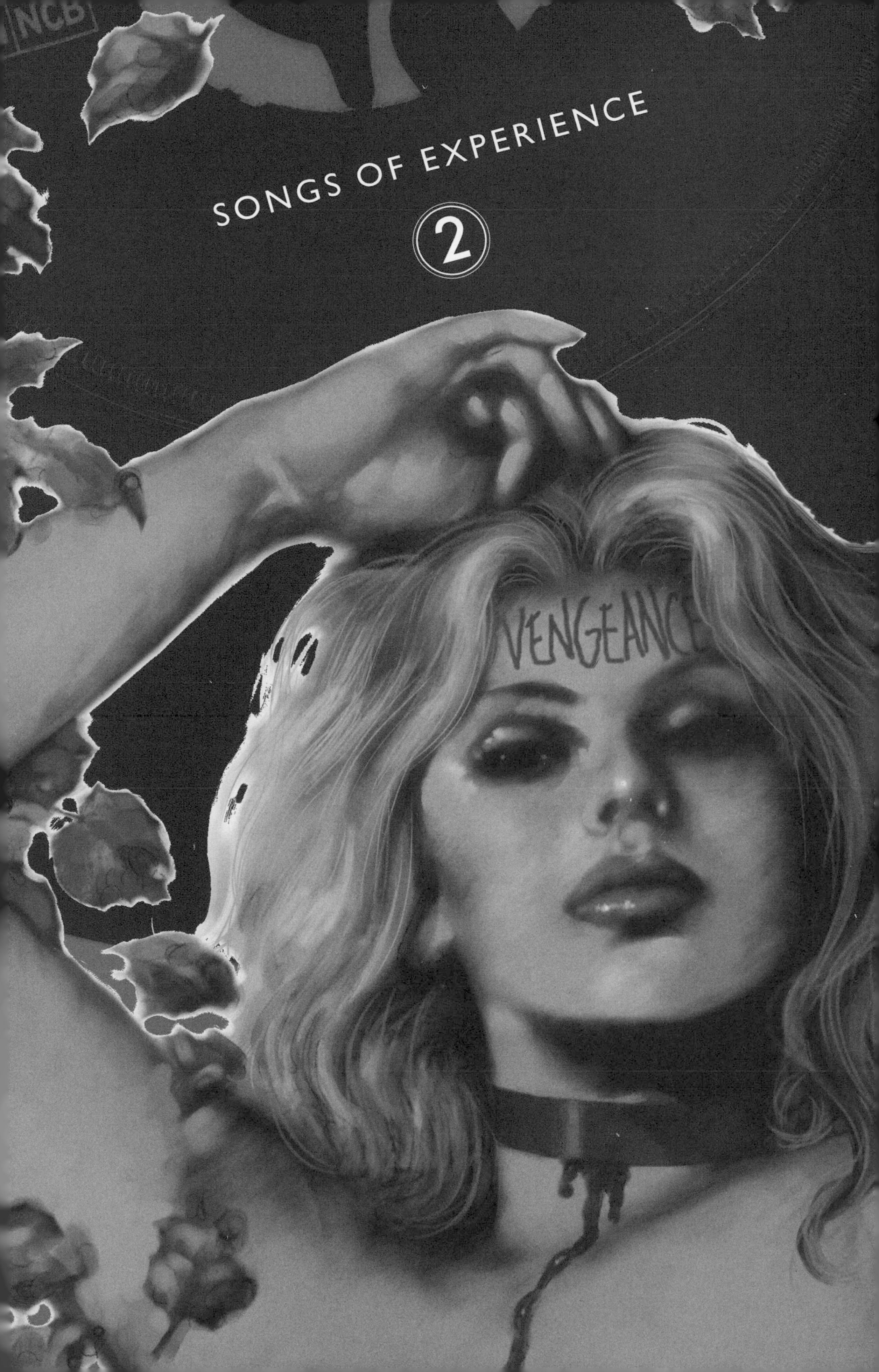
NCB
SONGS OF EXPERIENCE
2
VENGEANCE

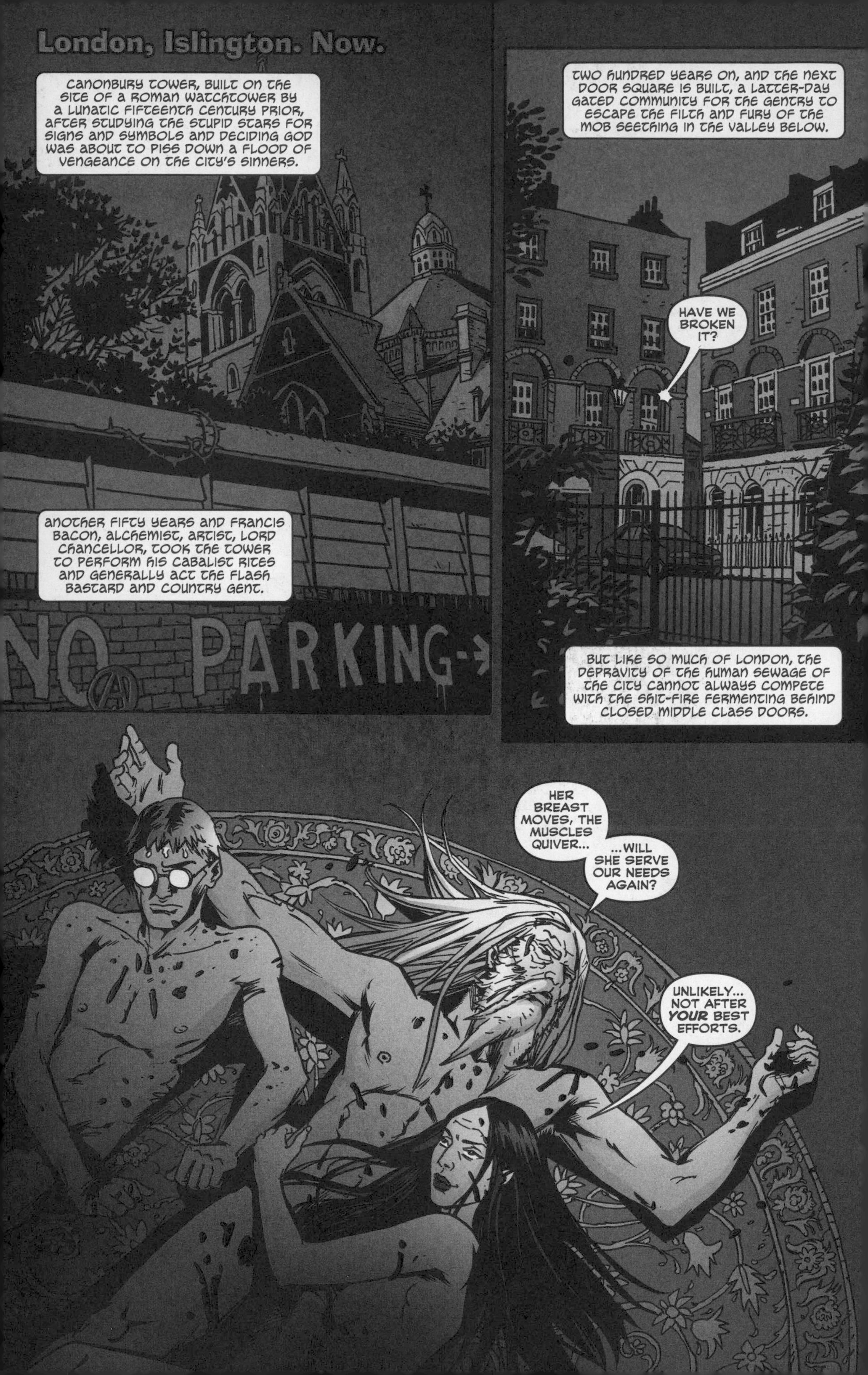
London, Islington. Now.
Canonbury Tower, built on the site of a Roman watchtower by a lunatic fifteenth century prior, after studying the stupid stars for signs and symbols and deciding God was about to piss down a flood of vengeance on the city's sinners.
Another fifty years and Francis Bacon, alchemist, artist, Lord Chancellor, took the tower to perform his cabalist rites and generally act the flash bastard and country gent.
NO PARKING
Two hundred years on, and the next door square is built, a latter-day gated community for the gentry to escape the filth and fury of the mob seething in the valley below.
HAVE WE BROKEN IT?
But like so much of London, the depravity of the human sewage of the city cannot always compete with the shit-fire fermenting behind closed middle class doors.
HER BREAST MOVES, THE MUSCLES QUIVER...
...WILL SHE SERVE OUR NEEDS AGAIN?
UNLIKELY... NOT AFTER YOUR BEST EFFORTS.

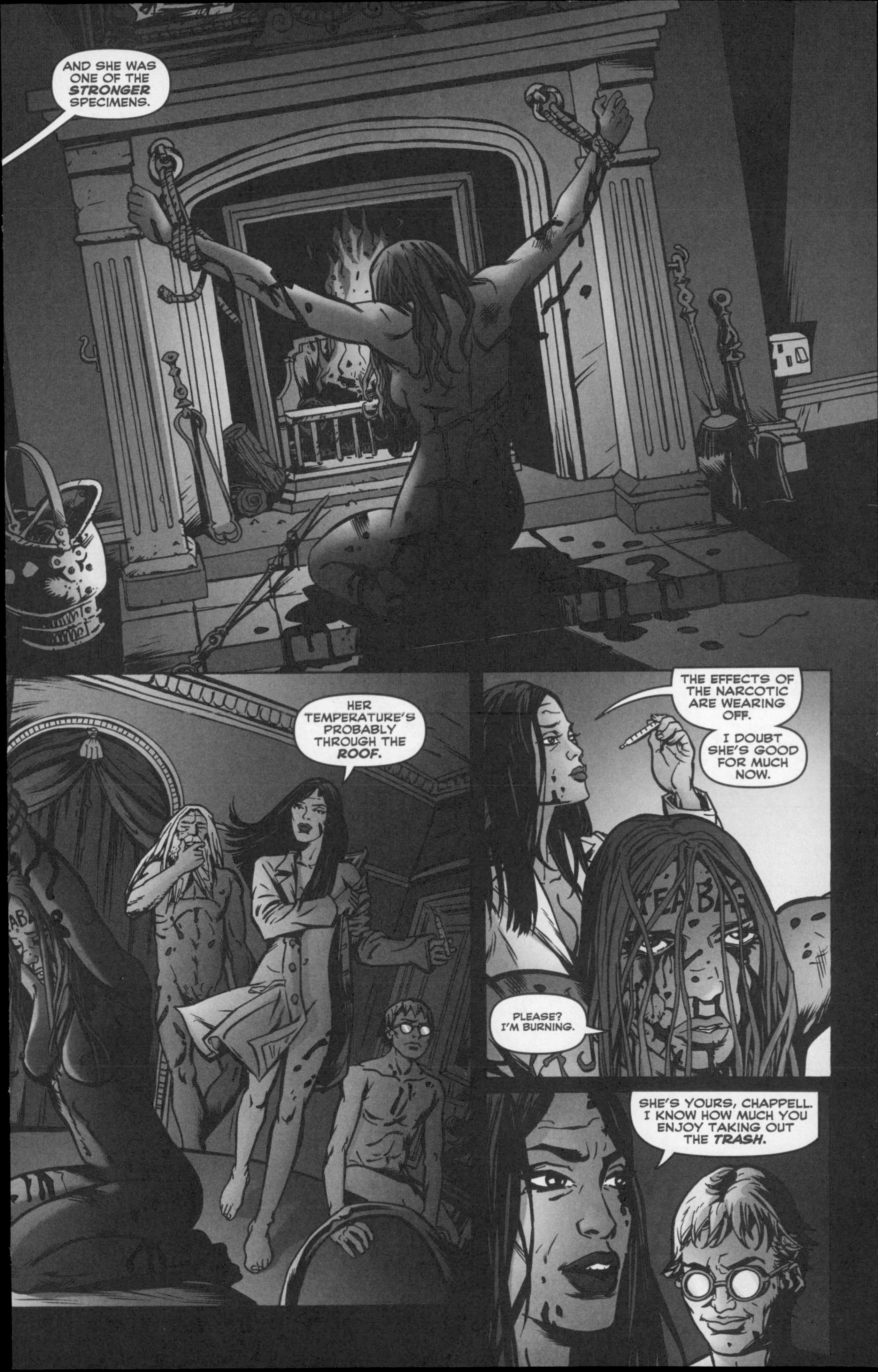
AND SHE WAS ONE OF THE STRONGER SPECIMENS.
HER TEMPERATURE'S PROBABLY THROUGH THE ROOF.
THE EFFECTS OF THE NARCOTIC ARE WEARING OFF.
I DOUBT SHE'S GOOD FOR MUCH NOW.
PLEASE? I'M BURNING.
SHE'S YOURS, CHAPPELL. I KNOW HOW MUCH YOU ENJOY TAKING OUT THE TRASH.

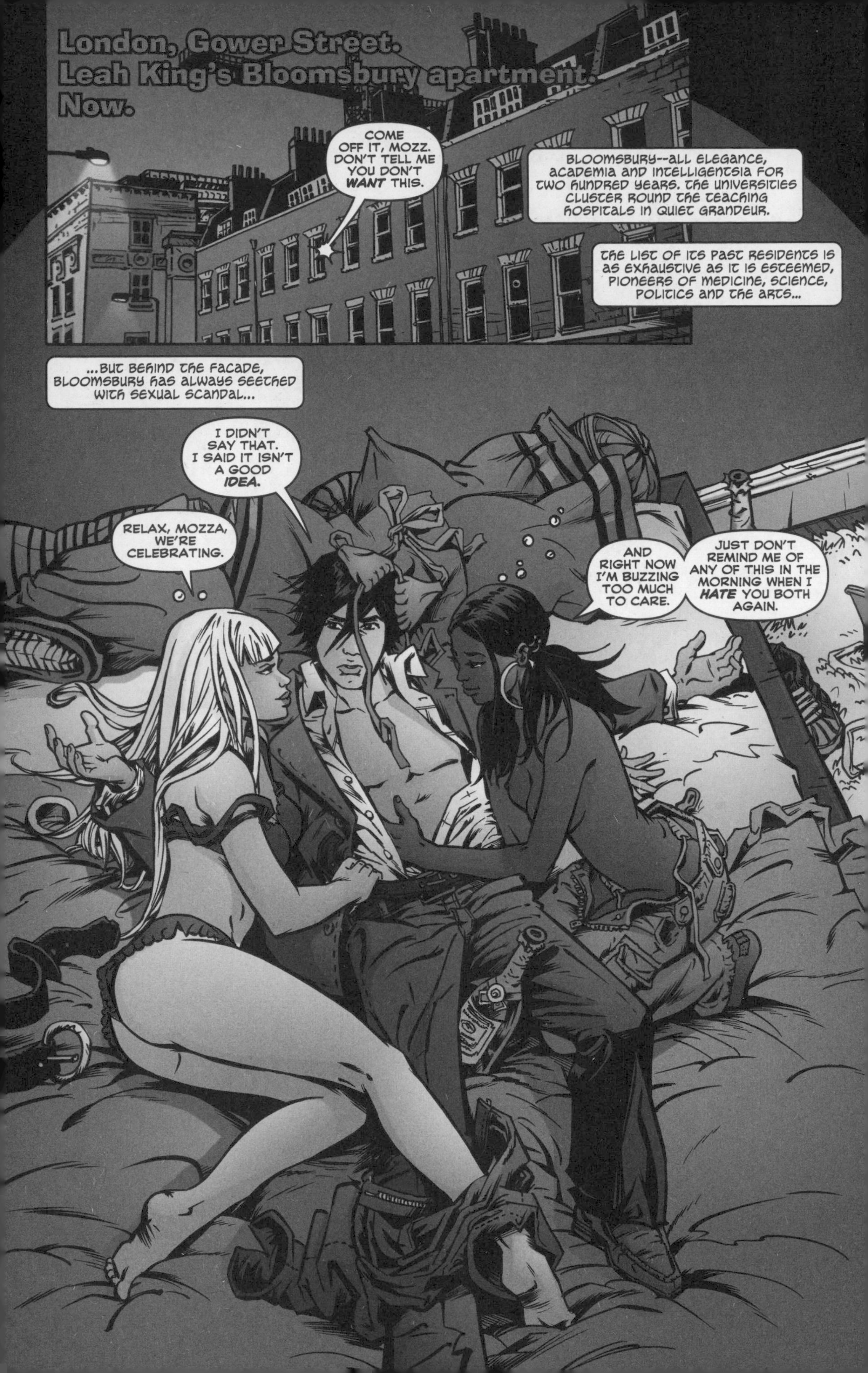
London, Gower Street.
Leah King's Bloomsbury apartment.
Now.
COME OFF IT, MOZZ. DON'T TELL ME YOU DON'T *WANT* THIS.
BLOOMSBURY--ALL ELEGANCE, ACADEMIA AND INTELLIGENTSIA FOR TWO HUNDRED YEARS. THE UNIVERSITIES CLUSTER ROUND THE TEACHING HOSPITALS IN QUIET GRANDEUR.
THE LIST OF ITS PAST RESIDENTS IS AS EXHAUSTIVE AS IT IS ESTEEMED, PIONEERS OF MEDICINE, SCIENCE, POLITICS AND THE ARTS...
...BUT BEHIND THE FACADE, BLOOMSBURY HAS ALWAYS SEETHED WITH SEXUAL SCANDAL...
I DIDN'T SAY THAT. I SAID IT ISN'T A GOOD *IDEA*.
RELAX, MOZZA, WE'RE CELEBRATING.
AND RIGHT NOW I'M BUZZING TOO MUCH TO CARE.
JUST DON'T REMIND ME OF ANY OF THIS IN THE MORNING WHEN I *HATE* YOU BOTH AGAIN.

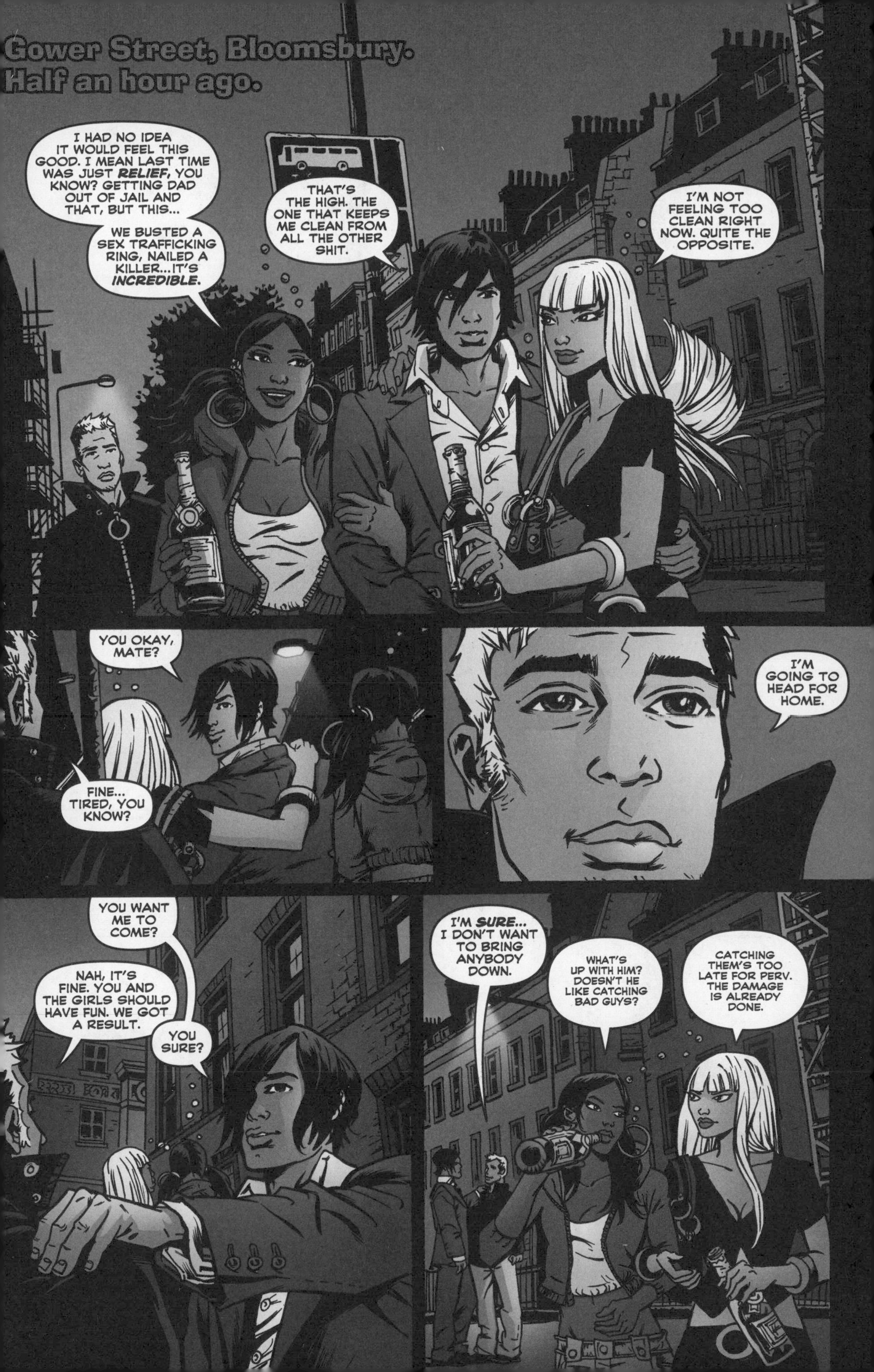

Gower Street, Bloomsbury.
Half an hour ago.
I HAD NO IDEA IT WOULD FEEL THIS GOOD. I MEAN LAST TIME WAS JUST RELIEF, YOU KNOW? GETTING DAD OUT OF JAIL AND THAT, BUT THIS...
WE BUSTED A SEX TRAFFICKING RING, NAILED A KILLER...IT'S INCREDIBLE.
THAT'S THE HIGH. THE ONE THAT KEEPS ME CLEAN FROM ALL THE OTHER SHIT.
I'M NOT FEELING TOO CLEAN RIGHT NOW. QUITE THE OPPOSITE.
YOU OKAY, MATE?
FINE... TIRED, YOU KNOW?
I'M GOING TO HEAD FOR HOME.
YOU WANT ME TO COME?
NAH, IT'S FINE. YOU AND THE GIRLS SHOULD HAVE FUN. WE GOT A RESULT.
YOU SURE?
I'M SURE... I DON'T WANT TO BRING ANYBODY DOWN.
WHAT'S UP WITH HIM? DOESN'T HE LIKE CATCHING BAD GUYS?
CATCHING THEM'S TOO LATE FOR PERV. THE DAMAGE IS ALREADY DONE.

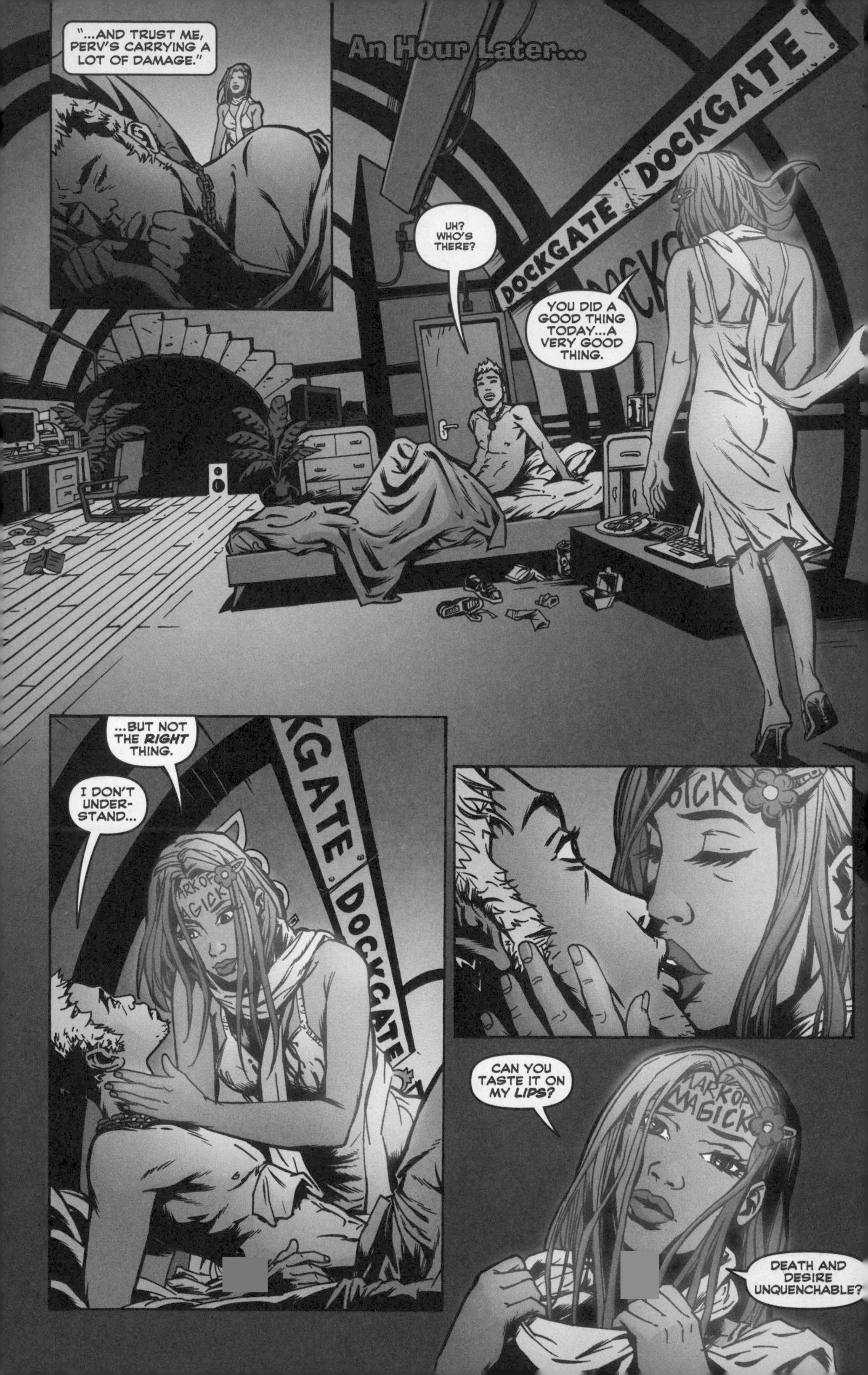
"...AND TRUST ME, PERV'S CARRYING A LOT OF DAMAGE."
An Hour Later...
DOCKGATE
DOCKGATE
UH? WHO'S THERE?
YOU DID A GOOD THING TODAY...A VERY GOOD THING.
...BUT NOT THE *RIGHT* THING.
I DON'T UNDER-STAND...
MARK OF MAGICK
CAN YOU TASTE IT ON MY *LIPS*?
DEATH AND DESIRE UNQUENCHABLE?

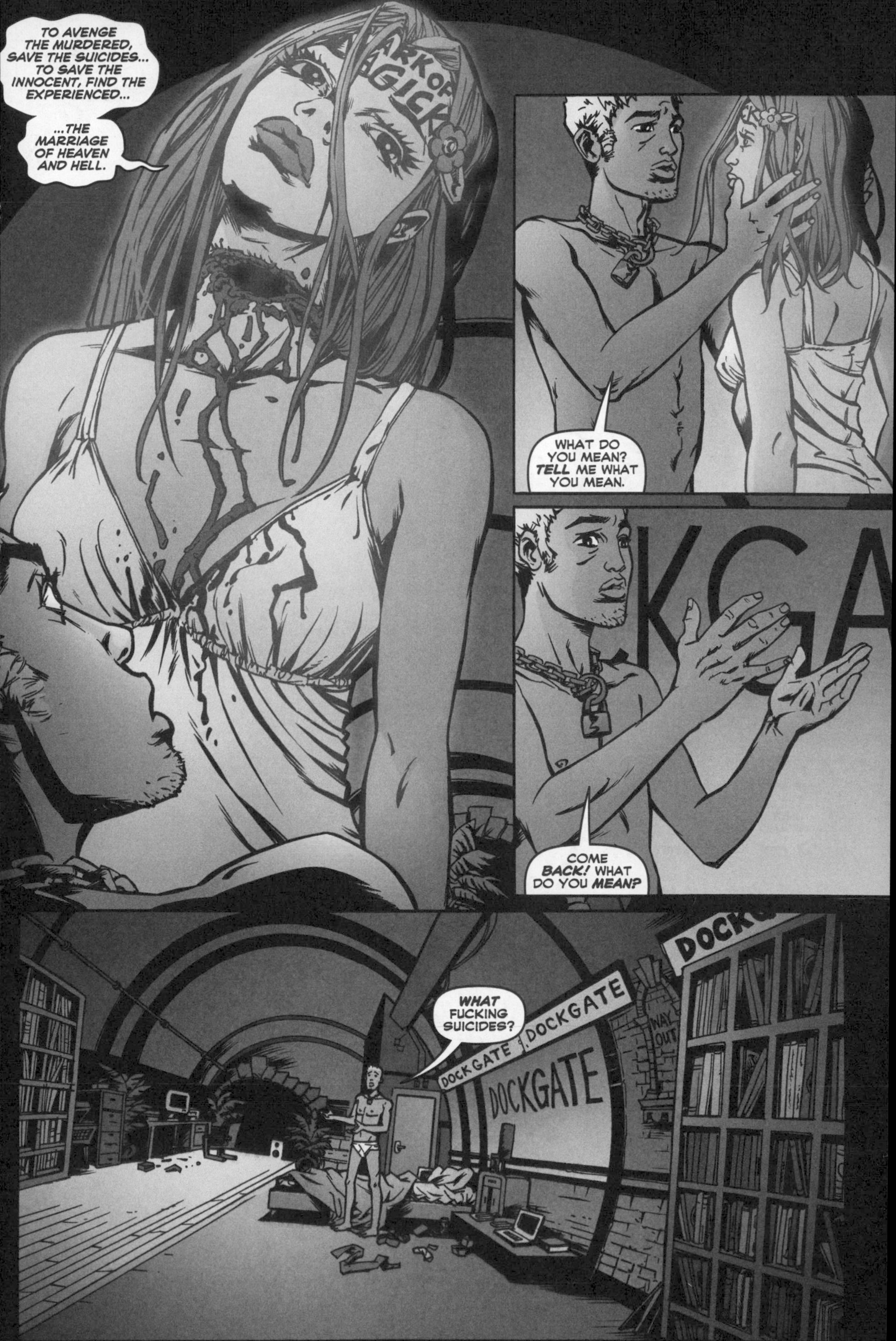
TO AVENGE THE MURDERED, SAVE THE SUICIDES... TO SAVE THE INNOCENT, FIND THE EXPERIENCED...
...THE MARRIAGE OF HEAVEN AND HELL.
WHAT DO YOU MEAN? **TELL** ME WHAT YOU MEAN.
COME **BACK!** WHAT DO YOU **MEAN?**
DOCK
DOCKGATE
WHAT FUCKING SUICIDES?
DOCK GATE
DOCKGATE
WAY OUT

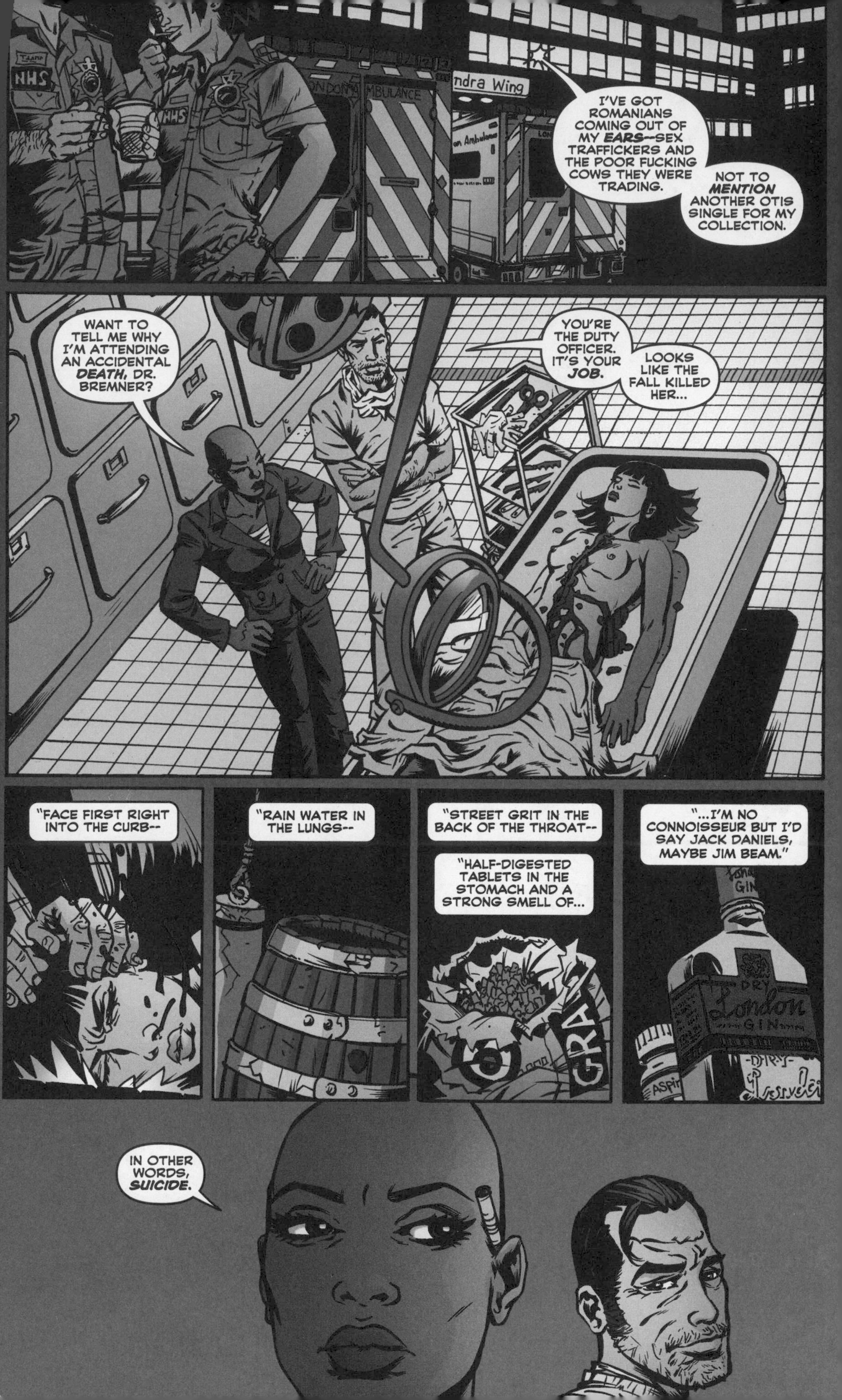
NHS
NHS
LONDON AMBULANCE
ndra Wing
I'VE GOT ROMANIANS COMING OUT OF MY EARS--SEX TRAFFICKERS AND THE POOR FUCKING COWS THEY WERE TRADING.
NOT TO MENTION ANOTHER OTIS SINGLE FOR MY COLLECTION.
WANT TO TELL ME WHY I'M ATTENDING AN ACCIDENTAL DEATH, DR. BREMNER?
YOU'RE THE DUTY OFFICER. IT'S YOUR JOB.
LOOKS LIKE THE FALL KILLED HER...
"FACE FIRST RIGHT INTO THE CURB--
"RAIN WATER IN THE LUNGS--
"STREET GRIT IN THE BACK OF THE THROAT--
"HALF-DIGESTED TABLETS IN THE STOMACH AND A STRONG SMELL OF...
"...I'M NO CONNOISSEUR BUT I'D SAY JACK DANIELS, MAYBE JIM BEAM."
DRY London GIN
IN OTHER WORDS, SUICIDE.

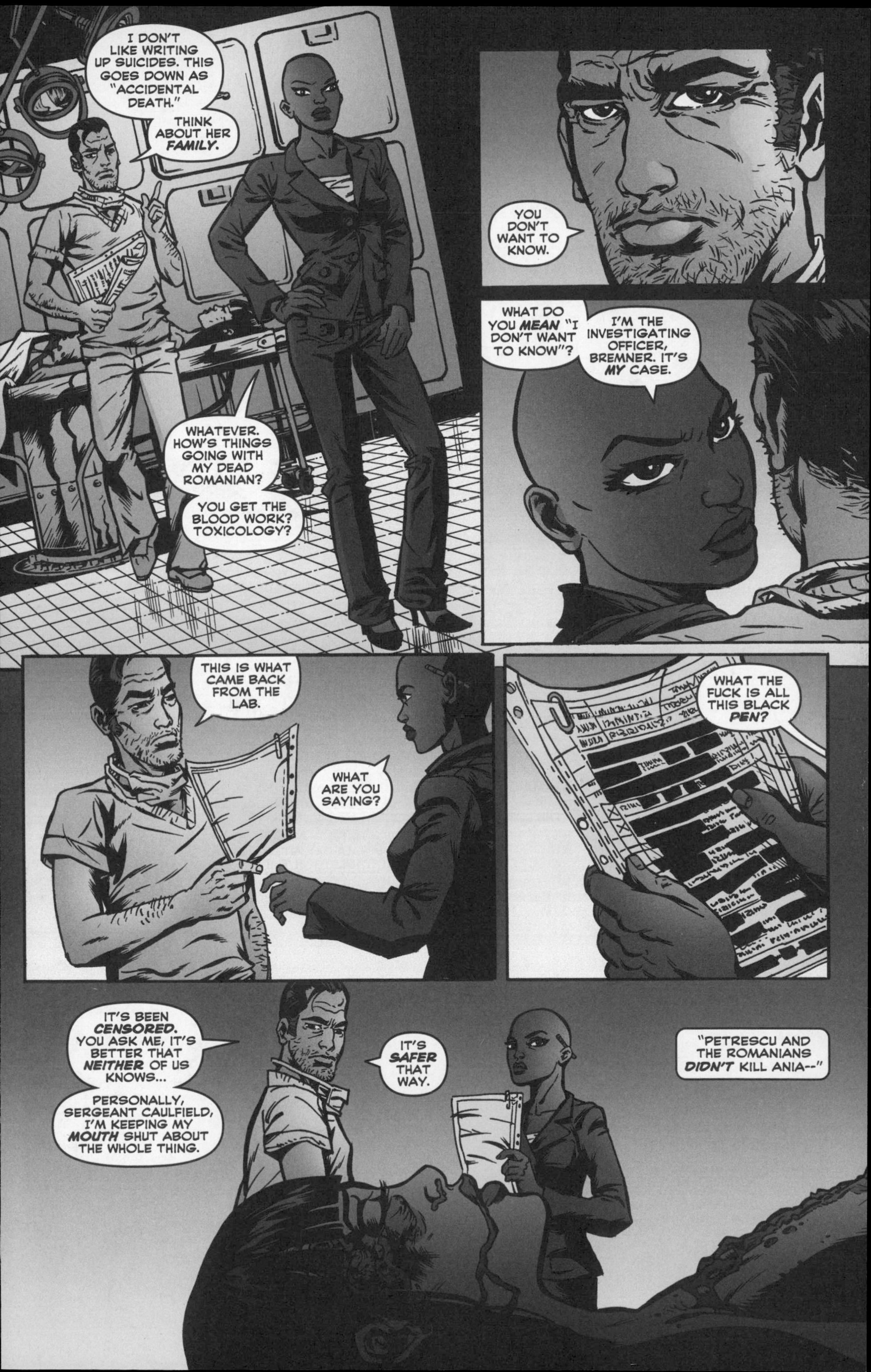
I DON'T LIKE WRITING UP SUICIDES. THIS GOES DOWN AS "ACCIDENTAL DEATH."
THINK ABOUT HER *FAMILY*.
WHATEVER. HOW'S THINGS GOING WITH MY DEAD ROMANIAN?
YOU GET THE BLOOD WORK? TOXICOLOGY?
YOU DON'T WANT TO KNOW.
WHAT DO YOU *MEAN* "I DON'T WANT TO KNOW"?
I'M THE INVESTIGATING OFFICER, BREMNER. IT'S *MY* CASE.
THIS IS WHAT CAME BACK FROM THE LAB.
WHAT ARE YOU SAYING?
WHAT THE FUCK IS ALL THIS BLACK *PEN?*
IT'S BEEN *CENSORED.* YOU ASK ME, IT'S BETTER THAT *NEITHER* OF US KNOWS...
IT'S *SAFER* THAT WAY.
PERSONALLY, SERGEANT CAULFIELD, I'M KEEPING MY *MOUTH* SHUT ABOUT THE WHOLE THING.
"PETRESCU AND THE ROMANIANS *DIDN'T* KILL ANIA--"

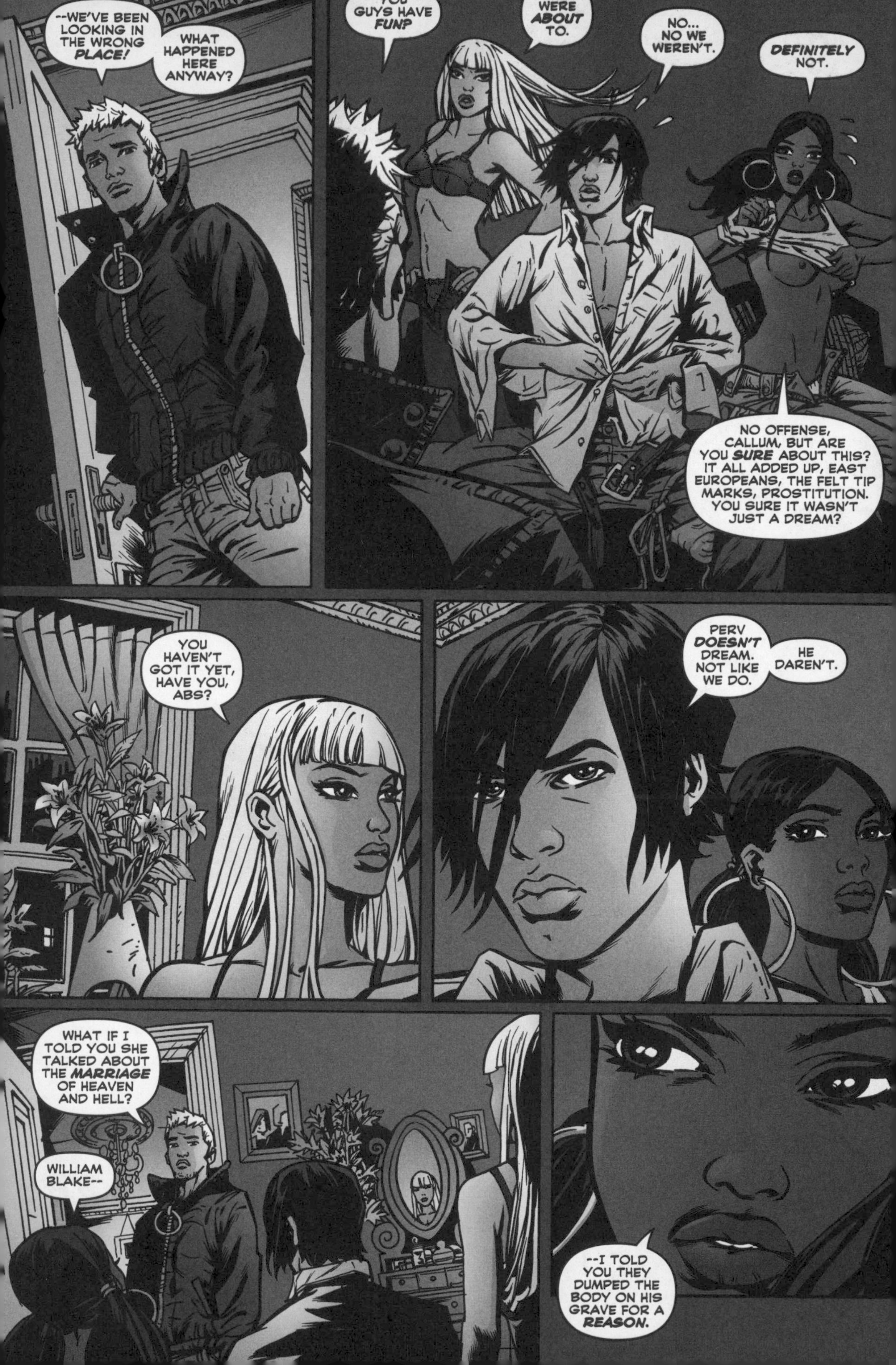
--WE'VE BEEN LOOKING IN THE WRONG *PLACE!*
WHAT HAPPENED HERE ANYWAY?
YOU GUYS HAVE *FUN?*
WE WERE *ABOUT* TO.
NO... NO WE WEREN'T.
DEFINITELY NOT.
NO OFFENSE, CALLUM, BUT ARE YOU *SURE* ABOUT THIS? IT ALL ADDED UP, EAST EUROPEANS, THE FELT TIP MARKS, PROSTITUTION. YOU SURE IT WASN'T JUST A DREAM?
YOU HAVEN'T GOT IT YET, HAVE YOU, ABS?
PERV *DOESN'T* DREAM. NOT LIKE WE DO.
HE DAREN'T.
WHAT IF I TOLD YOU SHE TALKED ABOUT THE *MARRIAGE* OF HEAVEN AND HELL?
WILLIAM BLAKE--
--I TOLD YOU THEY DUMPED THE BODY ON HIS GRAVE FOR A *REASON.*

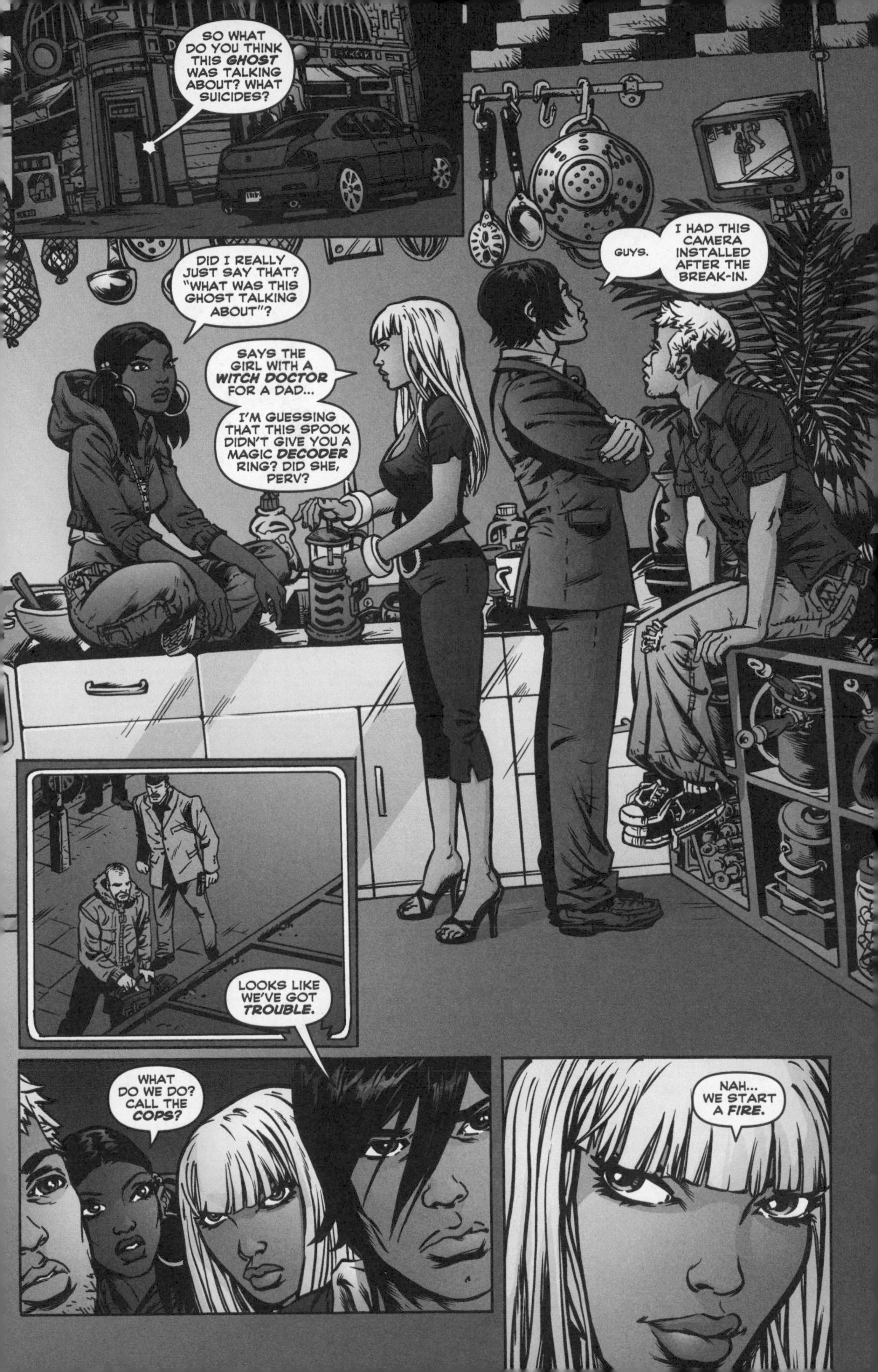
SO WHAT DO YOU THINK THIS GHOST WAS TALKING ABOUT? WHAT SUICIDES?
DID I REALLY JUST SAY THAT? "WHAT WAS THIS GHOST TALKING ABOUT"?
SAYS THE GIRL WITH A WITCH DOCTOR FOR A DAD...
I'M GUESSING THAT THIS SPOOK DIDN'T GIVE YOU A MAGIC DECODER RING? DID SHE, PERV?
GUYS.
I HAD THIS CAMERA INSTALLED AFTER THE BREAK-IN.
LOOKS LIKE WE'VE GOT TROUBLE.
WHAT DO WE DO? CALL THE COPS?
NAH... WE START A FIRE.

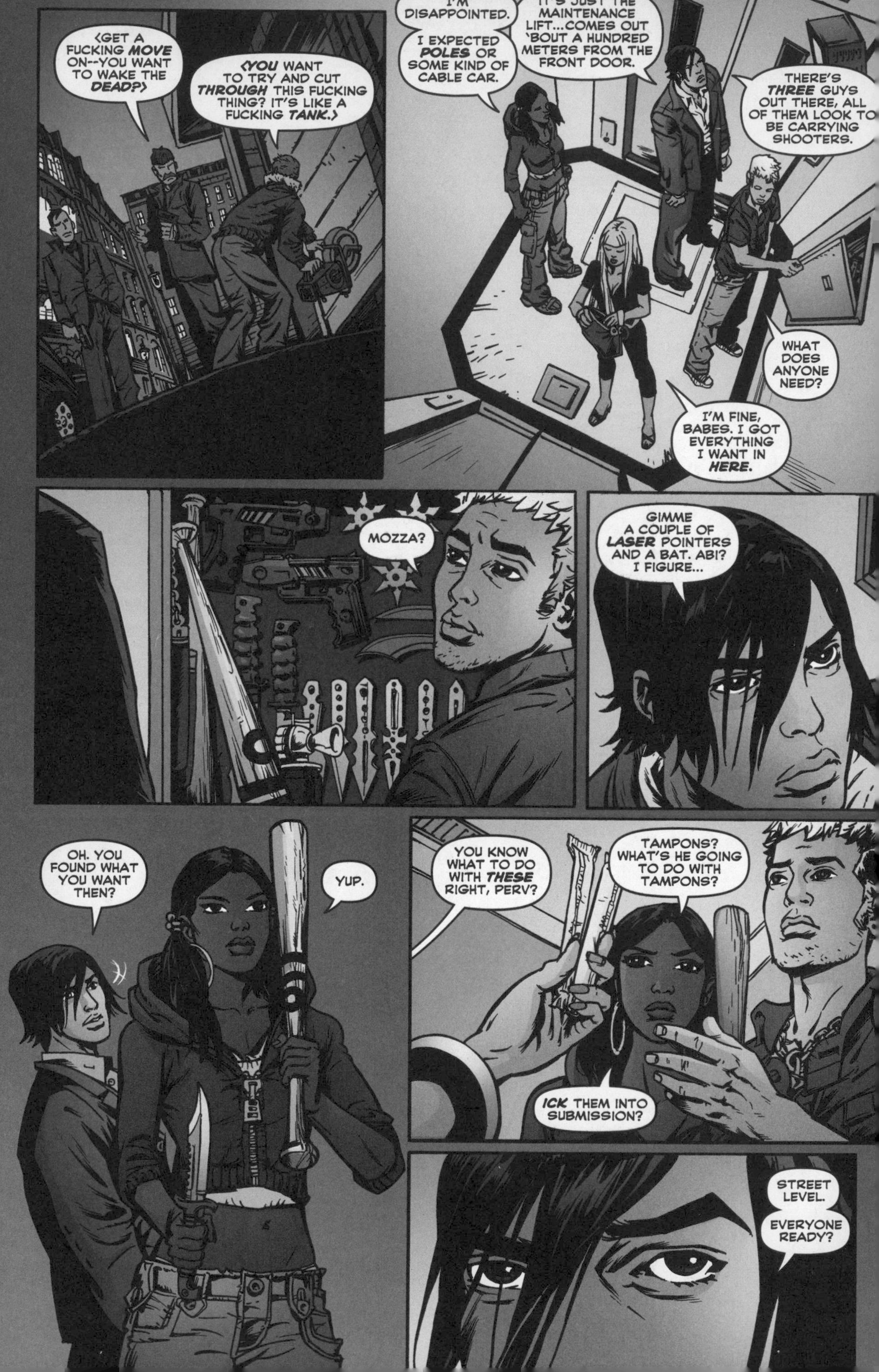

<GET A FUCKING MOVE ON--YOU WANT TO WAKE THE DEAD?>
<YOU WANT TO TRY AND CUT THROUGH THIS FUCKING THING? IT'S LIKE A FUCKING TANK.>
I'M DISAPPOINTED.
I EXPECTED POLES OR SOME KIND OF CABLE CAR.
IT'S JUST THE MAINTENANCE LIFT...COMES OUT 'BOUT A HUNDRED METERS FROM THE FRONT DOOR.
THERE'S THREE GUYS OUT THERE, ALL OF THEM LOOK TO BE CARRYING SHOOTERS.
WHAT DOES ANYONE NEED?
I'M FINE, BABES. I GOT EVERYTHING I WANT IN HERE.
MOZZA?
GIMME A COUPLE OF LASER POINTERS AND A BAT. ABI? I FIGURE...
OH. YOU FOUND WHAT YOU WANT THEN?
YUP.
YOU KNOW WHAT TO DO WITH THESE RIGHT, PERV?
TAMPONS? WHAT'S HE GOING TO DO WITH TAMPONS?
ICK THEM INTO SUBMISSION?
STREET LEVEL.
EVERYONE READY?

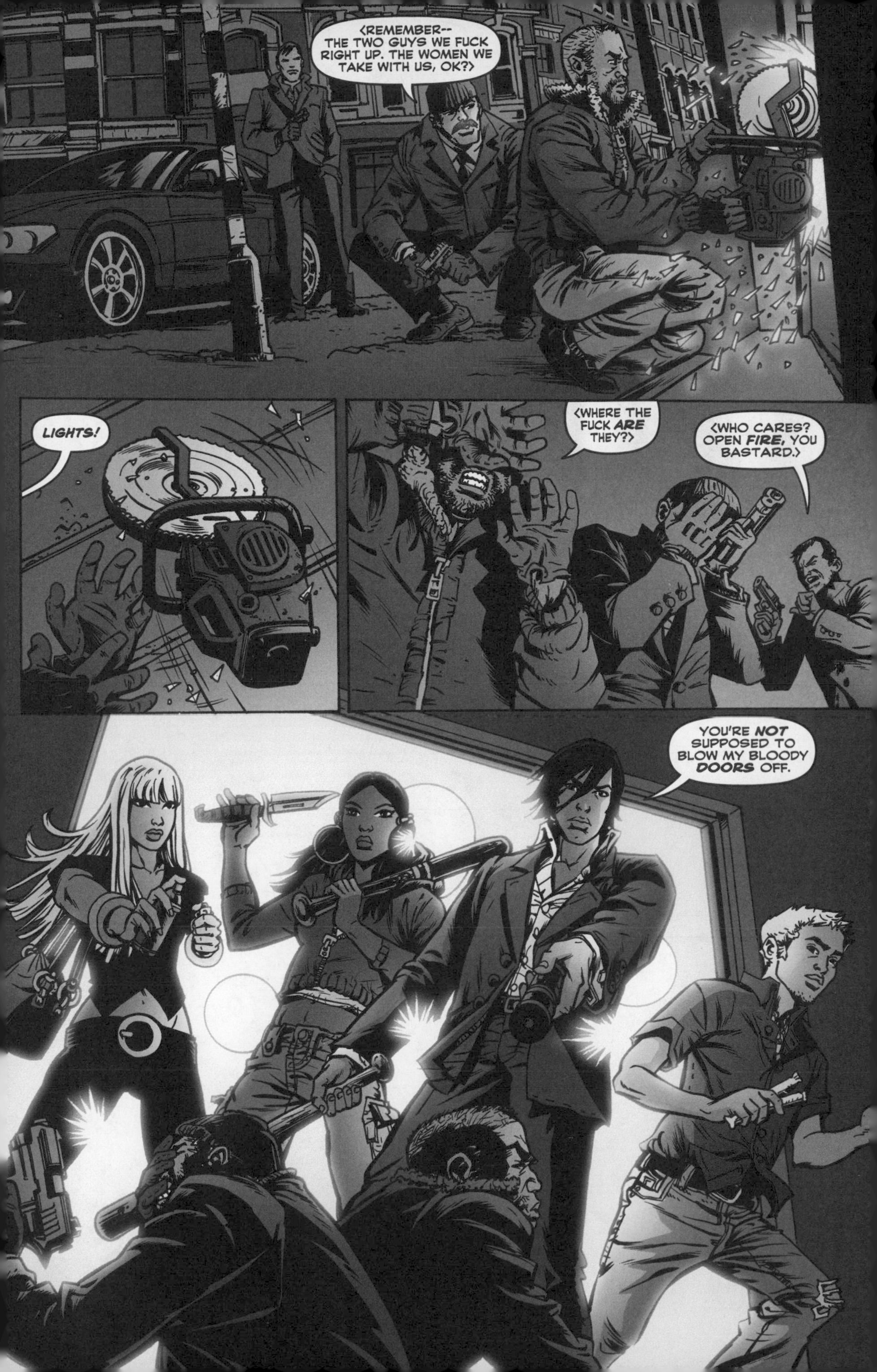

<REMEMBER-- THE TWO GUYS WE FUCK RIGHT UP. THE WOMEN WE TAKE WITH US, OK?>
LIGHTS!
<WHERE THE FUCK ARE THEY?>
<WHO CARES? OPEN FIRE, YOU BASTARD.>
YOU'RE NOT SUPPOSED TO BLOW MY BLOODY DOORS OFF.

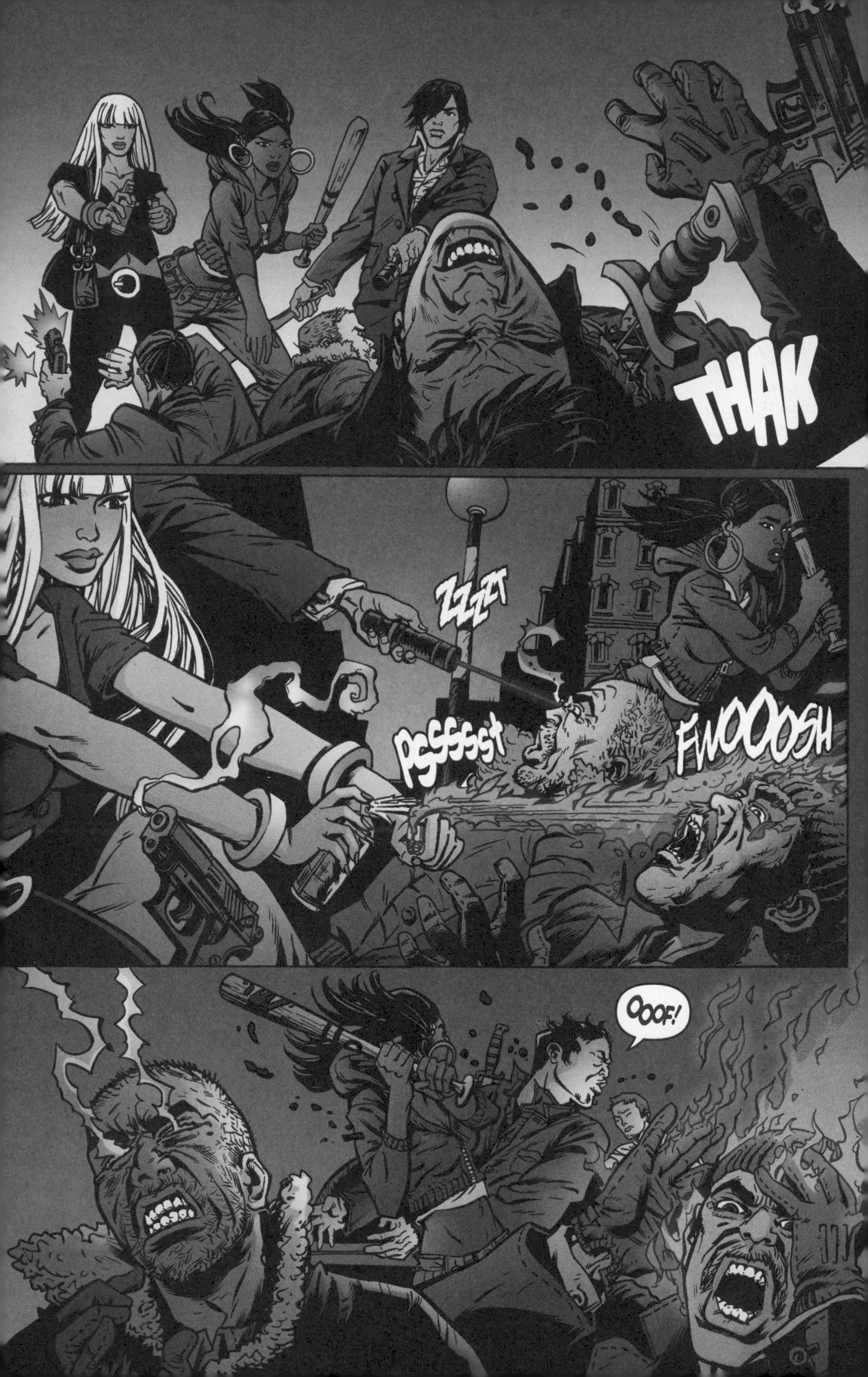
THAK
ZZZZT
PSSSSST
FWOOOSH
OOOF!

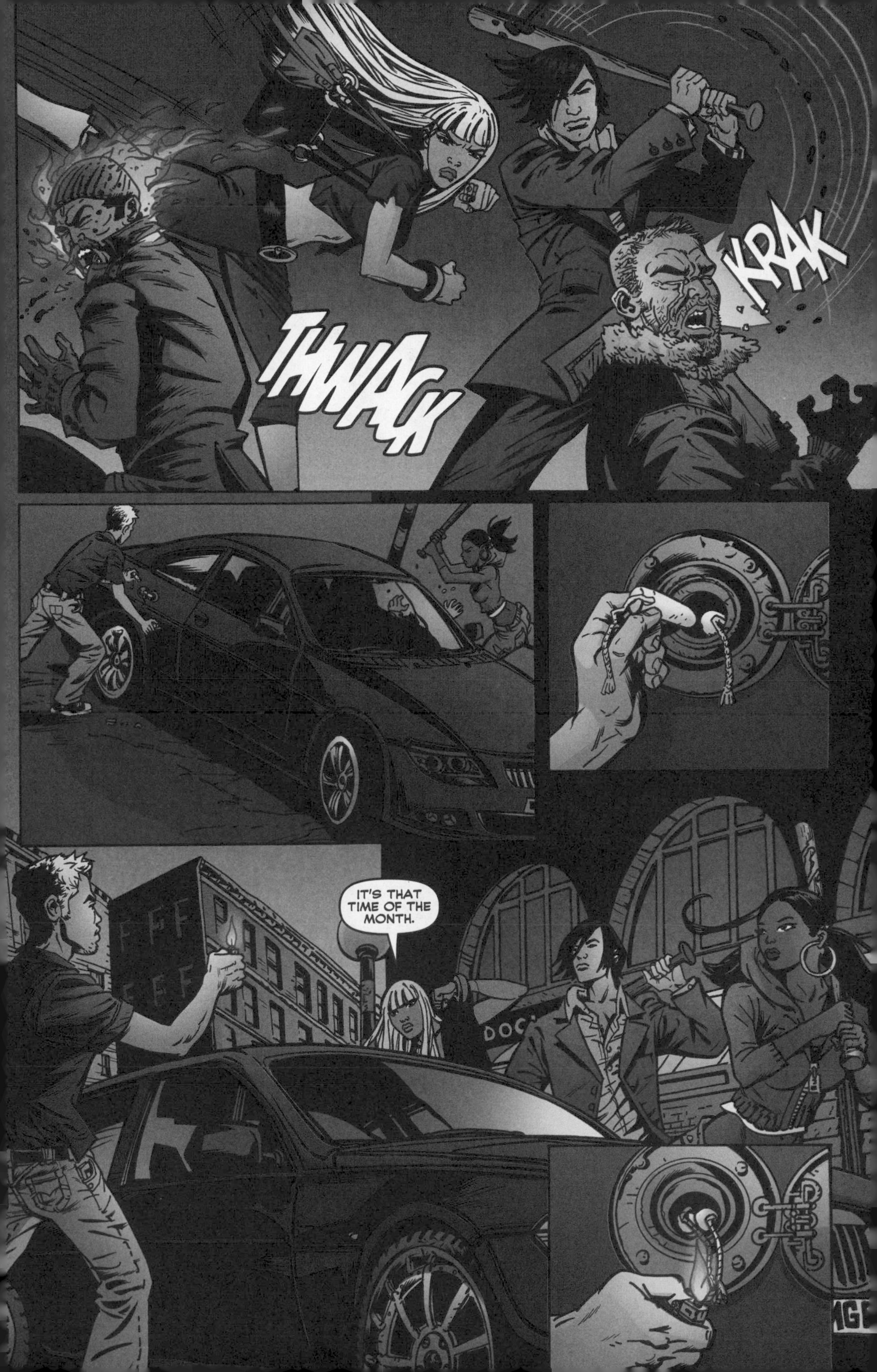
THWACK
KRAK
IT'S THAT TIME OF THE MONTH.

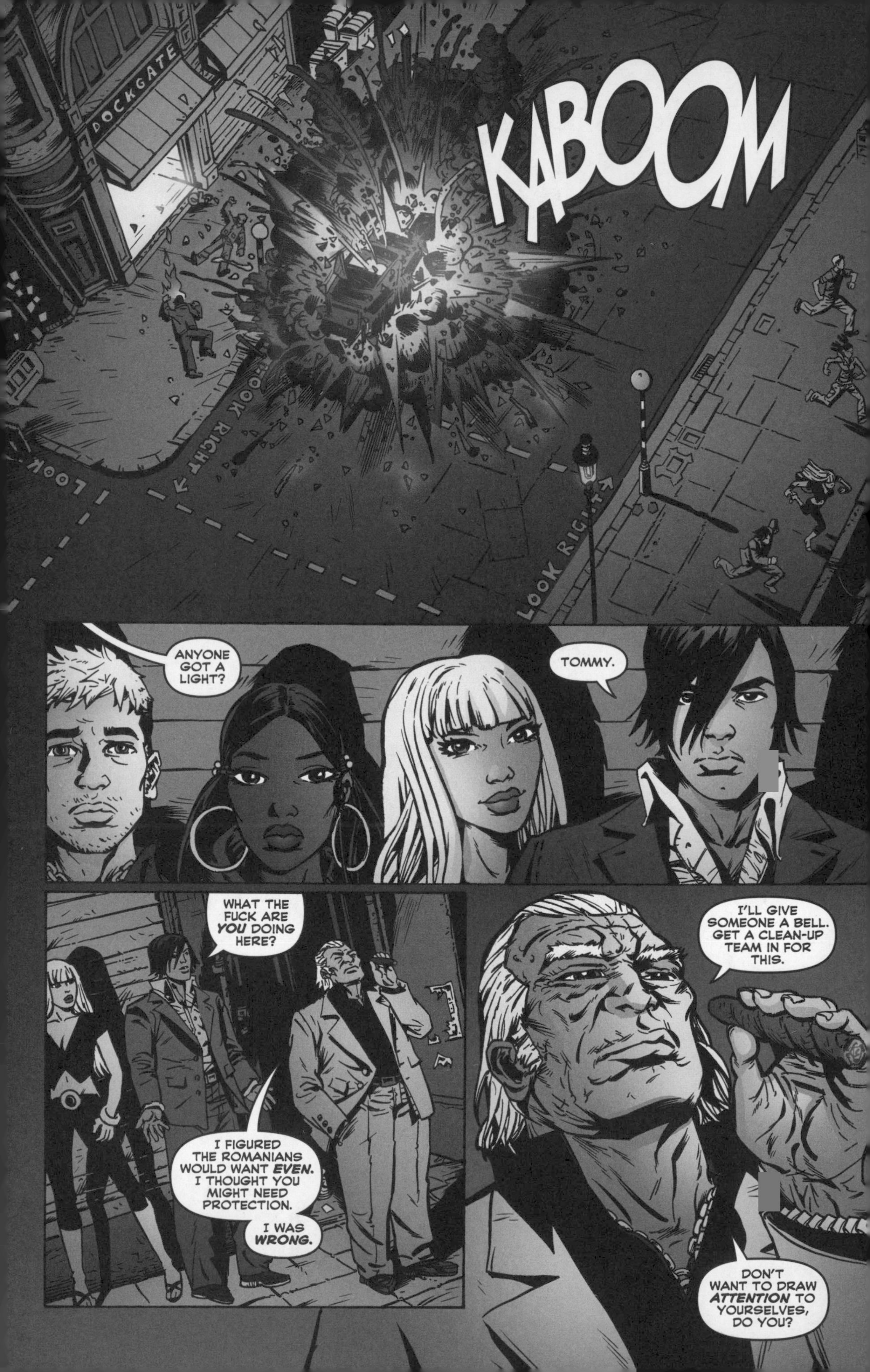
DOCKGATE
KABOOM
LOOK RIGHT
LOOK
LOOK RIGHT
ANYONE GOT A LIGHT?
TOMMY.
WHAT THE FUCK ARE YOU DOING HERE?
I FIGURED THE ROMANIANS WOULD WANT EVEN. I THOUGHT YOU MIGHT NEED PROTECTION.
I WAS WRONG.
I'LL GIVE SOMEONE A BELL. GET A CLEAN-UP TEAM IN FOR THIS.
DON'T WANT TO DRAW ATTENTION TO YOURSELVES, DO YOU?

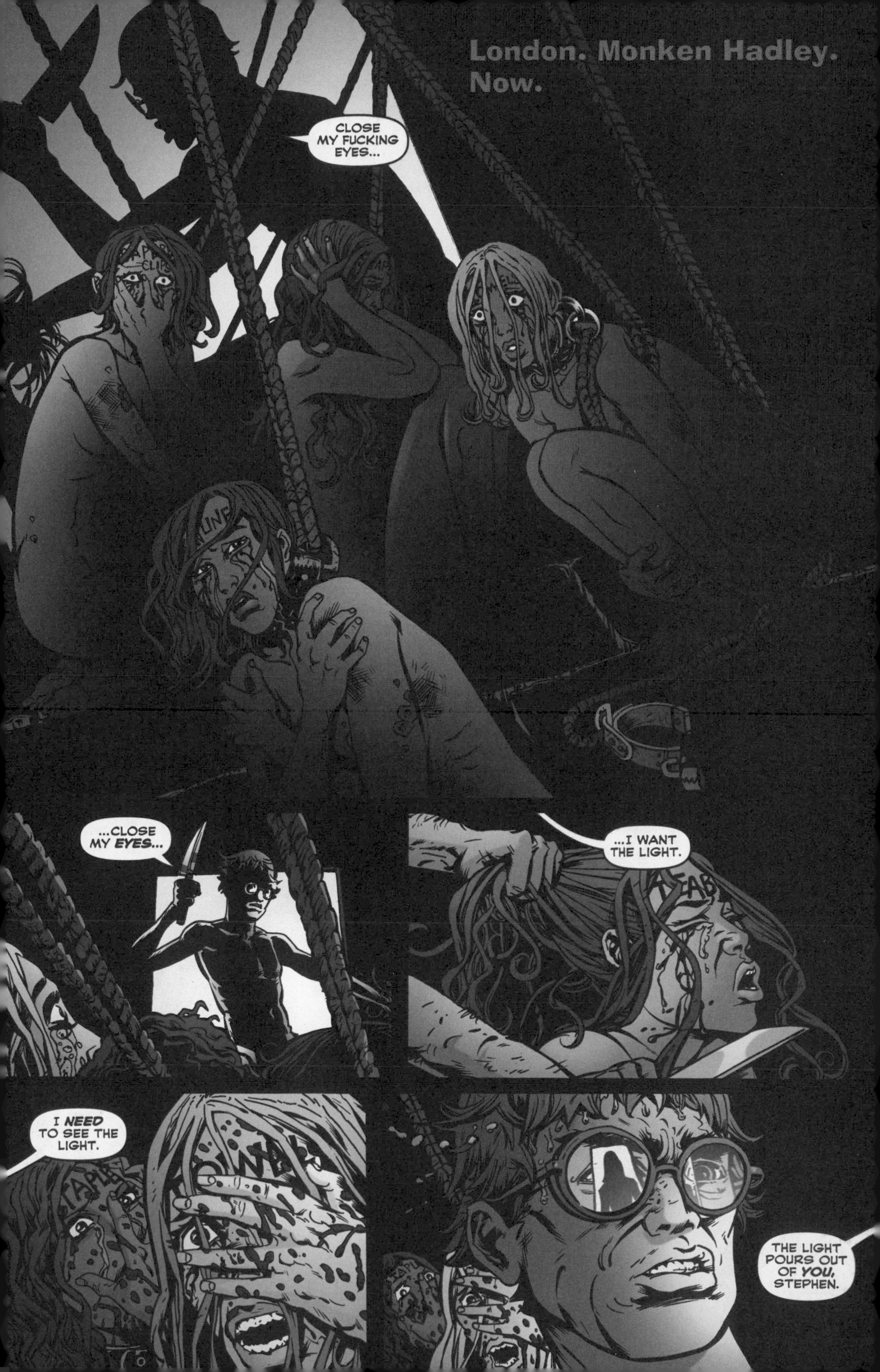
London. Monken Hadley.
Now.
CLOSE MY FUCKING EYES...
...CLOSE MY EYES...
...I WANT THE LIGHT.
I NEED TO SEE THE LIGHT.
THE LIGHT POURS OUT OF YOU, STEPHEN.

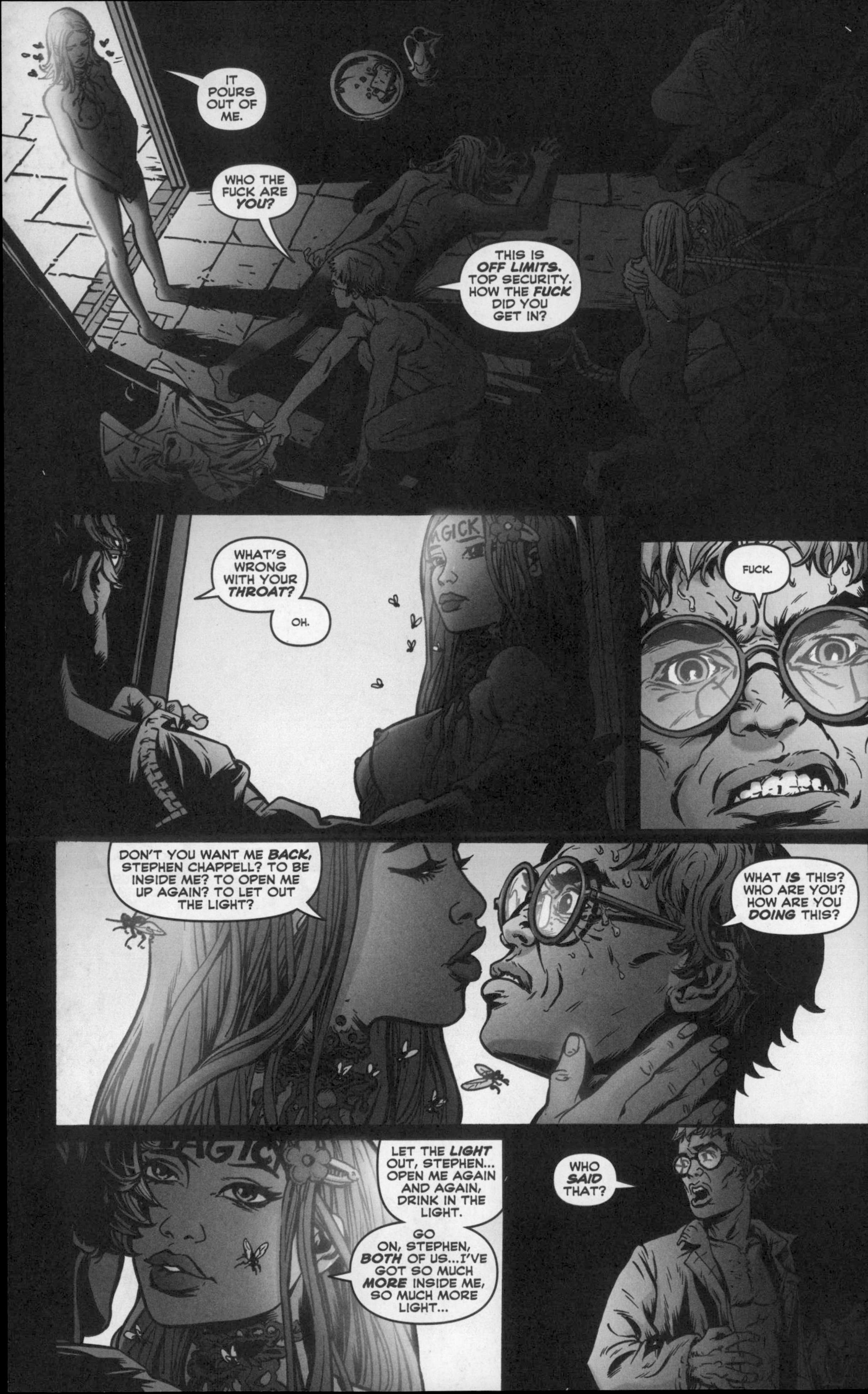
IT POURS OUT OF ME.
WHO THE FUCK ARE *YOU?*
THIS IS *OFF LIMITS.* TOP SECURITY. HOW THE *FUCK* DID YOU GET IN?
WHAT'S WRONG WITH YOUR *THROAT?*
OH.
FUCK.
DON'T YOU WANT ME *BACK,* STEPHEN CHAPPELL? TO BE INSIDE ME? TO OPEN ME UP AGAIN? TO LET OUT THE LIGHT?
WHAT *IS* THIS? WHO ARE YOU? HOW ARE YOU *DOING* THIS?
LET THE *LIGHT* OUT, STEPHEN... OPEN ME AGAIN AND AGAIN, DRINK IN THE LIGHT.
GO ON, STEPHEN, *BOTH* OF US...I'VE GOT SO MUCH *MORE* INSIDE ME, SO MUCH MORE LIGHT...
WHO *SAID* THAT?

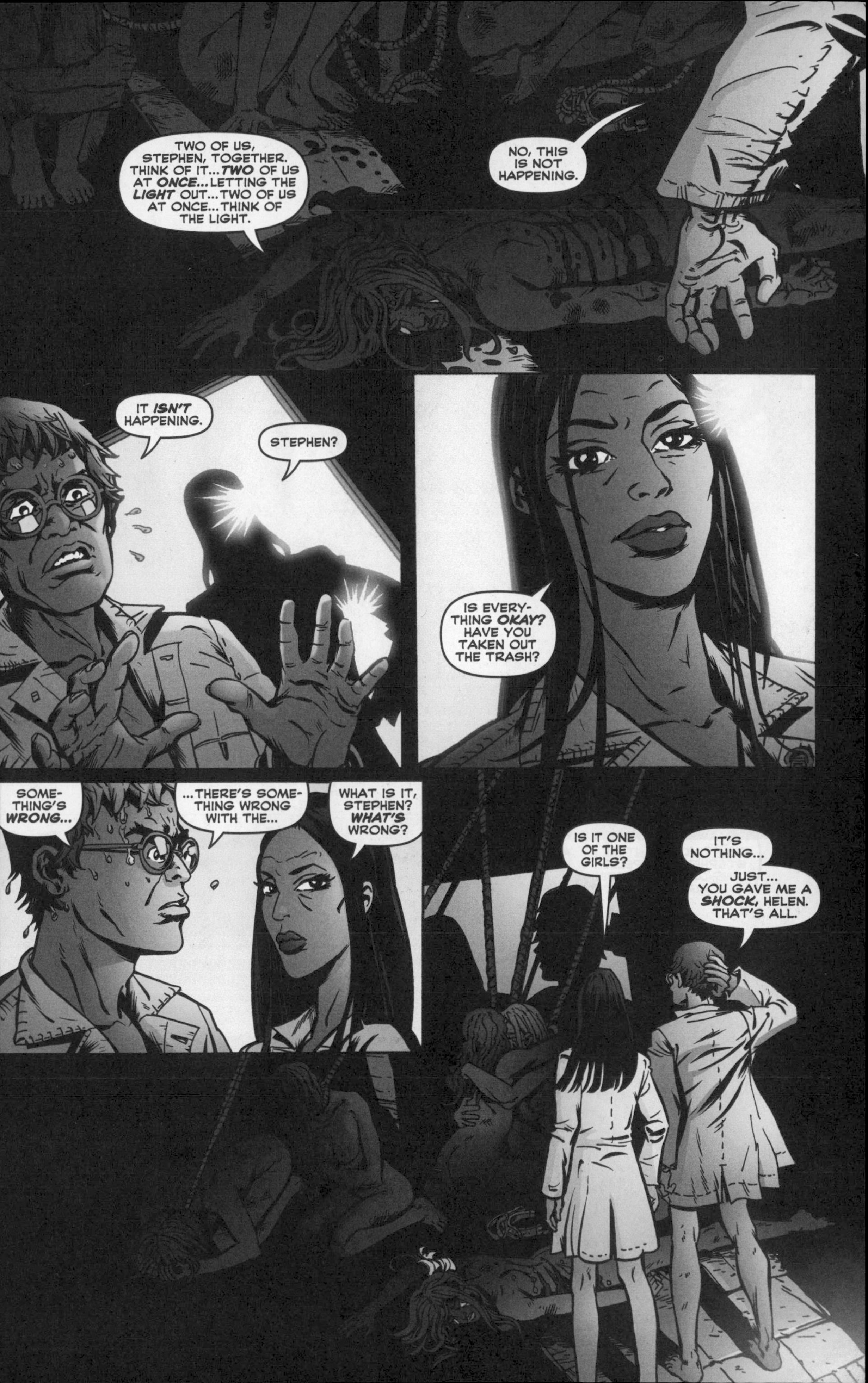
TWO OF US, STEPHEN, TOGETHER. THINK OF IT...TWO OF US AT ONCE...LETTING THE LIGHT OUT...TWO OF US AT ONCE...THINK OF THE LIGHT.
NO, THIS IS NOT HAPPENING.
IT ISN'T HAPPENING.
STEPHEN?
IS EVERY-THING OKAY? HAVE YOU TAKEN OUT THE TRASH?
SOME-THING'S WRONG...
...THERE'S SOME-THING WRONG WITH THE...
WHAT IS IT, STEPHEN? WHAT'S WRONG?
IS IT ONE OF THE GIRLS?
IT'S NOTHING...
JUST... YOU GAVE ME A SHOCK, HELEN. THAT'S ALL.

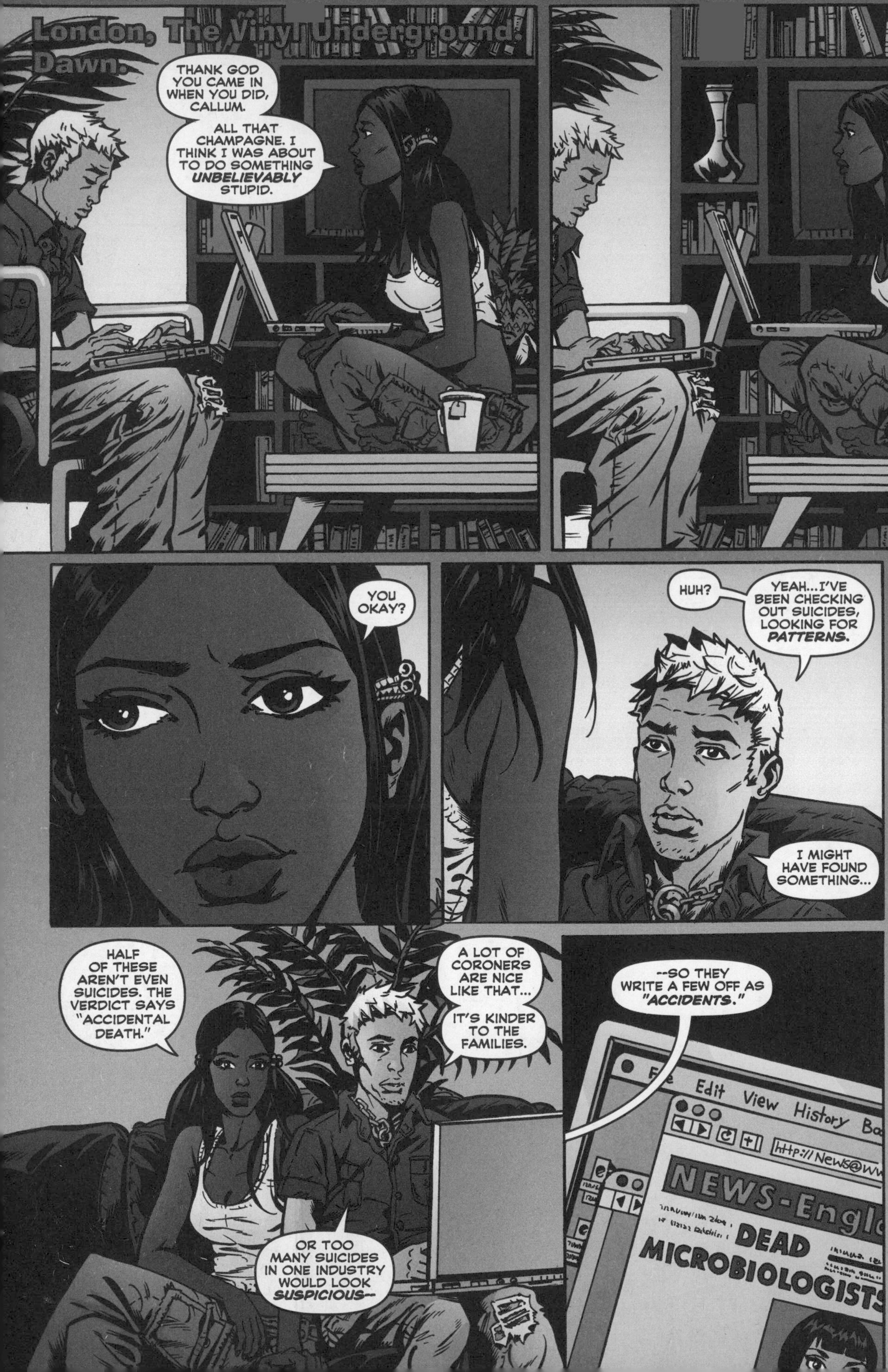
London, The Vinyl Underground. Dawn.
THANK GOD YOU CAME IN WHEN YOU DID, CALLUM.
ALL THAT CHAMPAGNE. I THINK I WAS ABOUT TO DO SOMETHING *UNBELIEVABLY* STUPID.
YOU OKAY?
HUH?
YEAH...I'VE BEEN CHECKING OUT SUICIDES, LOOKING FOR *PATTERNS.*
I MIGHT HAVE FOUND SOMETHING...
HALF OF THESE AREN'T EVEN SUICIDES. THE VERDICT SAYS "ACCIDENTAL DEATH."
A LOT OF CORONERS ARE NICE LIKE THAT...
IT'S KINDER TO THE FAMILIES.
OR TOO MANY SUICIDES IN ONE INDUSTRY WOULD LOOK *SUSPICIOUS*--
--SO THEY WRITE A FEW OFF AS *"ACCIDENTS."*
Edit View History
NEWS-Engl
DEAD MICROBIOLOGISTS

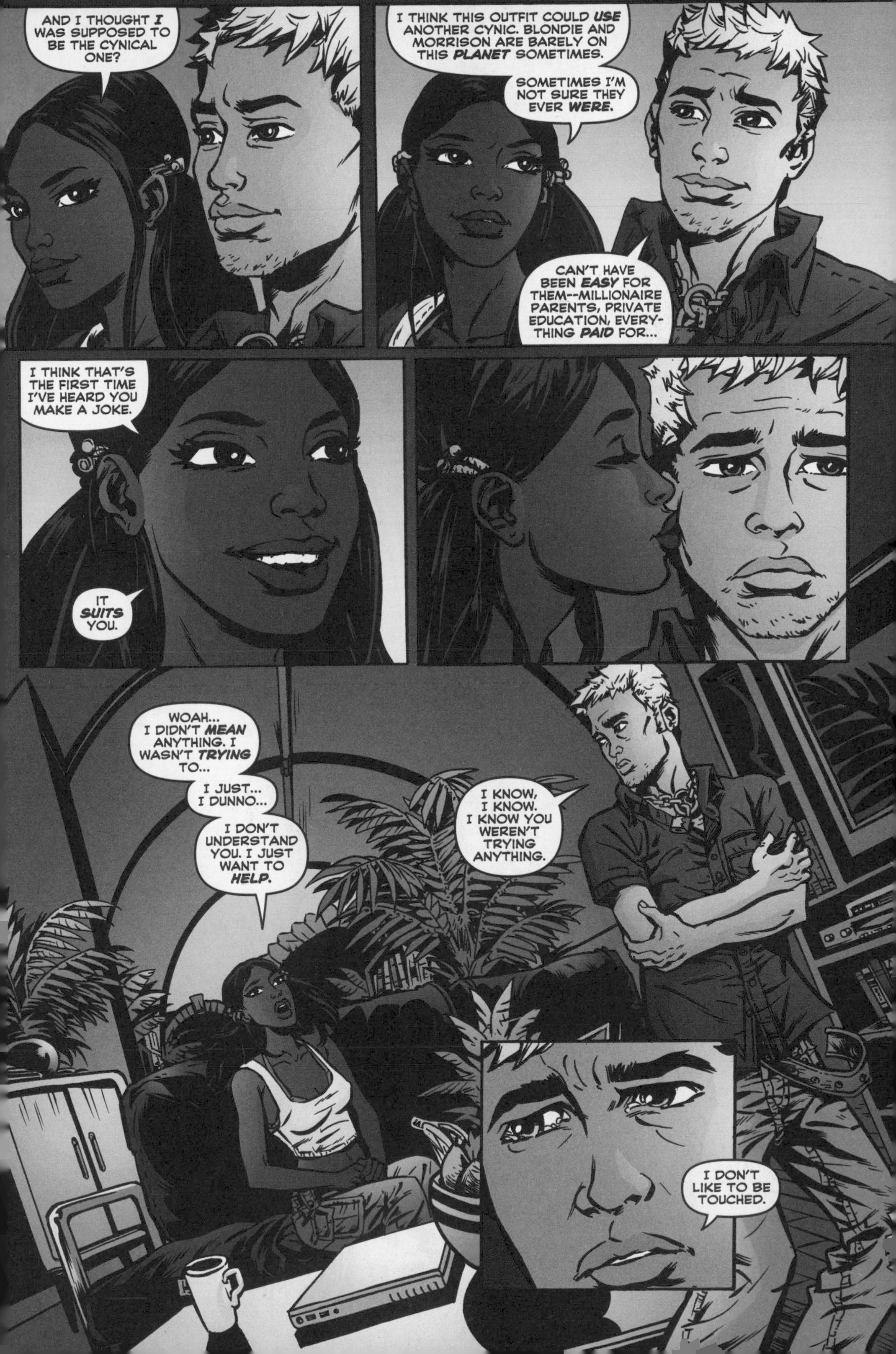
AND I THOUGHT I WAS SUPPOSED TO BE THE CYNICAL ONE?
I THINK THIS OUTFIT COULD USE ANOTHER CYNIC. BLONDIE AND MORRISON ARE BARELY ON THIS PLANET SOMETIMES.
SOMETIMES I'M NOT SURE THEY EVER WERE.
CAN'T HAVE BEEN EASY FOR THEM--MILLIONAIRE PARENTS, PRIVATE EDUCATION, EVERYTHING PAID FOR...
I THINK THAT'S THE FIRST TIME I'VE HEARD YOU MAKE A JOKE.
IT SUITS YOU.
WOAH... I DIDN'T MEAN ANYTHING. I WASN'T TRYING TO...
I JUST... I DUNNO...
I DON'T UNDERSTAND YOU. I JUST WANT TO HELP.
I KNOW, I KNOW. I KNOW YOU WEREN'T TRYING ANYTHING.
I DON'T LIKE TO BE TOUCHED.

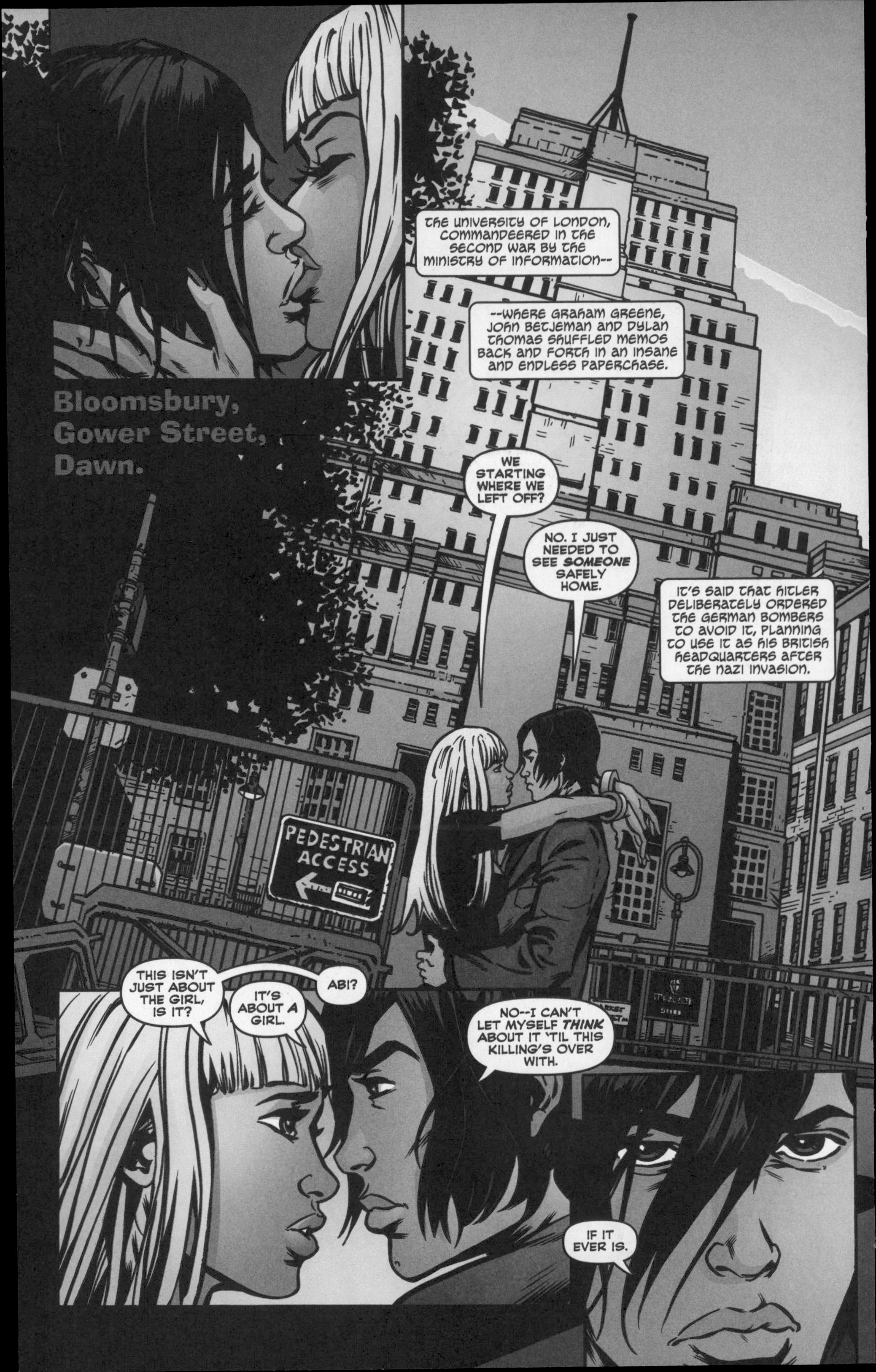
Bloomsbury, Gower Street, Dawn.
THE UNIVERSITY OF LONDON, COMMANDEERED IN THE SECOND WAR BY THE MINISTRY OF INFORMATION--
--WHERE GRAHAM GREENE, JOHN BETJEMAN AND DYLAN THOMAS SHUFFLED MEMOS BACK AND FORTH IN AN INSANE AND ENDLESS PAPERCHASE.
WE STARTING WHERE WE LEFT OFF?
NO. I JUST NEEDED TO SEE SOMEONE SAFELY HOME.
IT'S SAID THAT HITLER DELIBERATELY ORDERED THE GERMAN BOMBERS TO AVOID IT, PLANNING TO USE IT AS HIS BRITISH HEADQUARTERS AFTER THE NAZI INVASION.
PEDESTRIAN ACCESS
THIS ISN'T JUST ABOUT THE GIRL, IS IT?
ABI?
IT'S ABOUT A GIRL.
NO--I CAN'T LET MYSELF THINK ABOUT IT 'TIL THIS KILLING'S OVER WITH.
IF IT EVER IS.

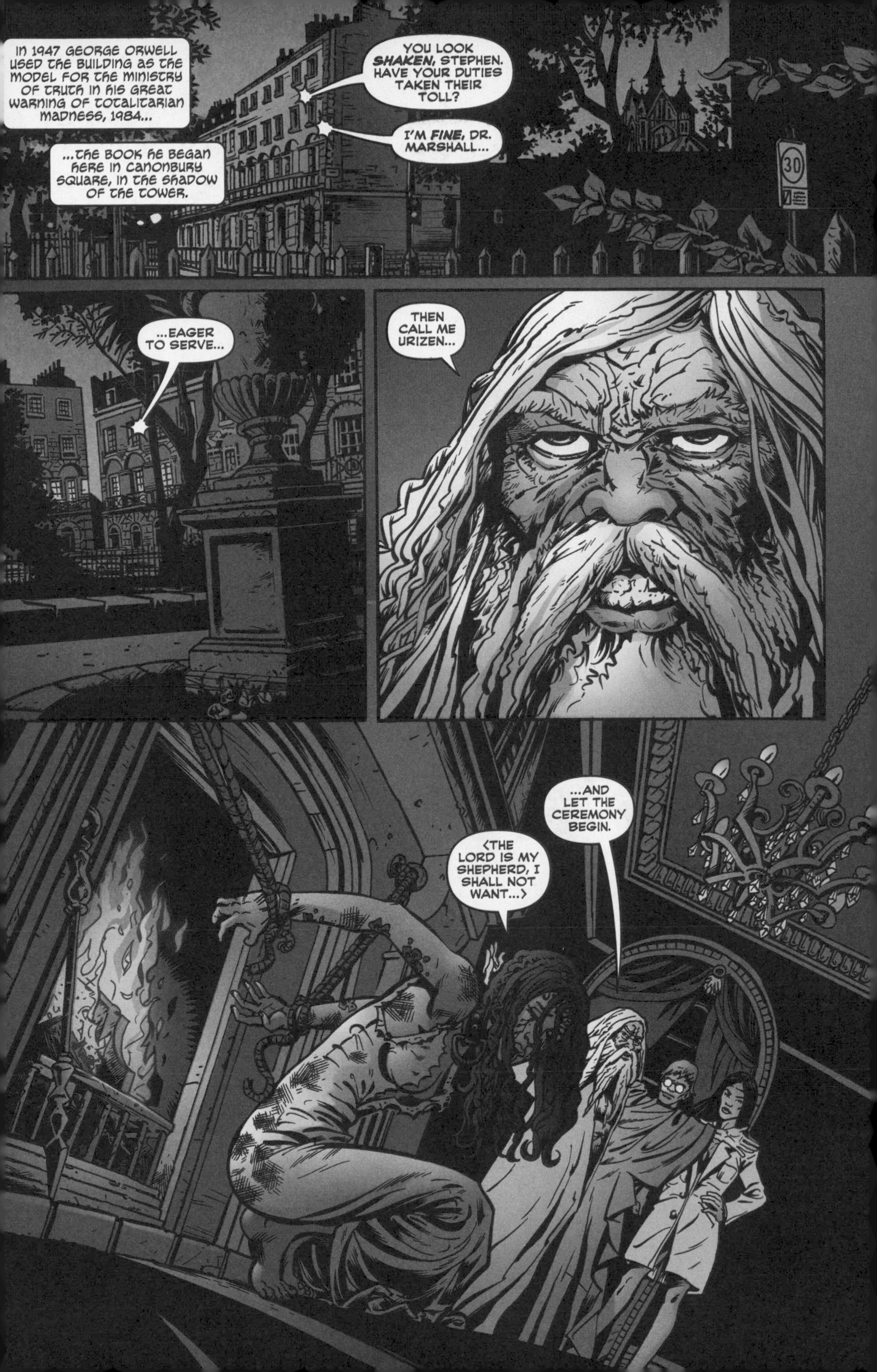
In 1947 George Orwell used the building as the model for the Ministry of Truth in his great warning of totalitarian madness, 1984...
YOU LOOK SHAKEN, STEPHEN. HAVE YOUR DUTIES TAKEN THEIR TOLL?
I'M FINE, DR. MARSHALL...
...the book he began here in Canonbury Square, in the shadow of the tower.
30
...EAGER TO SERVE...
THEN CALL ME URIZEN...
...AND LET THE CEREMONY BEGIN.
<THE LORD IS MY SHEPHERD, I SHALL NOT WANT...>

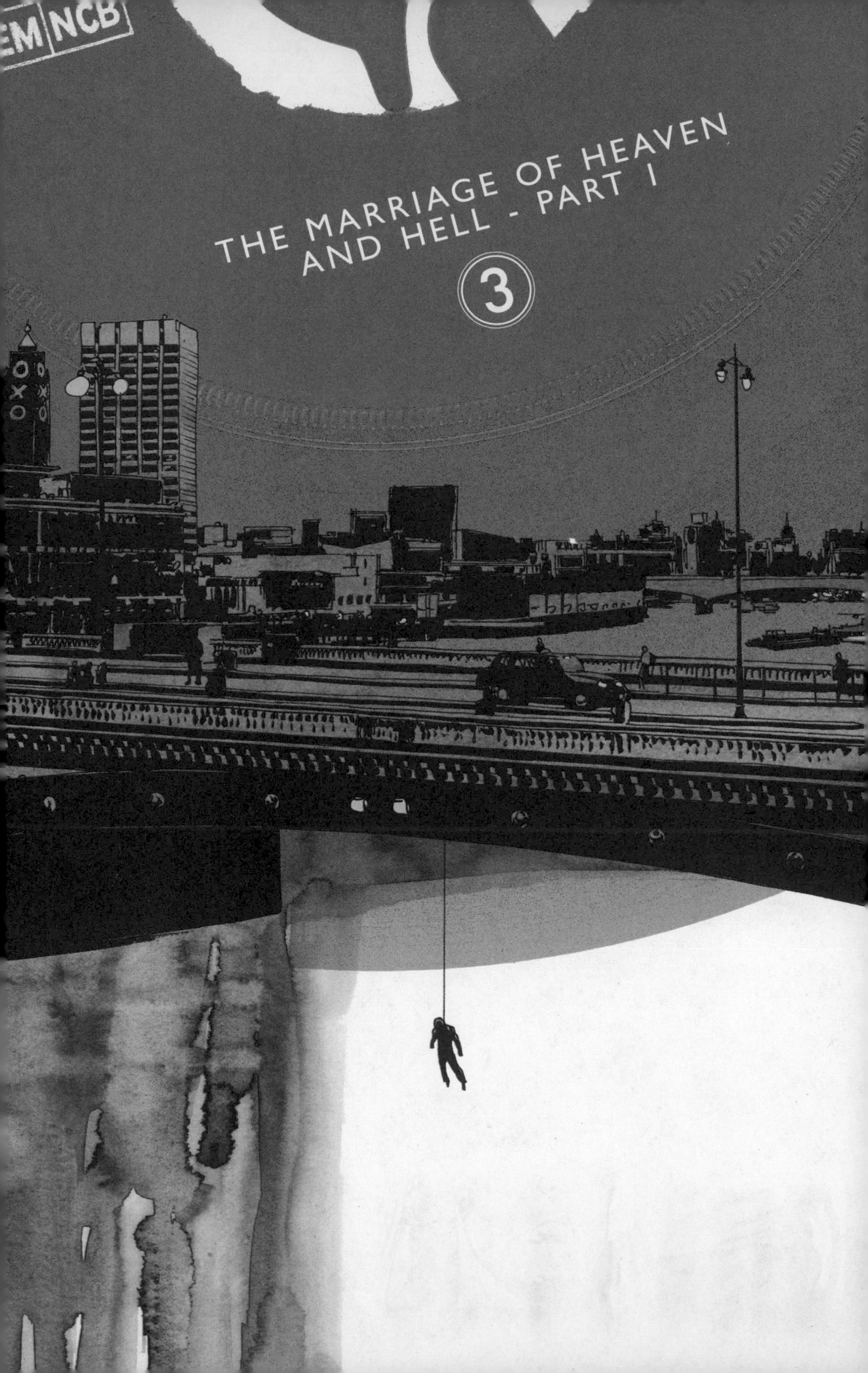
EM NCB
THE MARRIAGE OF HEAVEN
AND HELL - PART I
3

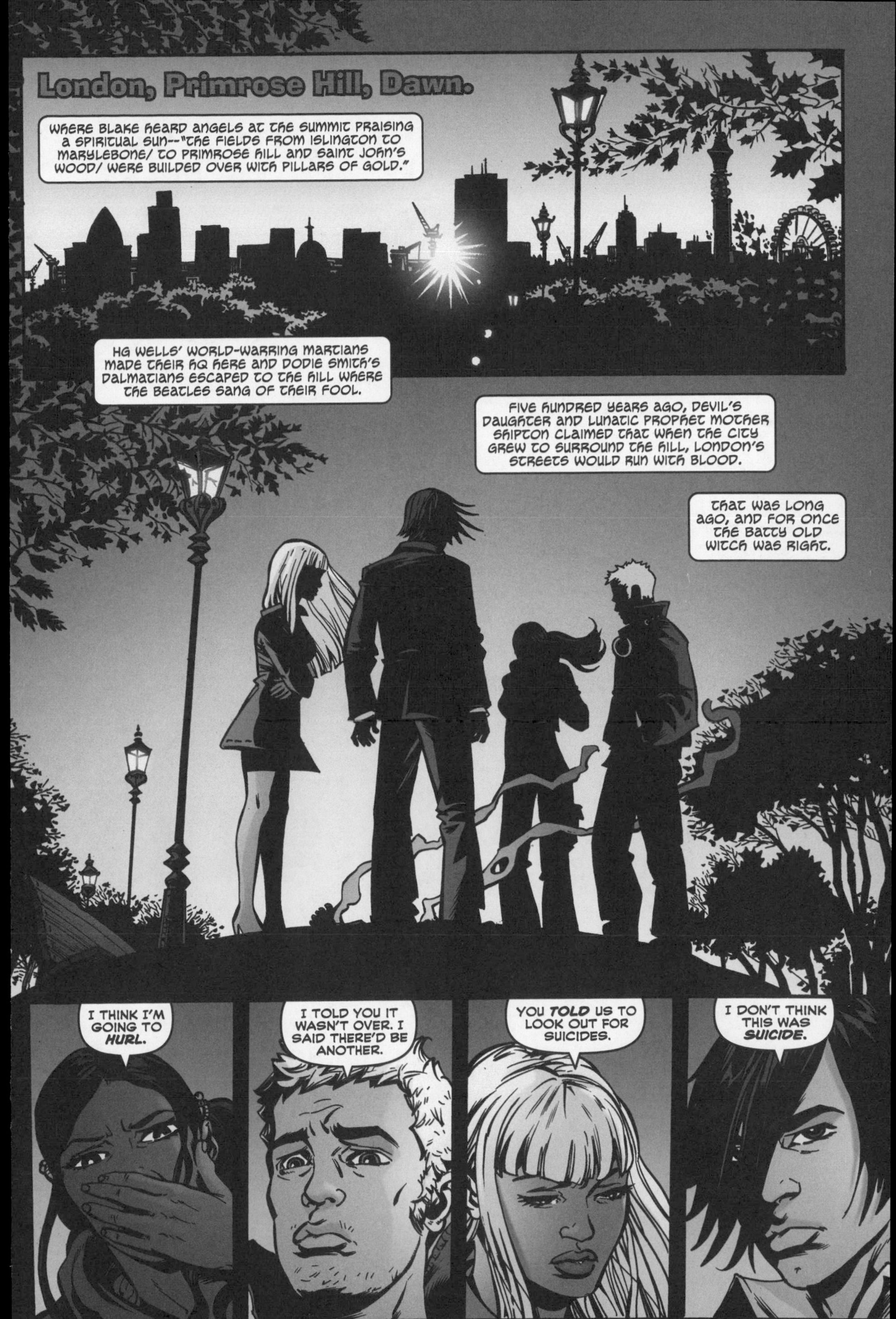

London, Primrose Hill, Dawn.
WHERE BLAKE HEARD ANGELS AT THE SUMMIT PRAISING A SPIRITUAL SUN--"THE FIELDS FROM ISLINGTON TO MARYLEBONE/ TO PRIMROSE HILL AND SAINT JOHN'S WOOD/ WERE BUILDED OVER WITH PILLARS OF GOLD."
HG WELLS' WORLD-WARRING MARTIANS MADE THEIR HQ HERE AND DODIE SMITH'S DALMATIANS ESCAPED TO THE HILL WHERE THE BEATLES SANG OF THEIR FOOL.
FIVE HUNDRED YEARS AGO, DEVIL'S DAUGHTER AND LUNATIC PROPHET MOTHER SHIPTON CLAIMED THAT WHEN THE CITY GREW TO SURROUND THE HILL, LONDON'S STREETS WOULD RUN WITH BLOOD.
THAT WAS LONG AGO, AND FOR ONCE THE BATTY OLD WITCH WAS RIGHT.
I THINK I'M GOING TO HURL.
I TOLD YOU IT WASN'T OVER. I SAID THERE'D BE ANOTHER.
YOU TOLD US TO LOOK OUT FOR SUICIDES.
I DON'T THINK THIS WAS SUICIDE.

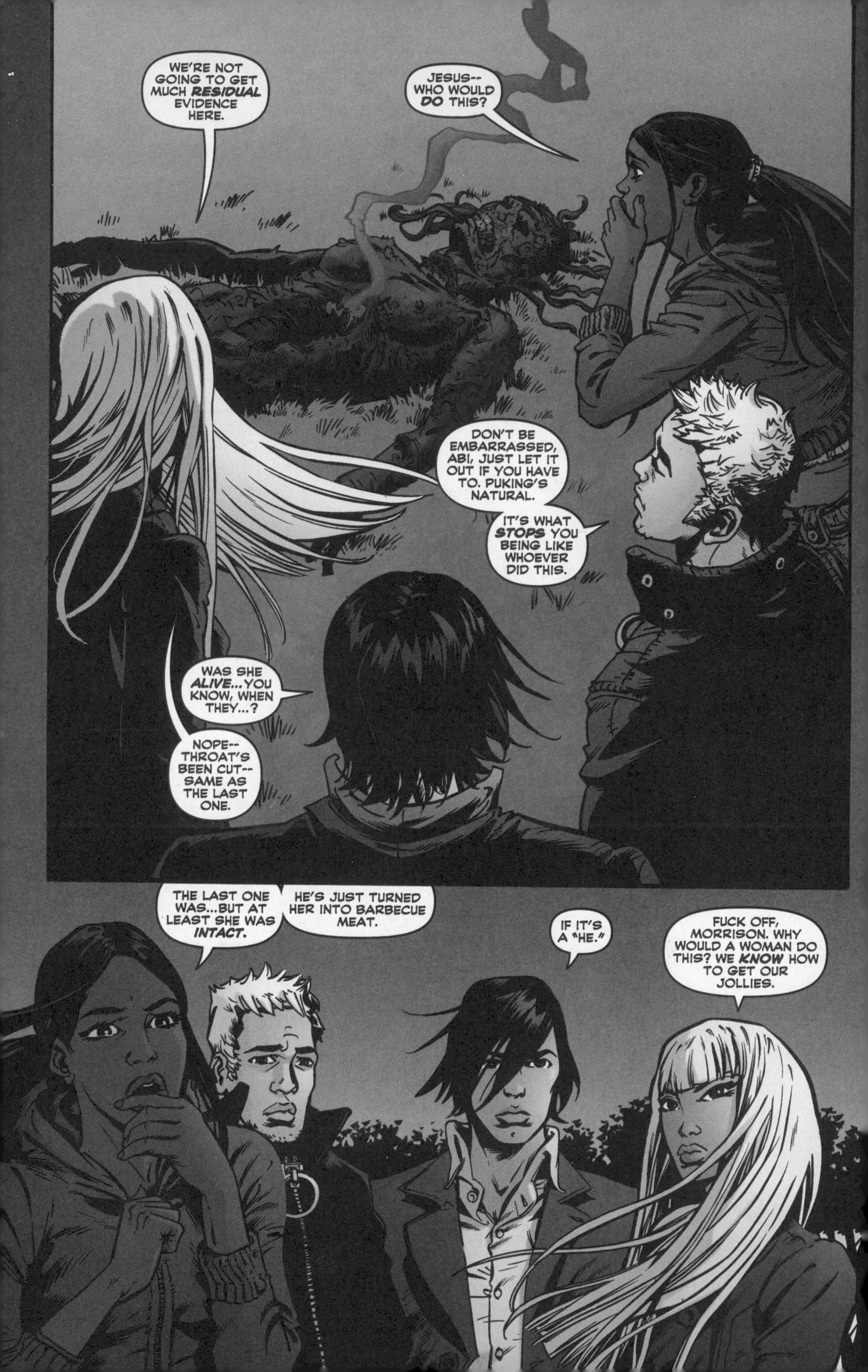
WE'RE NOT GOING TO GET MUCH RESIDUAL EVIDENCE HERE.
JESUS-- WHO WOULD DO THIS?
DON'T BE EMBARRASSED, ABI, JUST LET IT OUT IF YOU HAVE TO. PUKING'S NATURAL.
IT'S WHAT STOPS YOU BEING LIKE WHOEVER DID THIS.
WAS SHE ALIVE... YOU KNOW, WHEN THEY...?
NOPE-- THROAT'S BEEN CUT-- SAME AS THE LAST ONE.
THE LAST ONE WAS... BUT AT LEAST SHE WAS INTACT.
HE'S JUST TURNED HER INTO BARBECUE MEAT.
IF IT'S A "HE."
FUCK OFF, MORRISON. WHY WOULD A WOMAN DO THIS? WE KNOW HOW TO GET OUR JOLLIES.

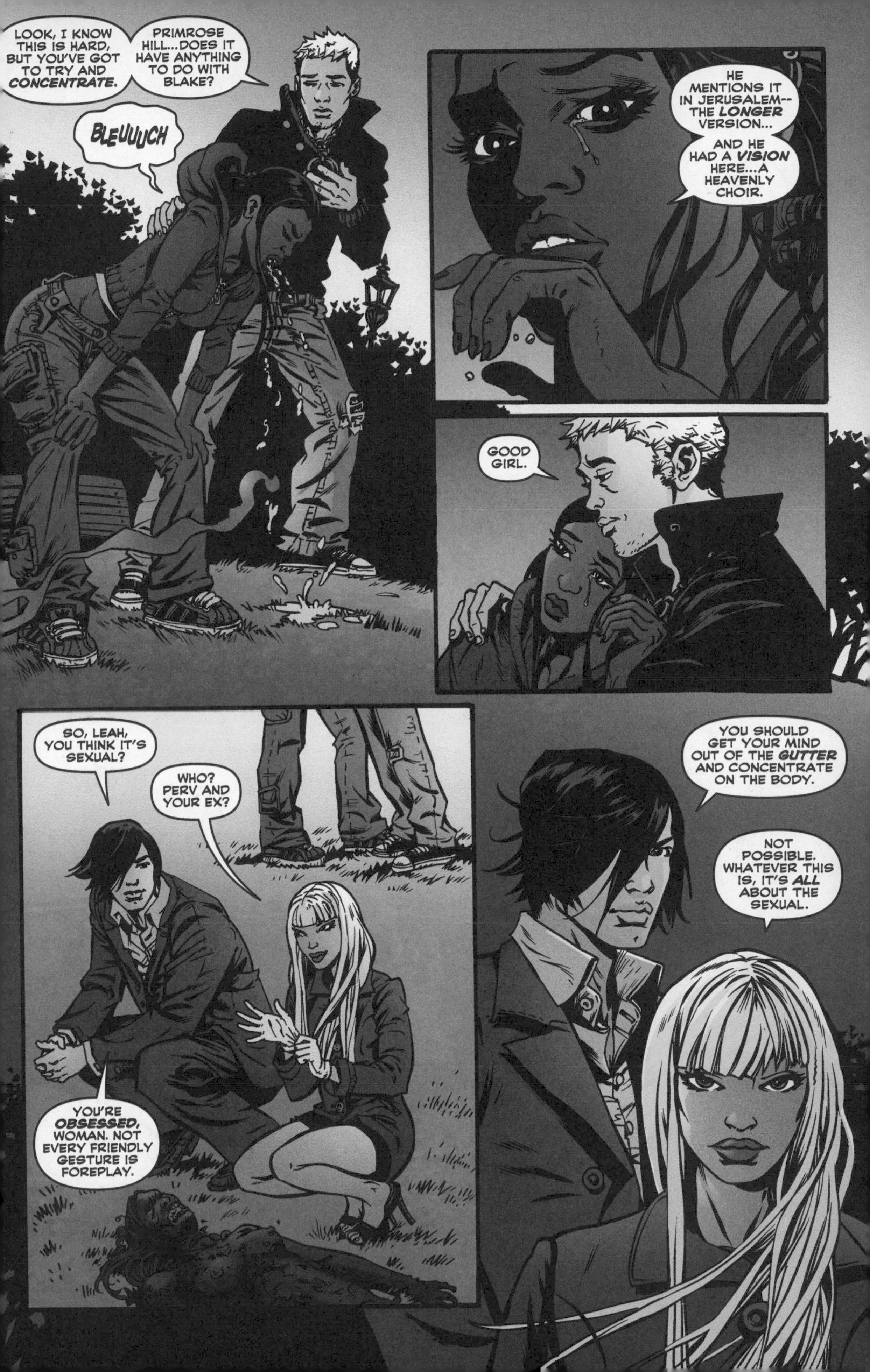
LOOK, I KNOW THIS IS HARD, BUT YOU'VE GOT TO TRY AND CONCENTRATE.
PRIMROSE HILL...DOES IT HAVE ANYTHING TO DO WITH BLAKE?
BLEUUUCH
HE MENTIONS IT IN JERUSALEM-- THE LONGER VERSION...
AND HE HAD A VISION HERE...A HEAVENLY CHOIR.
GOOD GIRL.
SO, LEAH, YOU THINK IT'S SEXUAL?
WHO? PERV AND YOUR EX?
YOU'RE OBSESSED, WOMAN. NOT EVERY FRIENDLY GESTURE IS FOREPLAY.
YOU SHOULD GET YOUR MIND OUT OF THE GUTTER AND CONCENTRATE ON THE BODY.
NOT POSSIBLE. WHATEVER THIS IS, IT'S ALL ABOUT THE SEXUAL.

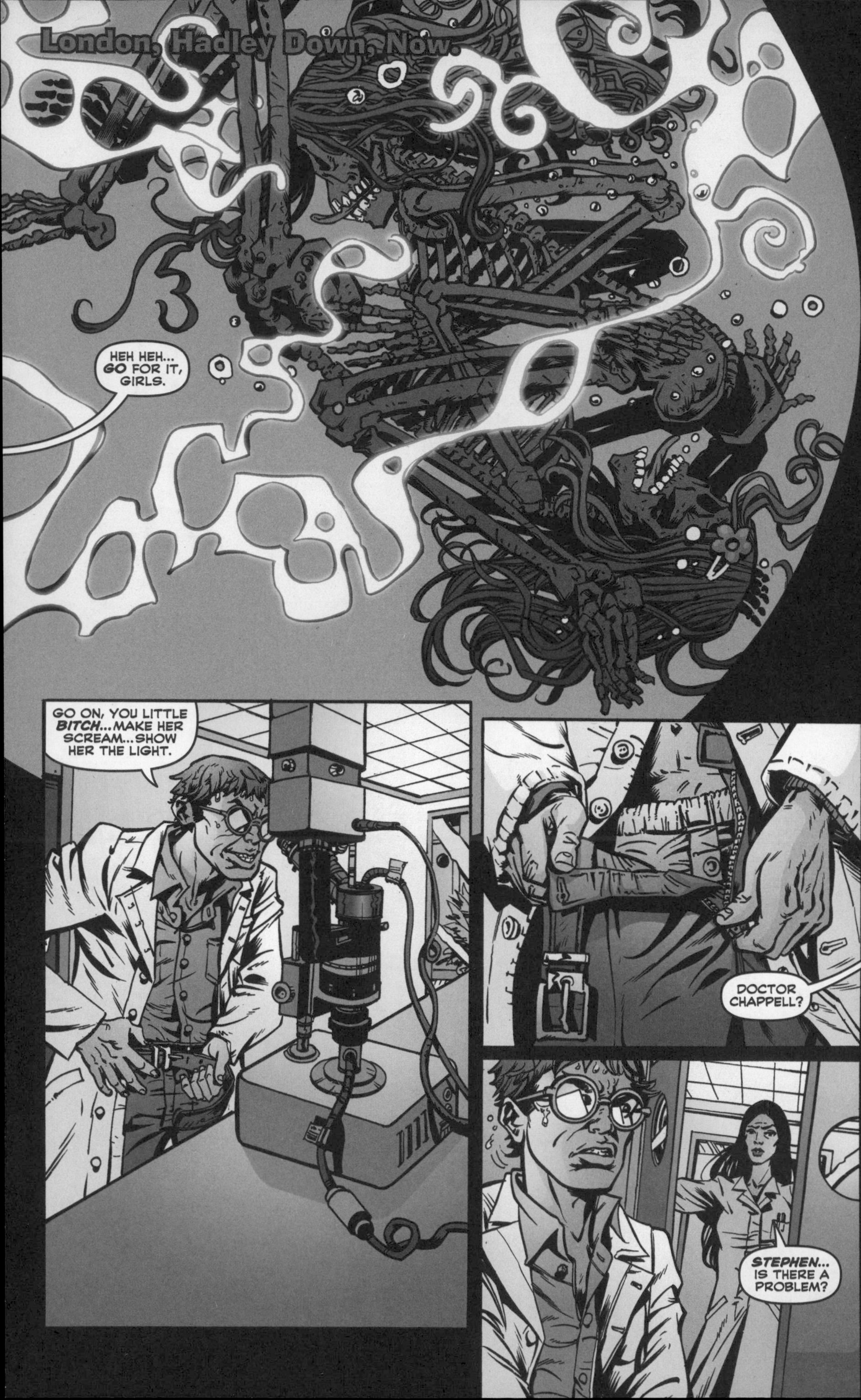
London, Hadley Down, Now.
HEH HEH... GO FOR IT, GIRLS.
GO ON, YOU LITTLE BITCH... MAKE HER SCREAM... SHOW HER THE LIGHT.
DOCTOR CHAPPELL?
STEPHEN... IS THERE A PROBLEM?

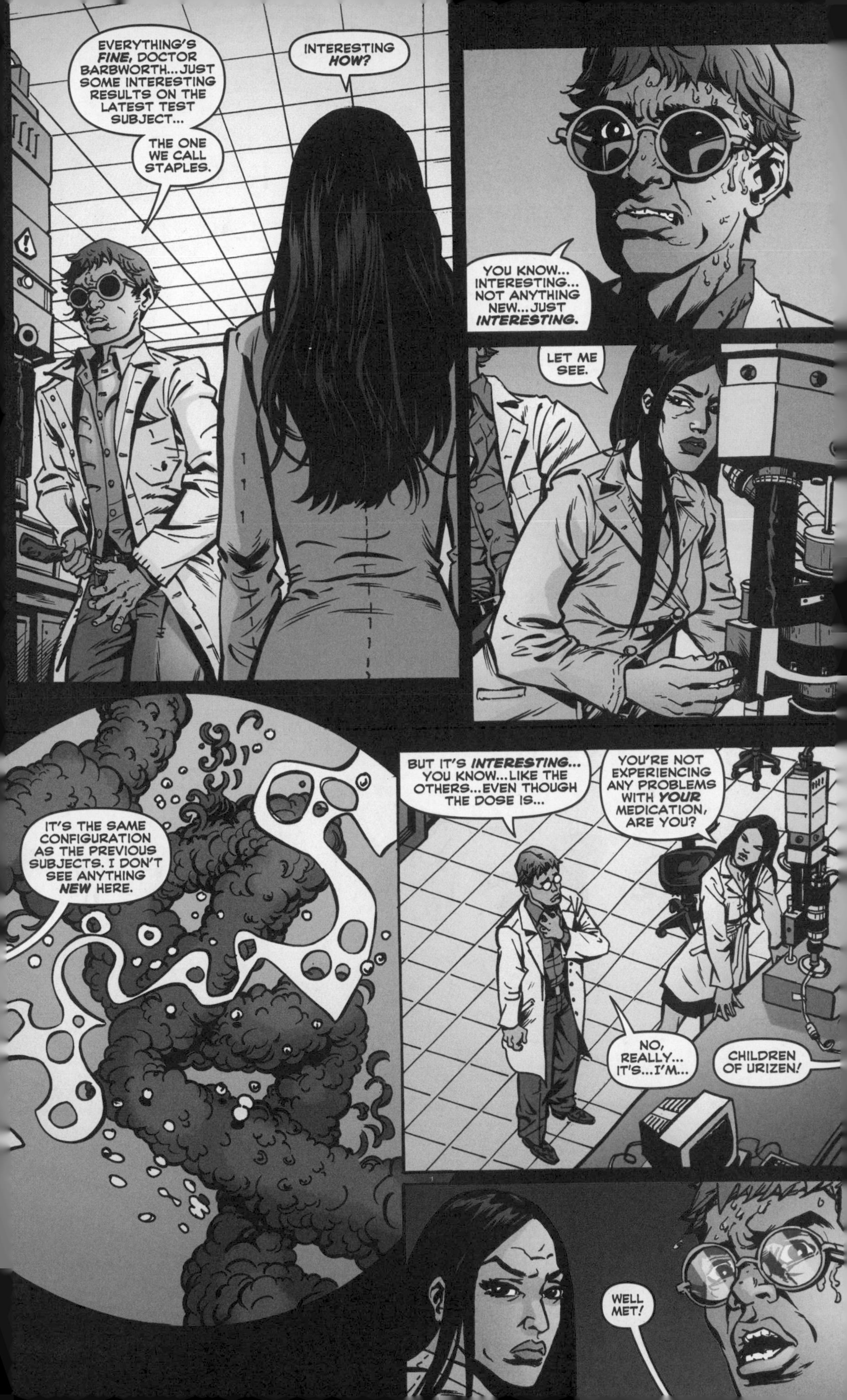
EVERYTHING'S FINE, DOCTOR BARBWORTH...JUST SOME INTERESTING RESULTS ON THE LATEST TEST SUBJECT...
THE ONE WE CALL STAPLES.
INTERESTING HOW?
YOU KNOW... INTERESTING... NOT ANYTHING NEW...JUST INTERESTING.
LET ME SEE.
IT'S THE SAME CONFIGURATION AS THE PREVIOUS SUBJECTS. I DON'T SEE ANYTHING NEW HERE.
BUT IT'S INTERESTING... YOU KNOW...LIKE THE OTHERS...EVEN THOUGH THE DOSE IS...
YOU'RE NOT EXPERIENCING ANY PROBLEMS WITH YOUR MEDICATION, ARE YOU?
NO, REALLY... IT'S...I'M...
CHILDREN OF URIZEN!
WELL MET!

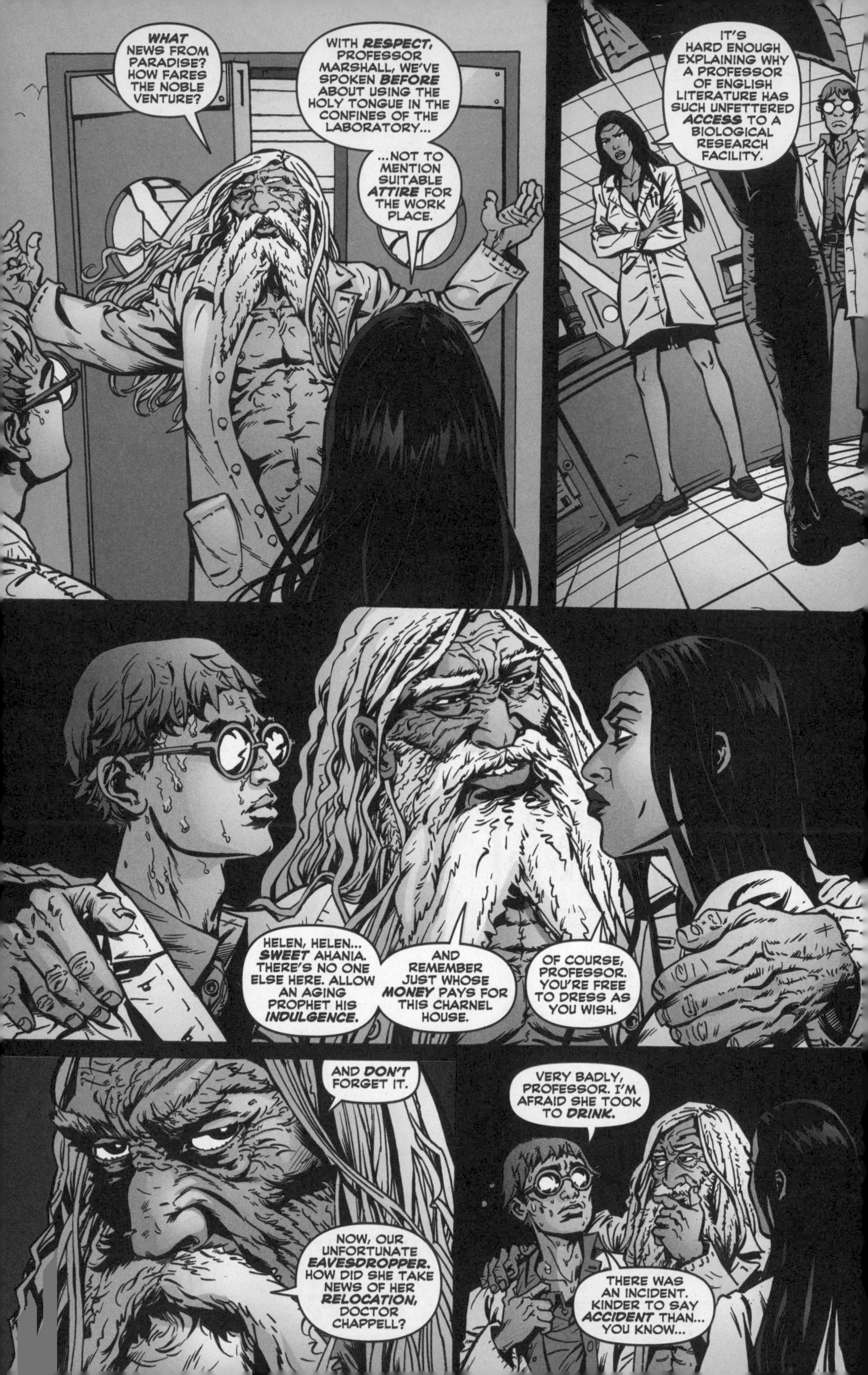
WHAT NEWS FROM PARADISE? HOW FARES THE NOBLE VENTURE?
WITH RESPECT, PROFESSOR MARSHALL, WE'VE SPOKEN BEFORE ABOUT USING THE HOLY TONGUE IN THE CONFINES OF THE LABORATORY...
...NOT TO MENTION SUITABLE ATTIRE FOR THE WORK PLACE.
IT'S HARD ENOUGH EXPLAINING WHY A PROFESSOR OF ENGLISH LITERATURE HAS SUCH UNFETTERED ACCESS TO A BIOLOGICAL RESEARCH FACILITY.
HELEN, HELEN... SWEET AHANIA. THERE'S NO ONE ELSE HERE. ALLOW AN AGING PROPHET HIS INDULGENCE.
AND REMEMBER JUST WHOSE MONEY PAYS FOR THIS CHARNEL HOUSE.
OF COURSE, PROFESSOR. YOU'RE FREE TO DRESS AS YOU WISH.
AND DON'T FORGET IT.
NOW, OUR UNFORTUNATE EAVESDROPPER. HOW DID SHE TAKE NEWS OF HER RELOCATION, DOCTOR CHAPPELL?
VERY BADLY, PROFESSOR. I'M AFRAID SHE TOOK TO DRINK.
THERE WAS AN INCIDENT. KINDER TO SAY ACCIDENT THAN... YOU KNOW...

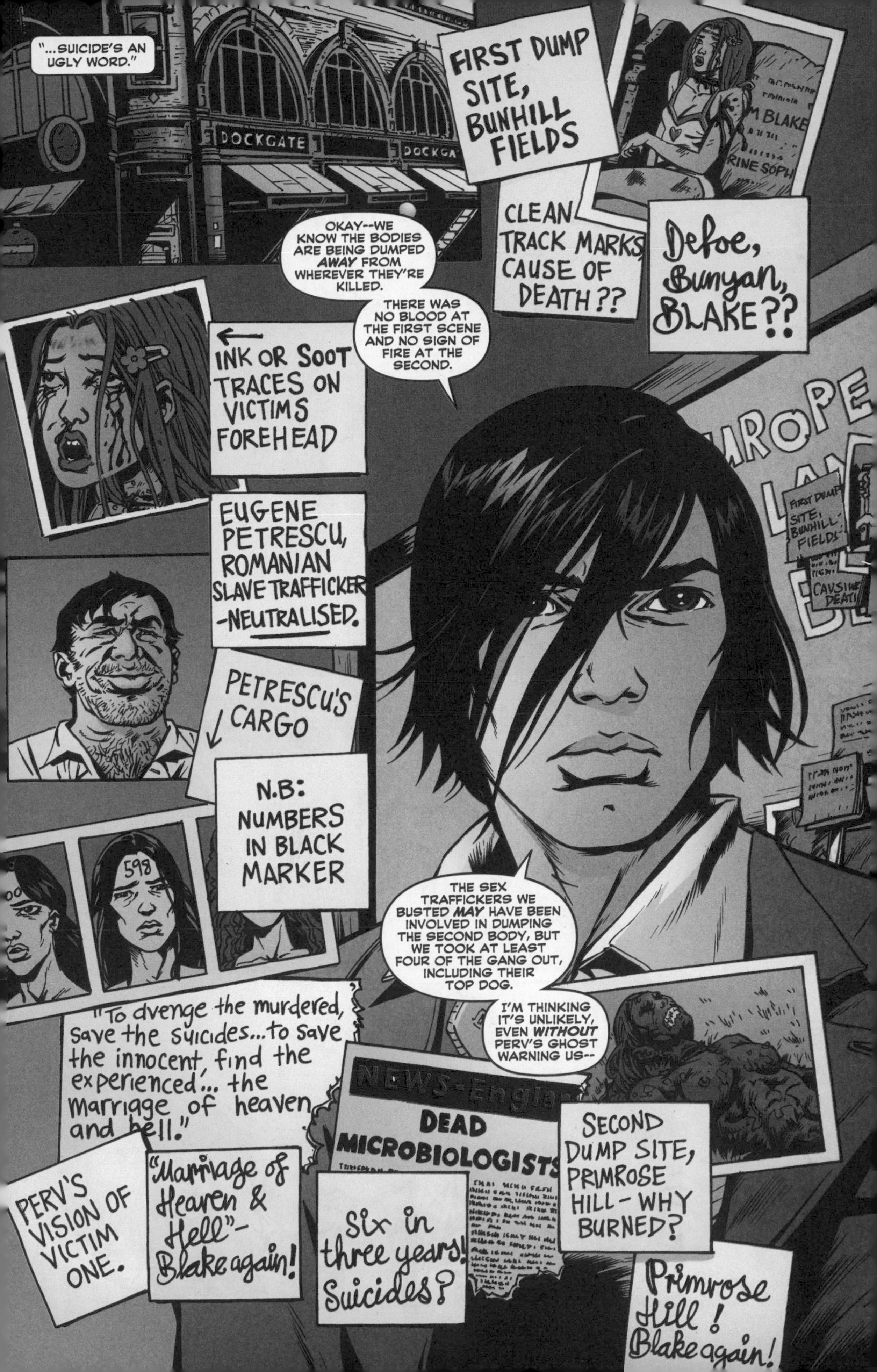
"...SUICIDE'S AN UGLY WORD."
DOCKGATE
FIRST DUMP SITE, BUNHILL FIELDS
OKAY--WE KNOW THE BODIES ARE BEING DUMPED AWAY FROM WHEREVER THEY'RE KILLED.
THERE WAS NO BLOOD AT THE FIRST SCENE AND NO SIGN OF FIRE AT THE SECOND.
CLEAN TRACK MARKS, CAUSE OF DEATH??
Defoe, Bunyan, BLAKE??
INK OR SOOT TRACES ON VICTIMS FOREHEAD
EUGENE PETRESCU, ROMANIAN SLAVE TRAFFICKER -NEUTRALISED.
PETRESCU'S CARGO
N.B: NUMBERS IN BLACK MARKER
598
THE SEX TRAFFICKERS WE BUSTED MAY HAVE BEEN INVOLVED IN DUMPING THE SECOND BODY, BUT WE TOOK AT LEAST FOUR OF THE GANG OUT, INCLUDING THEIR TOP DOG.
I'M THINKING IT'S UNLIKELY, EVEN WITHOUT PERV'S GHOST WARNING US--
"To avenge the murdered, save the suicides...to save the innocent, find the experienced... the marriage of heaven and hell."
DEAD MICROBIOLOGISTS
SECOND DUMP SITE, PRIMROSE HILL - WHY BURNED?
PERV'S VISION OF VICTIM ONE.
"Marriage of Heaven & Hell"- Blake again!
Six in three years! Suicides?
Primrose Hill! Blake again!

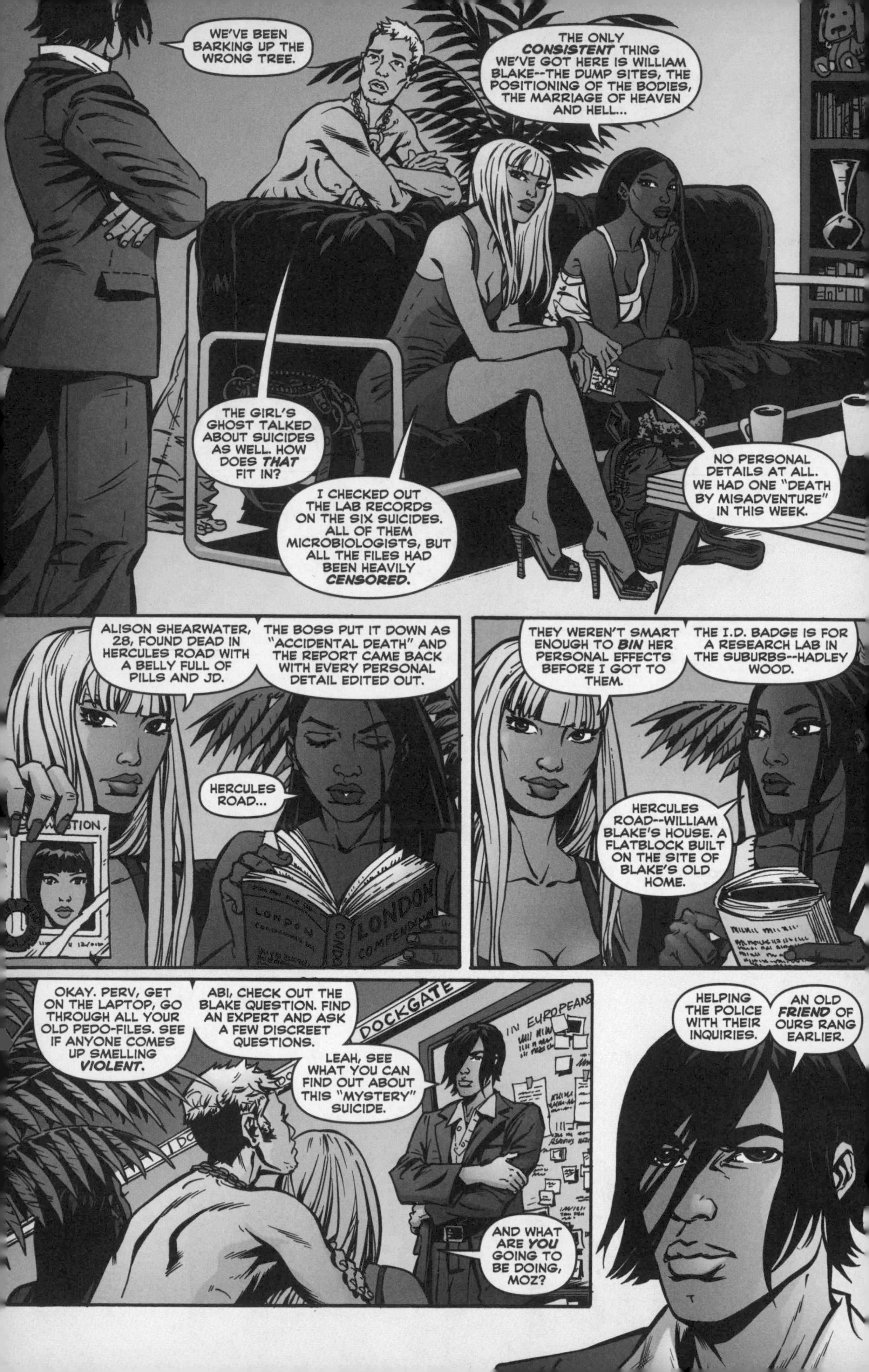
WE'VE BEEN BARKING UP THE WRONG TREE.
THE ONLY CONSISTENT THING WE'VE GOT HERE IS WILLIAM BLAKE--THE DUMP SITES, THE POSITIONING OF THE BODIES, THE MARRIAGE OF HEAVEN AND HELL...
THE GIRL'S GHOST TALKED ABOUT SUICIDES AS WELL. HOW DOES THAT FIT IN?
I CHECKED OUT THE LAB RECORDS ON THE SIX SUICIDES. ALL OF THEM MICROBIOLOGISTS, BUT ALL THE FILES HAD BEEN HEAVILY CENSORED.
NO PERSONAL DETAILS AT ALL. WE HAD ONE "DEATH BY MISADVENTURE" IN THIS WEEK.
ALISON SHEARWATER, 28, FOUND DEAD IN HERCULES ROAD WITH A BELLY FULL OF PILLS AND JD.
THE BOSS PUT IT DOWN AS "ACCIDENTAL DEATH" AND THE REPORT CAME BACK WITH EVERY PERSONAL DETAIL EDITED OUT.
HERCULES ROAD...
LONDON
LONDON COMPENDIUM
THEY WEREN'T SMART ENOUGH TO BIN HER PERSONAL EFFECTS BEFORE I GOT TO THEM.
THE I.D. BADGE IS FOR A RESEARCH LAB IN THE SUBURBS--HADLEY WOOD.
HERCULES ROAD--WILLIAM BLAKE'S HOUSE. A FLATBLOCK BUILT ON THE SITE OF BLAKE'S OLD HOME.
OKAY. PERV, GET ON THE LAPTOP, GO THROUGH ALL YOUR OLD PEDO-FILES. SEE IF ANYONE COMES UP SMELLING VIOLENT.
ABI, CHECK OUT THE BLAKE QUESTION. FIND AN EXPERT AND ASK A FEW DISCREET QUESTIONS.
LEAH, SEE WHAT YOU CAN FIND OUT ABOUT THIS "MYSTERY" SUICIDE.
DOCKGATE
AND WHAT ARE YOU GOING TO BE DOING, MOZ?
AN OLD FRIEND OF OURS RANG EARLIER.
HELPING THE POLICE WITH THEIR INQUIRIES.

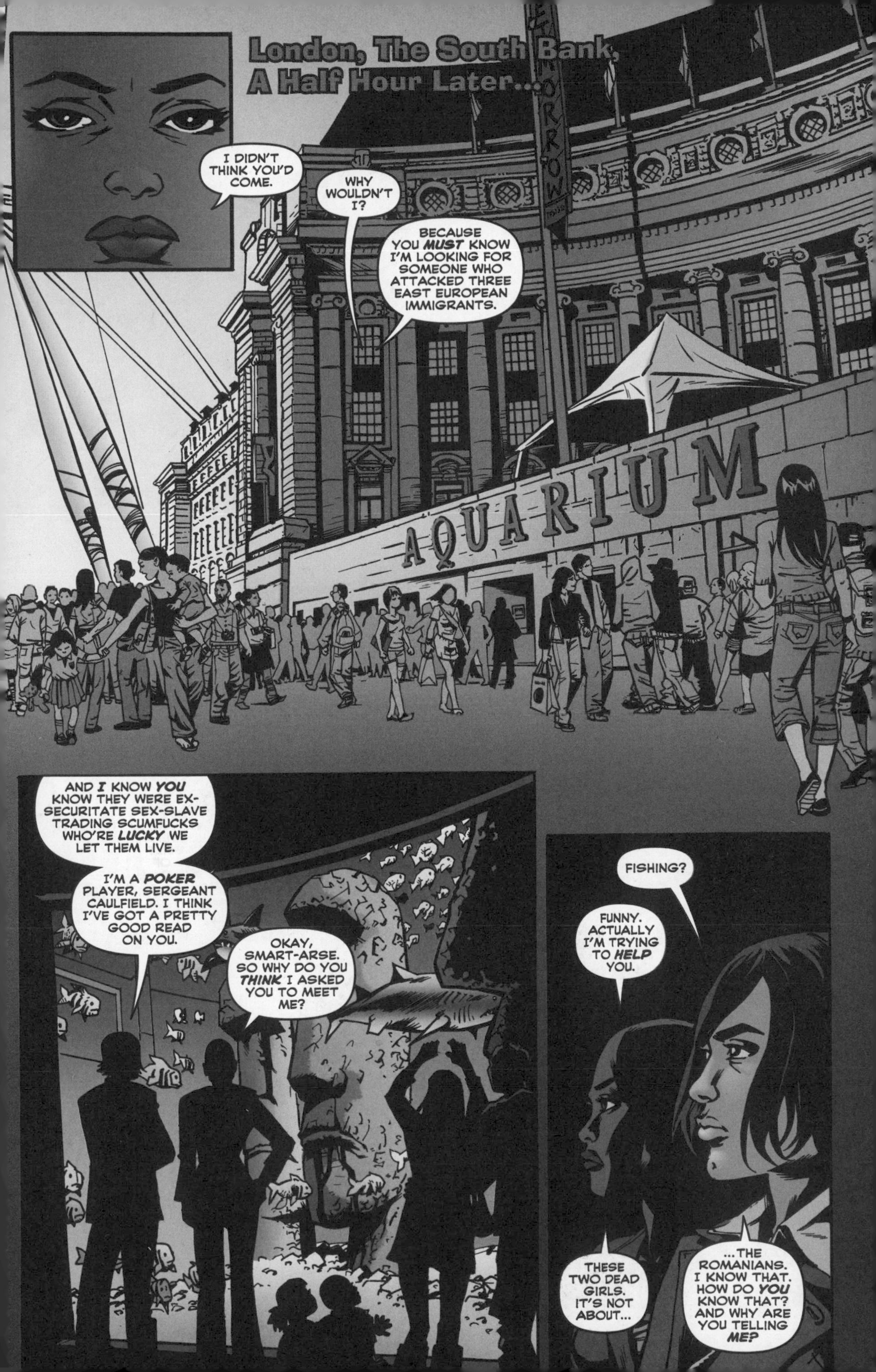
London, The South Bank, A Half Hour Later...
I DIDN'T THINK YOU'D COME.
WHY WOULDN'T I?
BECAUSE YOU MUST KNOW I'M LOOKING FOR SOMEONE WHO ATTACKED THREE EAST EUROPEAN IMMIGRANTS.
AQUARIUM
AND I KNOW YOU KNOW THEY WERE EX-SECURITATE SEX-SLAVE TRADING SCUMFUCKS WHO'RE LUCKY WE LET THEM LIVE.
I'M A POKER PLAYER, SERGEANT CAULFIELD. I THINK I'VE GOT A PRETTY GOOD READ ON YOU.
OKAY, SMART-ARSE. SO WHY DO YOU THINK I ASKED YOU TO MEET ME?
FISHING?
FUNNY. ACTUALLY I'M TRYING TO HELP YOU.
THESE TWO DEAD GIRLS. IT'S NOT ABOUT...
...THE ROMANIANS. I KNOW THAT. HOW DO YOU KNOW THAT? AND WHY ARE YOU TELLING ME?

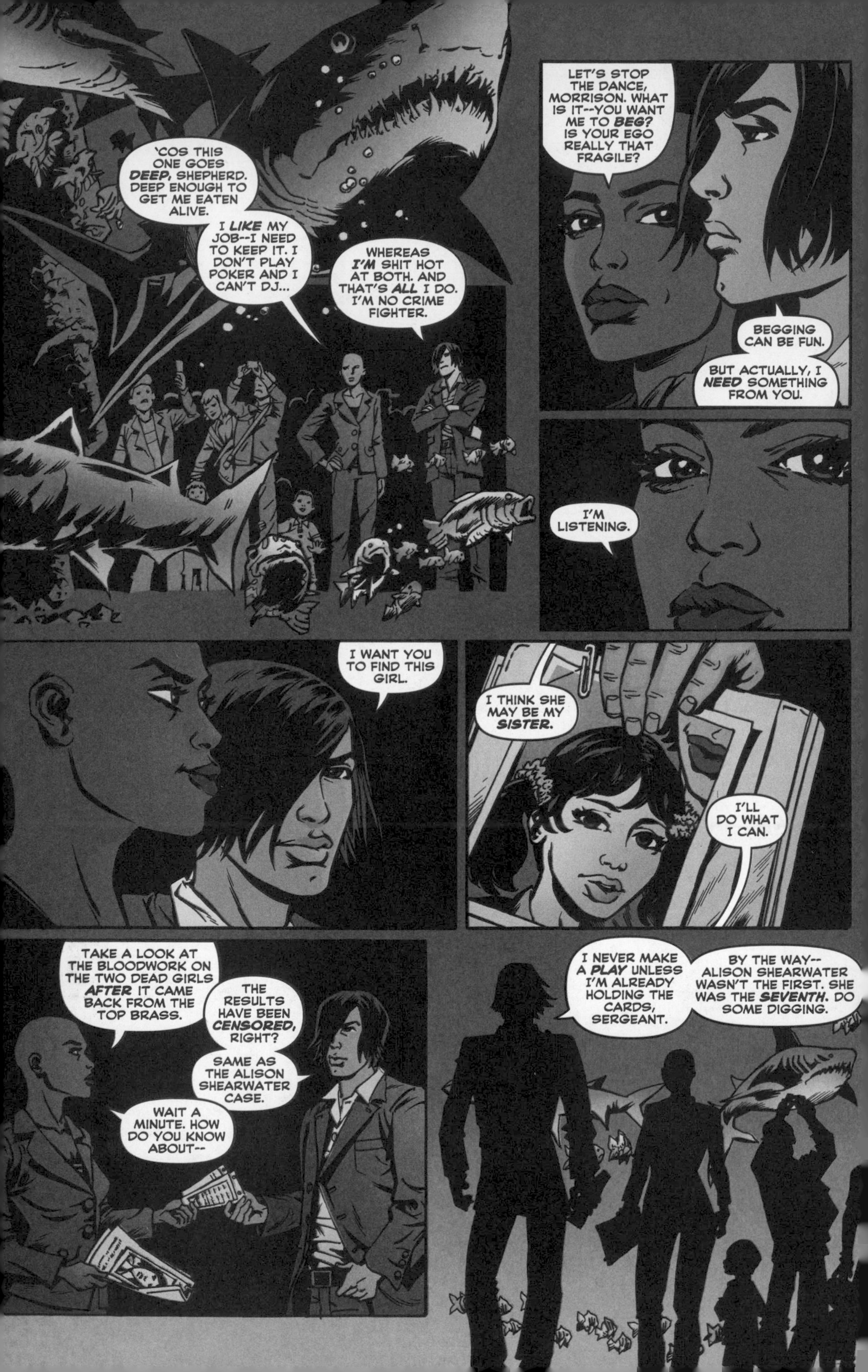

'COS THIS ONE GOES DEEP, SHEPHERD. DEEP ENOUGH TO GET ME EATEN ALIVE.
I LIKE MY JOB--I NEED TO KEEP IT. I DON'T PLAY POKER AND I CAN'T DJ...
WHEREAS I'M SHIT HOT AT BOTH. AND THAT'S ALL I DO. I'M NO CRIME FIGHTER.
LET'S STOP THE DANCE, MORRISON. WHAT IS IT--YOU WANT ME TO BEG? IS YOUR EGO REALLY THAT FRAGILE?
BEGGING CAN BE FUN.
BUT ACTUALLY, I NEED SOMETHING FROM YOU.
I'M LISTENING.
I WANT YOU TO FIND THIS GIRL.
I THINK SHE MAY BE MY SISTER.
I'LL DO WHAT I CAN.
TAKE A LOOK AT THE BLOODWORK ON THE TWO DEAD GIRLS AFTER IT CAME BACK FROM THE TOP BRASS.
THE RESULTS HAVE BEEN CENSORED, RIGHT?
SAME AS THE ALISON SHEARWATER CASE.
WAIT A MINUTE. HOW DO YOU KNOW ABOUT--
I NEVER MAKE A PLAY UNLESS I'M ALREADY HOLDING THE CARDS, SERGEANT.
BY THE WAY--ALISON SHEARWATER WASN'T THE FIRST. SHE WAS THE SEVENTH. DO SOME DIGGING.

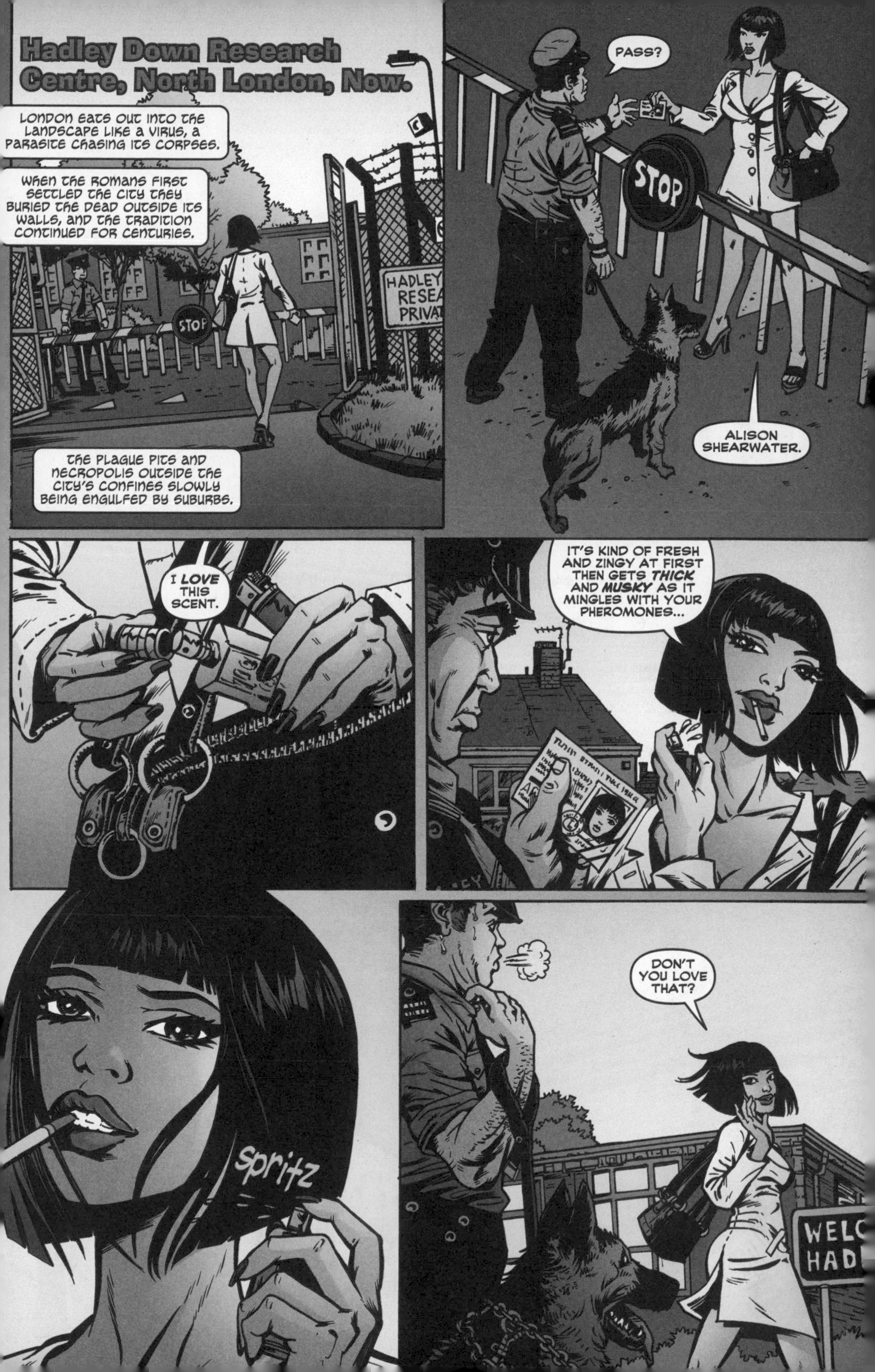
Hadley Down Research Centre, North London, Now.
LONDON EATS OUT INTO THE LANDSCAPE LIKE A VIRUS, A PARASITE CHASING ITS CORPSES.
WHEN THE ROMANS FIRST SETTLED THE CITY THEY BURIED THE DEAD OUTSIDE ITS WALLS, AND THE TRADITION CONTINUED FOR CENTURIES.
HADLEY
RESEA
PRIVAT
STOP
THE PLAGUE PITS AND NECROPOLIS OUTSIDE THE CITY'S CONFINES SLOWLY BEING ENGULFED BY SUBURBS.
PASS?
STOP
ALISON SHEARWATER.
I LOVE THIS SCENT.
IT'S KIND OF FRESH AND ZINGY AT FIRST THEN GETS THICK AND MUSKY AS IT MINGLES WITH YOUR PHEROMONES...
spritz
DON'T YOU LOVE THAT?
WELC
HAD

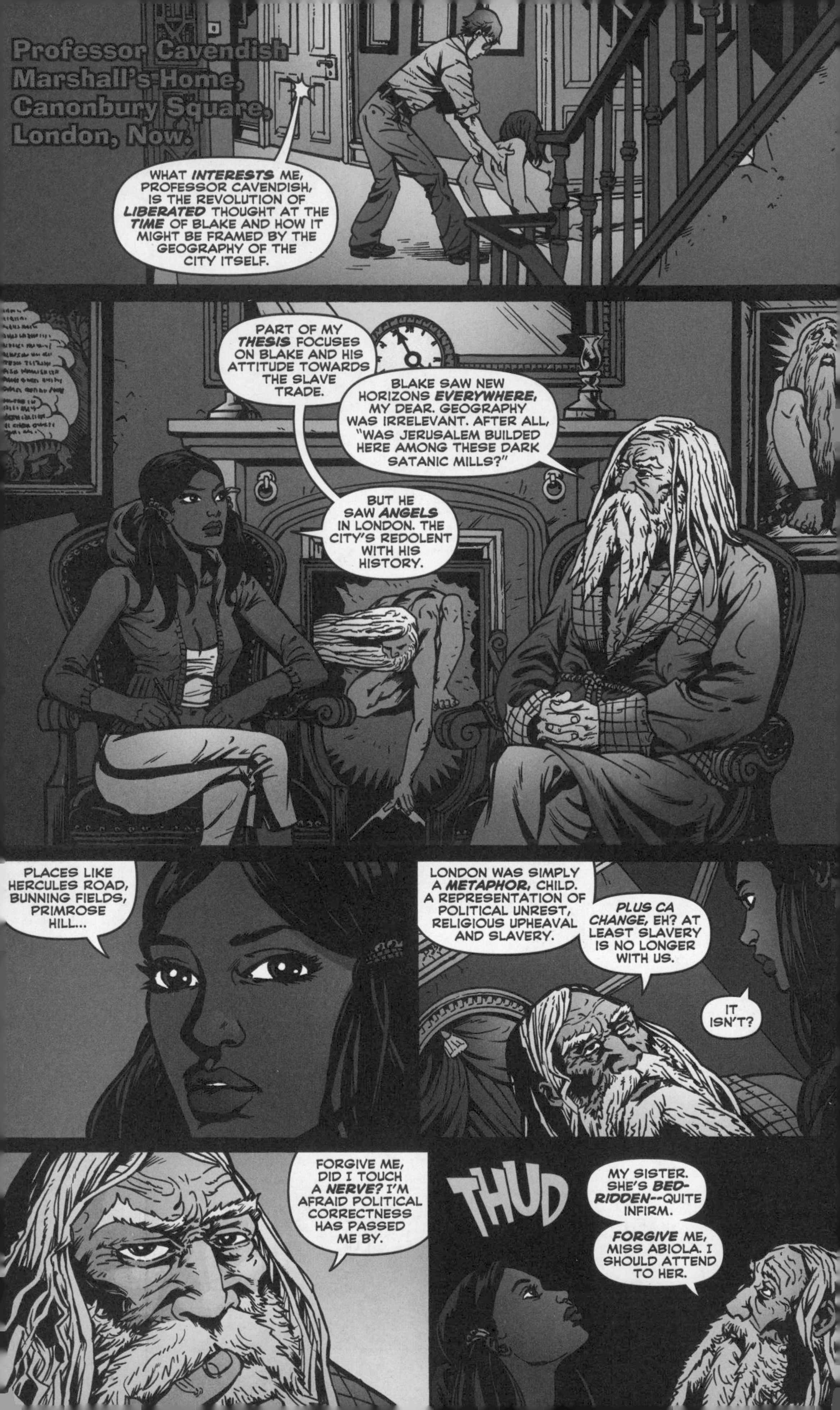

Professor Cavendish Marshall's Home, Canonbury Square, London, Now.
WHAT INTERESTS ME, PROFESSOR CAVENDISH, IS THE REVOLUTION OF LIBERATED THOUGHT AT THE TIME OF BLAKE AND HOW IT MIGHT BE FRAMED BY THE GEOGRAPHY OF THE CITY ITSELF.
PART OF MY THESIS FOCUSES ON BLAKE AND HIS ATTITUDE TOWARDS THE SLAVE TRADE.
BLAKE SAW NEW HORIZONS EVERYWHERE, MY DEAR. GEOGRAPHY WAS IRRELEVANT. AFTER ALL, "WAS JERUSALEM BUILDED HERE AMONG THESE DARK SATANIC MILLS?"
BUT HE SAW ANGELS IN LONDON. THE CITY'S REDOLENT WITH HIS HISTORY.
PLACES LIKE HERCULES ROAD, BUNNING FIELDS, PRIMROSE HILL...
LONDON WAS SIMPLY A METAPHOR, CHILD. A REPRESENTATION OF POLITICAL UNREST, RELIGIOUS UPHEAVAL AND SLAVERY.
PLUS CA CHANGE, EH? AT LEAST SLAVERY IS NO LONGER WITH US.
IT ISN'T?
FORGIVE ME, DID I TOUCH A NERVE? I'M AFRAID POLITICAL CORRECTNESS HAS PASSED ME BY.
THUD
MY SISTER. SHE'S BED-RIDDEN--QUITE INFIRM.
FORGIVE ME, MISS ABIOLA. I SHOULD ATTEND TO HER.

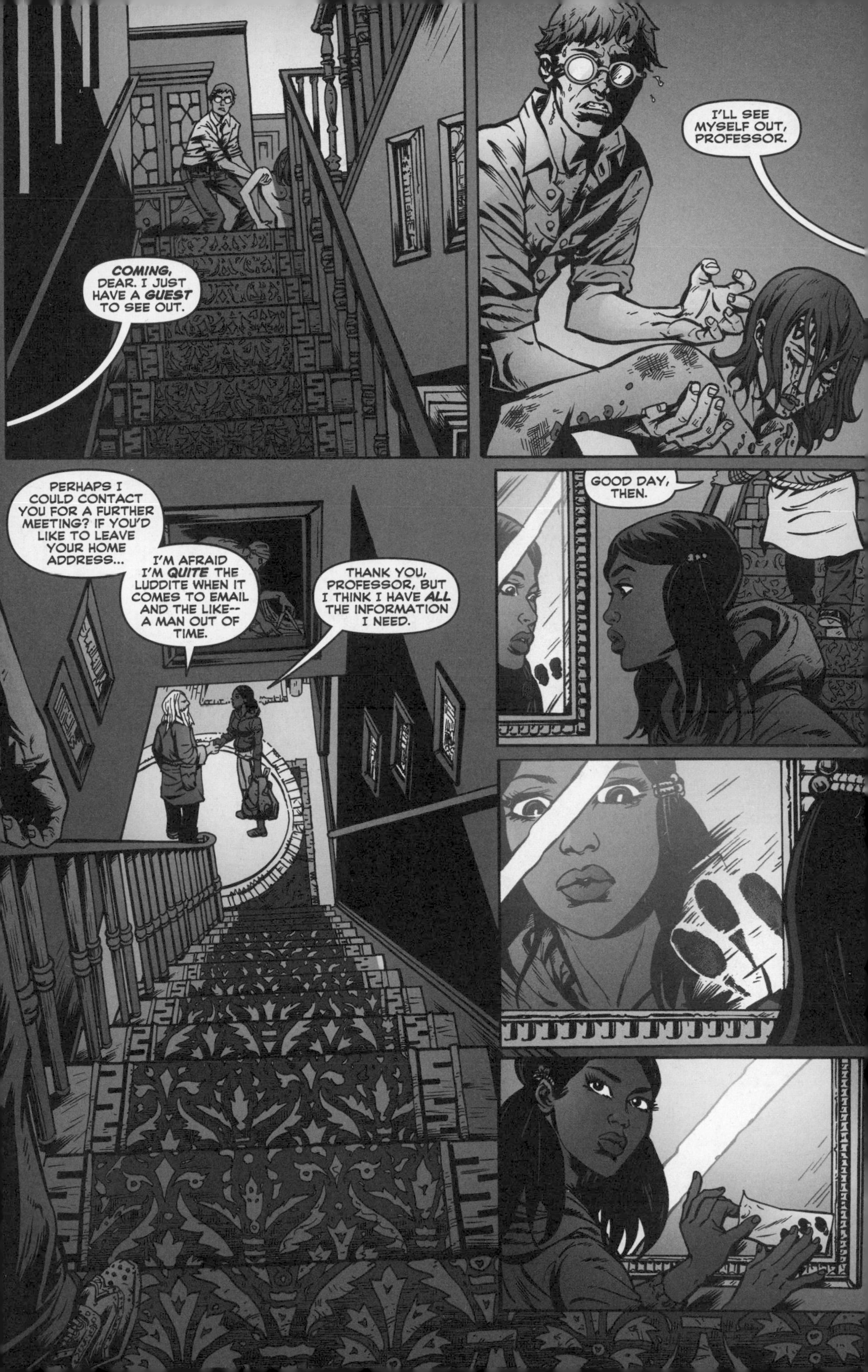

COMING, DEAR. I JUST HAVE A GUEST TO SEE OUT.
I'LL SEE MYSELF OUT, PROFESSOR.
PERHAPS I COULD CONTACT YOU FOR A FURTHER MEETING? IF YOU'D LIKE TO LEAVE YOUR HOME ADDRESS...
I'M AFRAID I'M QUITE THE LUDDITE WHEN IT COMES TO EMAIL AND THE LIKE-- A MAN OUT OF TIME.
THANK YOU, PROFESSOR, BUT I THINK I HAVE ALL THE INFORMATION I NEED.
GOOD DAY, THEN.

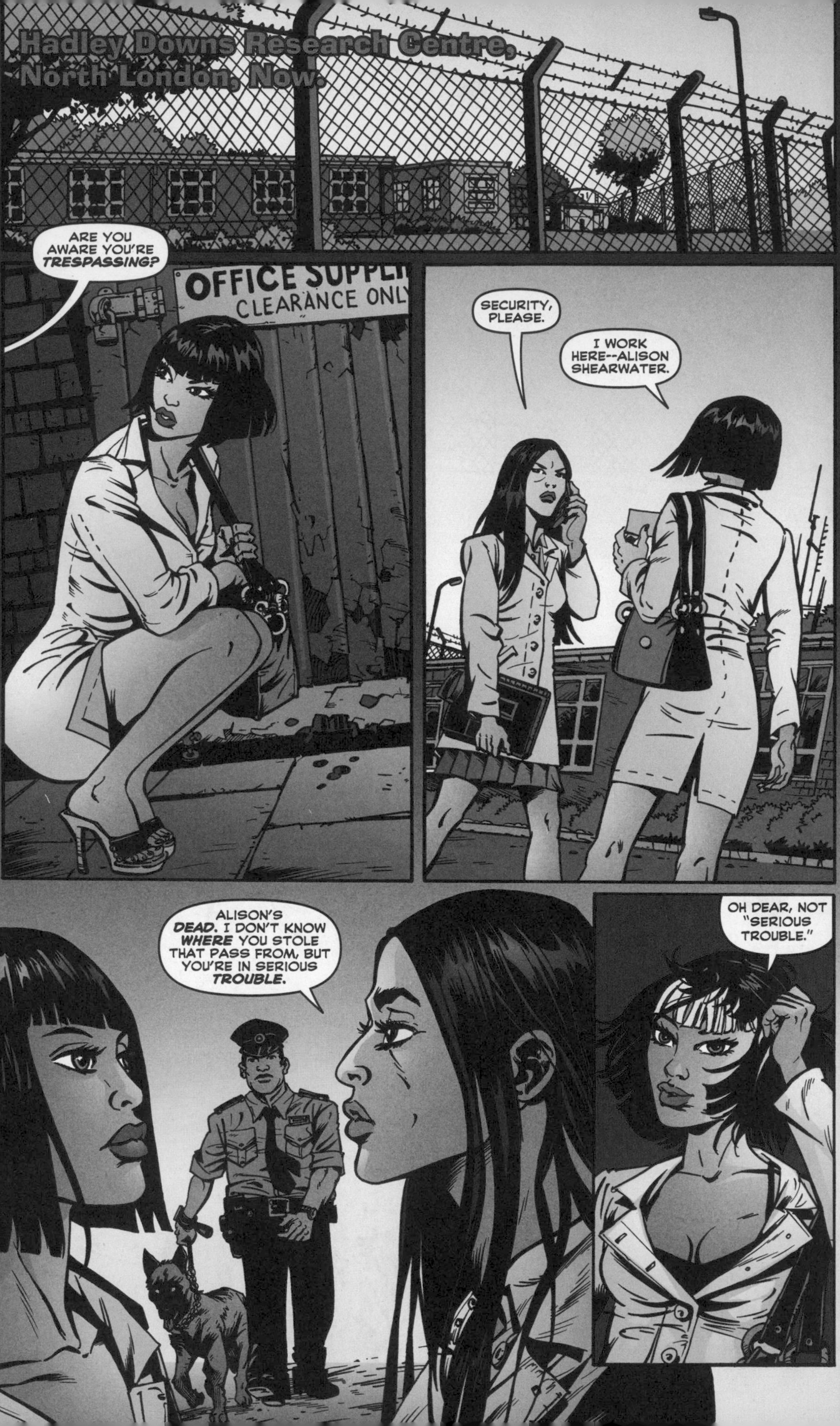
Hadley Downs Research Centre, North London, Now.
ARE YOU AWARE YOU'RE *TRESPASSING?*
OFFICE SUPPL
CLEARANCE ONLY
SECURITY, PLEASE.
I WORK HERE--ALISON SHEARWATER.
ALISON'S *DEAD.* I DON'T KNOW *WHERE* YOU STOLE THAT PASS FROM, BUT YOU'RE IN SERIOUS *TROUBLE.*
OH DEAR, NOT "SERIOUS TROUBLE."

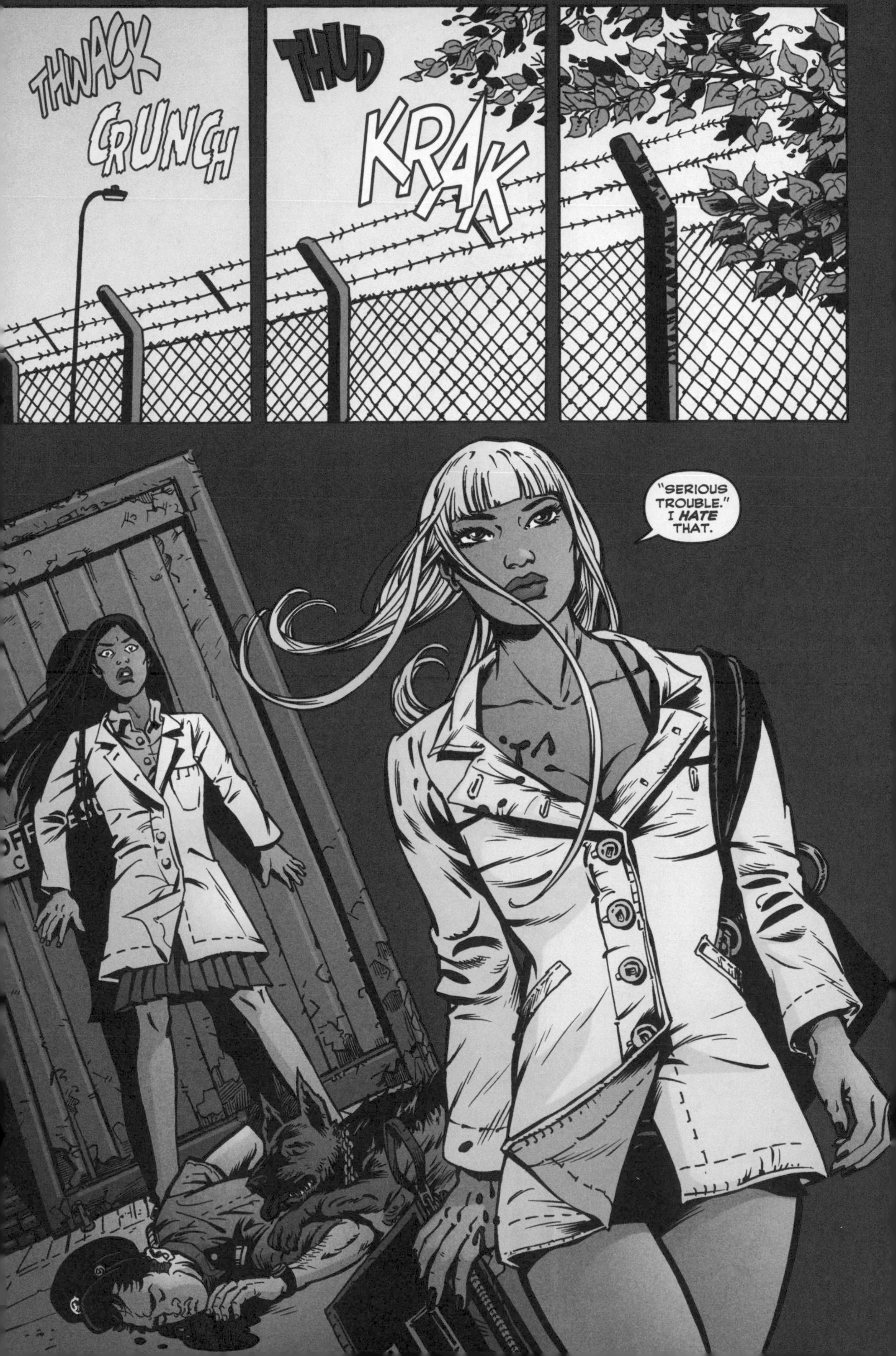
THWACK
CRUNCH
THUD
KRAK
"SERIOUS TROUBLE." I HATE THAT.

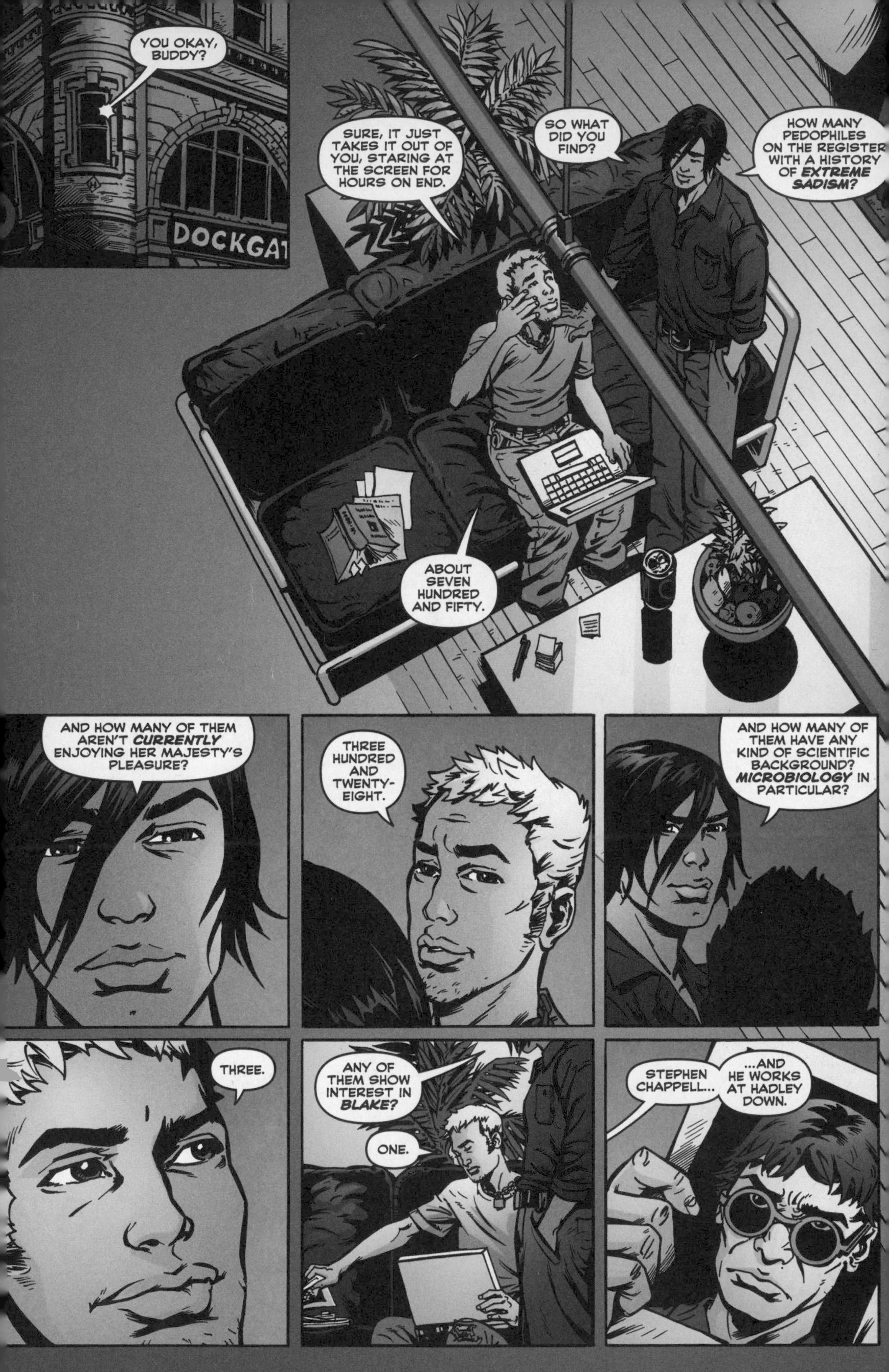
YOU OKAY, BUDDY?
DOCKGAT
SURE, IT JUST TAKES IT OUT OF YOU, STARING AT THE SCREEN FOR HOURS ON END.
SO WHAT DID YOU FIND?
HOW MANY PEDOPHILES ON THE REGISTER WITH A HISTORY OF EXTREME SADISM?
ABOUT SEVEN HUNDRED AND FIFTY.
AND HOW MANY OF THEM AREN'T CURRENTLY ENJOYING HER MAJESTY'S PLEASURE?
THREE HUNDRED AND TWENTY-EIGHT.
AND HOW MANY OF THEM HAVE ANY KIND OF SCIENTIFIC BACKGROUND? MICROBIOLOGY IN PARTICULAR?
THREE.
ANY OF THEM SHOW INTEREST IN BLAKE?
ONE.
STEPHEN CHAPPELL...
...AND HE WORKS AT HADLEY DOWN.

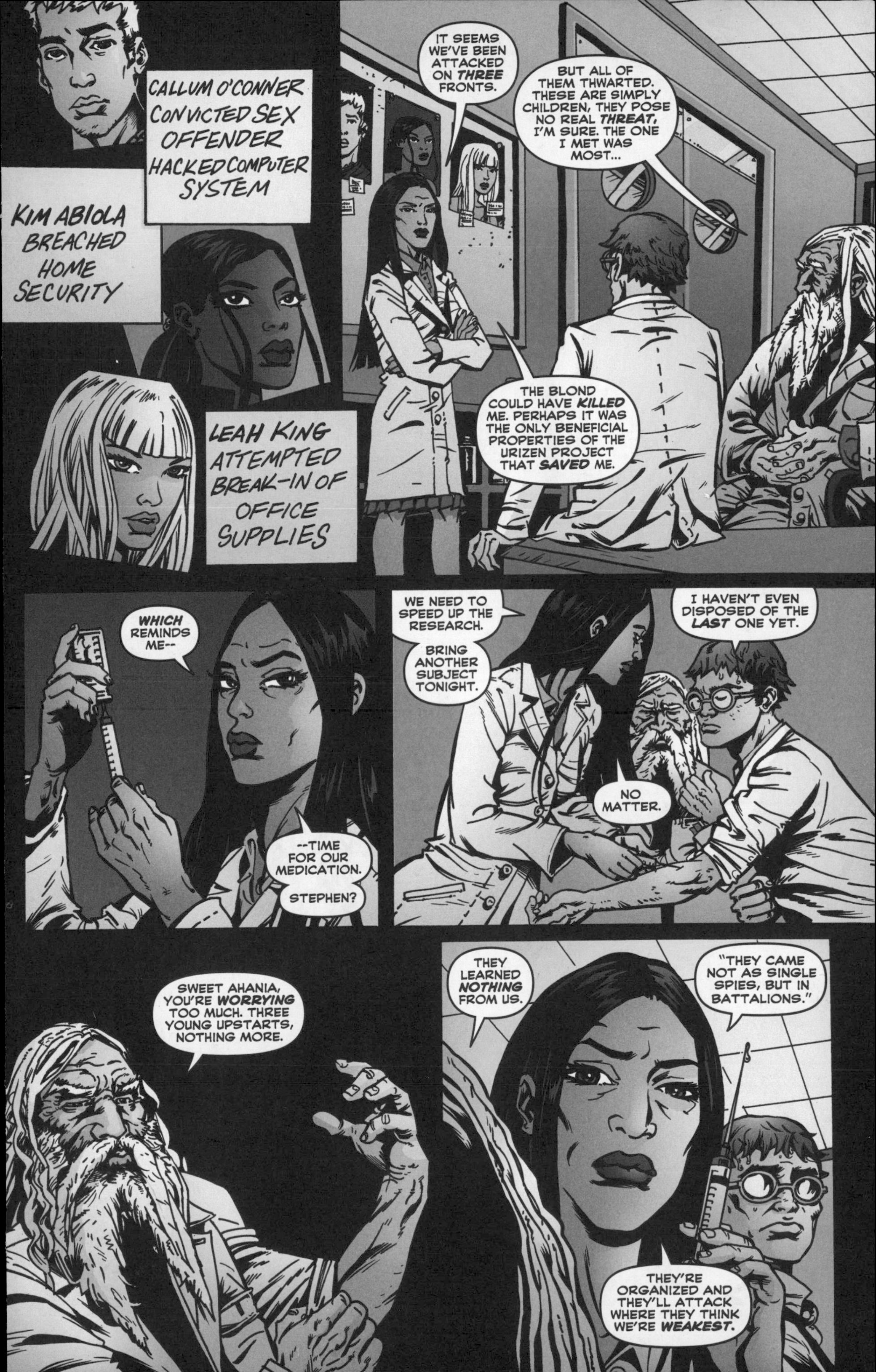
CALLUM O'CONNER
CONVICTED SEX OFFENDER
HACKED COMPUTER SYSTEM
KIM ABIOLA
BREACHED HOME SECURITY
LEAH KING
ATTEMPTED BREAK-IN OF OFFICE SUPPLIES
IT SEEMS WE'VE BEEN ATTACKED ON THREE FRONTS.
BUT ALL OF THEM THWARTED. THESE ARE SIMPLY CHILDREN, THEY POSE NO REAL THREAT, I'M SURE. THE ONE I MET WAS MOST...
THE BLOND COULD HAVE KILLED ME. PERHAPS IT WAS THE ONLY BENEFICIAL PROPERTIES OF THE URIZEN PROJECT THAT SAVED ME.
WHICH REMINDS ME--
--TIME FOR OUR MEDICATION.
STEPHEN?
WE NEED TO SPEED UP THE RESEARCH.
BRING ANOTHER SUBJECT TONIGHT.
I HAVEN'T EVEN DISPOSED OF THE LAST ONE YET.
NO MATTER.
SWEET AHANIA, YOU'RE WORRYING TOO MUCH. THREE YOUNG UPSTARTS, NOTHING MORE.
THEY LEARNED NOTHING FROM US.
"THEY CAME NOT AS SINGLE SPIES, BUT IN BATTALIONS."
THEY'RE ORGANIZED AND THEY'LL ATTACK WHERE THEY THINK WE'RE WEAKEST.

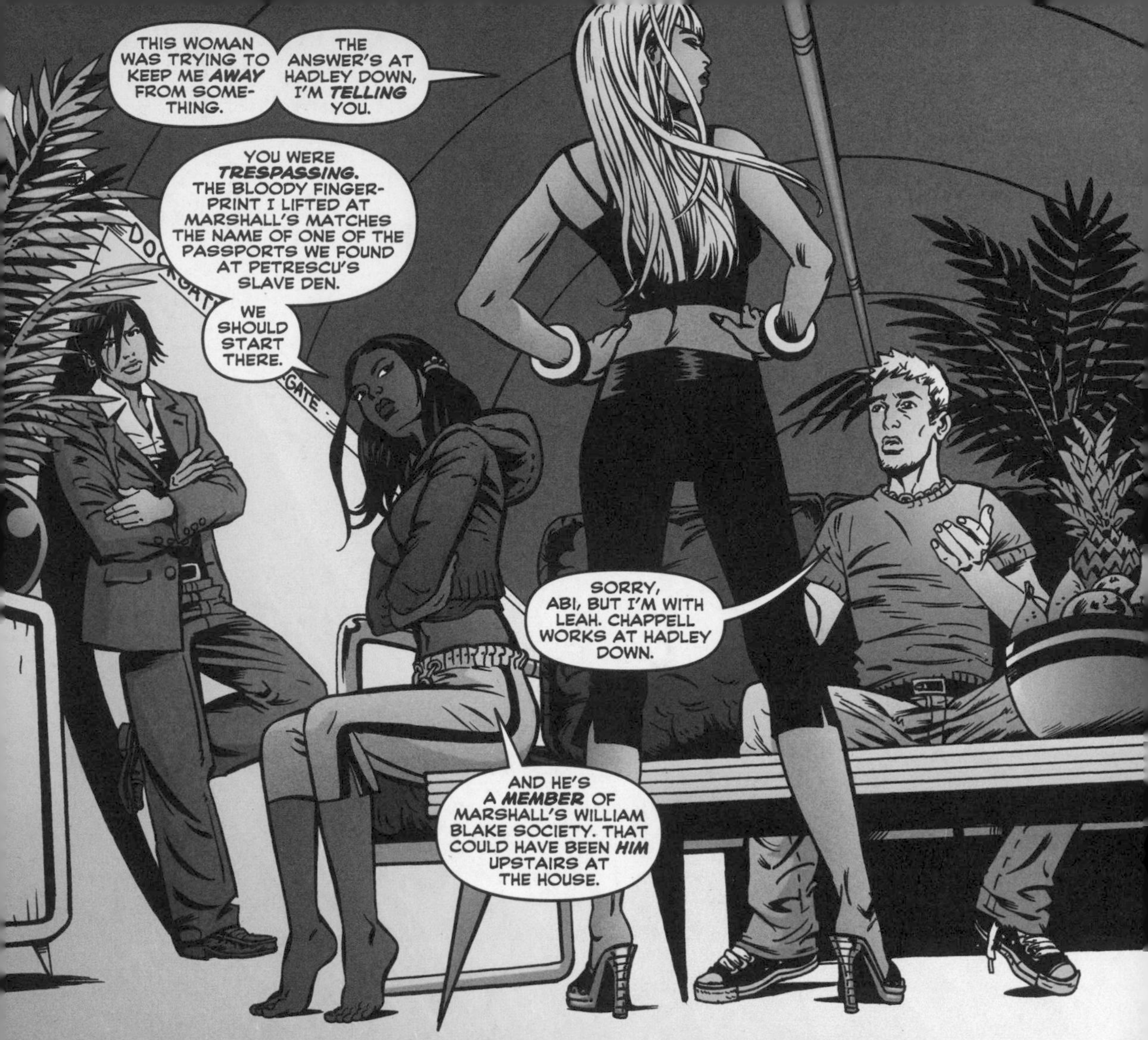
THIS WOMAN WAS TRYING TO KEEP ME *AWAY* FROM SOME-THING.
THE ANSWER'S AT HADLEY DOWN, I'M *TELLING* YOU.
YOU WERE *TRESPASSING.* THE BLOODY FINGER-PRINT I LIFTED AT MARSHALL'S MATCHES THE NAME OF ONE OF THE PASSPORTS WE FOUND AT PETRESCU'S SLAVE DEN.
WE SHOULD START THERE.
SORRY, ABI, BUT I'M WITH LEAH. CHAPPELL WORKS AT HADLEY DOWN.
AND HE'S A *MEMBER* OF MARSHALL'S WILLIAM BLAKE SOCIETY. THAT COULD HAVE BEEN *HIM* UPSTAIRS AT THE HOUSE.

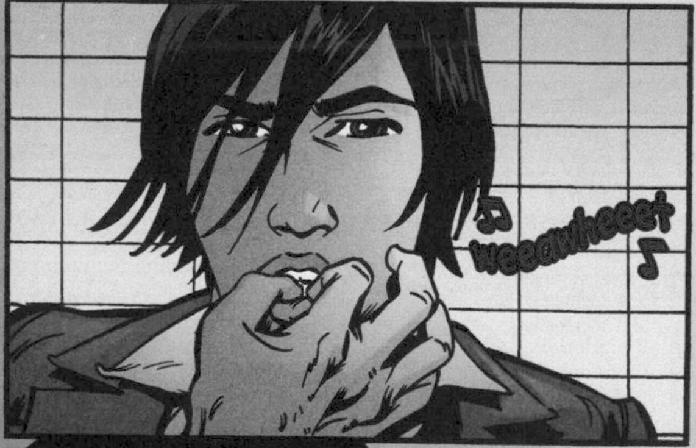
weeawheeet

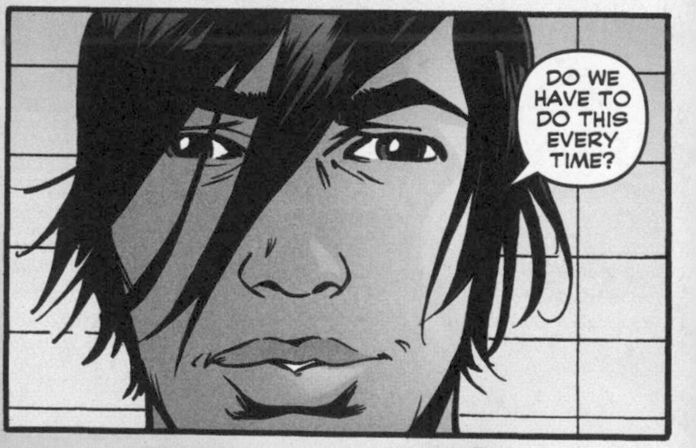
DO WE HAVE TO DO THIS EVERY TIME?

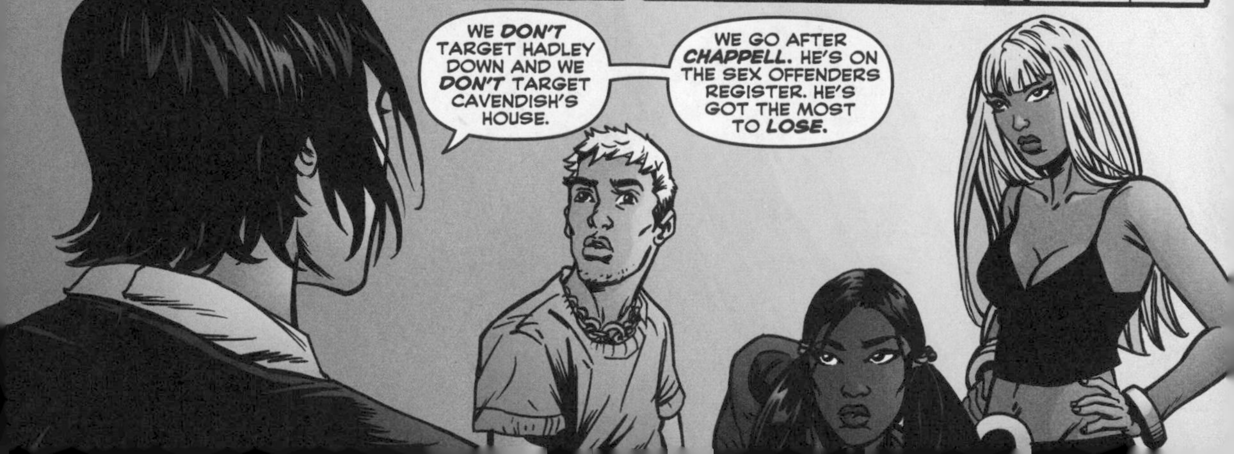
WE *DON'T* TARGET HADLEY DOWN AND WE *DON'T* TARGET CAVENDISH'S HOUSE.
WE GO AFTER *CHAPPELL.* HE'S ON THE SEX OFFENDERS REGISTER. HE'S GOT THE MOST TO *LOSE.*

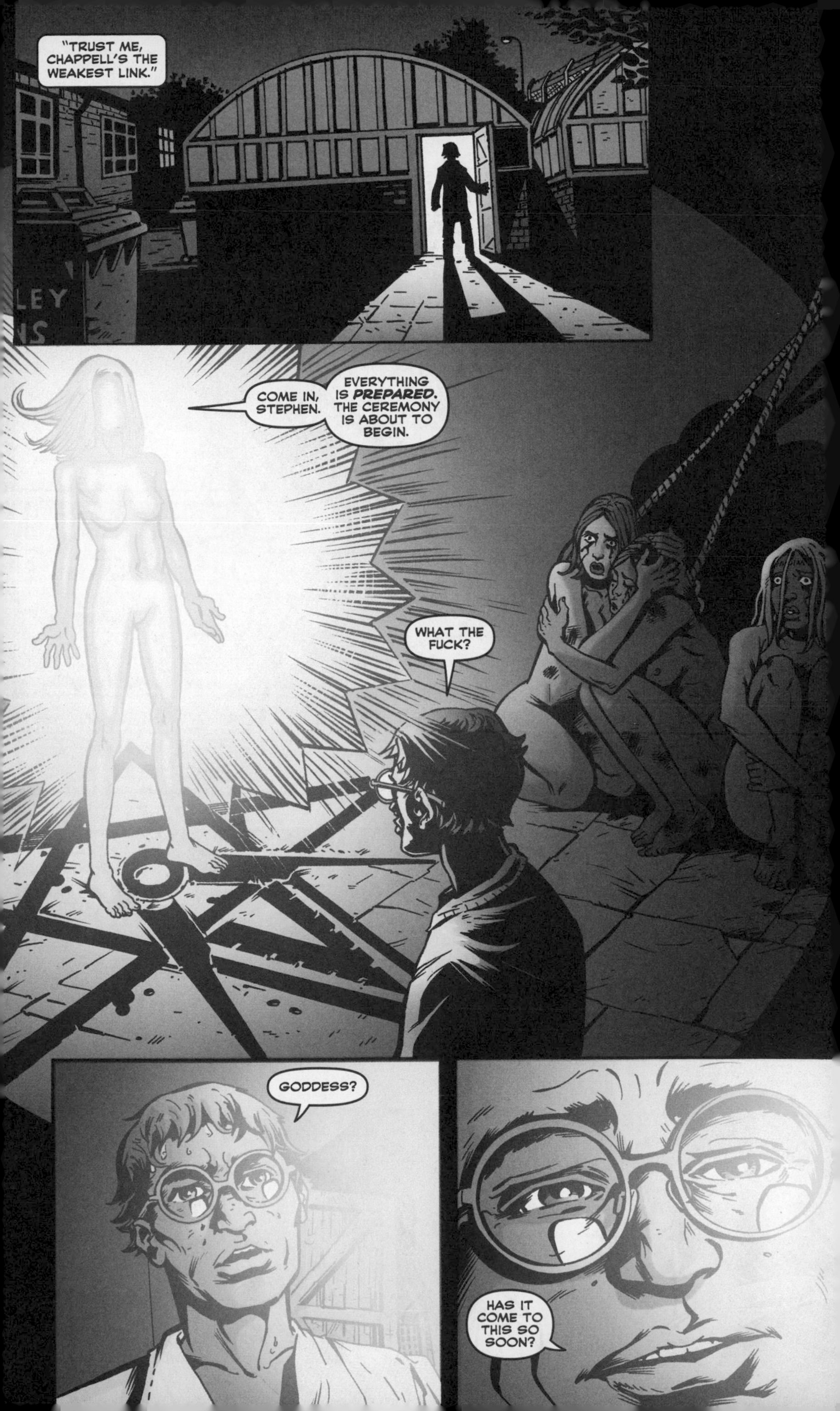
"TRUST ME, CHAPPELL'S THE WEAKEST LINK."
LEY
COME IN, STEPHEN.
EVERYTHING IS **PREPARED**. THE CEREMONY IS ABOUT TO BEGIN.
WHAT THE FUCK?
GODDESS?
HAS IT COME TO THIS SO SOON?

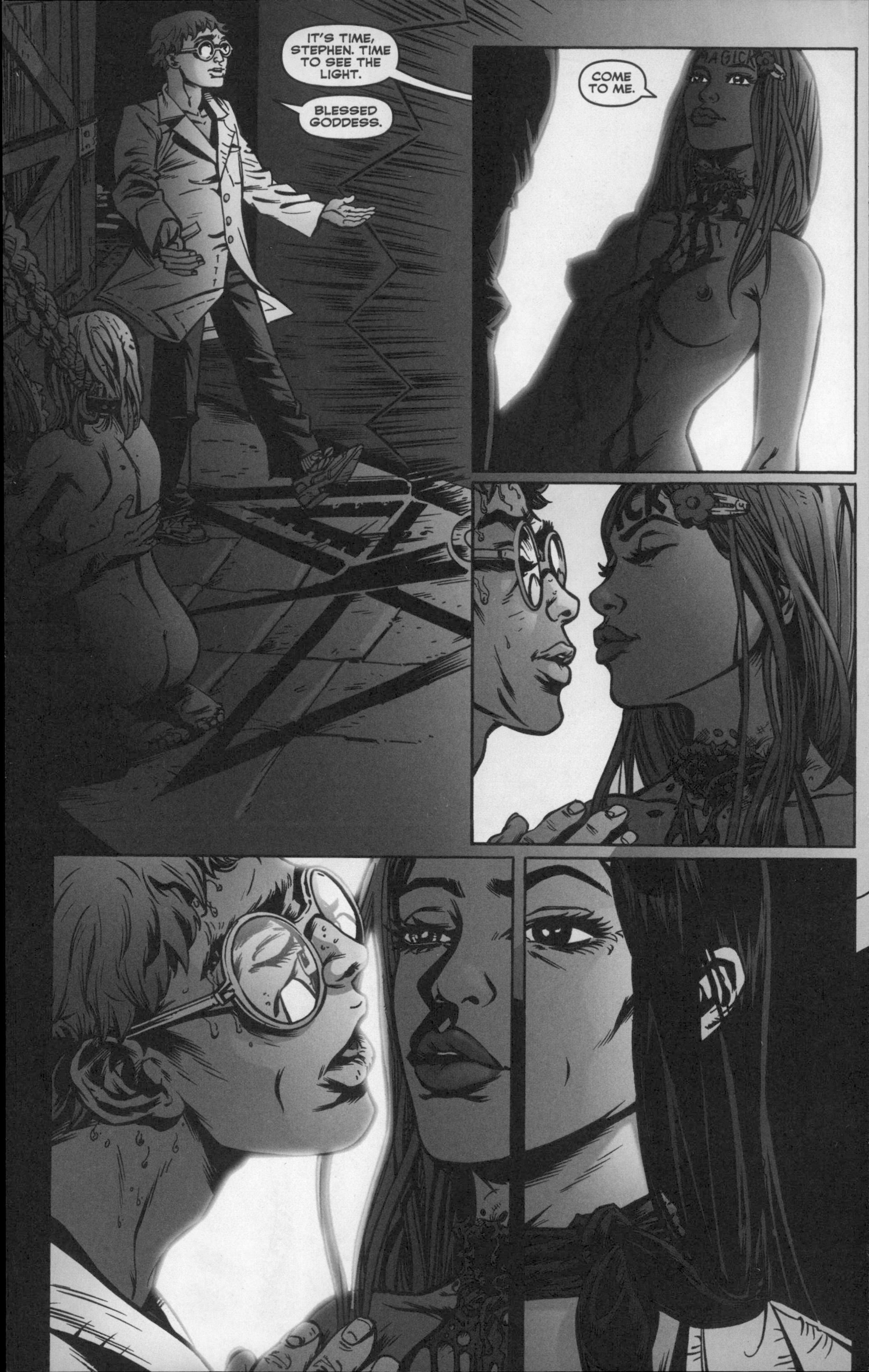
IT'S TIME, STEPHEN. TIME TO SEE THE LIGHT.
BLESSED GODDESS.
COME TO ME.
MAGICK

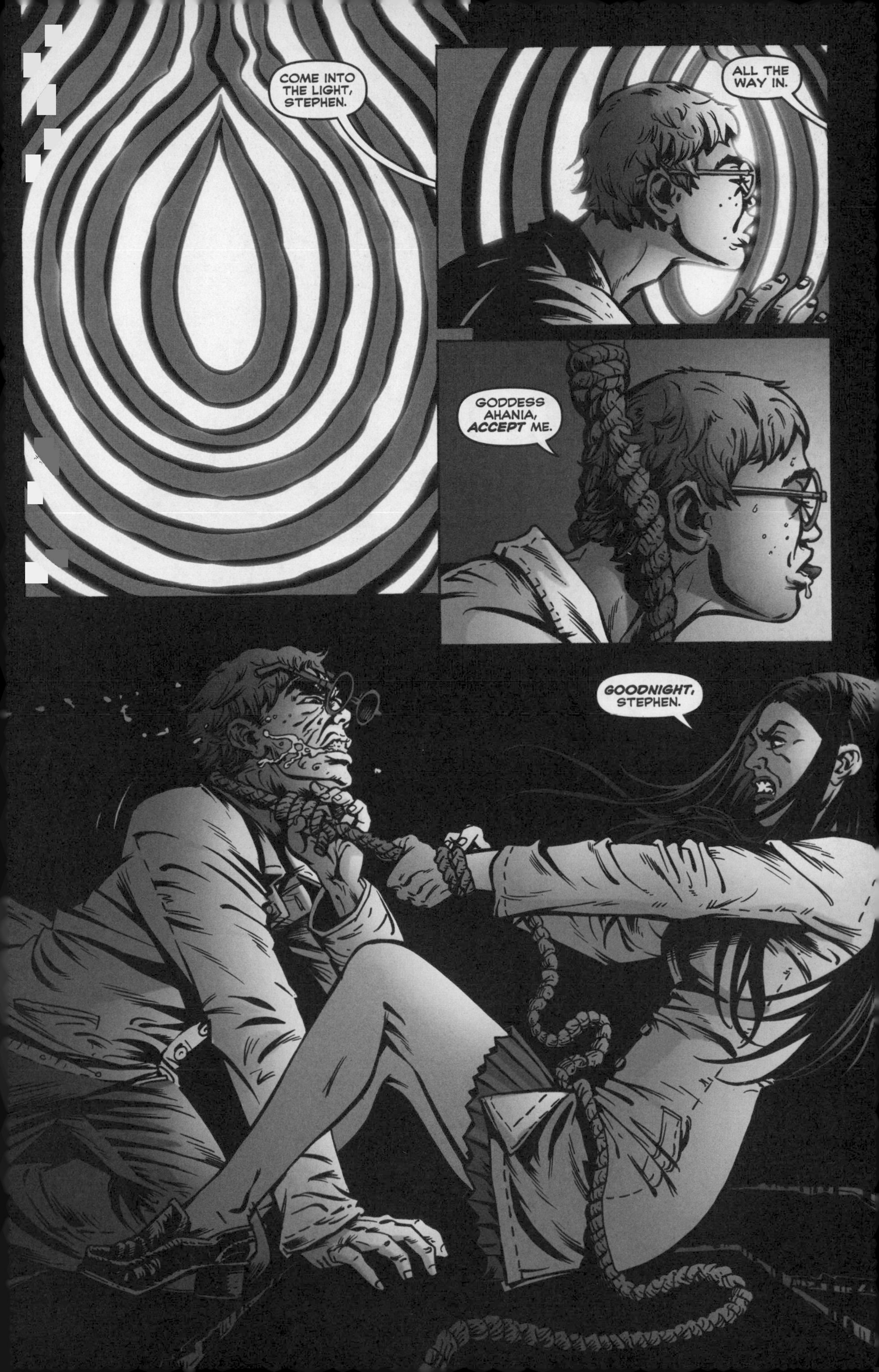
COME INTO THE LIGHT, STEPHEN.
ALL THE WAY IN.
GODDESS AHANIA, *ACCEPT* ME.
GOODNIGHT, STEPHEN.

Blackfriars Bridge, London, Now.

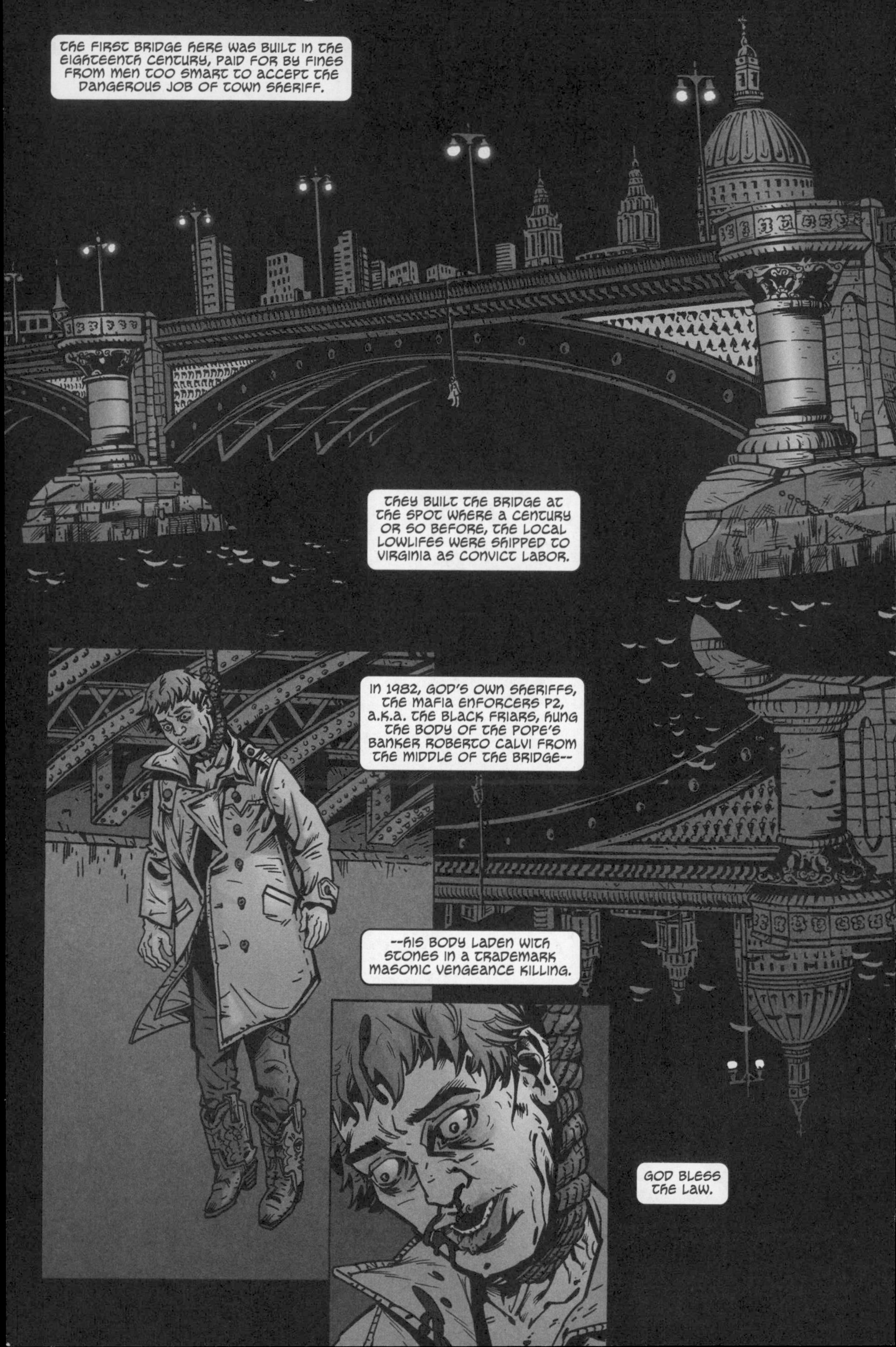
THE FIRST BRIDGE HERE WAS BUILT IN THE EIGHTEENTH CENTURY, PAID FOR BY FINES FROM MEN TOO SMART TO ACCEPT THE DANGEROUS JOB OF TOWN SHERIFF.
THEY BUILT THE BRIDGE AT THE SPOT WHERE A CENTURY OR SO BEFORE, THE LOCAL LOWLIFES WERE SHIPPED TO VIRGINIA AS CONVICT LABOR.
IN 1982, GOD'S OWN SHERIFFS, THE MAFIA ENFORCERS P2, A.K.A. THE BLACK FRIARS, HUNG THE BODY OF THE POPE'S BANKER ROBERTO CALVI FROM THE MIDDLE OF THE BRIDGE--
--HIS BODY LADEN WITH STONES IN A TRADEMARK MASONIC VENGEANCE KILLING.
GOD BLESS THE LAW.

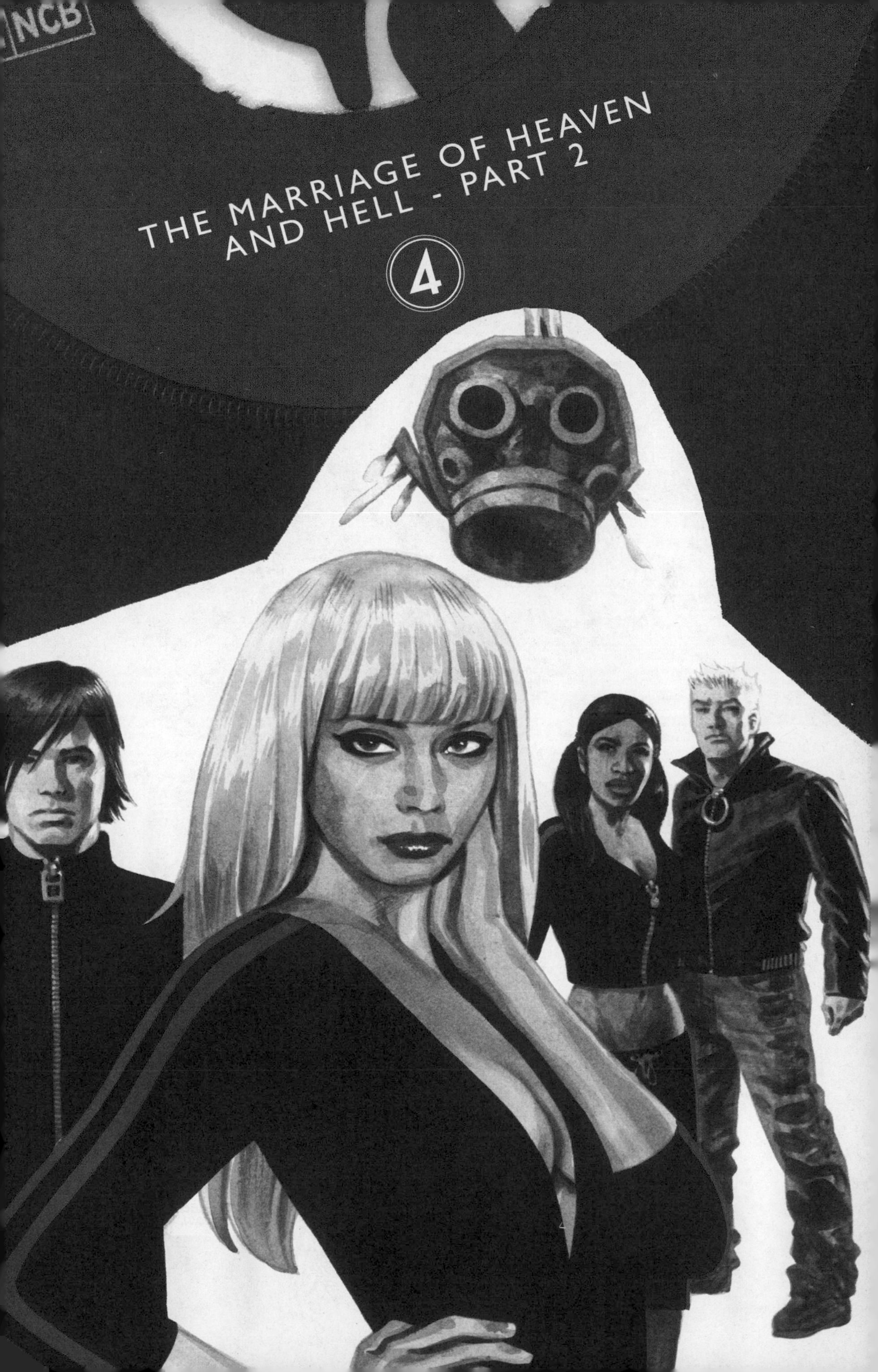
NCB
THE MARRIAGE OF HEAVEN
AND HELL - PART 2
4

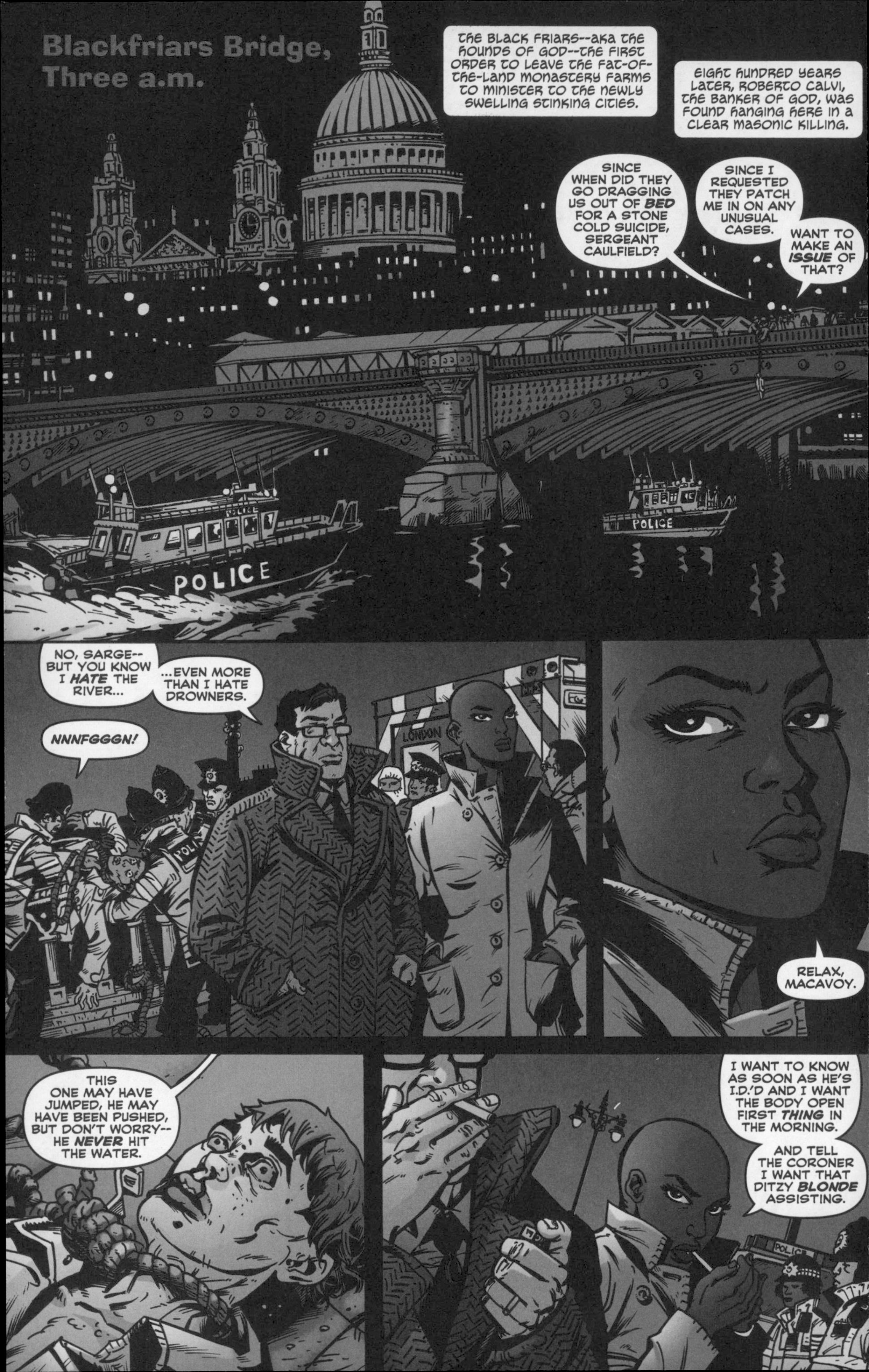

Blackfriars Bridge, Three a.m.
THE BLACK FRIARS--AKA THE HOUNDS OF GOD--THE FIRST ORDER TO LEAVE THE FAT-OF-THE-LAND MONASTERY FARMS TO MINISTER TO THE NEWLY SWELLING STINKING CITIES.
EIGHT HUNDRED YEARS LATER, ROBERTO CALVI, THE BANKER OF GOD, WAS FOUND HANGING HERE IN A CLEAR MASONIC KILLING.
SINCE WHEN DID THEY GO DRAGGING US OUT OF BED FOR A STONE COLD SUICIDE, SERGEANT CAULFIELD?
SINCE I REQUESTED THEY PATCH ME IN ON ANY UNUSUAL CASES.
WANT TO MAKE AN ISSUE OF THAT?
POLICE
POLICE
NO, SARGE--BUT YOU KNOW I HATE THE RIVER...
...EVEN MORE THAN I HATE DROWNERS.
NNNFGGGN!
RELAX, MACAVOY.
THIS ONE MAY HAVE JUMPED, HE MAY HAVE BEEN PUSHED, BUT DON'T WORRY--HE NEVER HIT THE WATER.
I WANT TO KNOW AS SOON AS HE'S I.D.'D AND I WANT THE BODY OPEN FIRST THING IN THE MORNING.
AND TELL THE CORONER I WANT THAT DITZY BLONDE ASSISTING.

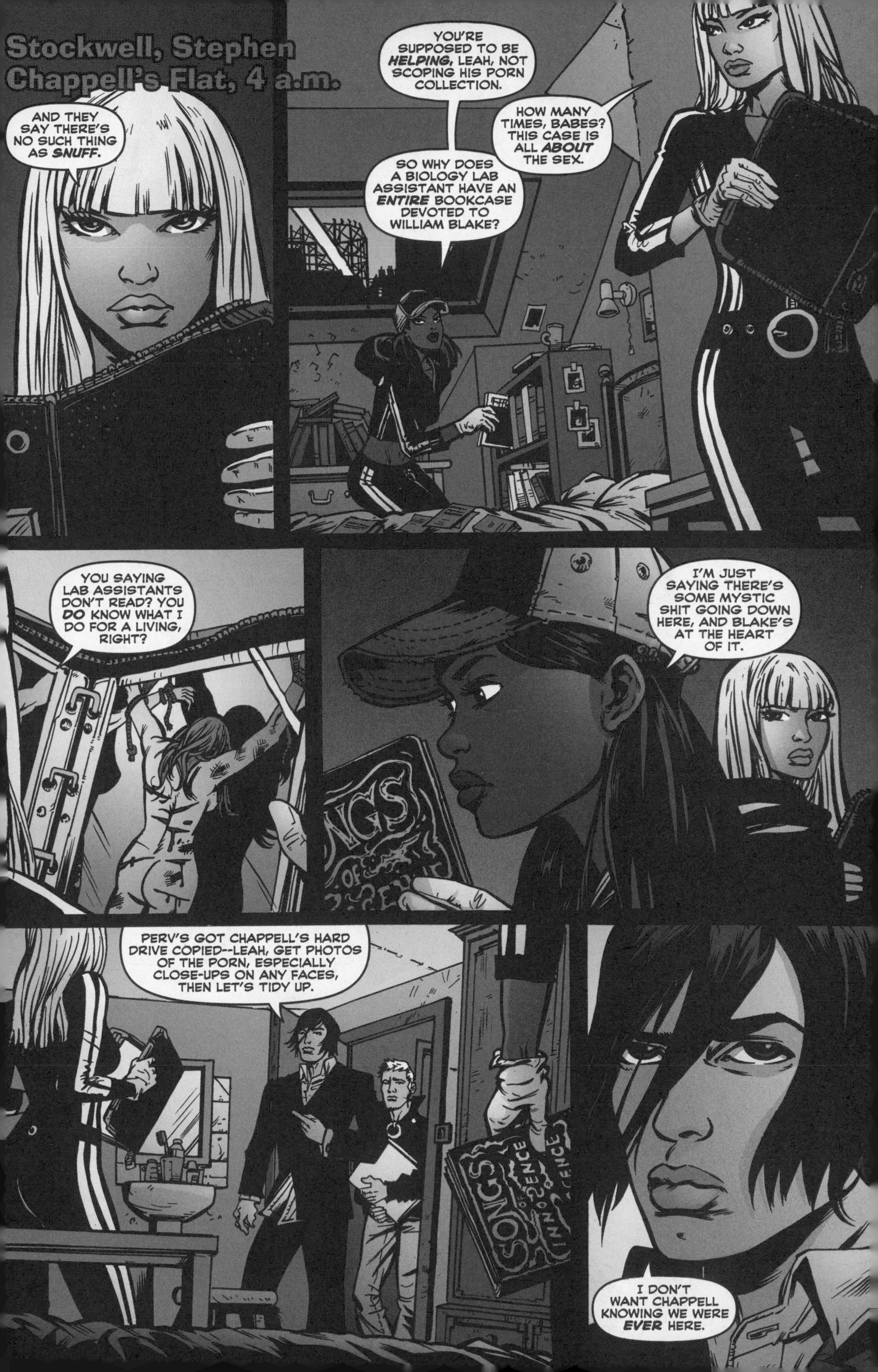

Stockwell, Stephen Chappell's Flat, 4 a.m.
AND THEY SAY THERE'S NO SUCH THING AS SNUFF.
YOU'RE SUPPOSED TO BE HELPING, LEAH, NOT SCOPING HIS PORN COLLECTION.
HOW MANY TIMES, BABES? THIS CASE IS ALL ABOUT THE SEX.
SO WHY DOES A BIOLOGY LAB ASSISTANT HAVE AN ENTIRE BOOKCASE DEVOTED TO WILLIAM BLAKE?
YOU SAYING LAB ASSISTANTS DON'T READ? YOU DO KNOW WHAT I DO FOR A LIVING, RIGHT?
I'M JUST SAYING THERE'S SOME MYSTIC SHIT GOING DOWN HERE, AND BLAKE'S AT THE HEART OF IT.
PERV'S GOT CHAPPELL'S HARD DRIVE COPIED--LEAH, GET PHOTOS OF THE PORN, ESPECIALLY CLOSE-UPS ON ANY FACES, THEN LET'S TIDY UP.
SONGS OF INNOCENCE
I DON'T WANT CHAPPELL KNOWING WE WERE EVER HERE.

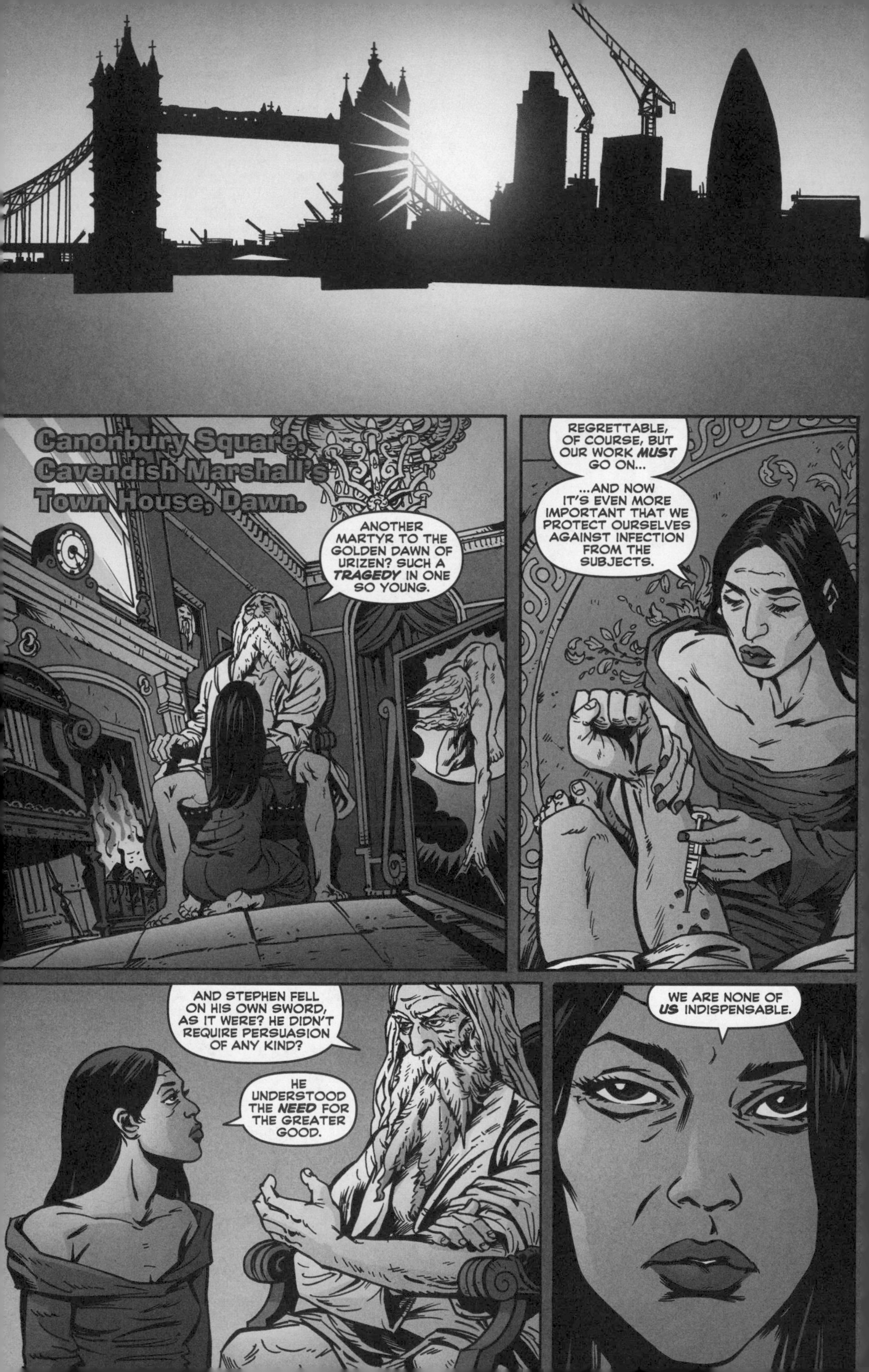
Canonbury Square, Cavendish Marshall's Town House, Dawn.
ANOTHER MARTYR TO THE GOLDEN DAWN OF URIZEN? SUCH A TRAGEDY IN ONE SO YOUNG.
REGRETTABLE, OF COURSE, BUT OUR WORK MUST GO ON...
...AND NOW IT'S EVEN MORE IMPORTANT THAT WE PROTECT OURSELVES AGAINST INFECTION FROM THE SUBJECTS.
AND STEPHEN FELL ON HIS OWN SWORD, AS IT WERE? HE DIDN'T REQUIRE PERSUASION OF ANY KIND?
HE UNDERSTOOD THE NEED FOR THE GREATER GOOD.
WE ARE NONE OF US INDISPENSABLE.

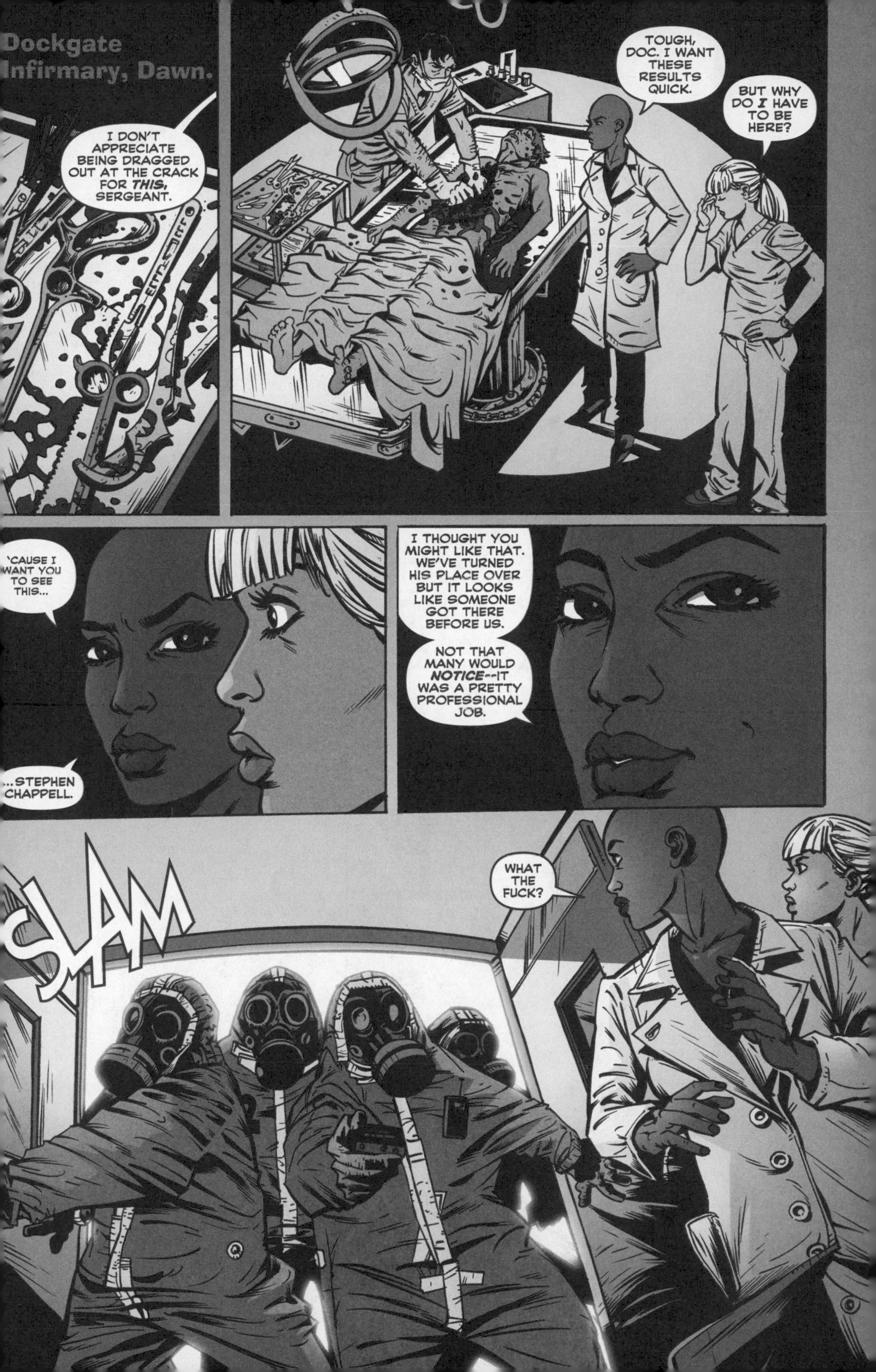
Dockgate Infirmary, Dawn.
I DON'T APPRECIATE BEING DRAGGED OUT AT THE CRACK FOR THIS, SERGEANT.
TOUGH, DOC. I WANT THESE RESULTS QUICK.
BUT WHY DO I HAVE TO BE HERE?
'CAUSE I WANT YOU TO SEE THIS...
...STEPHEN CHAPPELL.
I THOUGHT YOU MIGHT LIKE THAT. WE'VE TURNED HIS PLACE OVER BUT IT LOOKS LIKE SOMEONE GOT THERE BEFORE US.
NOT THAT MANY WOULD NOTICE--IT WAS A PRETTY PROFESSIONAL JOB.
SLAM
WHAT THE FUCK?

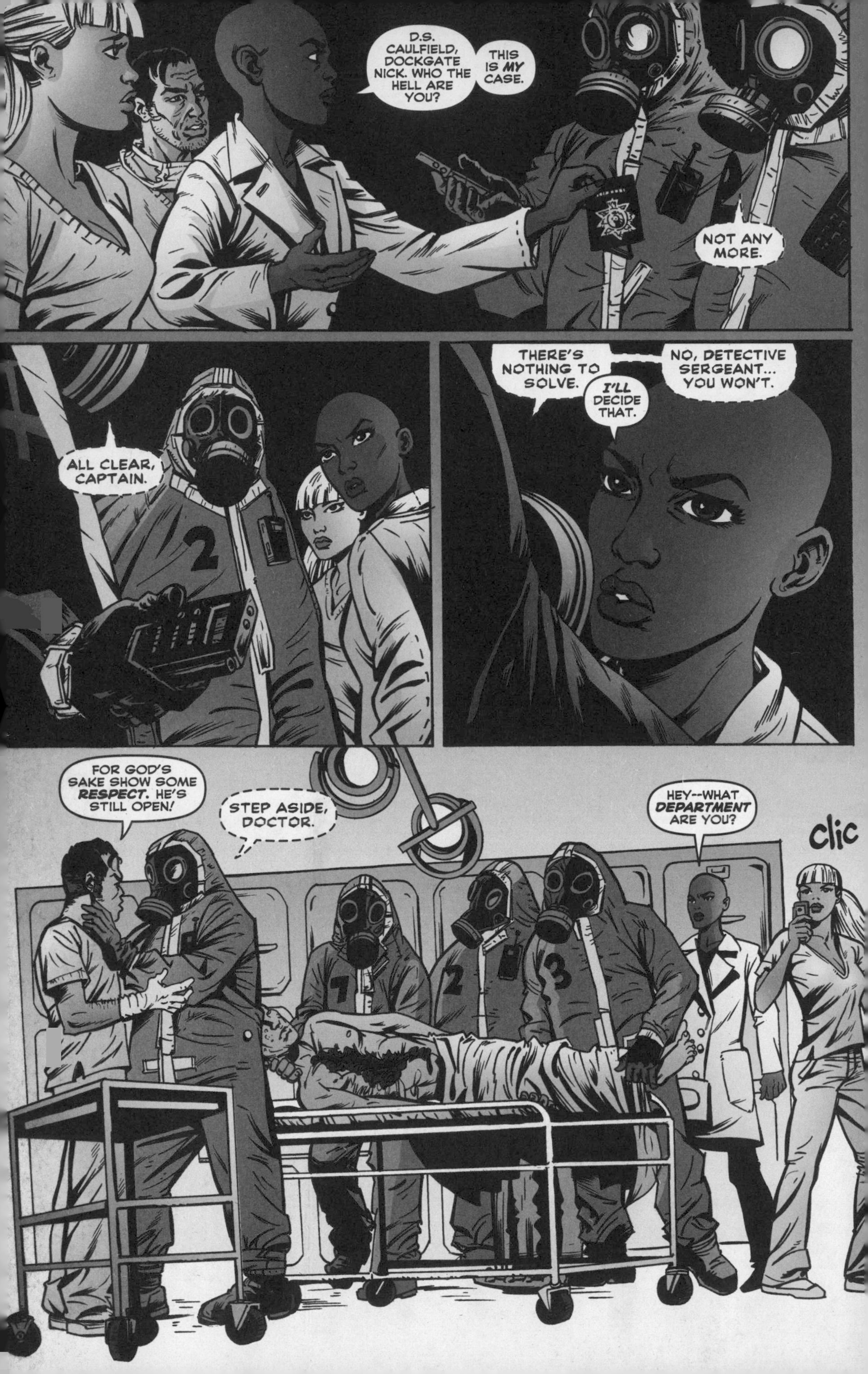
D.S. CAULFIELD, DOCKGATE NICK. WHO THE HELL ARE YOU?
THIS IS MY CASE.
NOT ANY MORE.
ALL CLEAR, CAPTAIN.
THERE'S NOTHING TO SOLVE.
I'LL DECIDE THAT.
NO, DETECTIVE SERGEANT... YOU WON'T.
FOR GOD'S SAKE SHOW SOME RESPECT. HE'S STILL OPEN!
STEP ASIDE, DOCTOR.
HEY--WHAT DEPARTMENT ARE YOU?
Clic

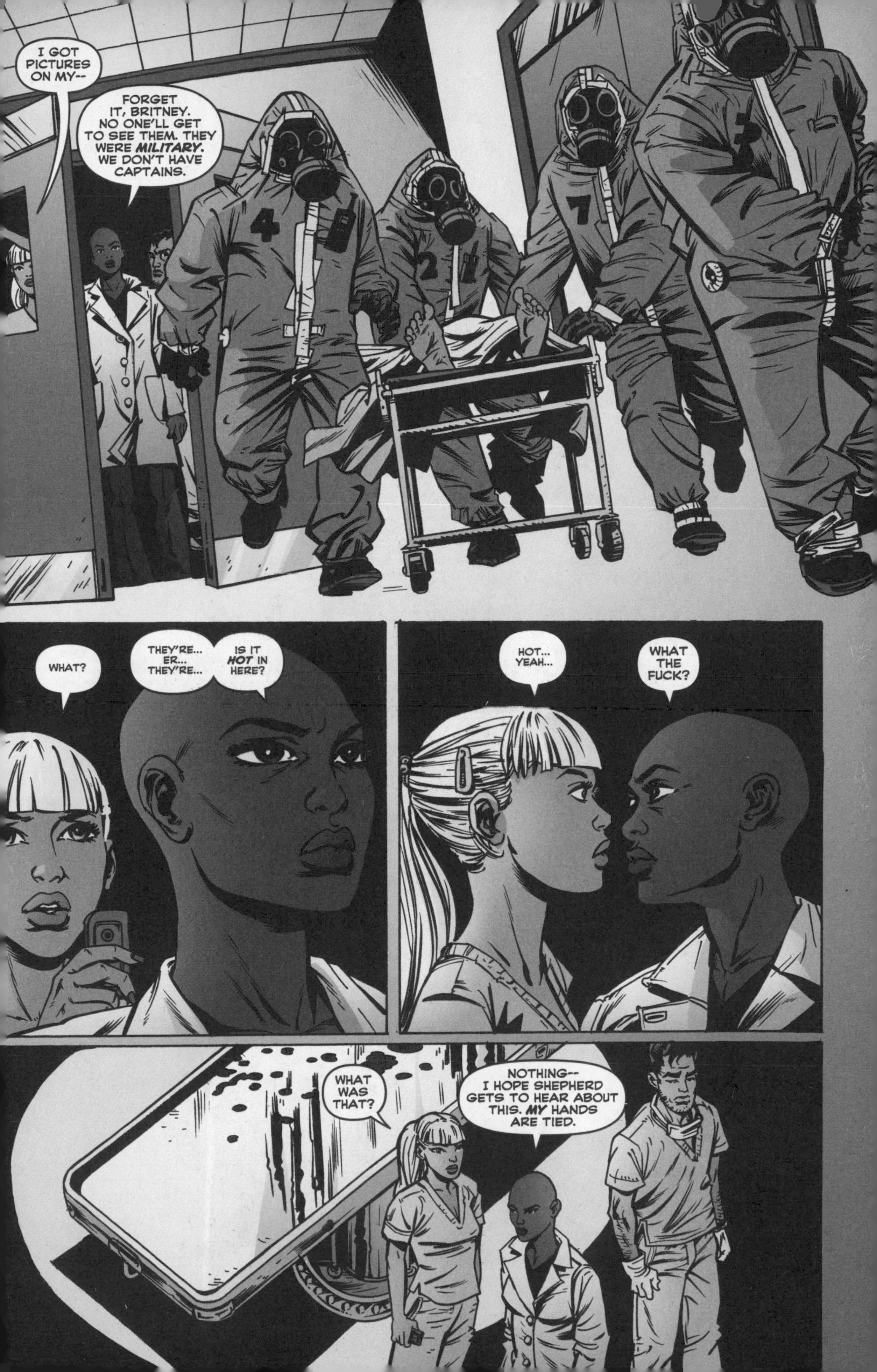
I GOT PICTURES ON MY--
FORGET IT, BRITNEY. NO ONE'LL GET TO SEE THEM. THEY WERE ***MILITARY***. WE DON'T HAVE CAPTAINS.
4
2
7
WHAT?
THEY'RE... ER... THEY'RE...
IS IT ***HOT*** IN HERE?
HOT... YEAH...
WHAT THE FUCK?
WHAT WAS THAT?
NOTHING-- I HOPE SHEPHERD GETS TO HEAR ABOUT THIS. ***MY*** HANDS ARE TIED.

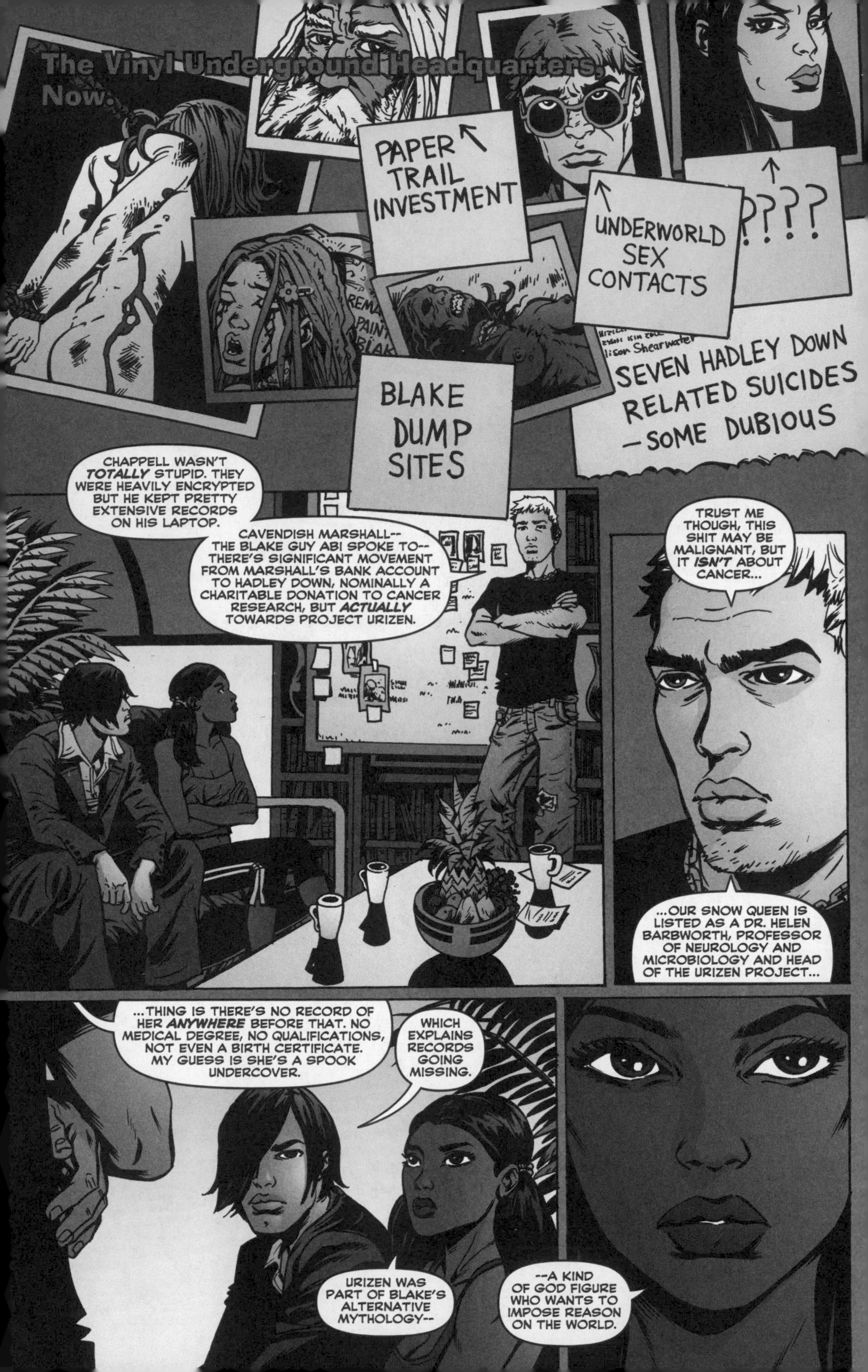
The Vinyl Underground Headquarters, Now.
PAPER TRAIL INVESTMENT
UNDERWORLD SEX CONTACTS
????
BLAKE DUMP SITES
SEVEN HADLEY DOWN RELATED SUICIDES —SOME DUBIOUS
CHAPPELL WASN'T TOTALLY STUPID. THEY WERE HEAVILY ENCRYPTED BUT HE KEPT PRETTY EXTENSIVE RECORDS ON HIS LAPTOP.
CAVENDISH MARSHALL-- THE BLAKE GUY ABI SPOKE TO-- THERE'S SIGNIFICANT MOVEMENT FROM MARSHALL'S BANK ACCOUNT TO HADLEY DOWN, NOMINALLY A CHARITABLE DONATION TO CANCER RESEARCH, BUT ACTUALLY TOWARDS PROJECT URIZEN.
TRUST ME THOUGH, THIS SHIT MAY BE MALIGNANT, BUT IT ISN'T ABOUT CANCER...
...OUR SNOW QUEEN IS LISTED AS A DR. HELEN BARBWORTH, PROFESSOR OF NEUROLOGY AND MICROBIOLOGY AND HEAD OF THE URIZEN PROJECT...
...THING IS THERE'S NO RECORD OF HER ANYWHERE BEFORE THAT. NO MEDICAL DEGREE, NO QUALIFICATIONS, NOT EVEN A BIRTH CERTIFICATE. MY GUESS IS SHE'S A SPOOK UNDERCOVER.
WHICH EXPLAINS RECORDS GOING MISSING.
URIZEN WAS PART OF BLAKE'S ALTERNATIVE MYTHOLOGY--
--A KIND OF GOD FIGURE WHO WANTS TO IMPOSE REASON ON THE WORLD.

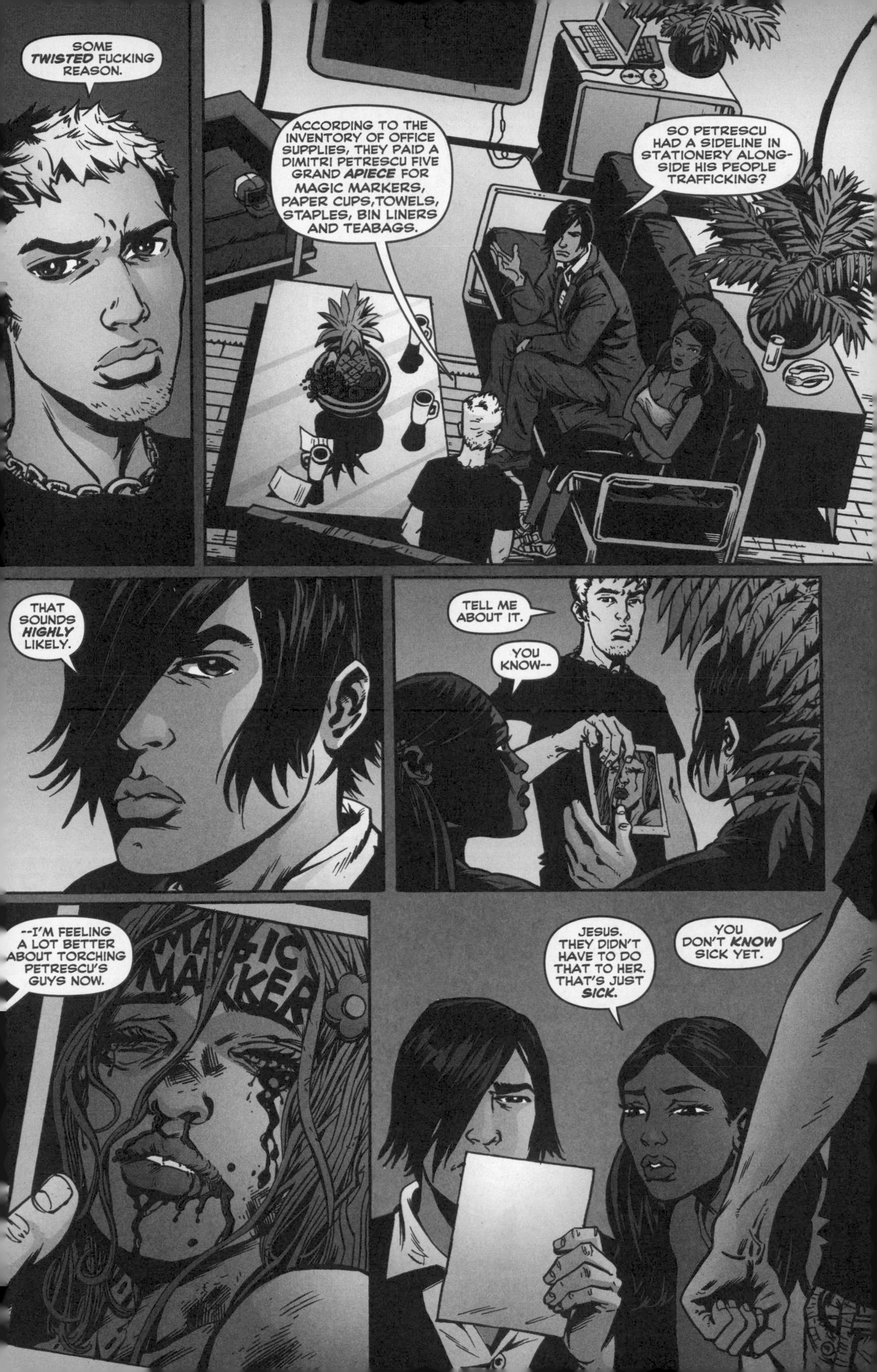
SOME TWISTED FUCKING REASON.
ACCORDING TO THE INVENTORY OF OFFICE SUPPLIES, THEY PAID A DIMITRI PETRESCU FIVE GRAND APIECE FOR MAGIC MARKERS, PAPER CUPS,TOWELS, STAPLES, BIN LINERS AND TEABAGS.
SO PETRESCU HAD A SIDELINE IN STATIONERY ALONG-SIDE HIS PEOPLE TRAFFICKING?
THAT SOUNDS HIGHLY LIKELY.
TELL ME ABOUT IT.
YOU KNOW--
--I'M FEELING A LOT BETTER ABOUT TORCHING PETRESCU'S GUYS NOW.
MAGIC MARKER
JESUS. THEY DIDN'T HAVE TO DO THAT TO HER. THAT'S JUST SICK.
YOU DON'T KNOW SICK YET.

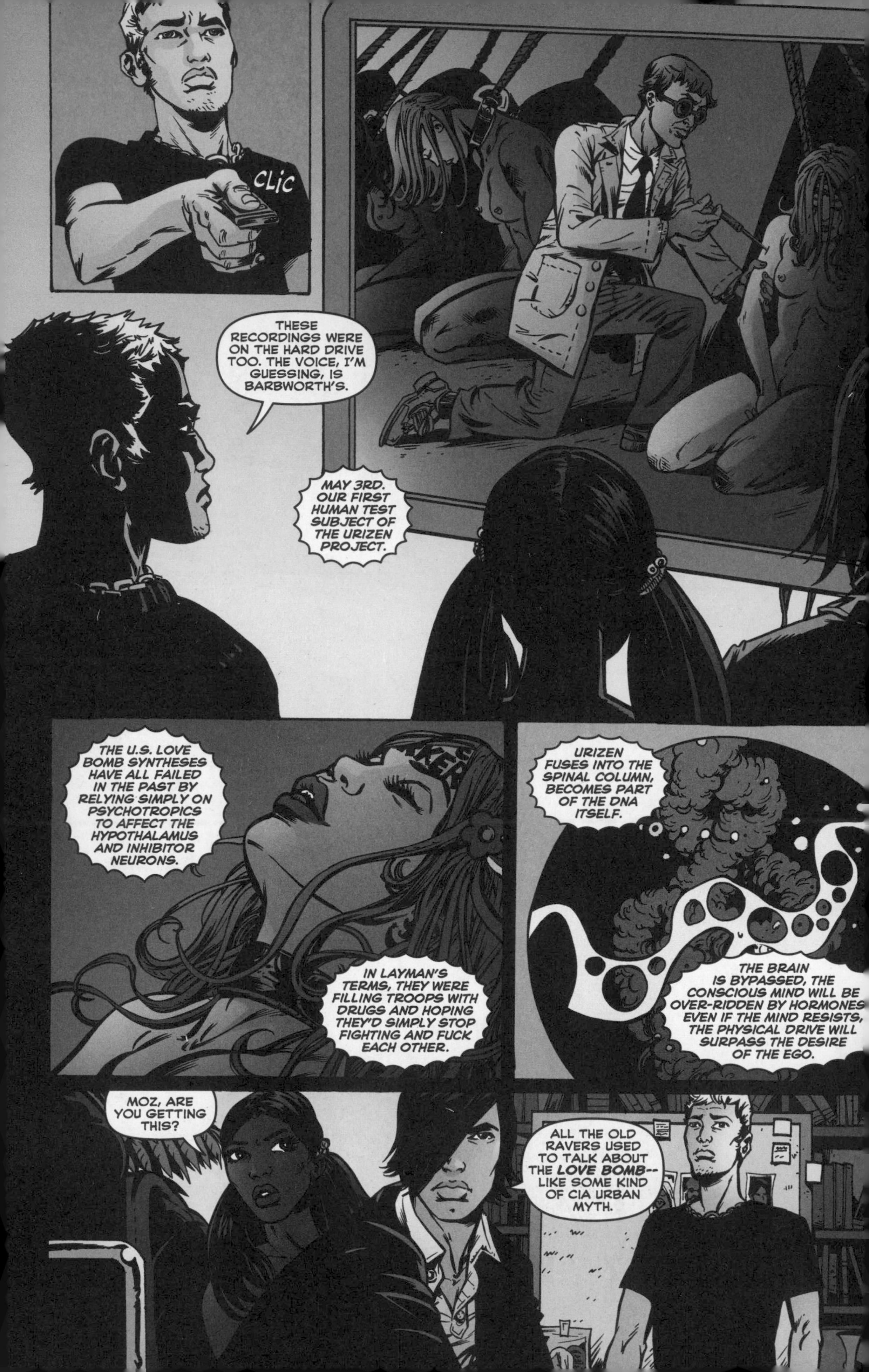
CLIC
THESE RECORDINGS WERE ON THE HARD DRIVE TOO. THE VOICE, I'M GUESSING, IS BARBWORTH'S.
MAY 3RD. OUR FIRST HUMAN TEST SUBJECT OF THE URIZEN PROJECT.
THE U.S. LOVE BOMB SYNTHESES HAVE ALL FAILED IN THE PAST BY RELYING SIMPLY ON PSYCHOTROPICS TO AFFECT THE HYPOTHALAMUS AND INHIBITOR NEURONS.
IN LAYMAN'S TERMS, THEY WERE FILLING TROOPS WITH DRUGS AND HOPING THEY'D SIMPLY STOP FIGHTING AND FUCK EACH OTHER.
URIZEN FUSES INTO THE SPINAL COLUMN, BECOMES PART OF THE DNA ITSELF.
THE BRAIN IS BYPASSED, THE CONSCIOUS MIND WILL BE OVER-RIDDEN BY HORMONES. EVEN IF THE MIND RESISTS, THE PHYSICAL DRIVE WILL SURPASS THE DESIRE OF THE EGO.
MOZ, ARE YOU GETTING THIS?
ALL THE OLD RAVERS USED TO TALK ABOUT THE LOVE BOMB-- LIKE SOME KIND OF CIA URBAN MYTH.

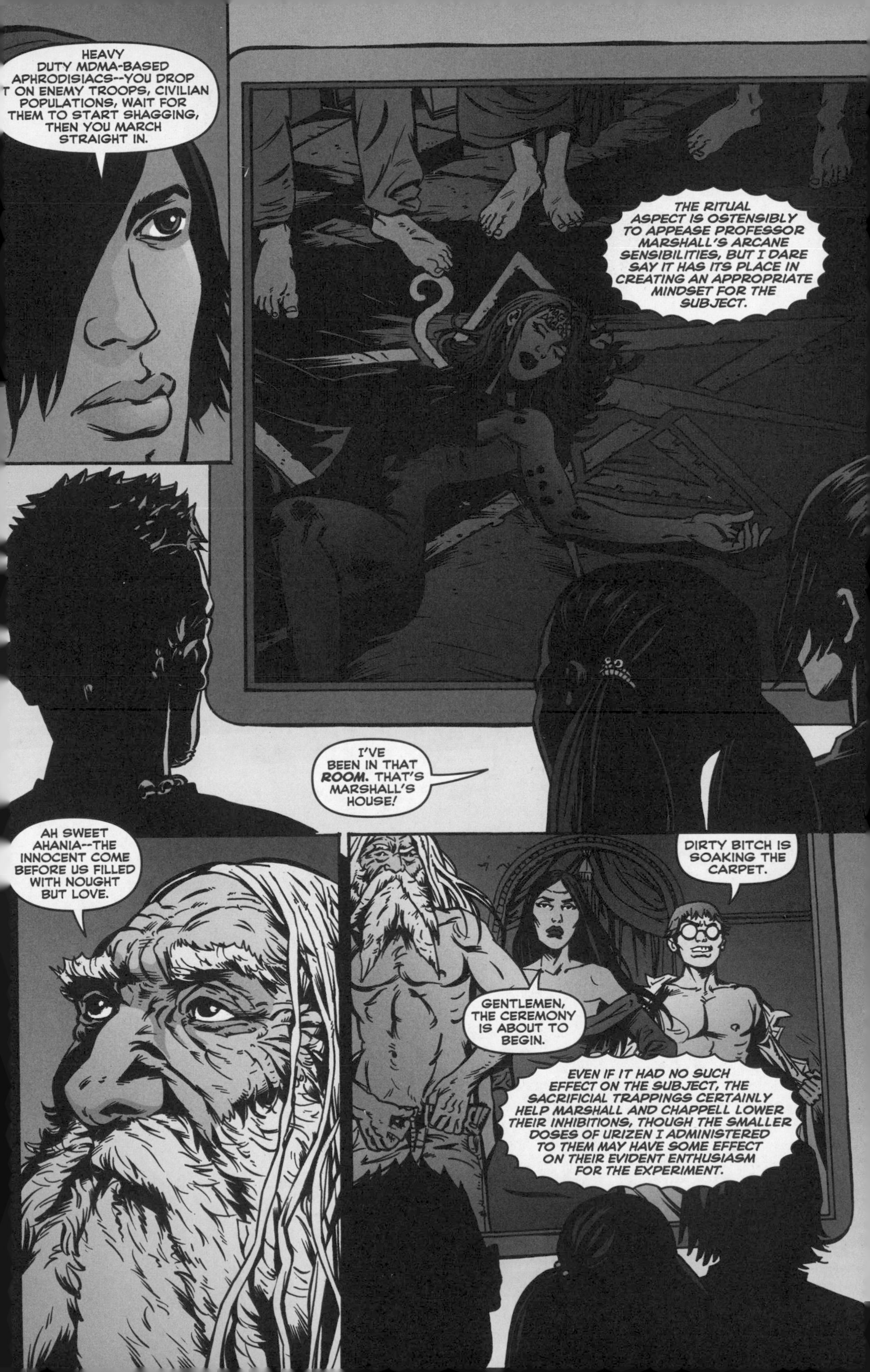
HEAVY DUTY MDMA-BASED APHRODISIACS--YOU DROP T ON ENEMY TROOPS, CIVILIAN POPULATIONS, WAIT FOR THEM TO START SHAGGING, THEN YOU MARCH STRAIGHT IN.
THE RITUAL ASPECT IS OSTENSIBLY TO APPEASE PROFESSOR MARSHALL'S ARCANE SENSIBILITIES, BUT I DARE SAY IT HAS ITS PLACE IN CREATING AN APPROPRIATE MINDSET FOR THE SUBJECT.
I'VE BEEN IN THAT ROOM. THAT'S MARSHALL'S HOUSE!
AH SWEET AHANIA--THE INNOCENT COME BEFORE US FILLED WITH NOUGHT BUT LOVE.
DIRTY BITCH IS SOAKING THE CARPET.
GENTLEMEN, THE CEREMONY IS ABOUT TO BEGIN.
EVEN IF IT HAD NO SUCH EFFECT ON THE SUBJECT, THE SACRIFICIAL TRAPPINGS CERTAINLY HELP MARSHALL AND CHAPPELL LOWER THEIR INHIBITIONS, THOUGH THE SMALLER DOSES OF URIZEN I ADMINISTERED TO THEM MAY HAVE SOME EFFECT ON THEIR EVIDENT ENTHUSIASM FOR THE EXPERIMENT.

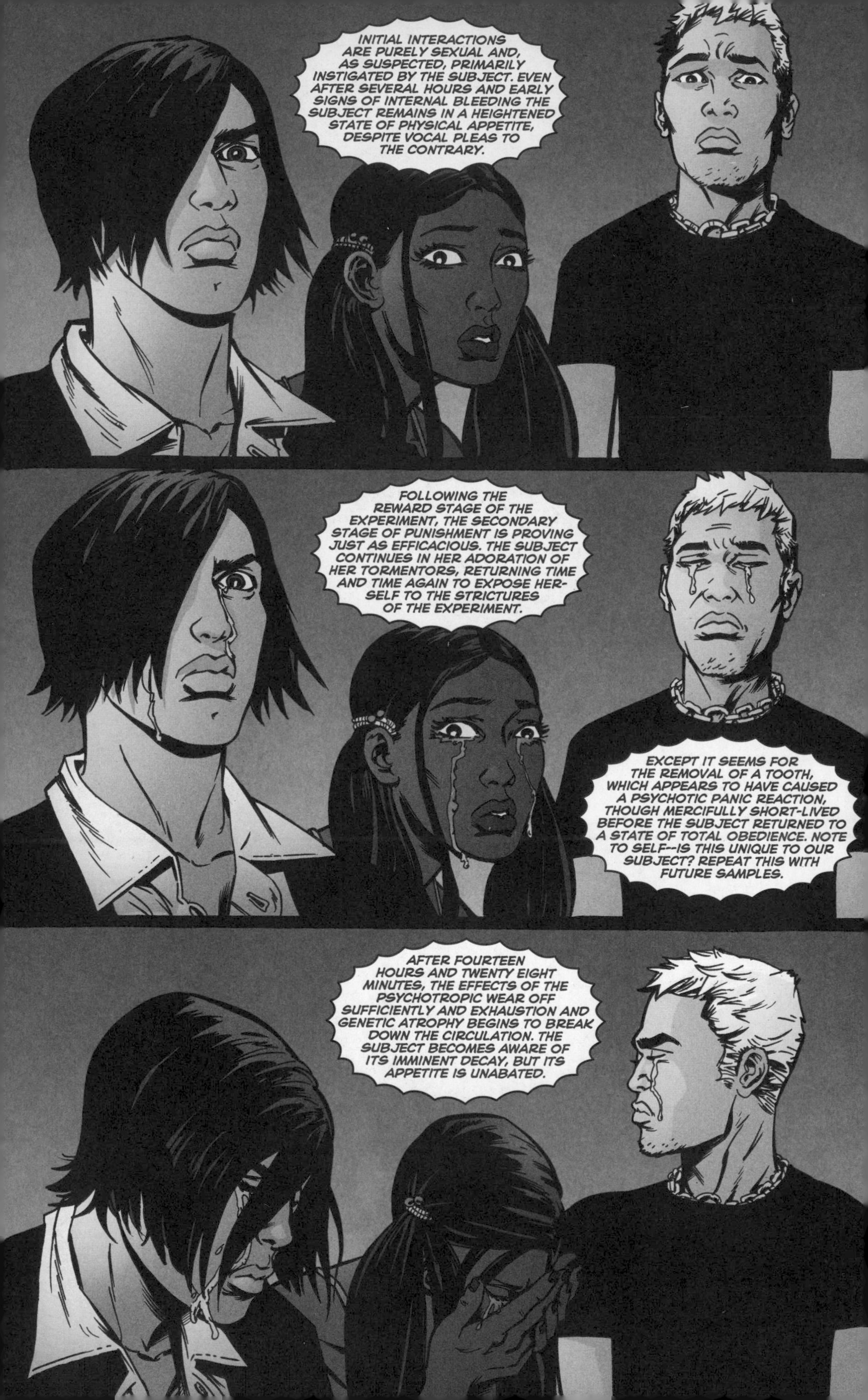
INITIAL INTERACTIONS ARE PURELY SEXUAL AND, AS SUSPECTED, PRIMARILY INSTIGATED BY THE SUBJECT. EVEN AFTER SEVERAL HOURS AND EARLY SIGNS OF INTERNAL BLEEDING THE SUBJECT REMAINS IN A HEIGHTENED STATE OF PHYSICAL APPETITE, DESPITE VOCAL PLEAS TO THE CONTRARY.
FOLLOWING THE REWARD STAGE OF THE EXPERIMENT, THE SECONDARY STAGE OF PUNISHMENT IS PROVING JUST AS EFFICACIOUS. THE SUBJECT CONTINUES IN HER ADORATION OF HER TORMENTORS, RETURNING TIME AND TIME AGAIN TO EXPOSE HER-SELF TO THE STRICTURES OF THE EXPERIMENT.
EXCEPT IT SEEMS FOR THE REMOVAL OF A TOOTH, WHICH APPEARS TO HAVE CAUSED A PSYCHOTIC PANIC REACTION, THOUGH MERCIFULLY SHORT-LIVED BEFORE THE SUBJECT RETURNED TO A STATE OF TOTAL OBEDIENCE. NOTE TO SELF--IS THIS UNIQUE TO OUR SUBJECT? REPEAT THIS WITH FUTURE SAMPLES.
AFTER FOURTEEN HOURS AND TWENTY EIGHT MINUTES, THE EFFECTS OF THE PSYCHOTROPIC WEAR OFF SUFFICIENTLY AND EXHAUSTION AND GENETIC ATROPHY BEGINS TO BREAK DOWN THE CIRCULATION. THE SUBJECT BECOMES AWARE OF ITS IMMINENT DECAY, BUT ITS APPETITE IS UNABATED.

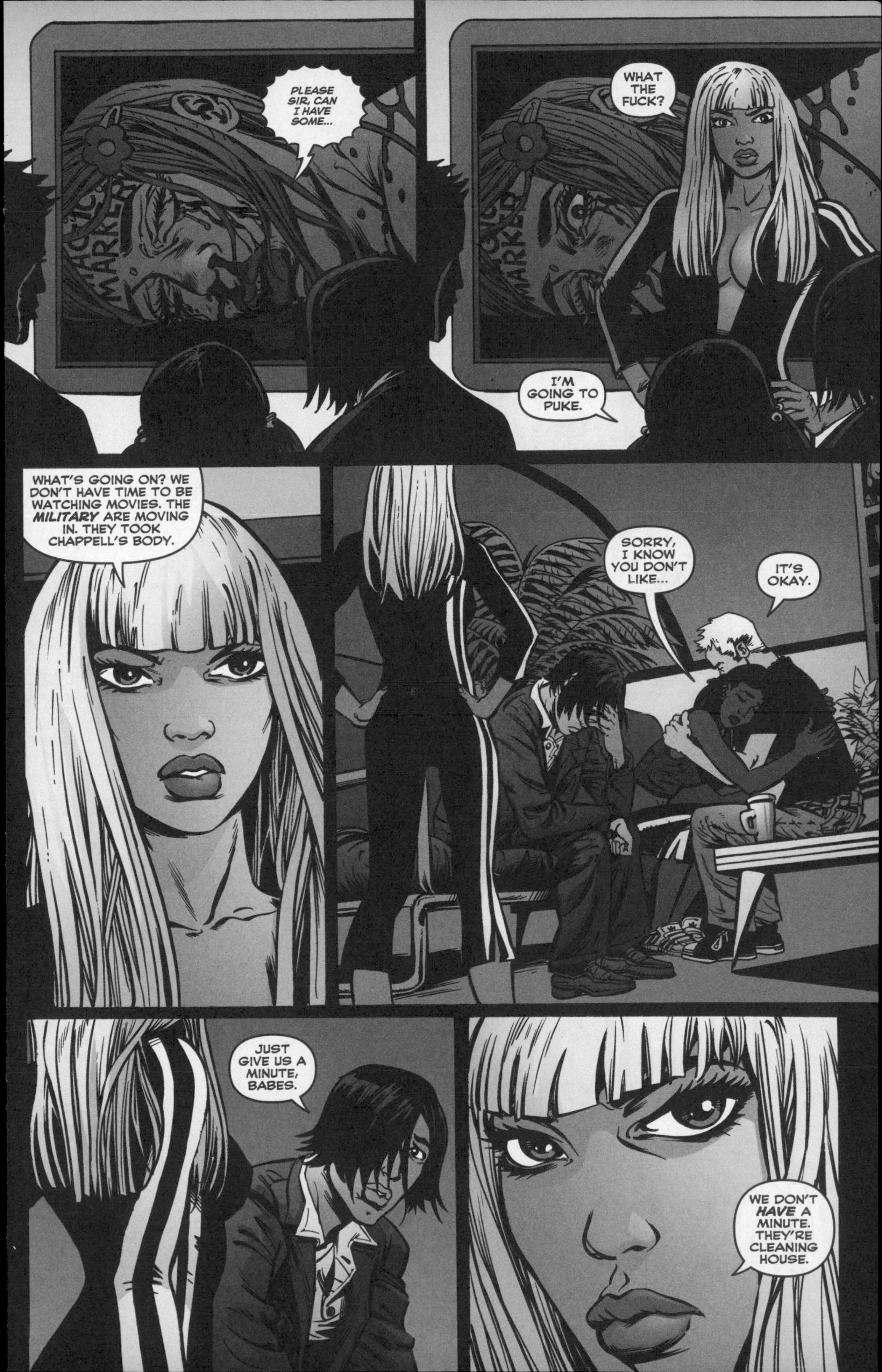
PLEASE SIR, CAN I HAVE SOME...
WHAT THE FUCK?
I'M GOING TO PUKE.
WHAT'S GOING ON? WE DON'T HAVE TIME TO BE WATCHING MOVIES. THE *MILITARY* ARE MOVING IN. THEY TOOK CHAPPELL'S BODY.
SORRY, I KNOW YOU DON'T LIKE...
IT'S OKAY.
JUST GIVE US A MINUTE, BABES.
WE DON'T *HAVE* A MINUTE. THEY'RE CLEANING HOUSE.

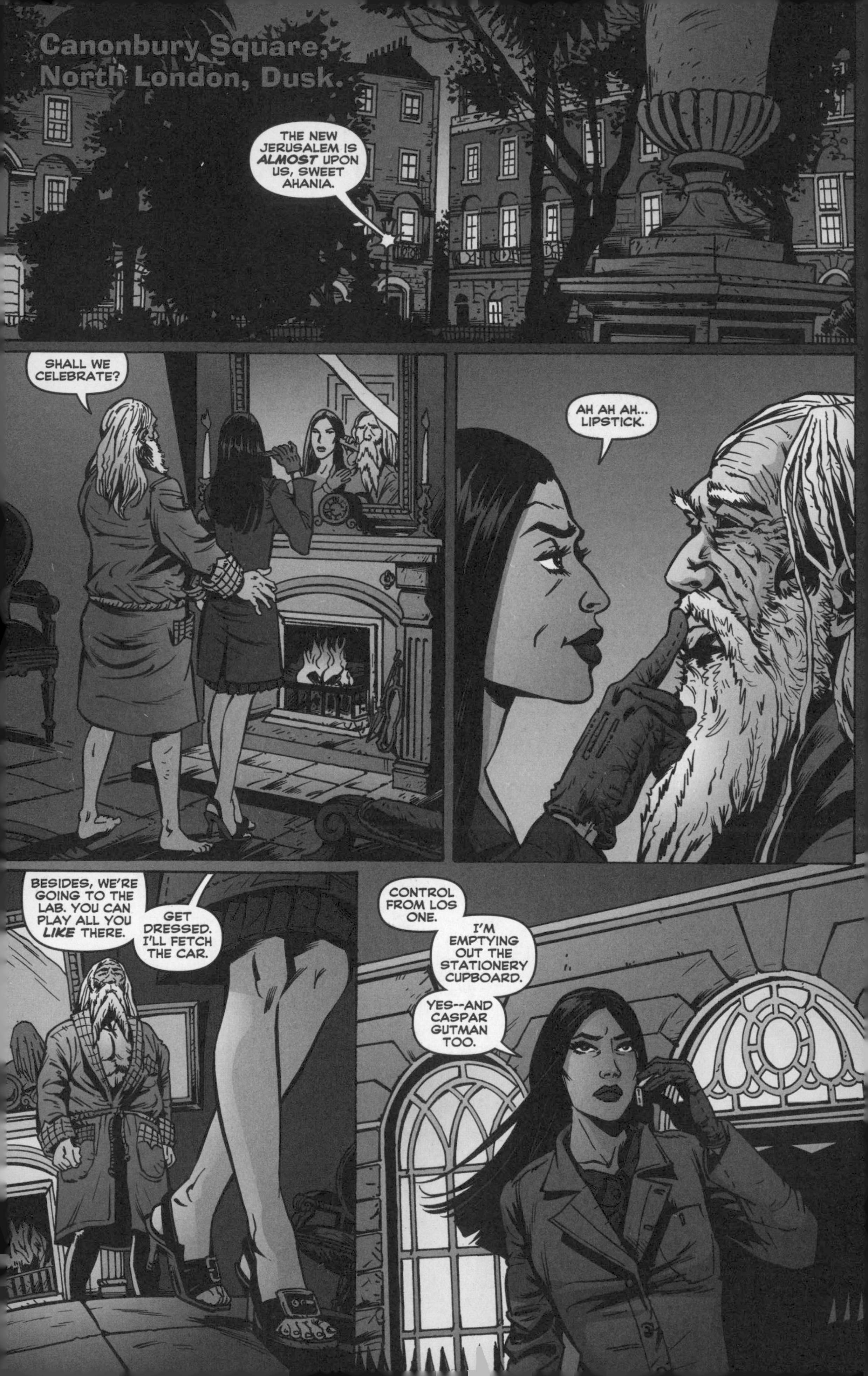

Canonbury Square, North London, Dusk.
THE NEW JERUSALEM IS ALMOST UPON US, SWEET AHANIA.
SHALL WE CELEBRATE?
AH AH AH... LIPSTICK.
BESIDES, WE'RE GOING TO THE LAB. YOU CAN PLAY ALL YOU LIKE THERE.
GET DRESSED. I'LL FETCH THE CAR.
CONTROL FROM LOS ONE.
I'M EMPTYING OUT THE STATIONERY CUPBOARD.
YES--AND CASPAR GUTMAN TOO.

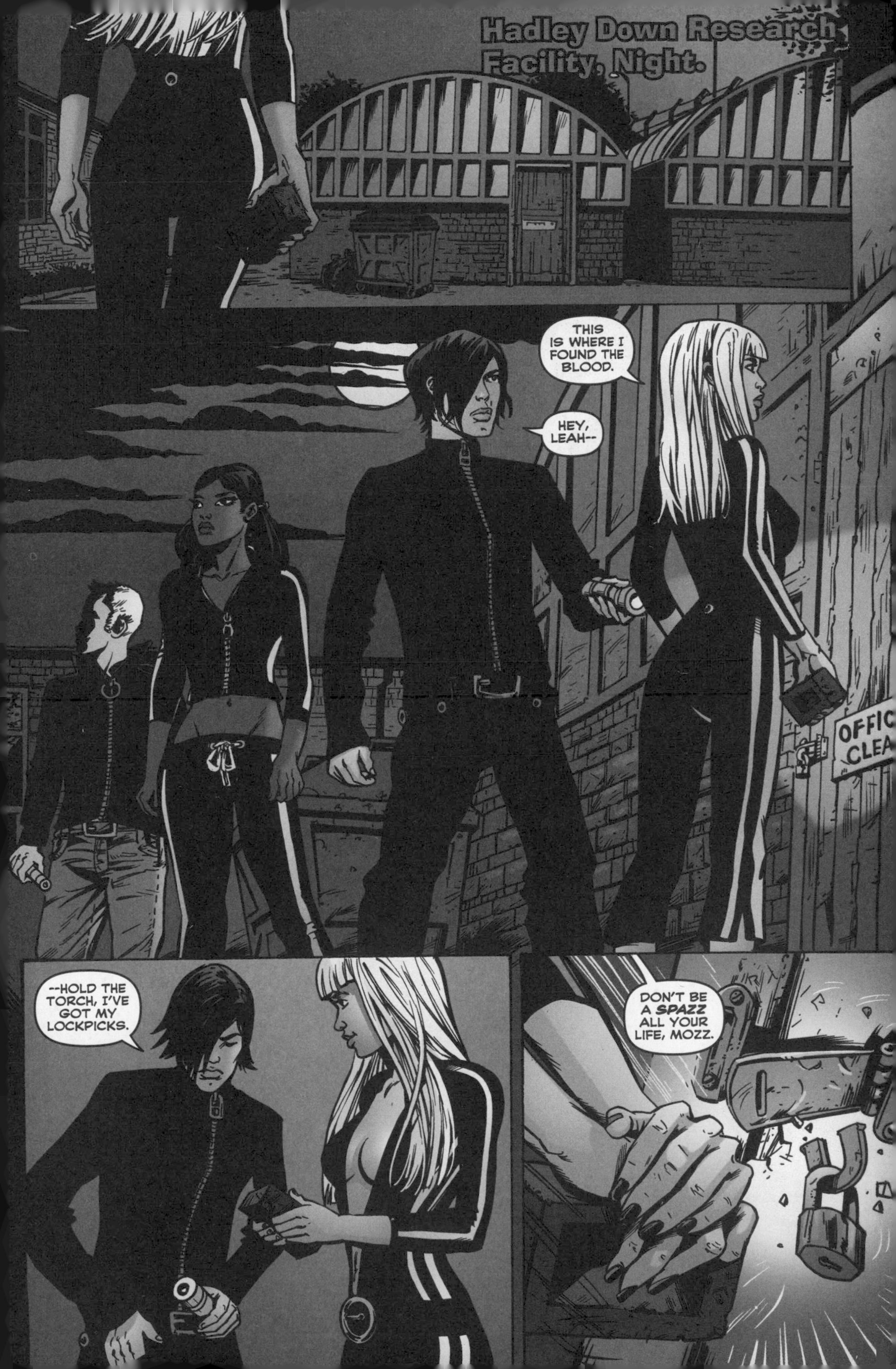

Hadley Down Research Facility, Night.
THIS IS WHERE I FOUND THE BLOOD.
HEY, LEAH--
OFFIC
CLEA
--HOLD THE TORCH, I'VE GOT MY LOCKPICKS.
DON'T BE A SPAZZ ALL YOUR LIFE, MOZZ.

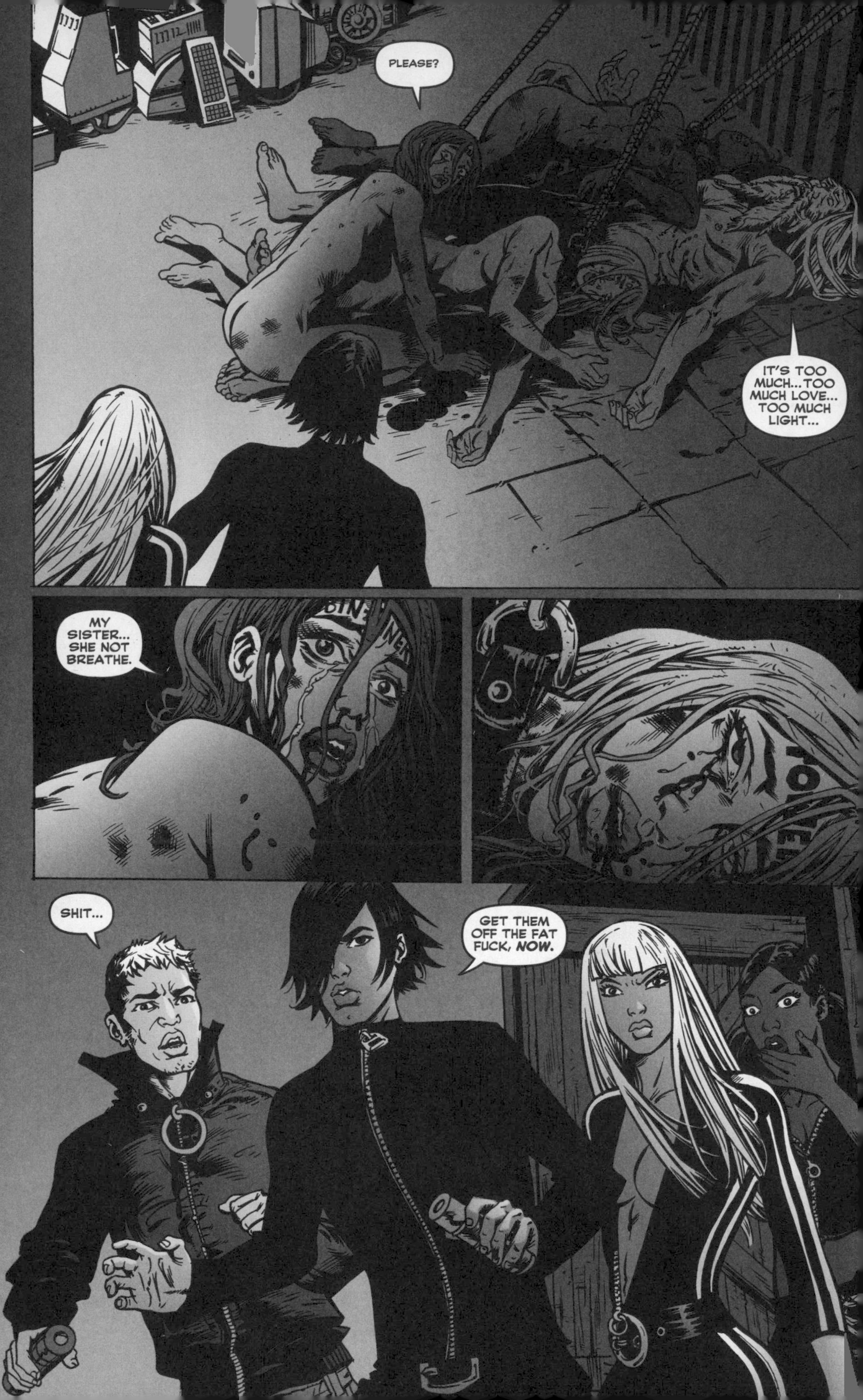
PLEASE?
IT'S TOO MUCH...TOO MUCH LOVE... TOO MUCH LIGHT...
MY SISTER... SHE NOT BREATHE.
SHIT...
GET THEM OFF THE FAT FUCK, *NOW.*

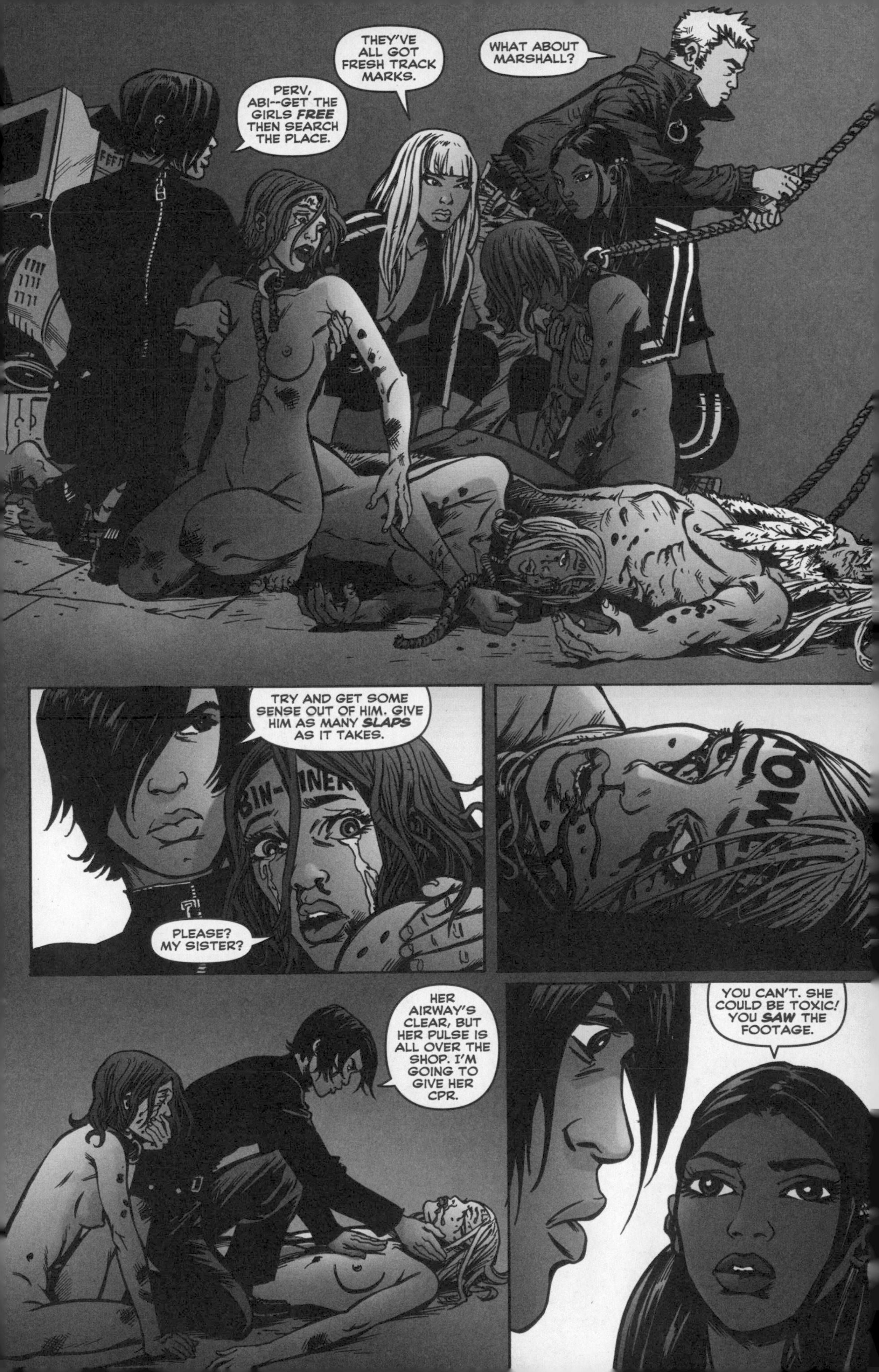
PERV, ABI--GET THE GIRLS FREE THEN SEARCH THE PLACE.
THEY'VE ALL GOT FRESH TRACK MARKS.
WHAT ABOUT MARSHALL?
TRY AND GET SOME SENSE OUT OF HIM. GIVE HIM AS MANY SLAPS AS IT TAKES.
PLEASE? MY SISTER?
HER AIRWAY'S CLEAR, BUT HER PULSE IS ALL OVER THE SHOP. I'M GOING TO GIVE HER CPR.
YOU CAN'T. SHE COULD BE TOXIC! YOU SAW THE FOOTAGE.

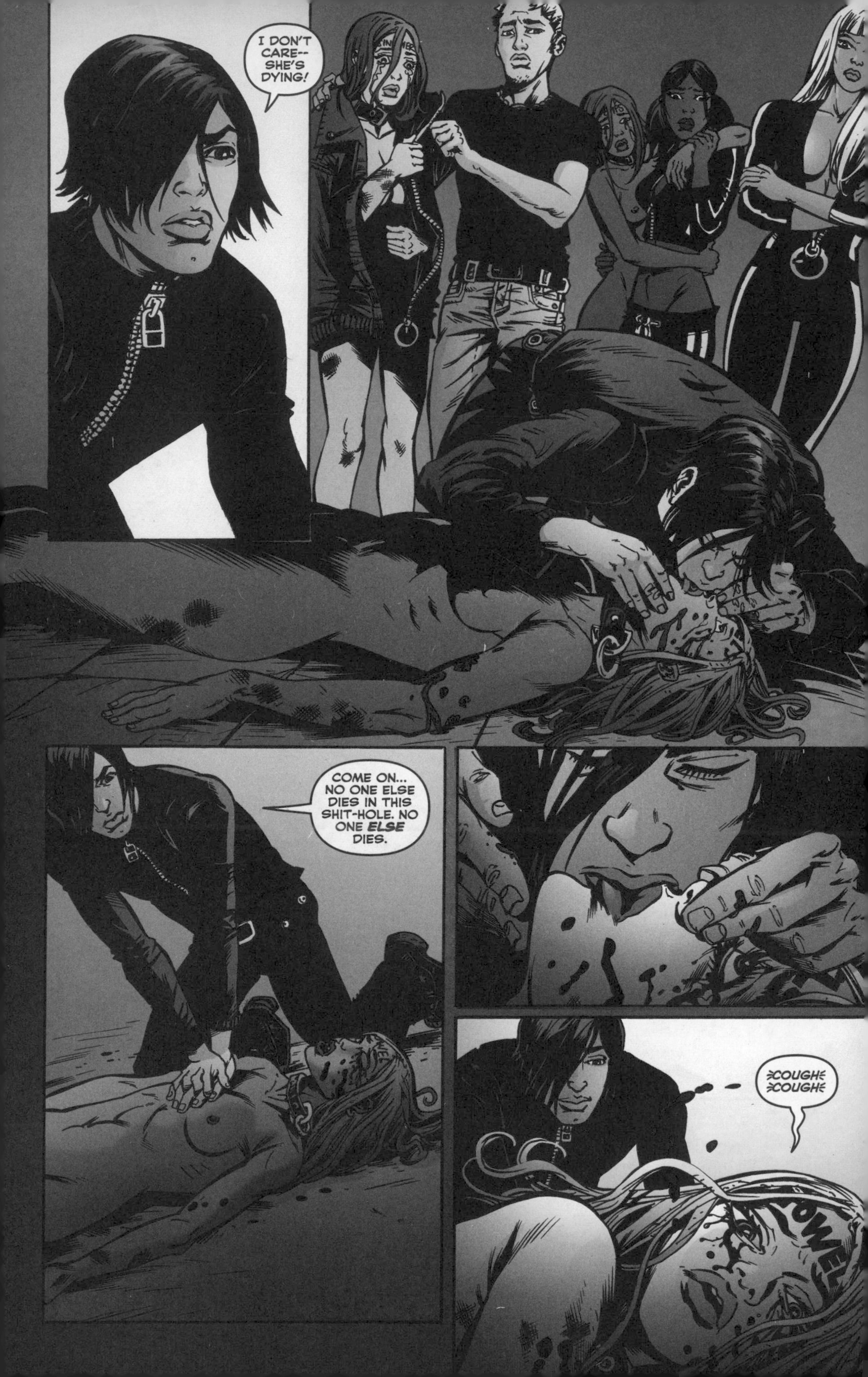
I DON'T CARE-- SHE'S DYING!
COME ON... NO ONE ELSE DIES IN THIS SHIT-HOLE. NO ONE ELSE DIES.
COUGH COUGH

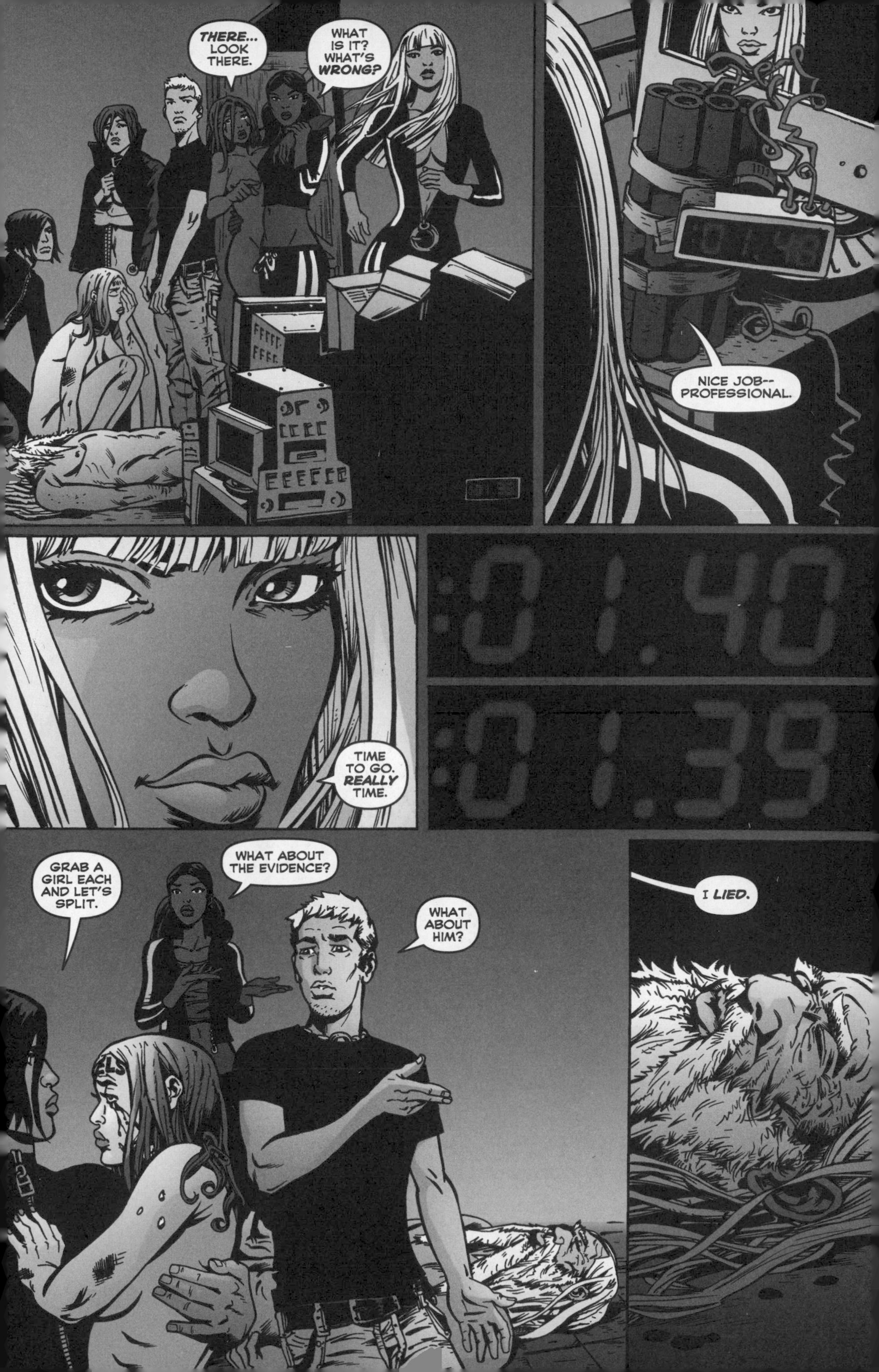
THERE... LOOK THERE.
WHAT IS IT? WHAT'S WRONG?
NICE JOB-- PROFESSIONAL.
TIME TO GO. REALLY TIME.
01.40
01.39
GRAB A GIRL EACH AND LET'S SPLIT.
WHAT ABOUT THE EVIDENCE?
WHAT ABOUT HIM?
I LIED.

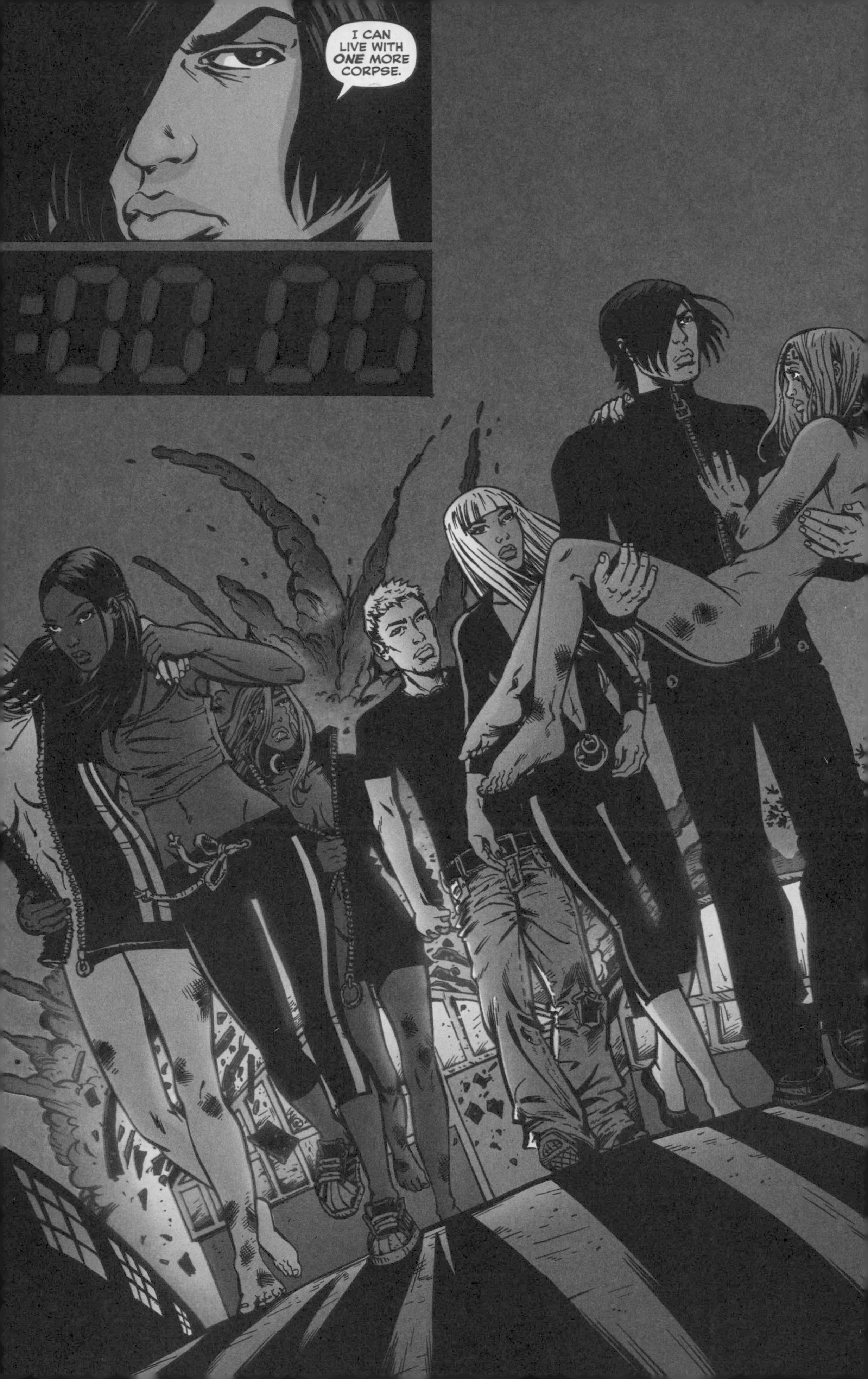

I CAN LIVE WITH ONE MORE CORPSE.

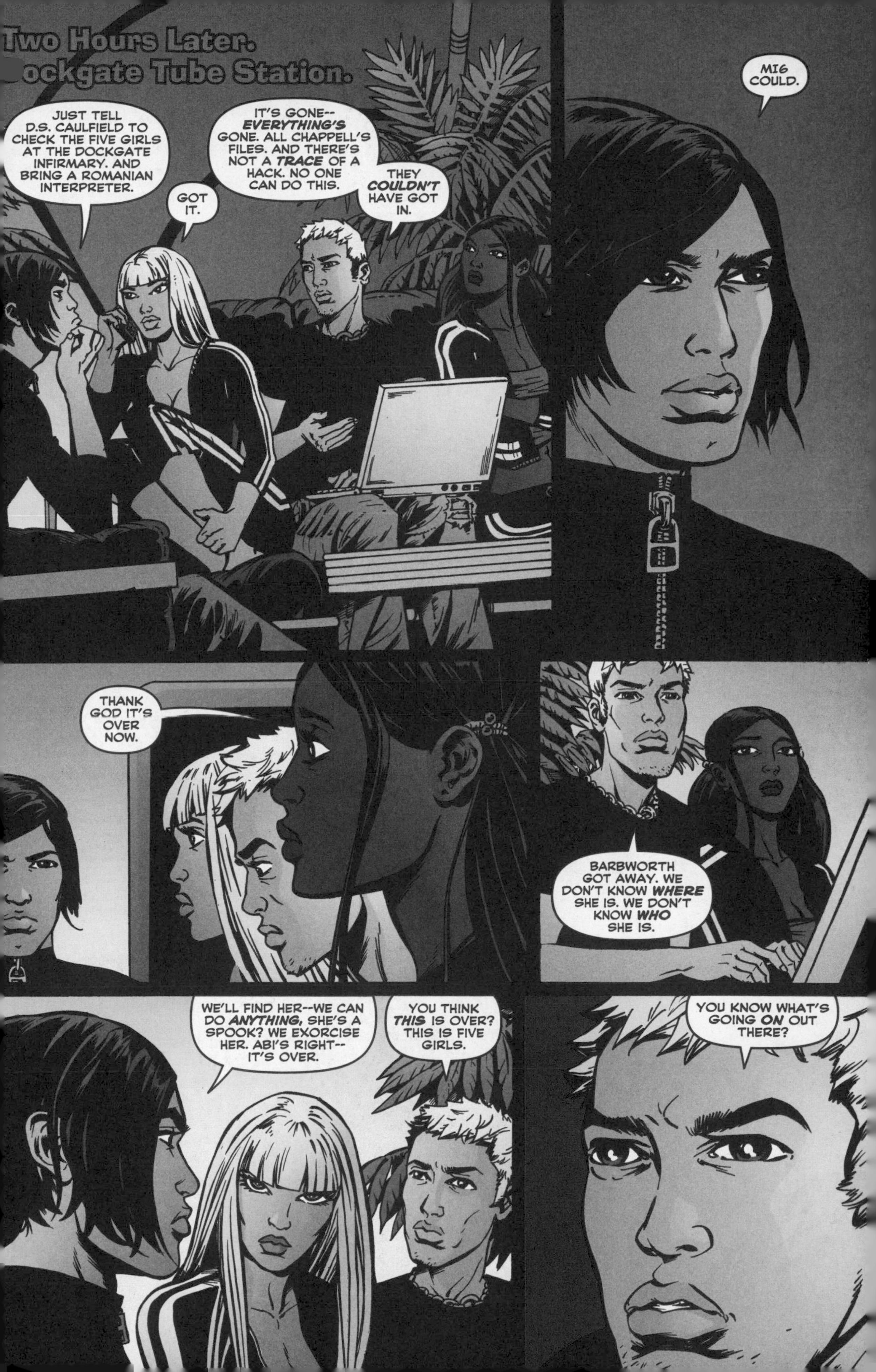

Two Hours Later.
ockgate Tube Station.
JUST TELL D.S. CAULFIELD TO CHECK THE FIVE GIRLS AT THE DOCKGATE INFIRMARY. AND BRING A ROMANIAN INTERPRETER.
GOT IT.
IT'S GONE-- EVERYTHING'S GONE. ALL CHAPPELL'S FILES. AND THERE'S NOT A TRACE OF A HACK. NO ONE CAN DO THIS.
THEY COULDN'T HAVE GOT IN.
MI6 COULD.
THANK GOD IT'S OVER NOW.
BARBWORTH GOT AWAY. WE DON'T KNOW WHERE SHE IS. WE DON'T KNOW WHO SHE IS.
WE'LL FIND HER--WE CAN DO ANYTHING, SHE'S A SPOOK? WE EXORCISE HER. ABI'S RIGHT-- IT'S OVER.
YOU THINK THIS IS OVER? THIS IS FIVE GIRLS.
YOU KNOW WHAT'S GOING ON OUT THERE?

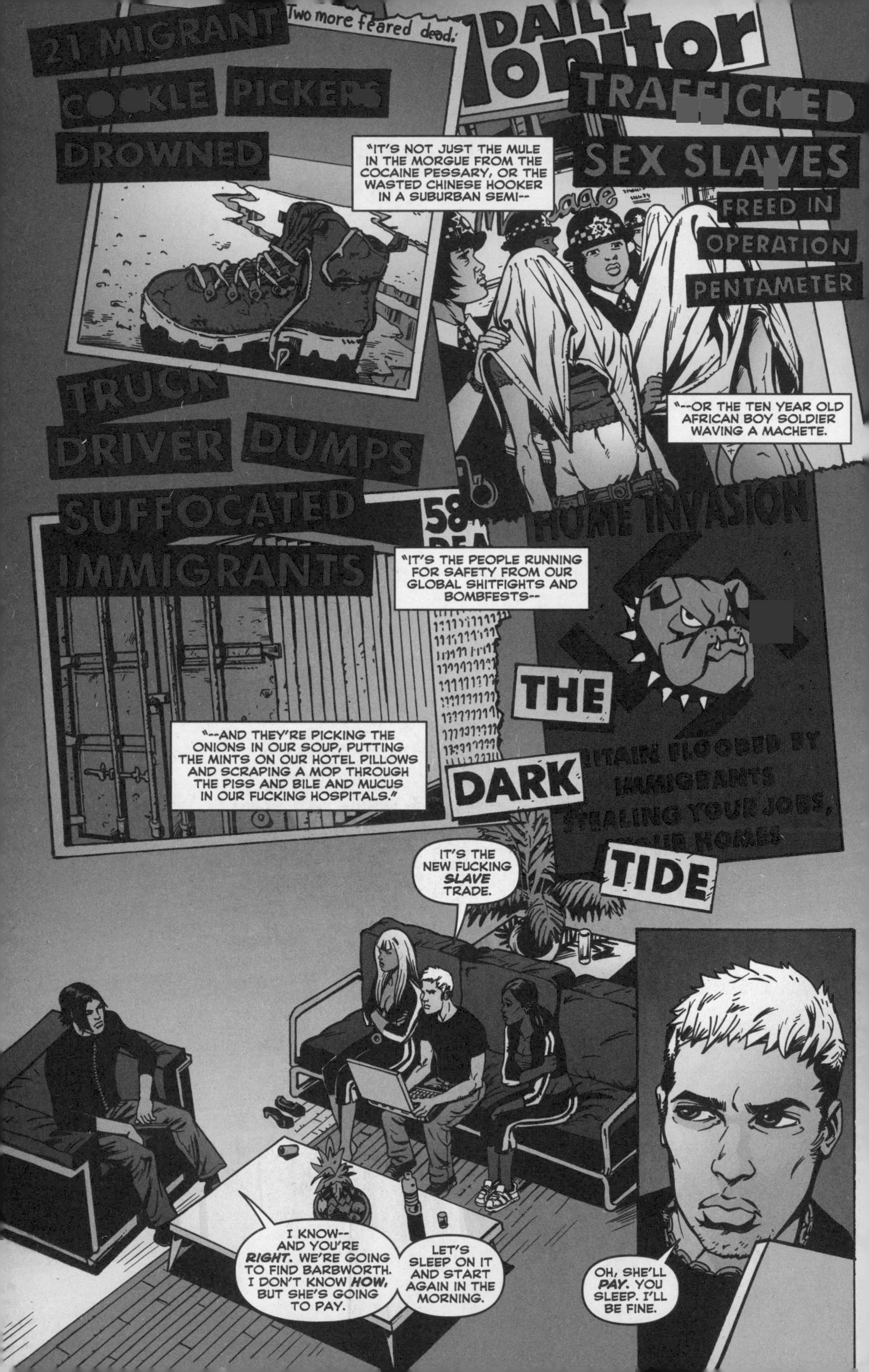
21 MIGRANT C[redacted]CKLE PICKER[redacted] DROWNED
Two more feared dead.
DAILY
TRAF[redacted]IC[redacted]ED SEX SLA[redacted]ES FREED IN OPERATION PENTAMETER
"IT'S NOT JUST THE MULE IN THE MORGUE FROM THE COCAINE PESSARY, OR THE WASTED CHINESE HOOKER IN A SUBURBAN SEMI--
"--OR THE TEN YEAR OLD AFRICAN BOY SOLDIER WAVING A MACHETE.
DRIVER DUMPS SUFFOCATED IMMIGRANTS
58
"IT'S THE PEOPLE RUNNING FOR SAFETY FROM OUR GLOBAL SHITFIGHTS AND BOMBFESTS--
"--AND THEY'RE PICKING THE ONIONS IN OUR SOUP, PUTTING THE MINTS ON OUR HOTEL PILLOWS AND SCRAPING A MOP THROUGH THE PISS AND BILE AND MUCUS IN OUR FUCKING HOSPITALS."
HOME INVASION
THE DARK TIDE
IMMIGRANTS STEALING YOUR JOBS,
IT'S THE NEW FUCKING *SLAVE* TRADE.
I KNOW-- AND YOU'RE *RIGHT.* WE'RE GOING TO FIND BARBWORTH. I DON'T KNOW *HOW,* BUT SHE'S GOING TO PAY.
LET'S SLEEP ON IT AND START AGAIN IN THE MORNING.
OH, SHE'LL *PAY.* YOU SLEEP. I'LL BE FINE.

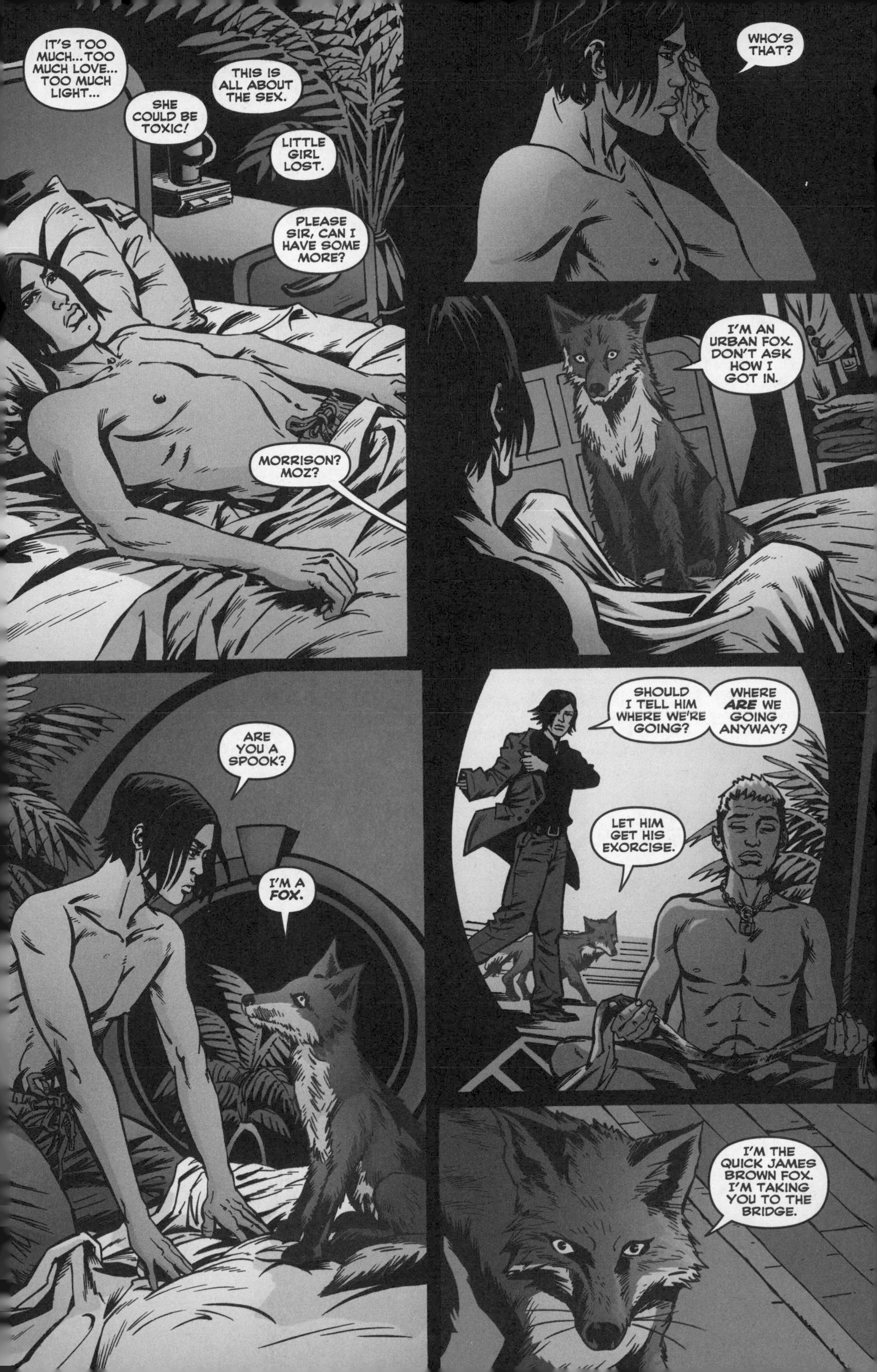
IT'S TOO MUCH...TOO MUCH LOVE... TOO MUCH LIGHT...
SHE COULD BE TOXIC!
THIS IS ALL ABOUT THE SEX.
LITTLE GIRL LOST.
PLEASE SIR, CAN I HAVE SOME MORE?
MORRISON? MOZ?
WHO'S THAT?
I'M AN URBAN FOX. DON'T ASK HOW I GOT IN.
ARE YOU A SPOOK?
I'M A *FOX.*
SHOULD I TELL HIM WHERE WE'RE GOING?
WHERE *ARE* WE GOING ANYWAY?
LET HIM GET HIS EXORCISE.
I'M THE QUICK JAMES BROWN FOX. I'M TAKING YOU TO THE BRIDGE.

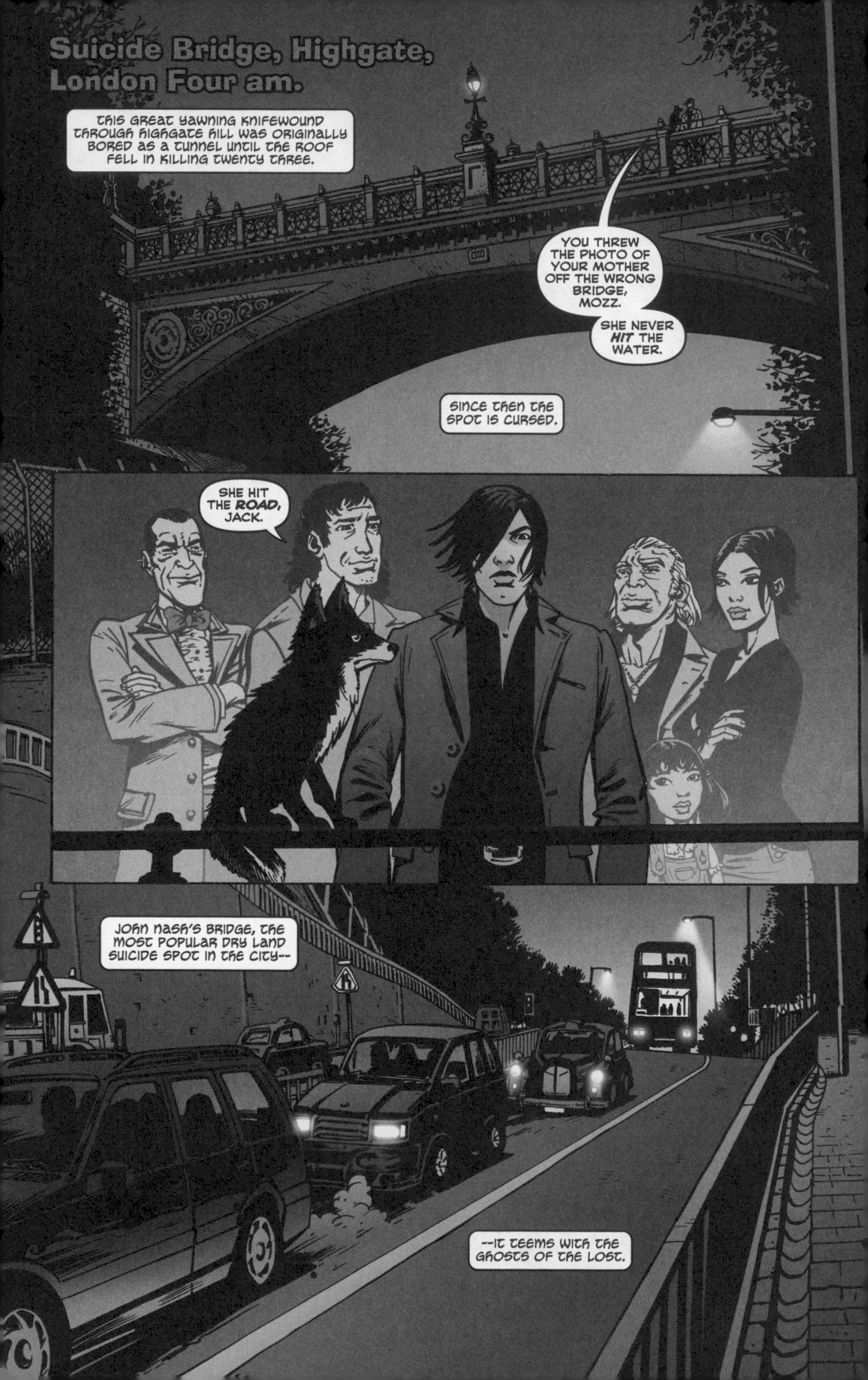
Suicide Bridge, Highgate, London Four am.
THIS GREAT YAWNING KNIFEWOUND THROUGH HIGHGATE HILL WAS ORIGINALLY BORED AS A TUNNEL UNTIL THE ROOF FELL IN KILLING TWENTY THREE.
YOU THREW THE PHOTO OF YOUR MOTHER OFF THE WRONG BRIDGE, MOZZ.
SHE NEVER HIT THE WATER.
SINCE THEN THE SPOT IS CURSED.
SHE HIT THE ROAD, JACK.
JOHN NASH'S BRIDGE, THE MOST POPULAR DRY LAND SUICIDE SPOT IN THE CITY--
--IT TEEMS WITH THE GHOSTS OF THE LOST.

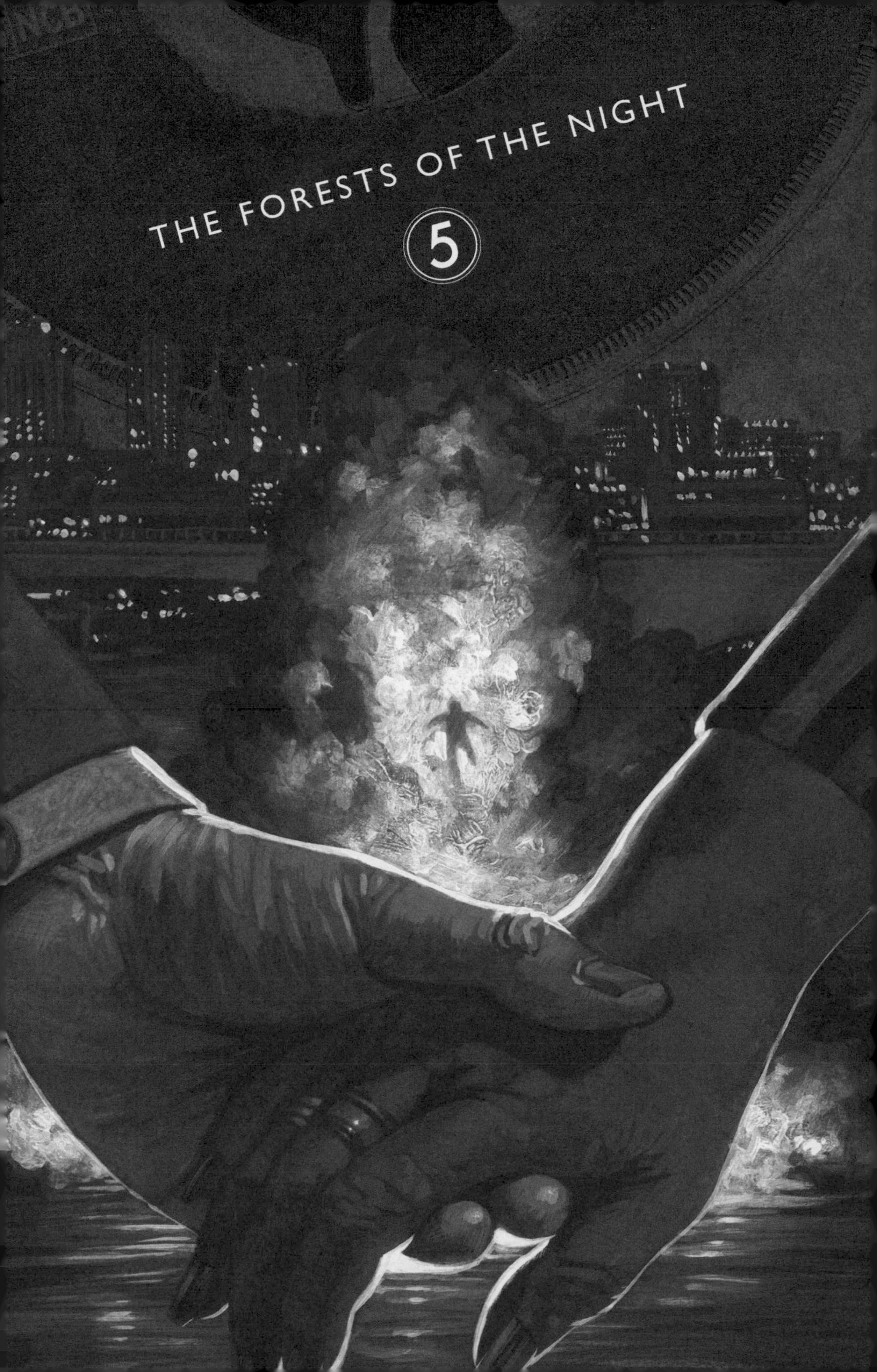
THE FORESTS OF THE NIGHT
5

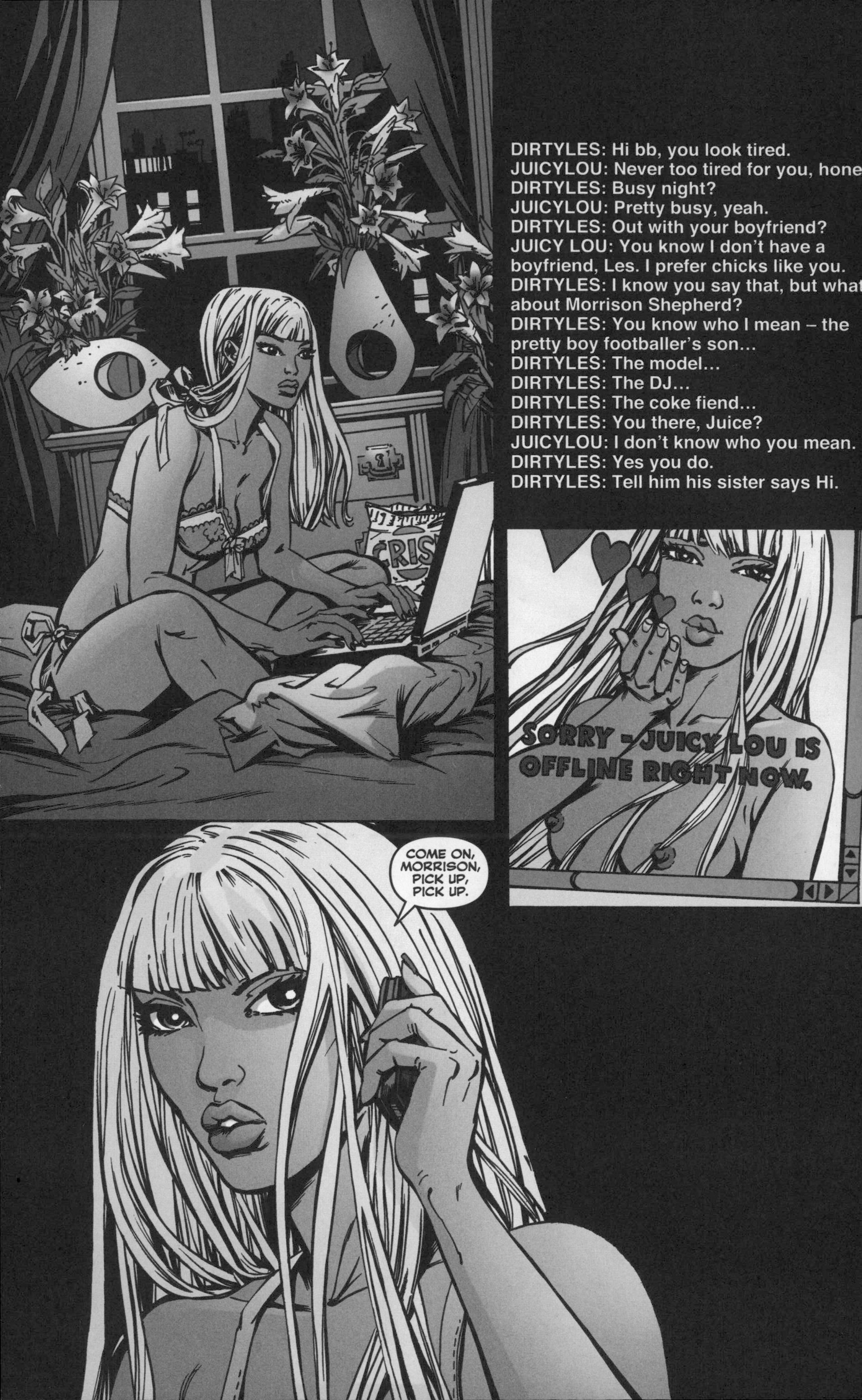
DIRTYLES: Hi bb, you look tired.
JUICYLOU: Never too tired for you, hone
DIRTYLES: Busy night?
JUICYLOU: Pretty busy, yeah.
DIRTYLES: Out with your boyfriend?
JUICY LOU: You know I don't have a boyfriend, Les. I prefer chicks like you.
DIRTYLES: I know you say that, but what about Morrison Shepherd?
DIRTYLES: You know who I mean – the pretty boy footballer's son…
DIRTYLES: The model…
DIRTYLES: The DJ…
DIRTYLES: The coke fiend…
DIRTYLES: You there, Juice?
JUICYLOU: I don't know who you mean.
DIRTYLES: Yes you do.
DIRTYLES: Tell him his sister says Hi.
SORRY – JUICY LOU IS OFFLINE RIGHT NOW.
COME ON, MORRISON, PICK UP, PICK UP.

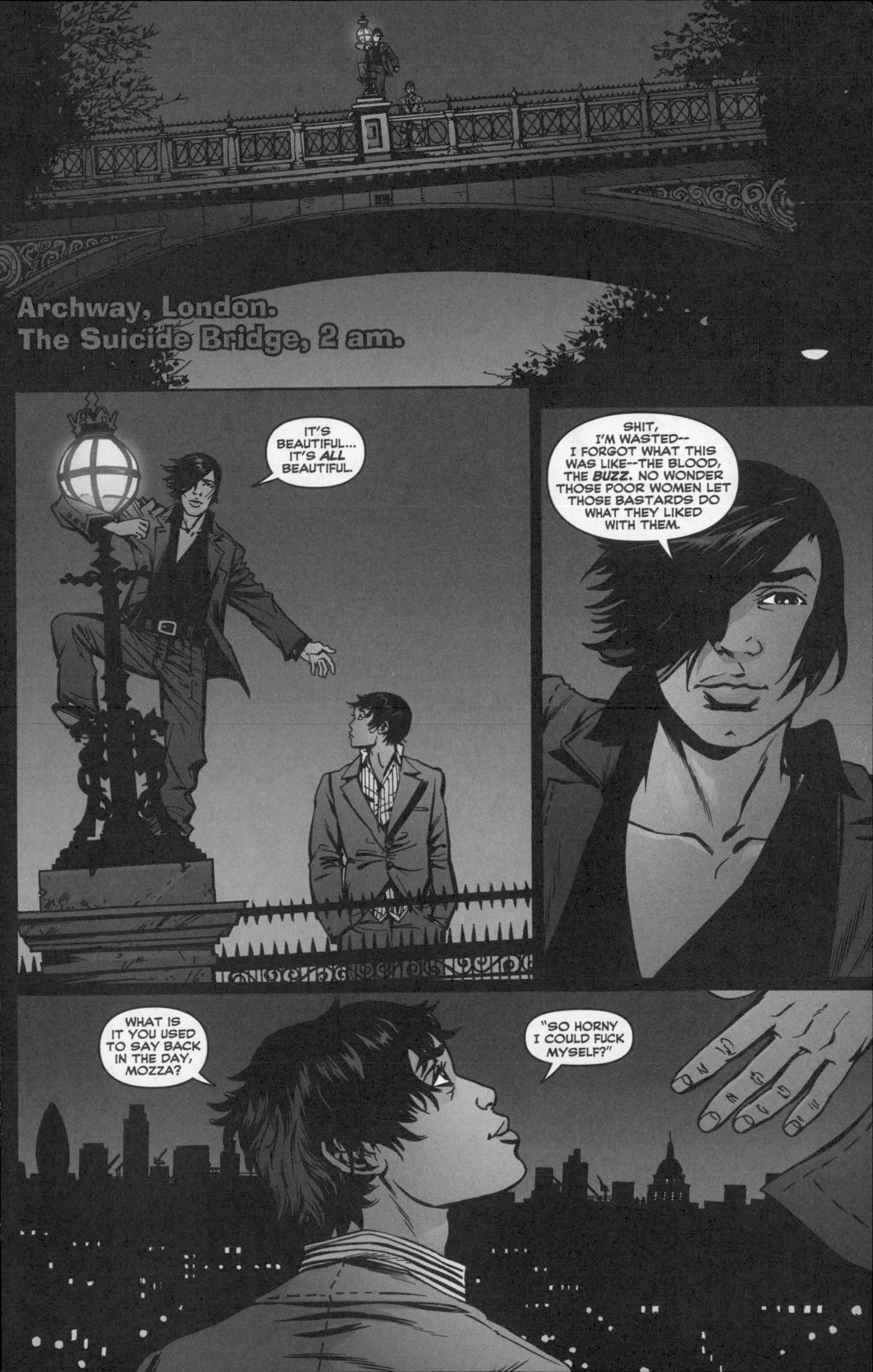
Archway, London.
The Suicide Bridge, 2 am.
IT'S BEAUTIFUL... IT'S *ALL* BEAUTIFUL.
SHIT, I'M WASTED-- I FORGOT WHAT THIS WAS LIKE--THE BLOOD, THE *BUZZ*. NO WONDER THOSE POOR WOMEN LET THOSE BASTARDS DO WHAT THEY LIKED WITH THEM.
WHAT IS IT YOU USED TO SAY BACK IN THE DAY, MOZZA?
"SO HORNY I COULD FUCK MYSELF?"

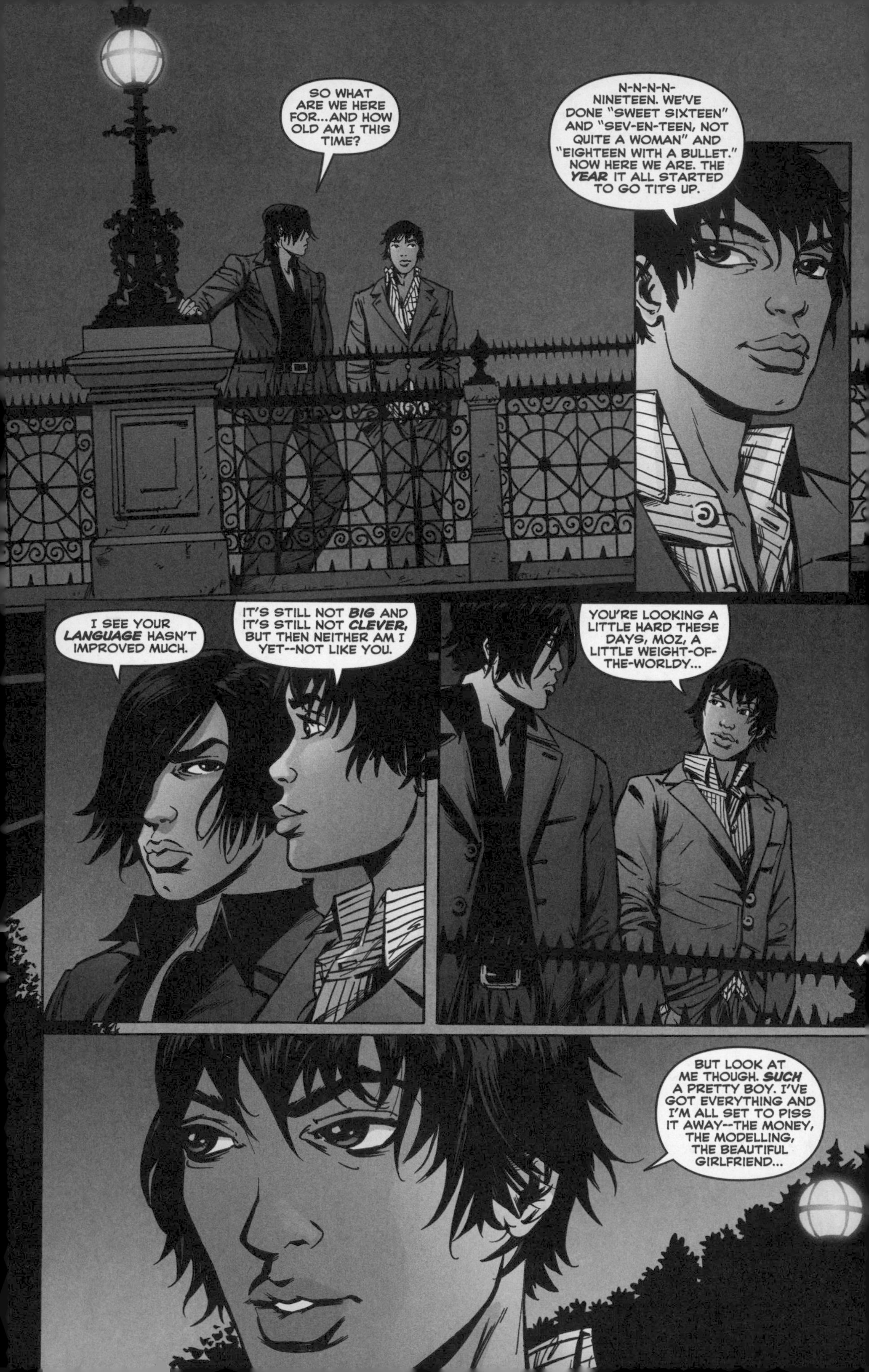
SO WHAT ARE WE HERE FOR...AND HOW OLD AM I THIS TIME?
N-N-N-N-NINETEEN. WE'VE DONE "SWEET SIXTEEN" AND "SEV-EN-TEEN, NOT QUITE A WOMAN" AND "EIGHTEEN WITH A BULLET." NOW HERE WE ARE. THE YEAR IT ALL STARTED TO GO TITS UP.
I SEE YOUR LANGUAGE HASN'T IMPROVED MUCH.
IT'S STILL NOT BIG AND IT'S STILL NOT CLEVER, BUT THEN NEITHER AM I YET--NOT LIKE YOU.
YOU'RE LOOKING A LITTLE HARD THESE DAYS, MOZ, A LITTLE WEIGHT-OF-THE-WORLDY...
BUT LOOK AT ME THOUGH. SUCH A PRETTY BOY. I'VE GOT EVERYTHING AND I'M ALL SET TO PISS IT AWAY--THE MONEY, THE MODELLING, THE BEAUTIFUL GIRLFRIEND...

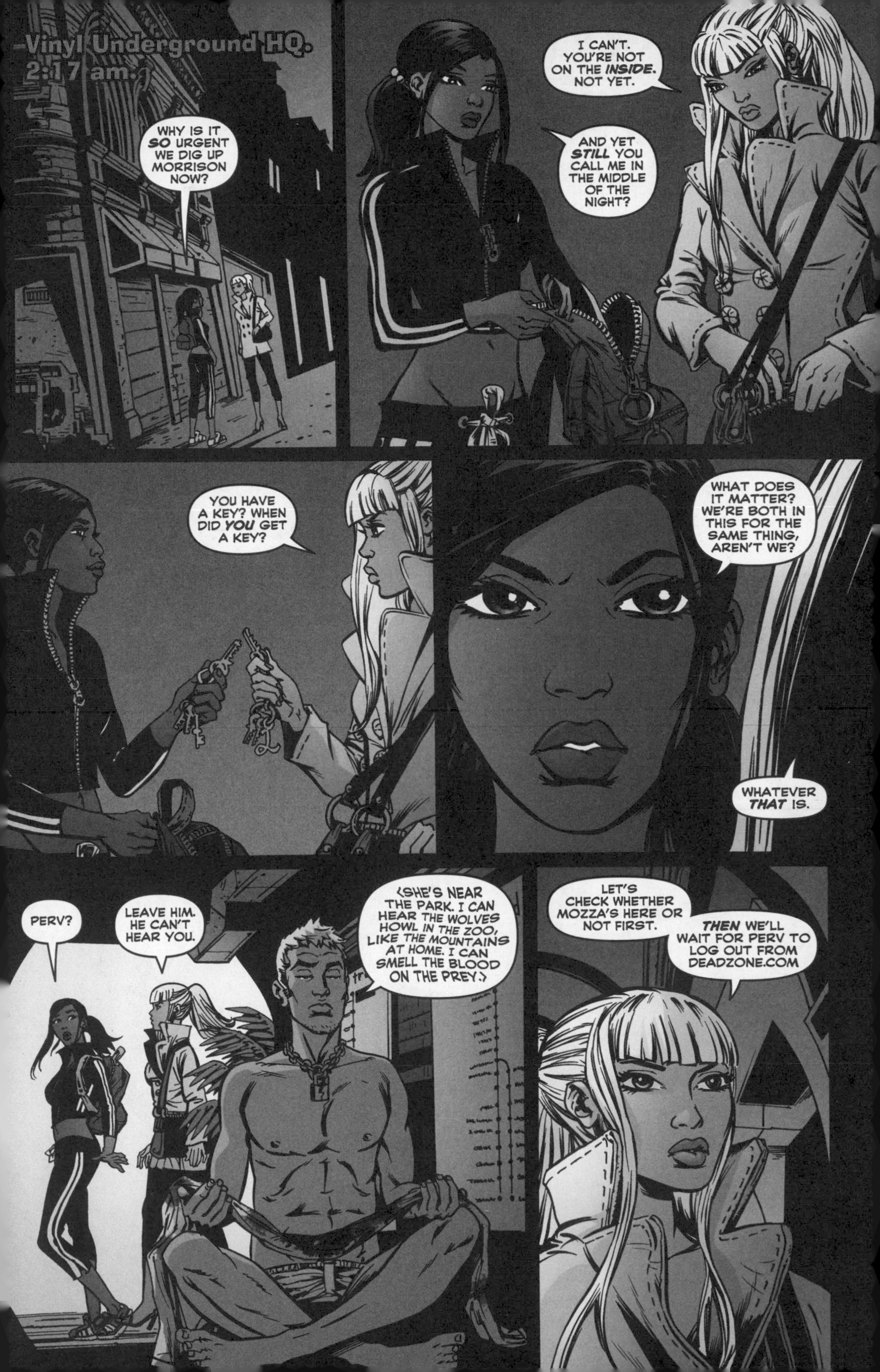

Vinyl Underground HQ. 2:17 am.
WHY IS IT SO URGENT WE DIG UP MORRISON NOW?
I CAN'T. YOU'RE NOT ON THE INSIDE. NOT YET.
AND YET STILL YOU CALL ME IN THE MIDDLE OF THE NIGHT?
YOU HAVE A KEY? WHEN DID YOU GET A KEY?
WHAT DOES IT MATTER? WE'RE BOTH IN THIS FOR THE SAME THING, AREN'T WE?
WHATEVER THAT IS.
PERV?
LEAVE HIM. HE CAN'T HEAR YOU.
<SHE'S NEAR THE PARK. I CAN HEAR THE WOLVES HOWL IN THE ZOO, LIKE THE MOUNTAINS AT HOME. I CAN SMELL THE BLOOD ON THE PREY.>
LET'S CHECK WHETHER MOZZA'S HERE OR NOT FIRST.
THEN WE'LL WAIT FOR PERV TO LOG OUT FROM DEADZONE.COM

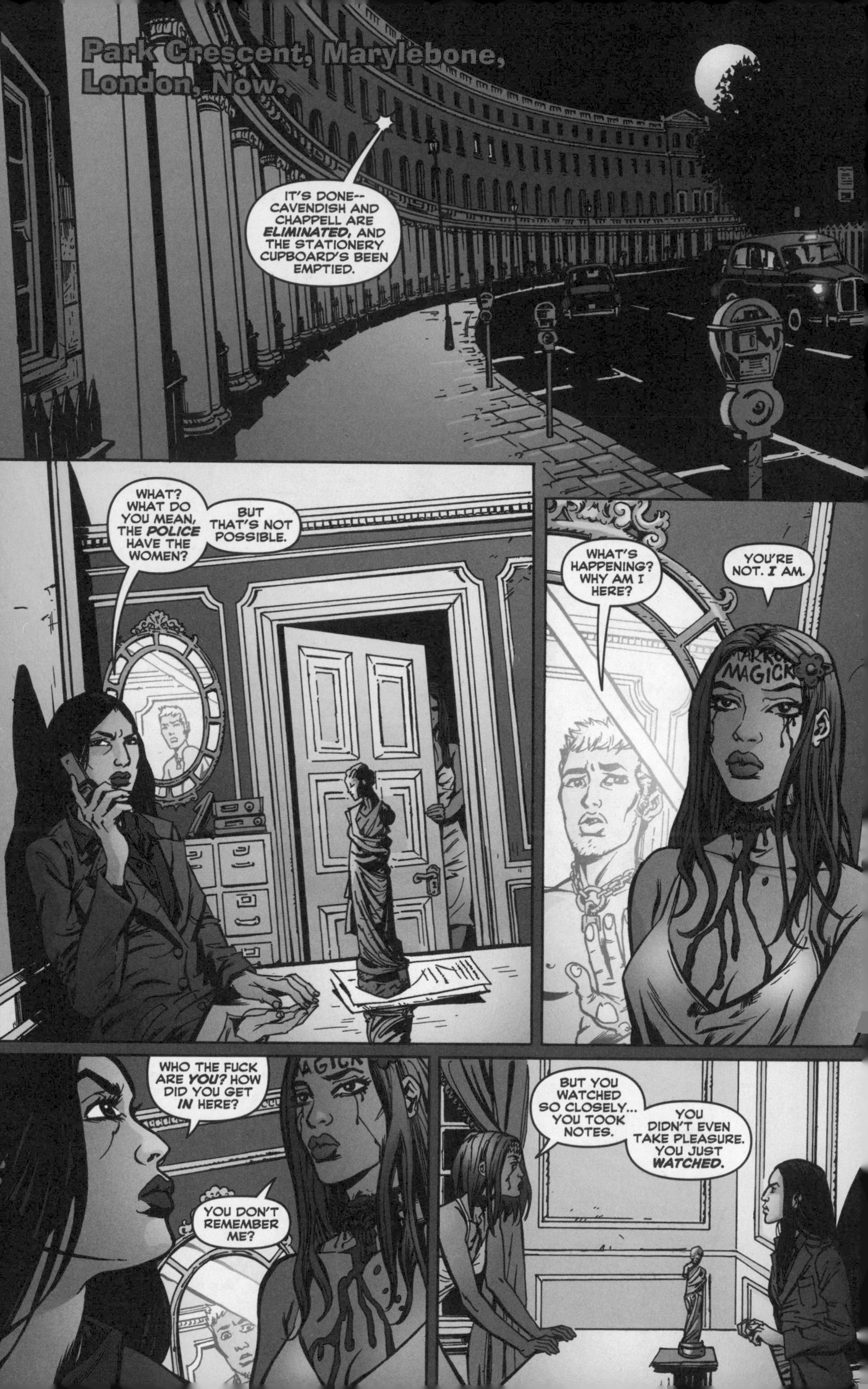
Park Crescent, Marylebone, London, Now.
IT'S DONE--CAVENDISH AND CHAPPELL ARE *ELIMINATED,* AND THE STATIONERY CUPBOARD'S BEEN EMPTIED.
WHAT? WHAT DO YOU MEAN, THE *POLICE* HAVE THE WOMEN?
BUT THAT'S NOT POSSIBLE.
WHAT'S HAPPENING? WHY AM I HERE?
YOU'RE NOT. *I* AM.
WHO THE FUCK ARE *YOU?* HOW DID YOU GET *IN* HERE?
YOU DON'T REMEMBER ME?
BUT YOU WATCHED SO CLOSELY... YOU TOOK NOTES.
YOU DIDN'T EVEN TAKE PLEASURE. YOU JUST ***WATCHED.***

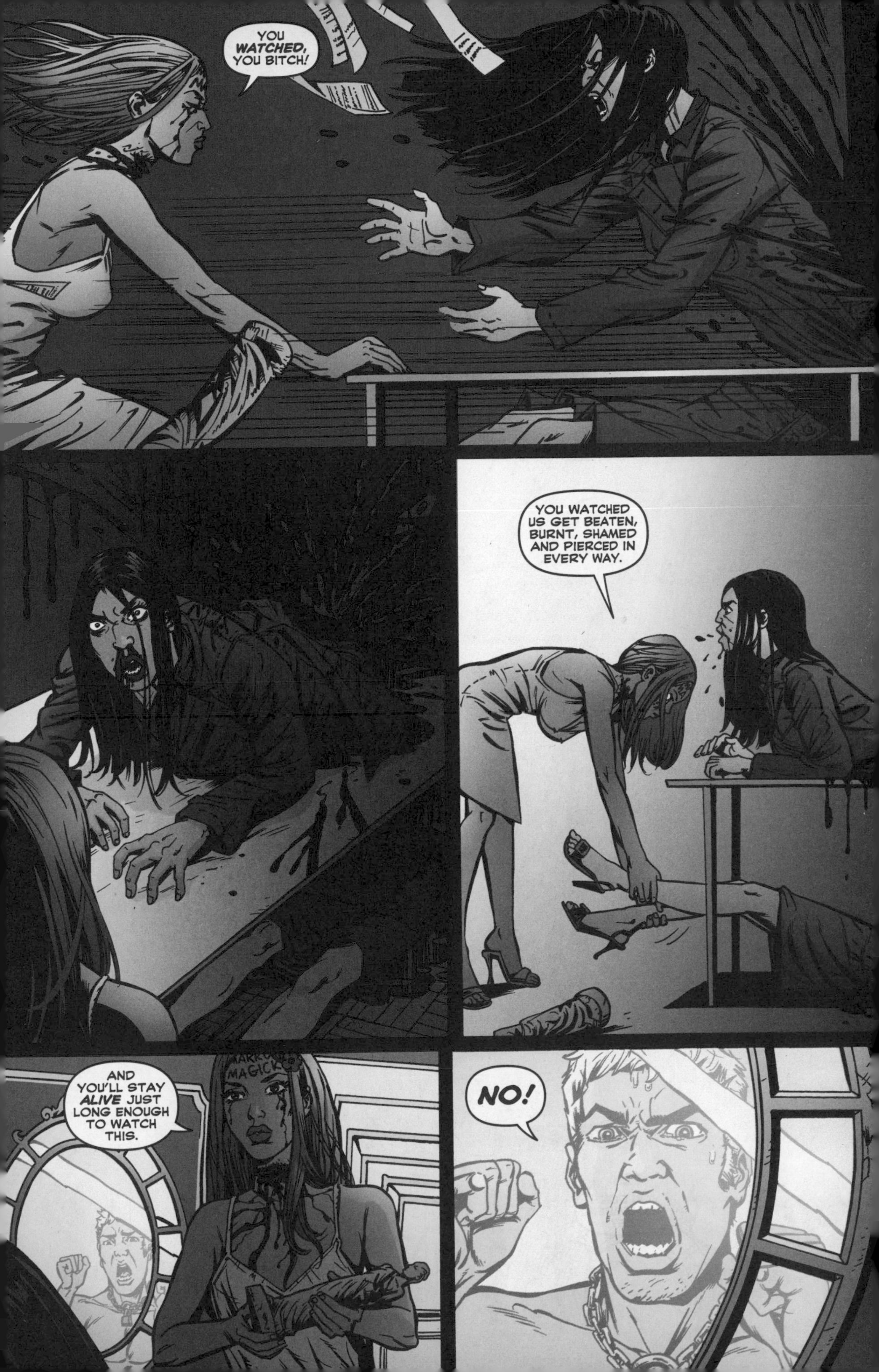
YOU WATCHED, YOU BITCH!
YOU WATCHED US GET BEATEN, BURNT, SHAMED AND PIERCED IN EVERY WAY.
AND YOU'LL STAY ALIVE JUST LONG ENOUGH TO WATCH THIS.
NO!

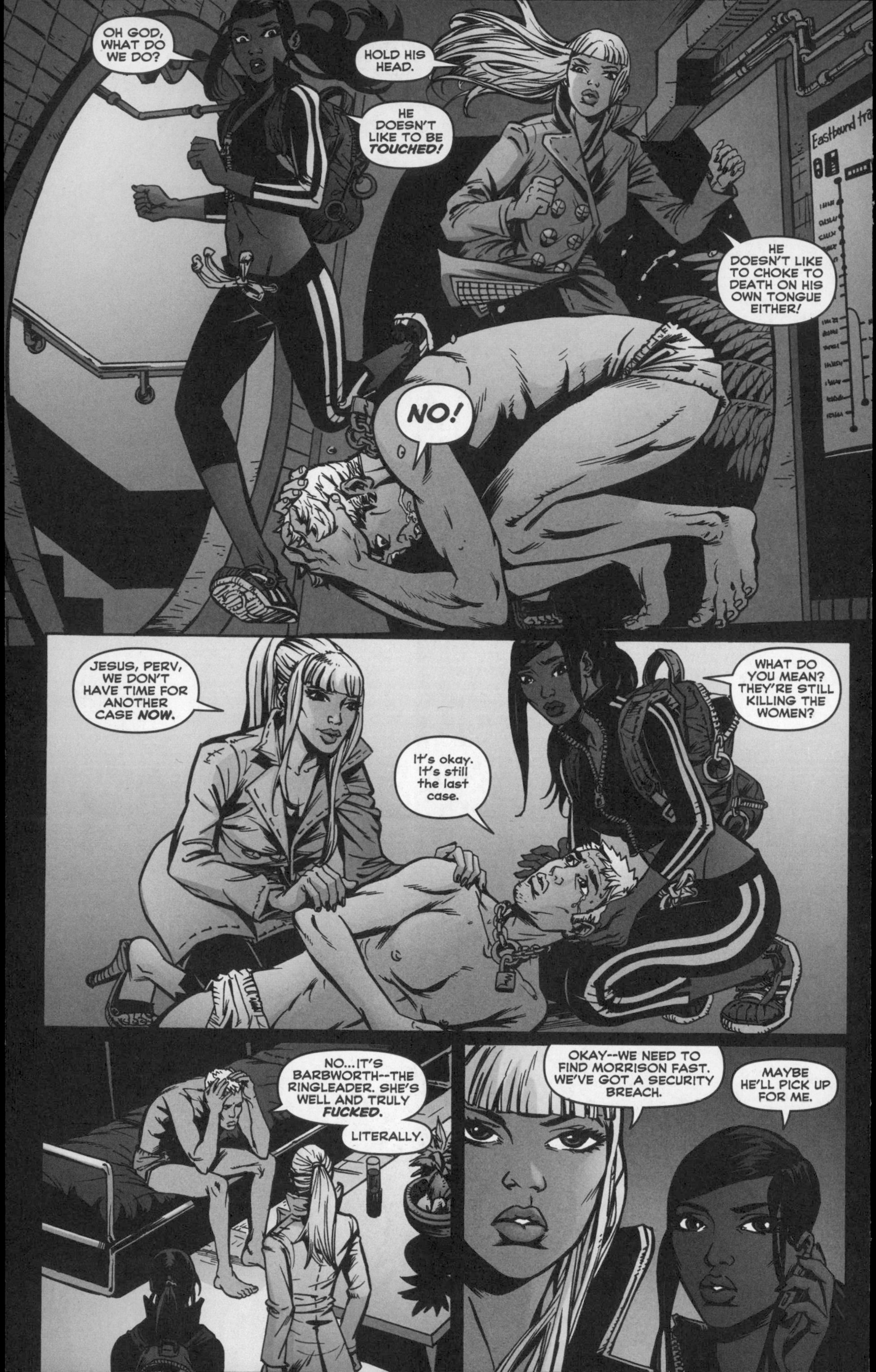

OH GOD, WHAT DO WE DO?
HOLD HIS HEAD.
HE DOESN'T LIKE TO BE TOUCHED!
HE DOESN'T LIKE TO CHOKE TO DEATH ON HIS OWN TONGUE EITHER!
NO!
Eastbound
JESUS, PERV, WE DON'T HAVE TIME FOR ANOTHER CASE NOW.
WHAT DO YOU MEAN? THEY'RE STILL KILLING THE WOMEN?
It's okay. It's still the last case.
NO...IT'S BARBWORTH--THE RINGLEADER. SHE'S WELL AND TRULY FUCKED.
LITERALLY.
OKAY--WE NEED TO FIND MORRISON FAST. WE'VE GOT A SECURITY BREACH.
MAYBE HE'LL PICK UP FOR ME.

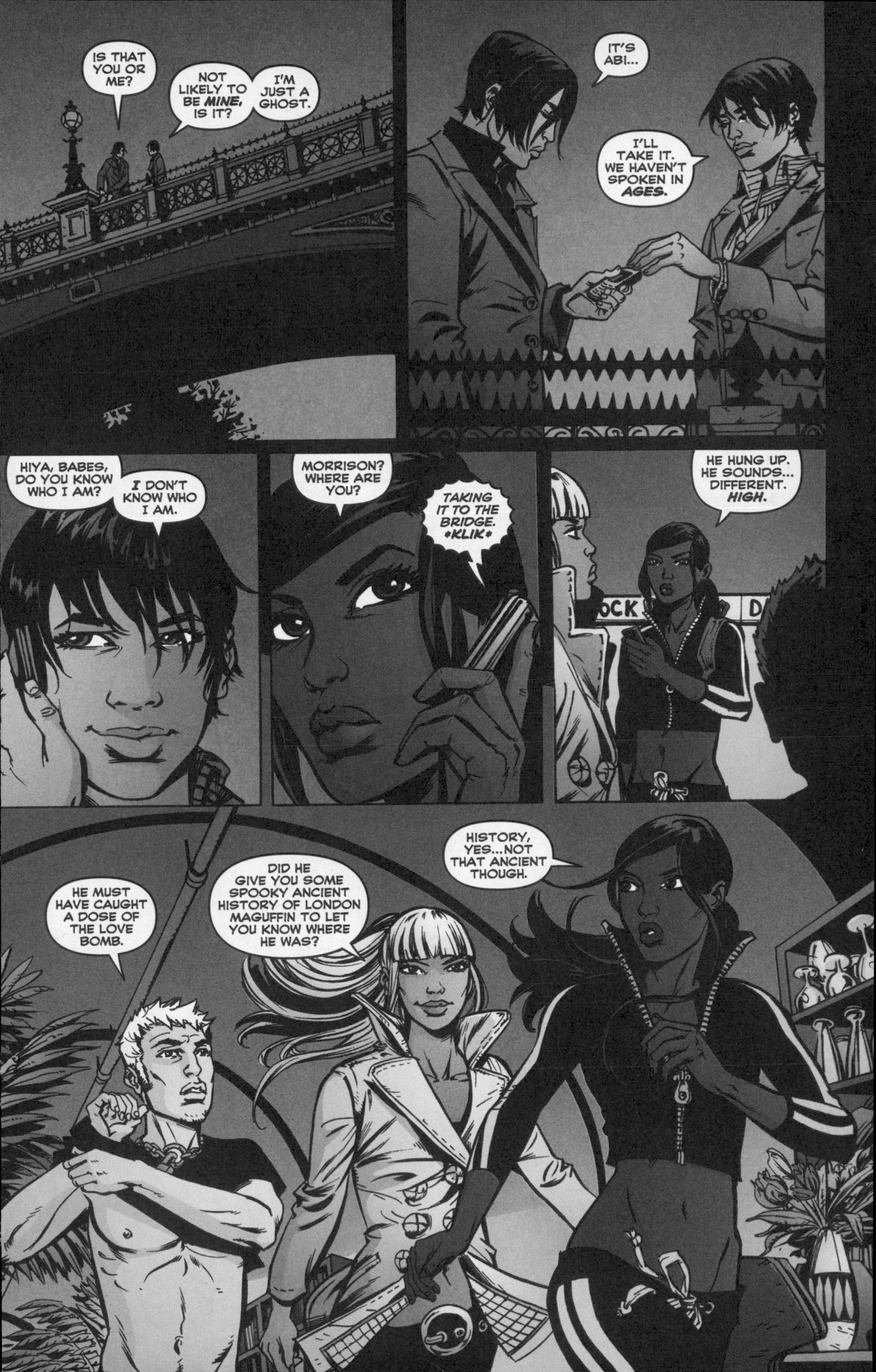
IS THAT YOU OR ME?
NOT LIKELY TO BE MINE, IS IT?
I'M JUST A GHOST.
IT'S ABI...
I'LL TAKE IT. WE HAVEN'T SPOKEN IN AGES.
HIYA, BABES, DO YOU KNOW WHO I AM?
I DON'T KNOW WHO I AM.
MORRISON? WHERE ARE YOU?
TAKING IT TO THE BRIDGE. *KLIK*
HE HUNG UP. HE SOUNDS... DIFFERENT. HIGH.
HE MUST HAVE CAUGHT A DOSE OF THE LOVE BOMB.
DID HE GIVE YOU SOME SPOOKY ANCIENT HISTORY OF LONDON MAGUFFIN TO LET YOU KNOW WHERE HE WAS?
HISTORY, YES...NOT THAT ANCIENT THOUGH.

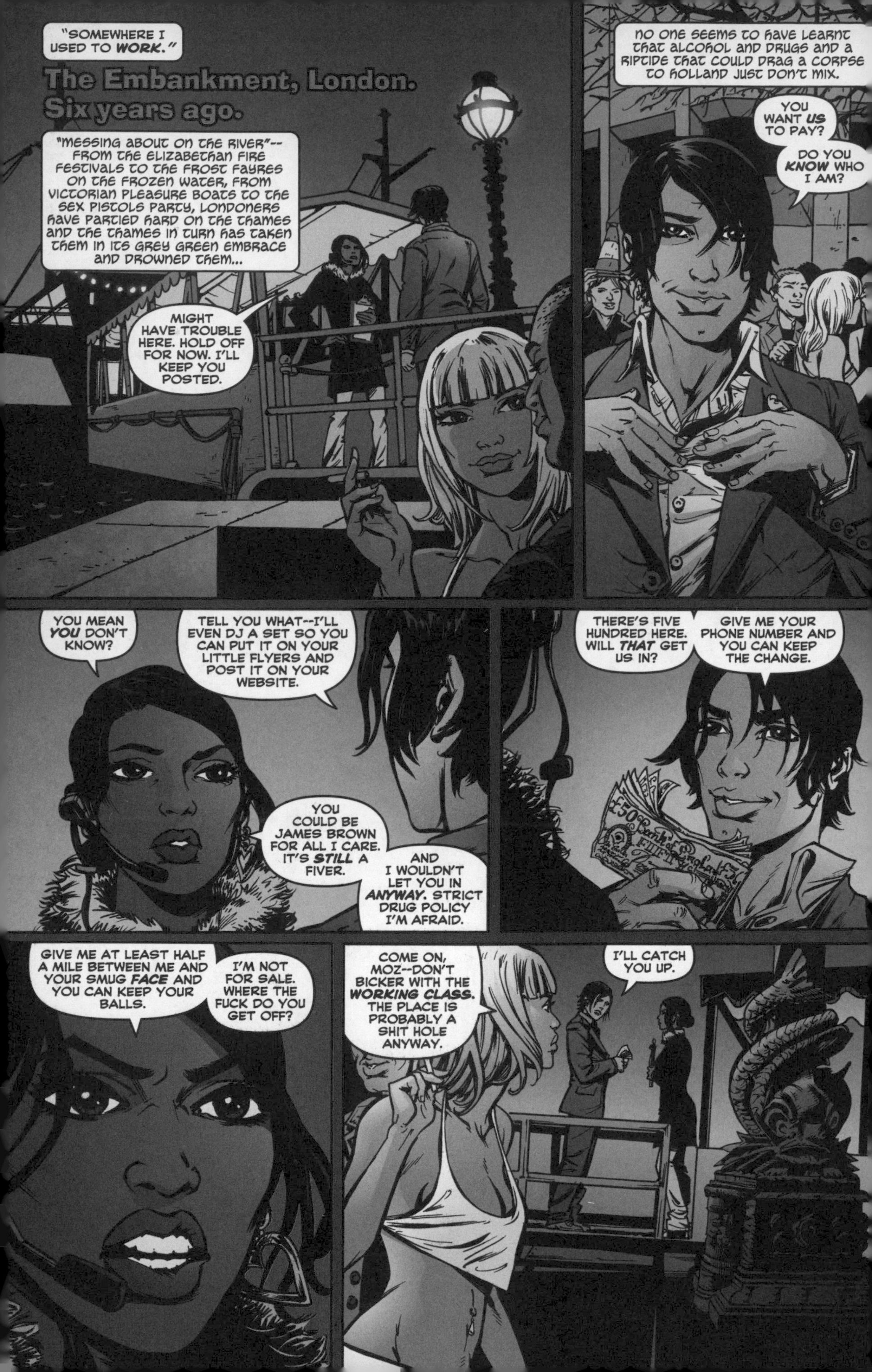
"SOMEWHERE I USED TO WORK."
The Embankment, London. Six years ago.
"MESSING ABOUT ON THE RIVER"--FROM THE ELIZABETHAN FIRE FESTIVALS TO THE FROST FAYRES ON THE FROZEN WATER, FROM VICTORIAN PLEASURE BOATS TO THE SEX PISTOLS PARTY, LONDONERS HAVE PARTIED HARD ON THE THAMES AND THE THAMES IN TURN HAS TAKEN THEM IN ITS GREY GREEN EMBRACE AND DROWNED THEM...
MIGHT HAVE TROUBLE HERE. HOLD OFF FOR NOW. I'LL KEEP YOU POSTED.
NO ONE SEEMS TO HAVE LEARNT THAT ALCOHOL AND DRUGS AND A RIPTIDE THAT COULD DRAG A CORPSE TO HOLLAND JUST DON'T MIX.
YOU WANT US TO PAY?
DO YOU KNOW WHO I AM?
YOU MEAN YOU DON'T KNOW?
TELL YOU WHAT--I'LL EVEN DJ A SET SO YOU CAN PUT IT ON YOUR LITTLE FLYERS AND POST IT ON YOUR WEBSITE.
YOU COULD BE JAMES BROWN FOR ALL I CARE. IT'S STILL A FIVER.
AND I WOULDN'T LET YOU IN ANYWAY. STRICT DRUG POLICY I'M AFRAID.
THERE'S FIVE HUNDRED HERE. WILL THAT GET US IN?
GIVE ME YOUR PHONE NUMBER AND YOU CAN KEEP THE CHANGE.
GIVE ME AT LEAST HALF A MILE BETWEEN ME AND YOUR SMUG FACE AND YOU CAN KEEP YOUR BALLS.
I'M NOT FOR SALE. WHERE THE FUCK DO YOU GET OFF?
COME ON, MOZ--DON'T BICKER WITH THE WORKING CLASS. THE PLACE IS PROBABLY A SHIT HOLE ANYWAY.
I'LL CATCH YOU UP.

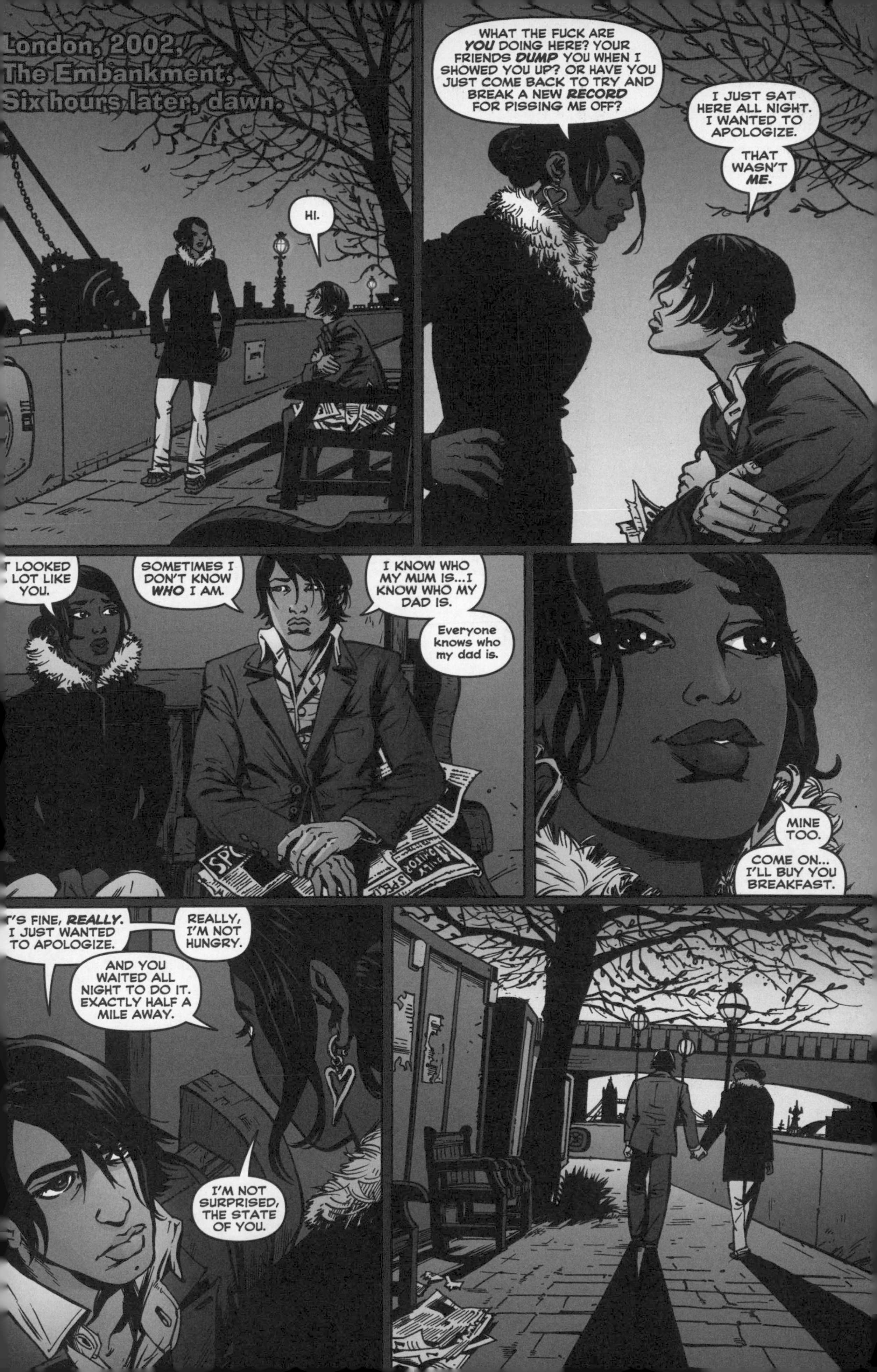

London, 2002, The Embankment, Six hours later, dawn.
HI.
WHAT THE FUCK ARE YOU DOING HERE? YOUR FRIENDS DUMP YOU WHEN I SHOWED YOU UP? OR HAVE YOU JUST COME BACK TO TRY AND BREAK A NEW RECORD FOR PISSING ME OFF?
I JUST SAT HERE ALL NIGHT. I WANTED TO APOLOGIZE.
THAT WASN'T ME.
T LOOKED LOT LIKE YOU.
SOMETIMES I DON'T KNOW WHO I AM.
I KNOW WHO MY MUM IS...I KNOW WHO MY DAD IS.
Everyone knows who my dad is.
MINE TOO.
COME ON... I'LL BUY YOU BREAKFAST.
'S FINE, REALLY. I JUST WANTED TO APOLOGIZE.
REALLY, I'M NOT HUNGRY.
AND YOU WAITED ALL NIGHT TO DO IT. EXACTLY HALF A MILE AWAY.
I'M NOT SURPRISED, THE STATE OF YOU.

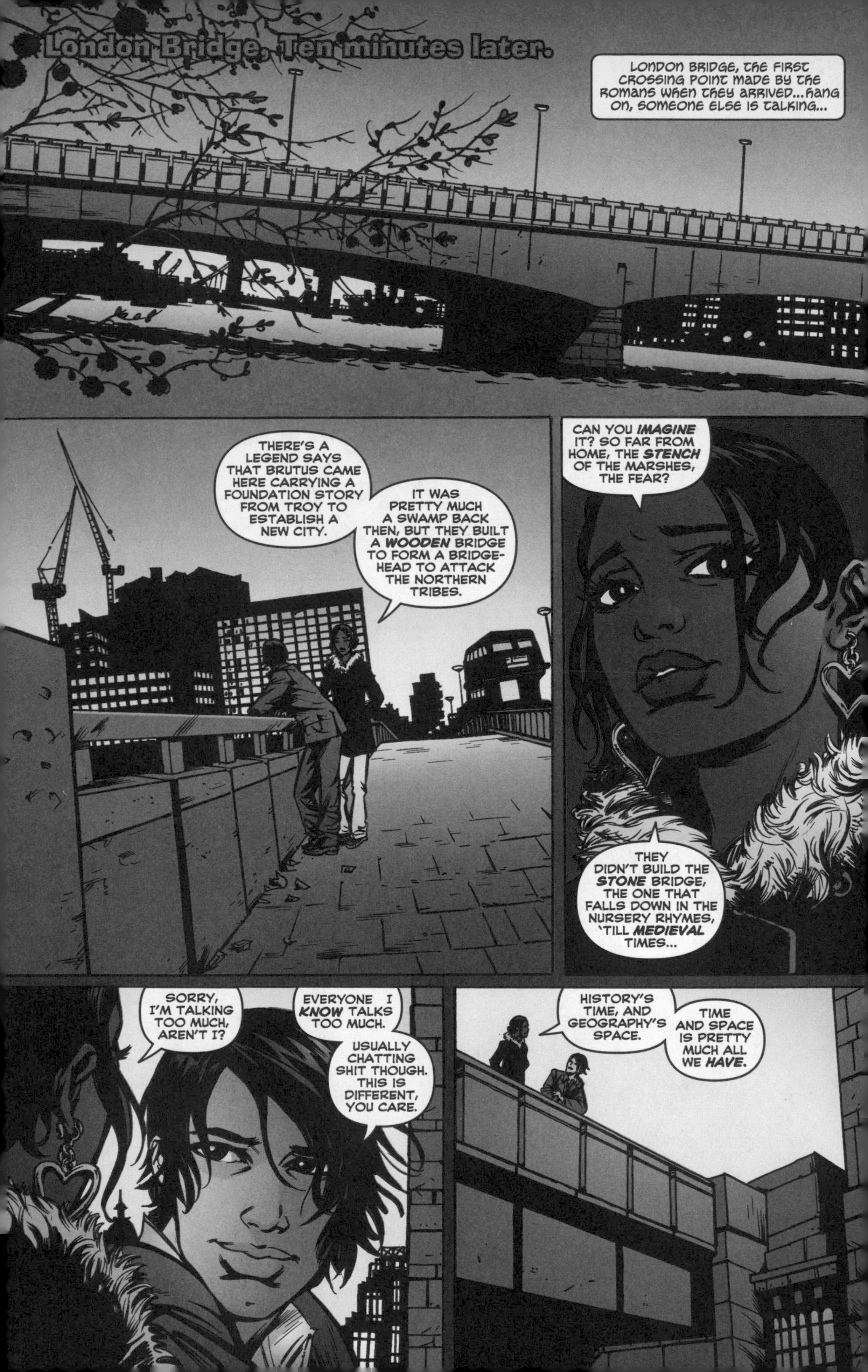
London Bridge. Ten minutes later.
LONDON BRIDGE, THE FIRST CROSSING POINT MADE BY THE ROMANS WHEN THEY ARRIVED...HANG ON, SOMEONE ELSE IS TALKING...
THERE'S A LEGEND SAYS THAT BRUTUS CAME HERE CARRYING A FOUNDATION STORY FROM TROY TO ESTABLISH A NEW CITY.
IT WAS PRETTY MUCH A SWAMP BACK THEN, BUT THEY BUILT A WOODEN BRIDGE TO FORM A BRIDGE-HEAD TO ATTACK THE NORTHERN TRIBES.
CAN YOU IMAGINE IT? SO FAR FROM HOME, THE STENCH OF THE MARSHES, THE FEAR?
THEY DIDN'T BUILD THE STONE BRIDGE, THE ONE THAT FALLS DOWN IN THE NURSERY RHYMES, 'TILL MEDIEVAL TIMES...
SORRY, I'M TALKING TOO MUCH, AREN'T I?
EVERYONE I KNOW TALKS TOO MUCH.
USUALLY CHATTING SHIT THOUGH. THIS IS DIFFERENT, YOU CARE.
HISTORY'S TIME, AND GEOGRAPHY'S SPACE.
TIME AND SPACE IS PRETTY MUCH ALL WE HAVE.

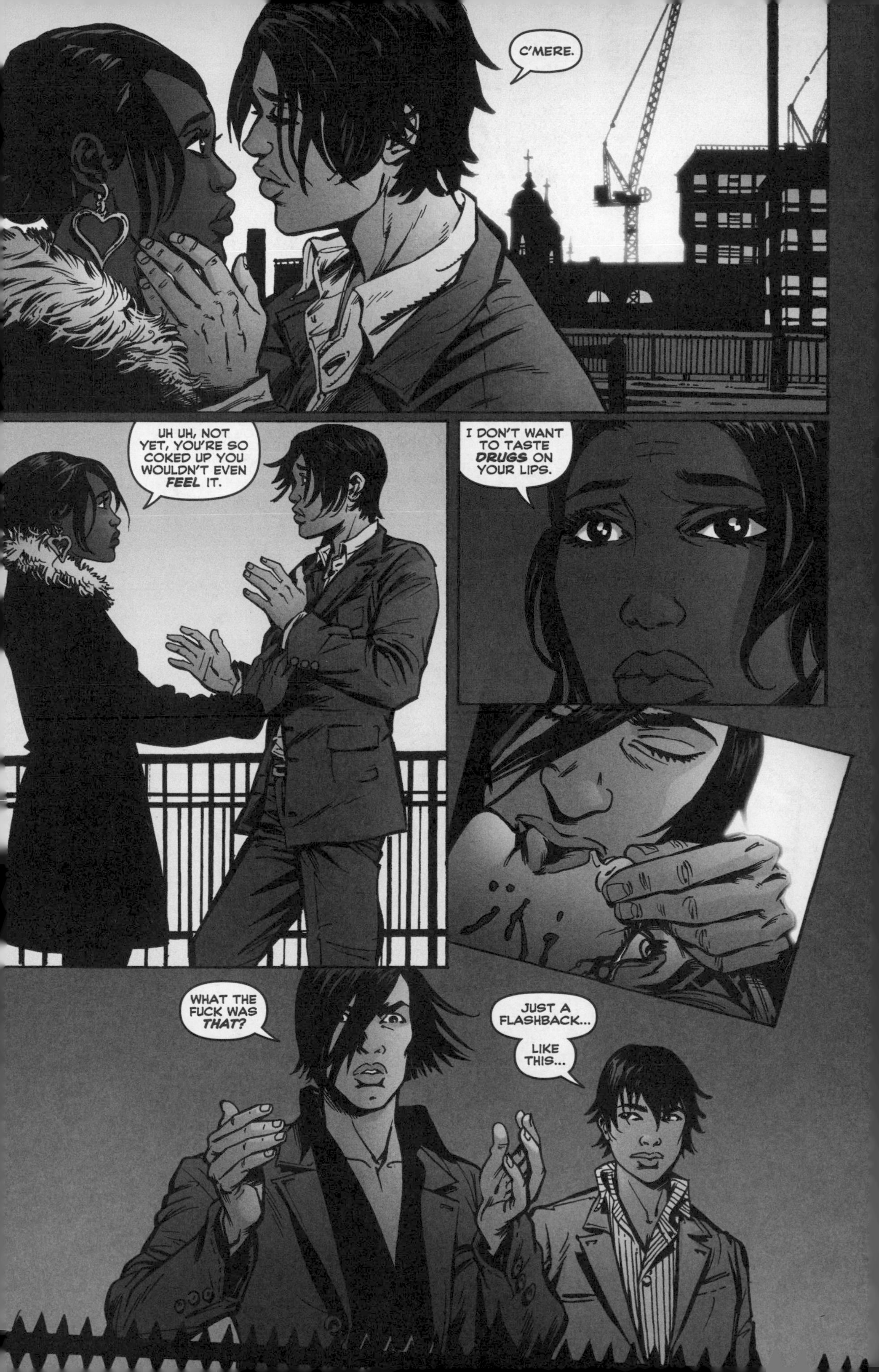
C'MERE.
UH UH, NOT YET, YOU'RE SO COKED UP YOU WOULDN'T EVEN *FEEL* IT.
I DON'T WANT TO TASTE *DRUGS* ON YOUR LIPS.
WHAT THE FUCK WAS *THAT*?
JUST A FLASHBACK...
LIKE THIS...

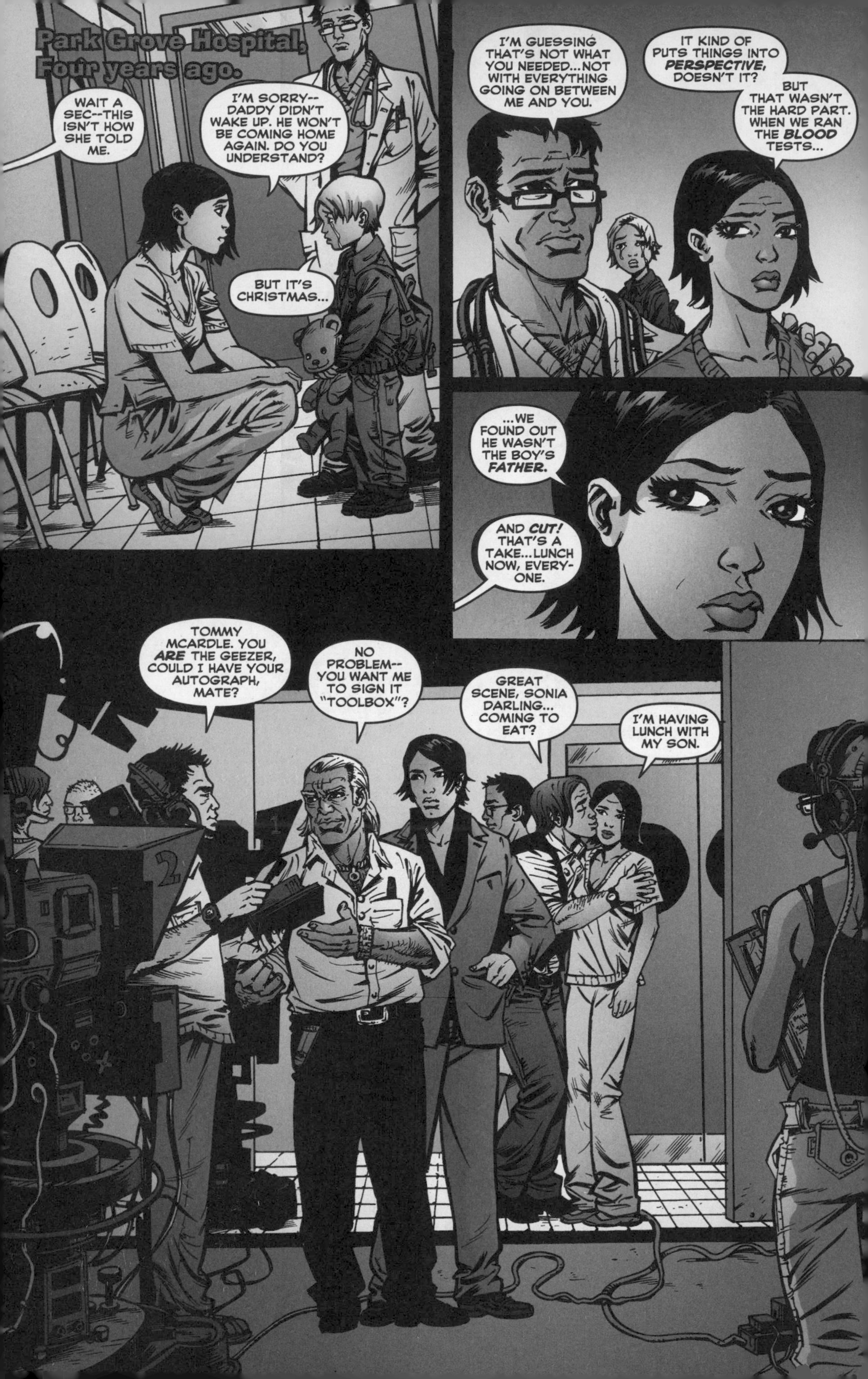
Park Grove Hospital, Four years ago.
WAIT A SEC--THIS ISN'T HOW SHE TOLD ME.
I'M SORRY--DADDY DIDN'T WAKE UP. HE WON'T BE COMING HOME AGAIN. DO YOU UNDERSTAND?
BUT IT'S CHRISTMAS...
I'M GUESSING THAT'S NOT WHAT YOU NEEDED...NOT WITH EVERYTHING GOING ON BETWEEN ME AND YOU.
IT KIND OF PUTS THINGS INTO PERSPECTIVE, DOESN'T IT?
BUT THAT WASN'T THE HARD PART. WHEN WE RAN THE BLOOD TESTS...
...WE FOUND OUT HE WASN'T THE BOY'S FATHER.
AND CUT! THAT'S A TAKE...LUNCH NOW, EVERY-ONE.
TOMMY MCARDLE. YOU ARE THE GEEZER, COULD I HAVE YOUR AUTOGRAPH, MATE?
NO PROBLEM--YOU WANT ME TO SIGN IT "TOOLBOX"?
GREAT SCENE, SONIA DARLING... COMING TO EAT?
I'M HAVING LUNCH WITH MY SON.

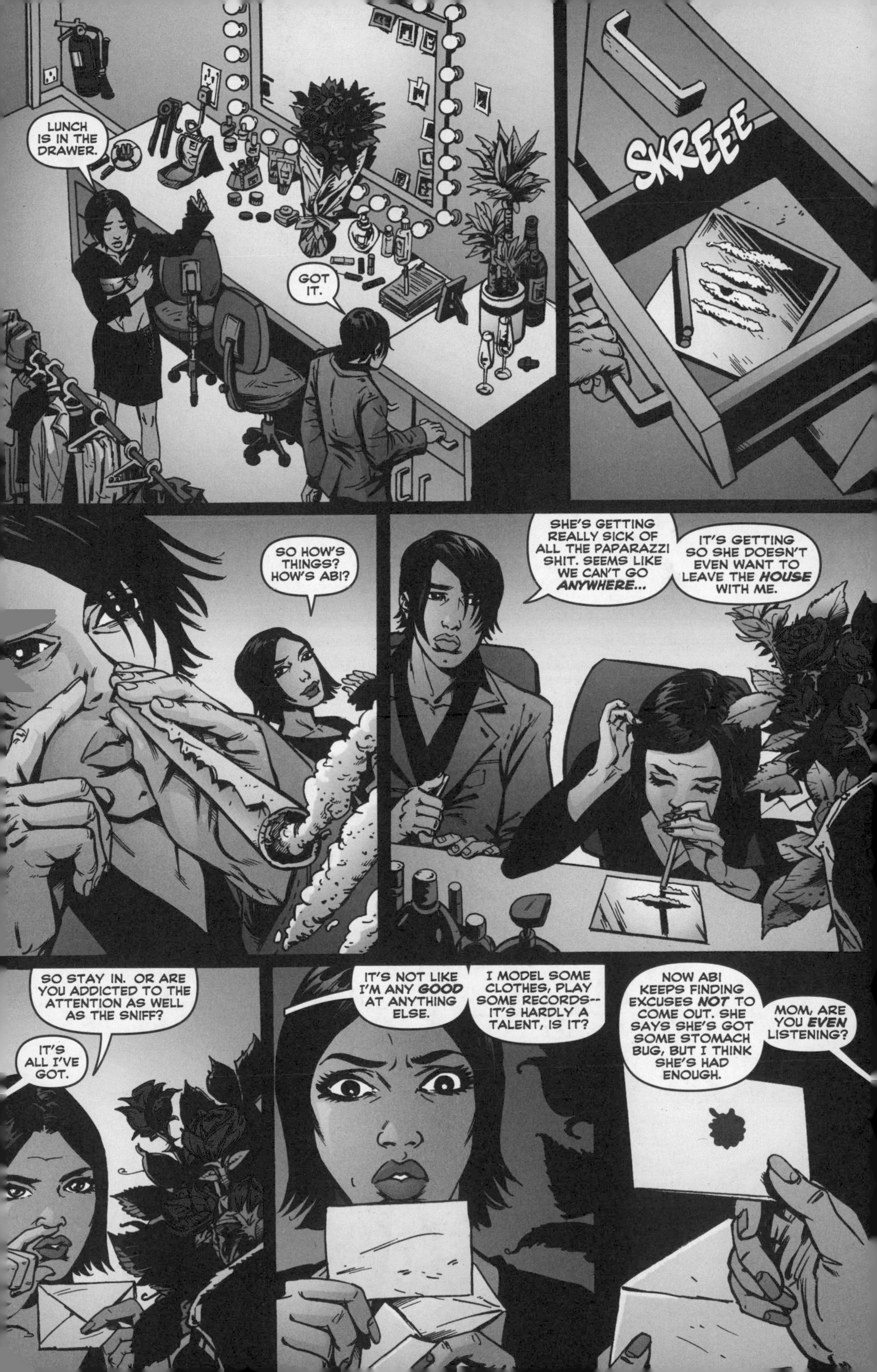
LUNCH IS IN THE DRAWER.
GOT IT.
SKREEE
SO HOW'S THINGS? HOW'S ABI?
SHE'S GETTING REALLY SICK OF ALL THE PAPARAZZI SHIT. SEEMS LIKE WE CAN'T GO ANYWHERE...
IT'S GETTING SO SHE DOESN'T EVEN WANT TO LEAVE THE HOUSE WITH ME.
SO STAY IN. OR ARE YOU ADDICTED TO THE ATTENTION AS WELL AS THE SNIFF?
IT'S ALL I'VE GOT.
IT'S NOT LIKE I'M ANY GOOD AT ANYTHING ELSE.
I MODEL SOME CLOTHES, PLAY SOME RECORDS-- IT'S HARDLY A TALENT, IS IT?
NOW ABI KEEPS FINDING EXCUSES NOT TO COME OUT. SHE SAYS SHE'S GOT SOME STOMACH BUG, BUT I THINK SHE'S HAD ENOUGH.
MOM, ARE YOU EVEN LISTENING?

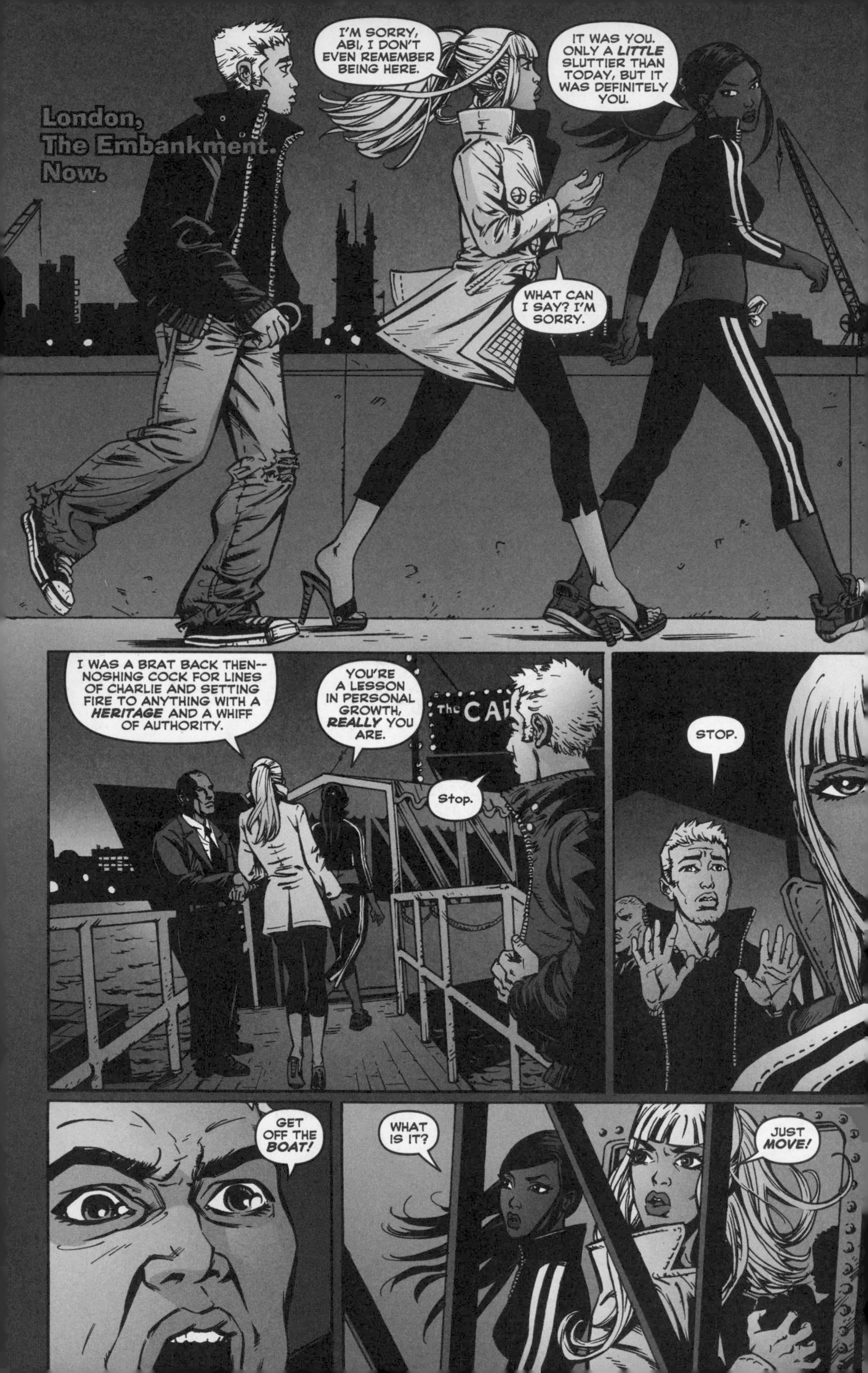
London, The Embankment. Now.
I'M SORRY, ABI, I DON'T EVEN REMEMBER BEING HERE.
IT WAS YOU. ONLY A LITTLE SLUTTIER THAN TODAY, BUT IT WAS DEFINITELY YOU.
WHAT CAN I SAY? I'M SORRY.
I WAS A BRAT BACK THEN-- NOSHING COCK FOR LINES OF CHARLIE AND SETTING FIRE TO ANYTHING WITH A HERITAGE AND A WHIFF OF AUTHORITY.
YOU'RE A LESSON IN PERSONAL GROWTH, REALLY YOU ARE.
Stop.
STOP.
GET OFF THE BOAT!
WHAT IS IT?
JUST MOVE!

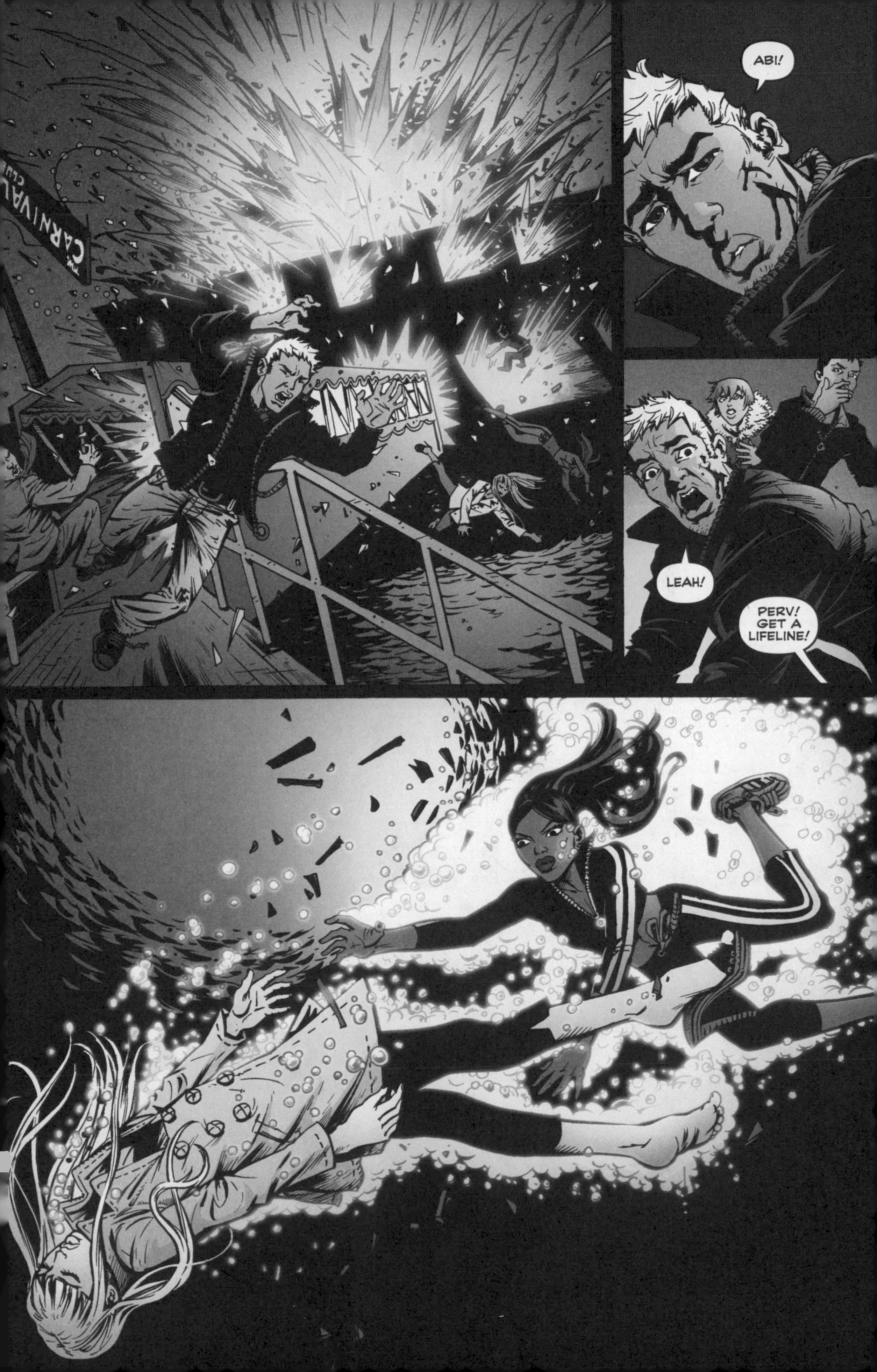
ABI!
LEAH!
PERV! GET A LIFELINE!

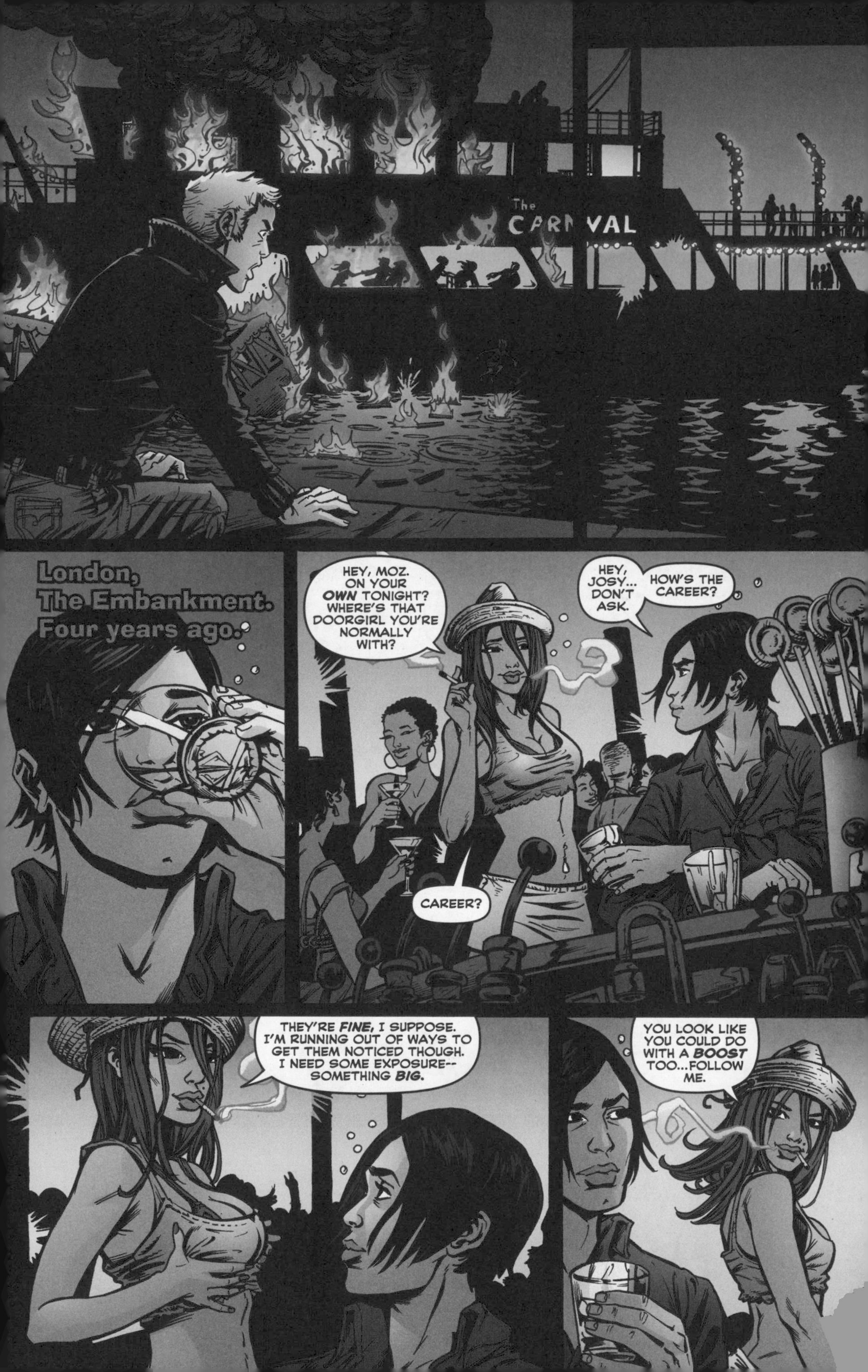

The CARNIVAL
London, The Embankment. Four years ago.
HEY, MOZ. ON YOUR OWN TONIGHT? WHERE'S THAT DOORGIRL YOU'RE NORMALLY WITH?
HEY, JOSY... DON'T ASK.
HOW'S THE CAREER?
CAREER?
THEY'RE FINE, I SUPPOSE. I'M RUNNING OUT OF WAYS TO GET THEM NOTICED THOUGH. I NEED SOME EXPOSURE-- SOMETHING BIG.
YOU LOOK LIKE YOU COULD DO WITH A BOOST TOO...FOLLOW ME.

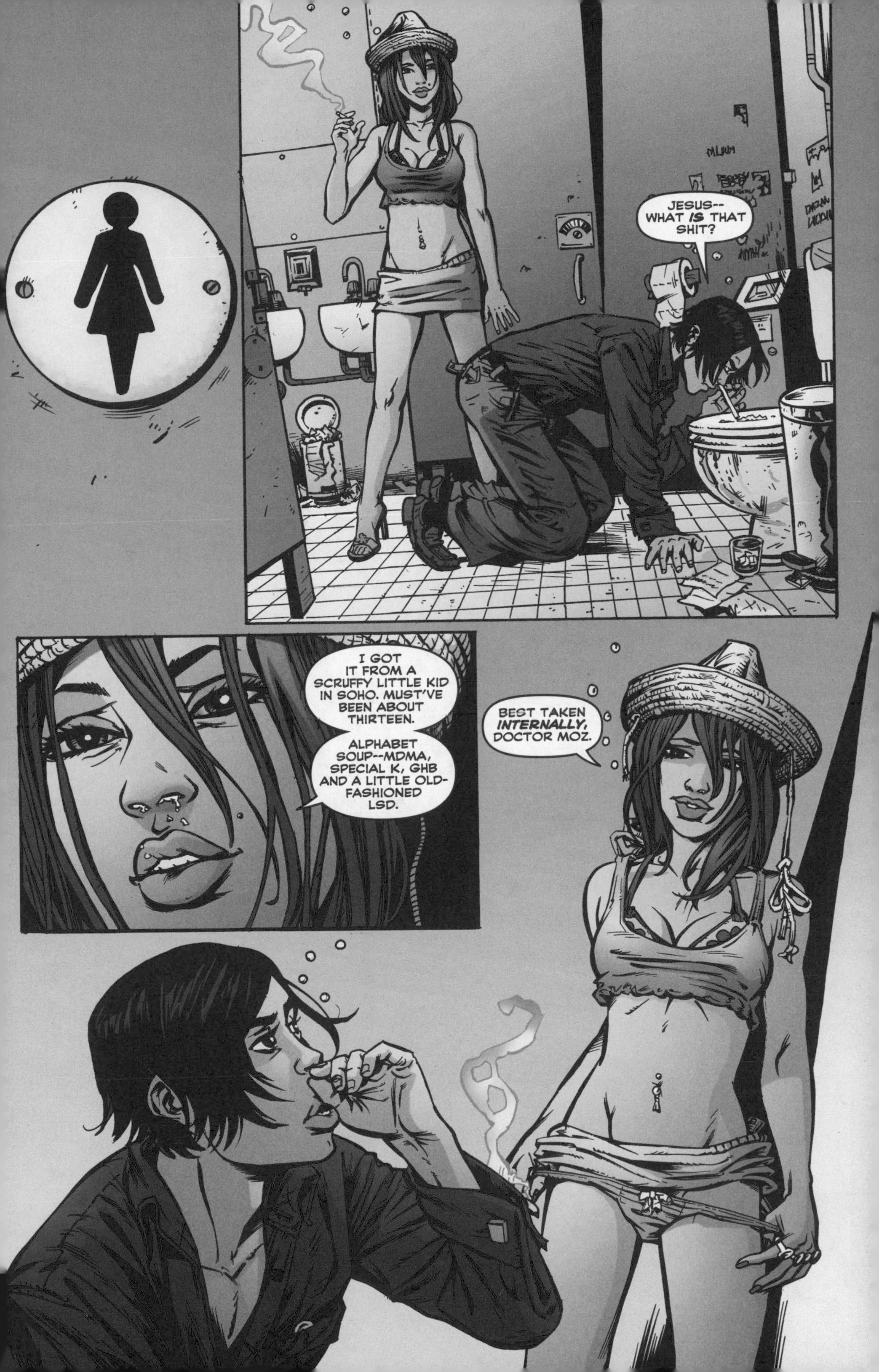
JESUS--
WHAT *IS* THAT SHIT?
I GOT IT FROM A SCRUFFY LITTLE KID IN SOHO. MUST'VE BEEN ABOUT THIRTEEN.
ALPHABET SOUP--MDMA, SPECIAL K, GHB AND A LITTLE OLD-FASHIONED LSD.
BEST TAKEN *INTERNALLY*, DOCTOR MOZ.

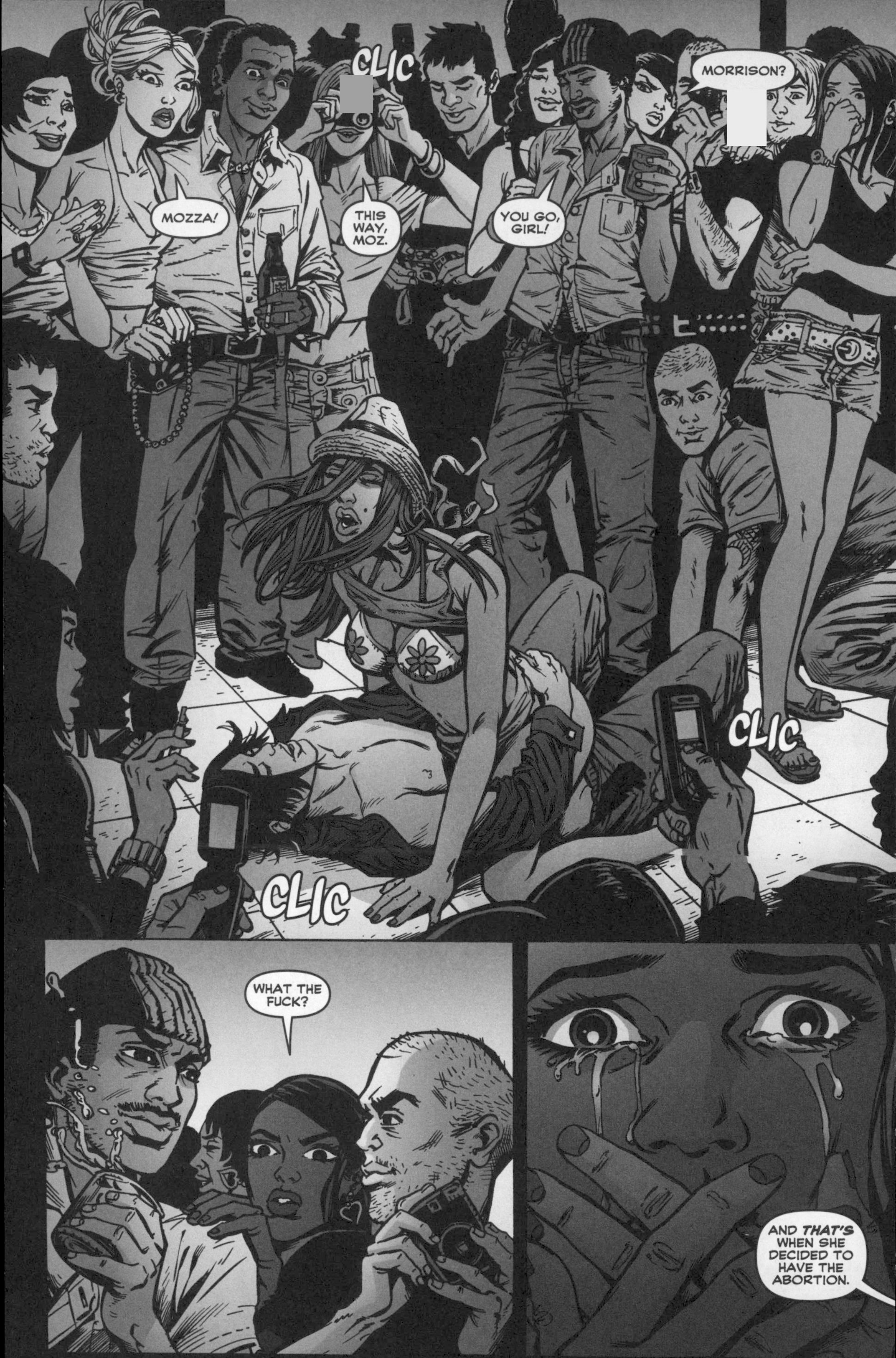
CLIC
MORRISON?
MOZZA!
THIS WAY, MOZ.
YOU GO, GIRL!
CLIC
CLIC
WHAT THE FUCK?
AND *THAT'S* WHEN SHE DECIDED TO HAVE THE ABORTION.

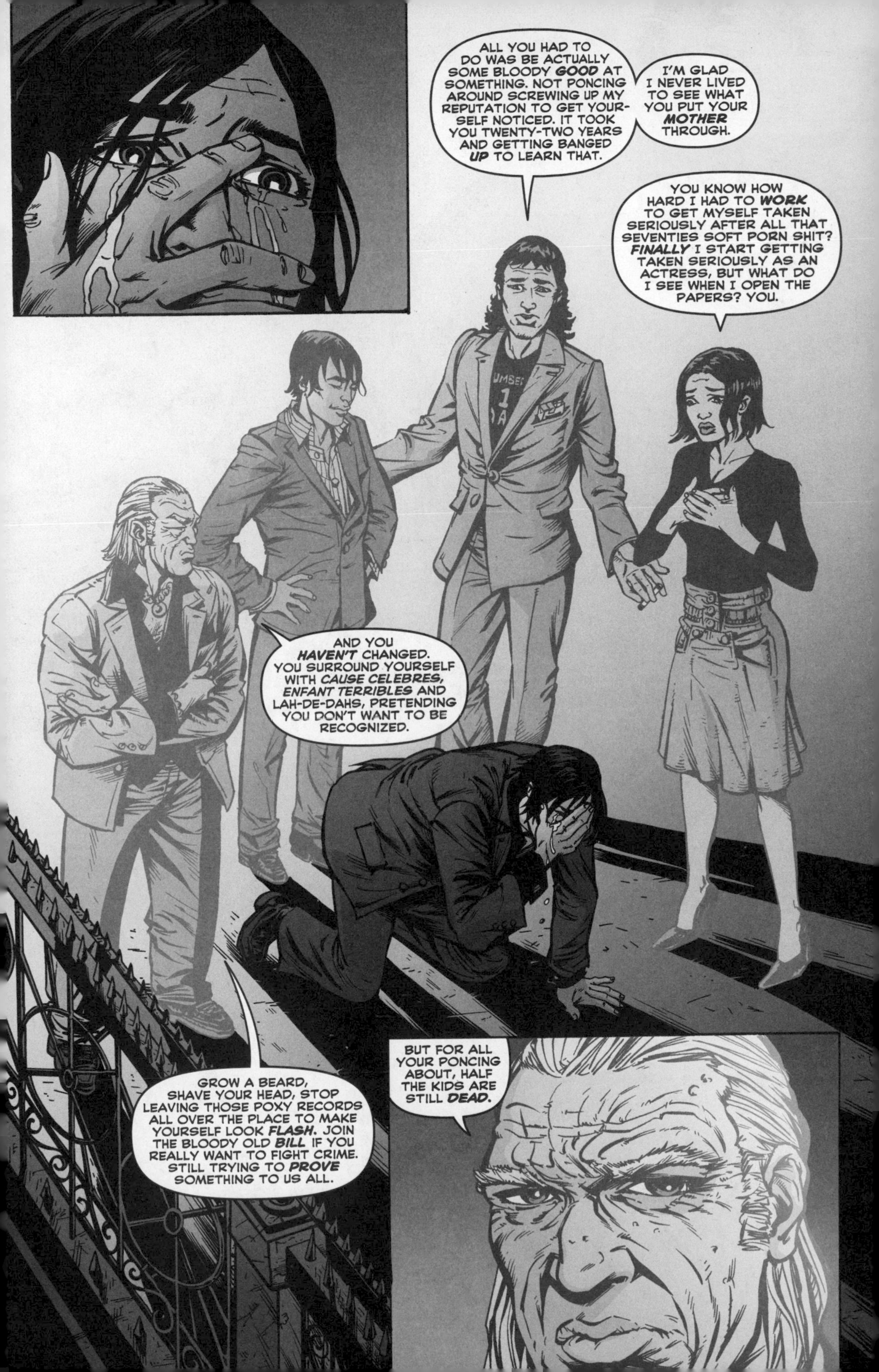
ALL YOU HAD TO DO WAS BE ACTUALLY SOME BLOODY GOOD AT SOMETHING. NOT PONCING AROUND SCREWING UP MY REPUTATION TO GET YOURSELF NOTICED. IT TOOK YOU TWENTY-TWO YEARS AND GETTING BANGED UP TO LEARN THAT.
I'M GLAD I NEVER LIVED TO SEE WHAT YOU PUT YOUR MOTHER THROUGH.
YOU KNOW HOW HARD I HAD TO WORK TO GET MYSELF TAKEN SERIOUSLY AFTER ALL THAT SEVENTIES SOFT PORN SHIT? FINALLY I START GETTING TAKEN SERIOUSLY AS AN ACTRESS, BUT WHAT DO I SEE WHEN I OPEN THE PAPERS? YOU.
AND YOU HAVEN'T CHANGED. YOU SURROUND YOURSELF WITH CAUSE CELEBRES, ENFANT TERRIBLES AND LAH-DE-DAHS, PRETENDING YOU DON'T WANT TO BE RECOGNIZED.
GROW A BEARD, SHAVE YOUR HEAD, STOP LEAVING THOSE POXY RECORDS ALL OVER THE PLACE TO MAKE YOURSELF LOOK FLASH. JOIN THE BLOODY OLD BILL IF YOU REALLY WANT TO FIGHT CRIME. STILL TRYING TO PROVE SOMETHING TO US ALL.
BUT FOR ALL YOUR PONCING ABOUT, HALF THE KIDS ARE STILL DEAD.

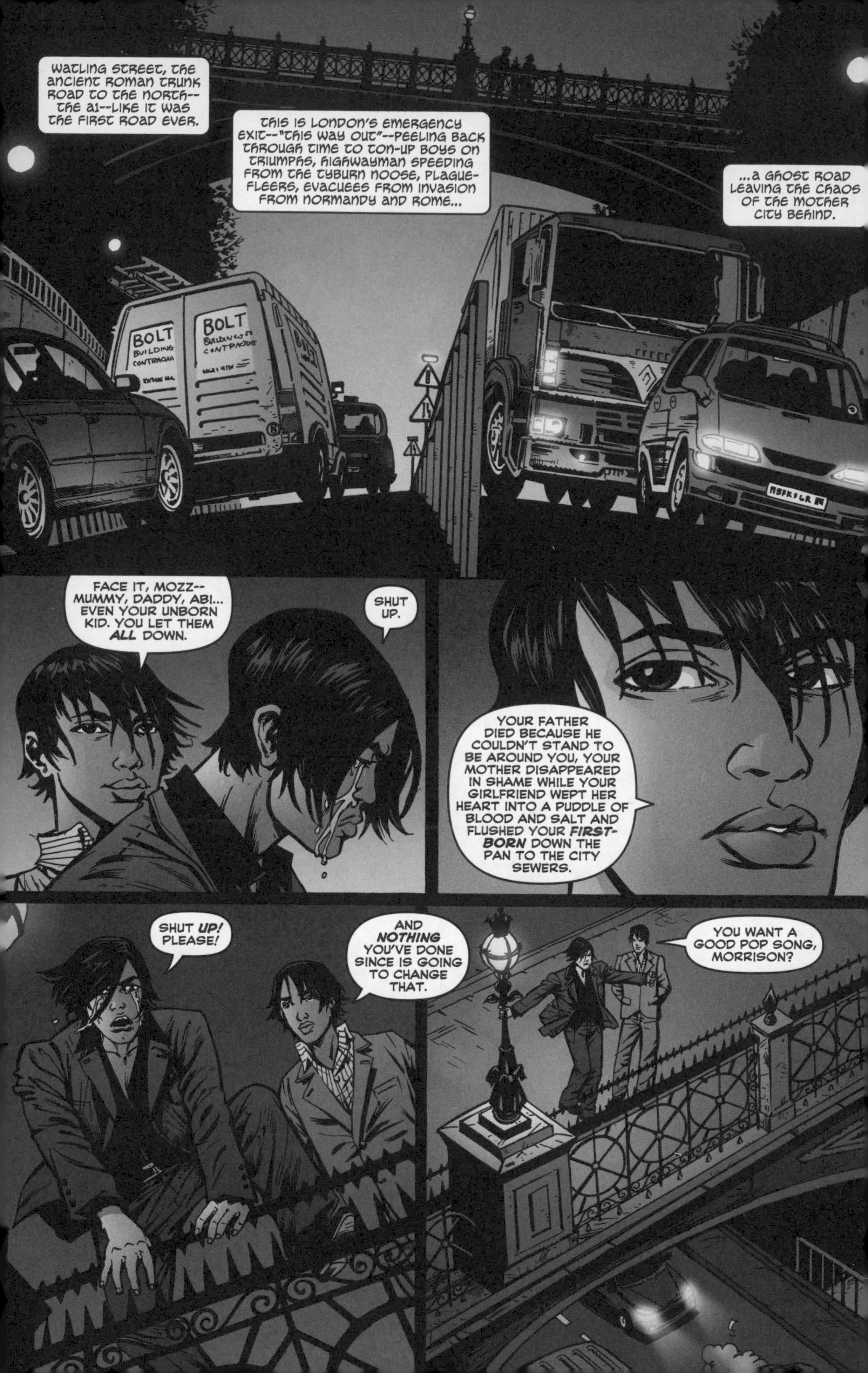
WATLING STREET, THE ANCIENT ROMAN TRUNK ROAD TO THE NORTH-- THE A1--LIKE IT WAS THE FIRST ROAD EVER.
THIS IS LONDON'S EMERGENCY EXIT--"THIS WAY OUT"--PEELING BACK THROUGH TIME TO TON-UP BOYS ON TRIUMPHS, HIGHWAYMAN SPEEDING FROM THE TYBURN NOOSE, PLAGUE-FLEERS, EVACUEES FROM INVASION FROM NORMANDY AND ROME...
...A GHOST ROAD LEAVING THE CHAOS OF THE MOTHER CITY BEHIND.
BOLT BUILDING CONTRACTORS
FACE IT, MOZZ-- MUMMY, DADDY, ABI... EVEN YOUR UNBORN KID. YOU LET THEM ALL DOWN.
SHUT UP.
YOUR FATHER DIED BECAUSE HE COULDN'T STAND TO BE AROUND YOU, YOUR MOTHER DISAPPEARED IN SHAME WHILE YOUR GIRLFRIEND WEPT HER HEART INTO A PUDDLE OF BLOOD AND SALT AND FLUSHED YOUR FIRST-BORN DOWN THE PAN TO THE CITY SEWERS.
SHUT UP! PLEASE!
AND NOTHING YOU'VE DONE SINCE IS GOING TO CHANGE THAT.
YOU WANT A GOOD POP SONG, MORRISON?

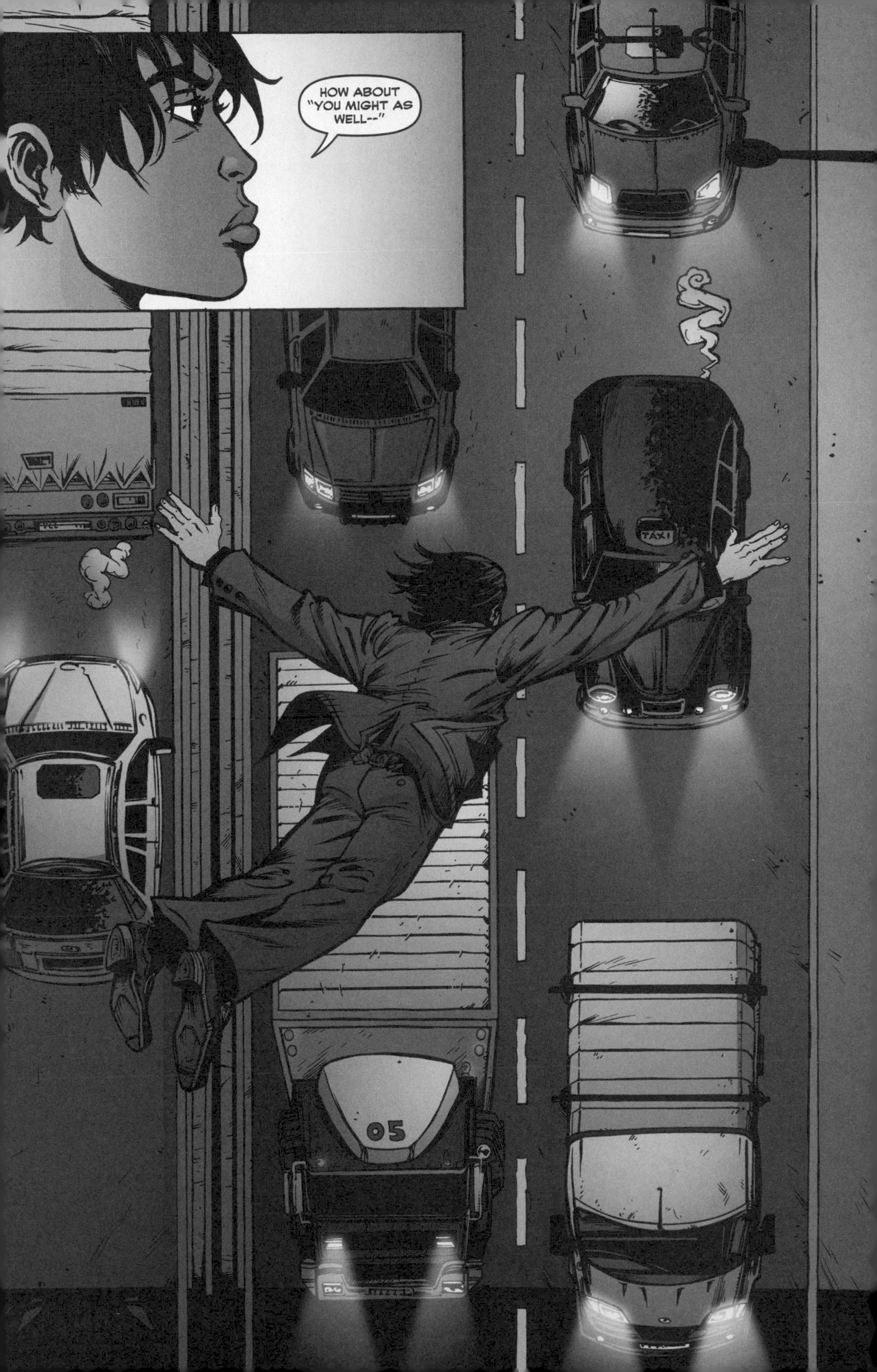
HOW ABOUT "YOU MIGHT AS WELL--"
TAXI
05

CAN'T STAND UP FOR FALLING DOWN

6

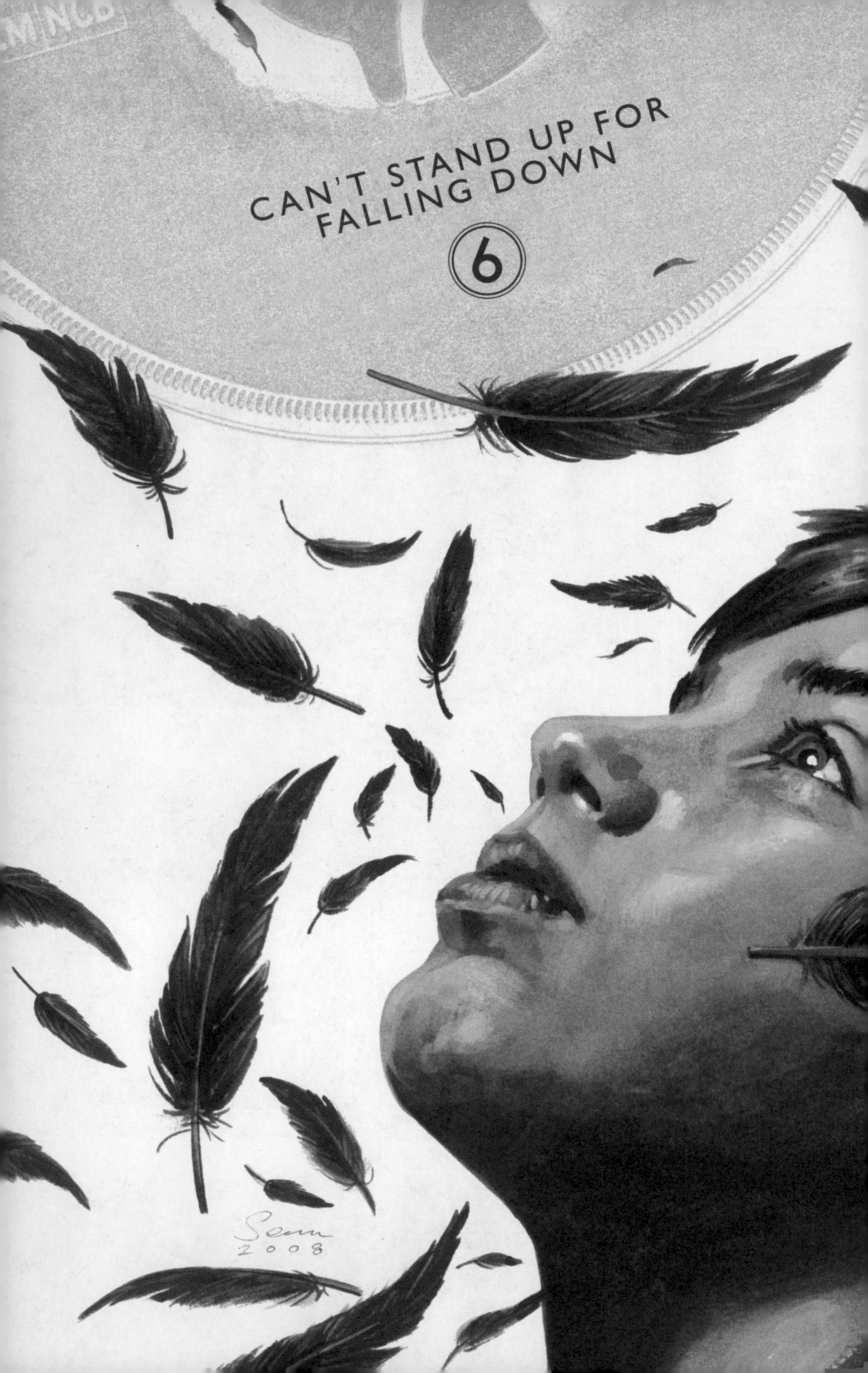
Sean
2008

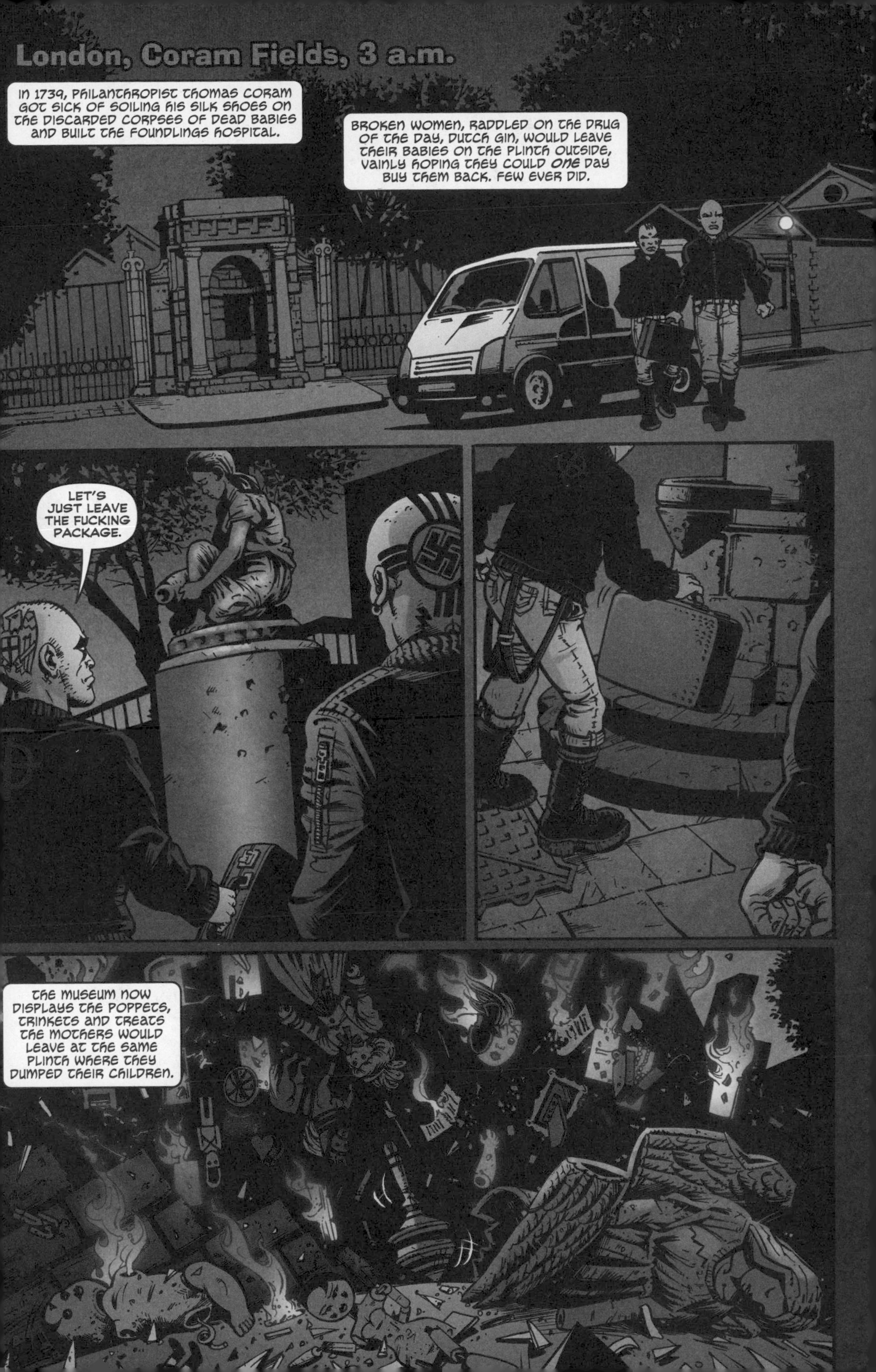
London, Coram Fields, 3 a.m.
In 1739, philanthropist Thomas Coram got sick of soiling his silk shoes on the discarded corpses of dead babies and built the Foundlings Hospital.
Broken women, raddled on the drug of the day, Dutch gin, would leave their babies on the plinth outside, vainly hoping they could *one* day buy them back. Few ever did.
LET'S JUST LEAVE THE FUCKING PACKAGE.
The museum now displays the poppets, trinkets and treats the mothers would leave at the same plinth where they dumped their children.

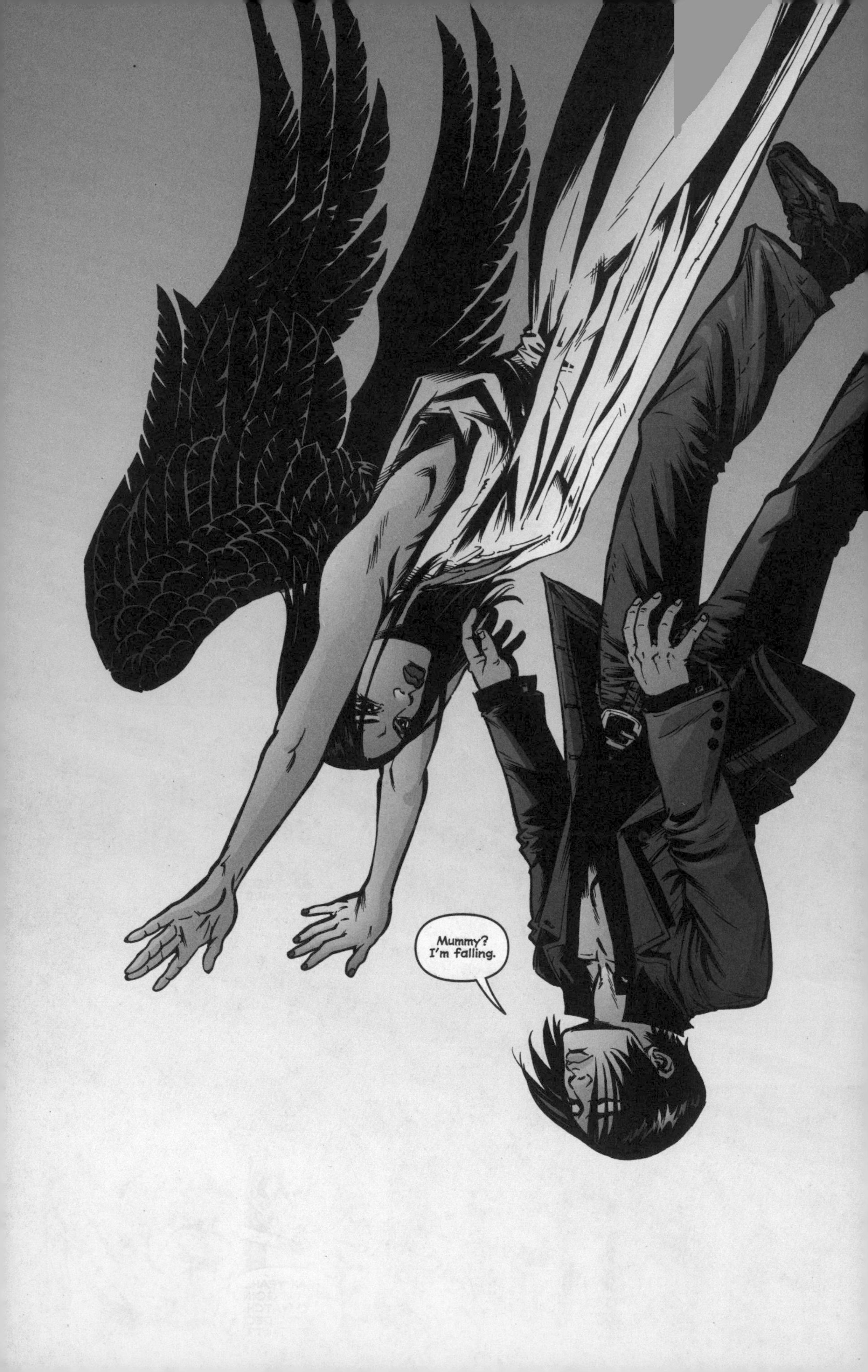
Mummy? I'm falling.

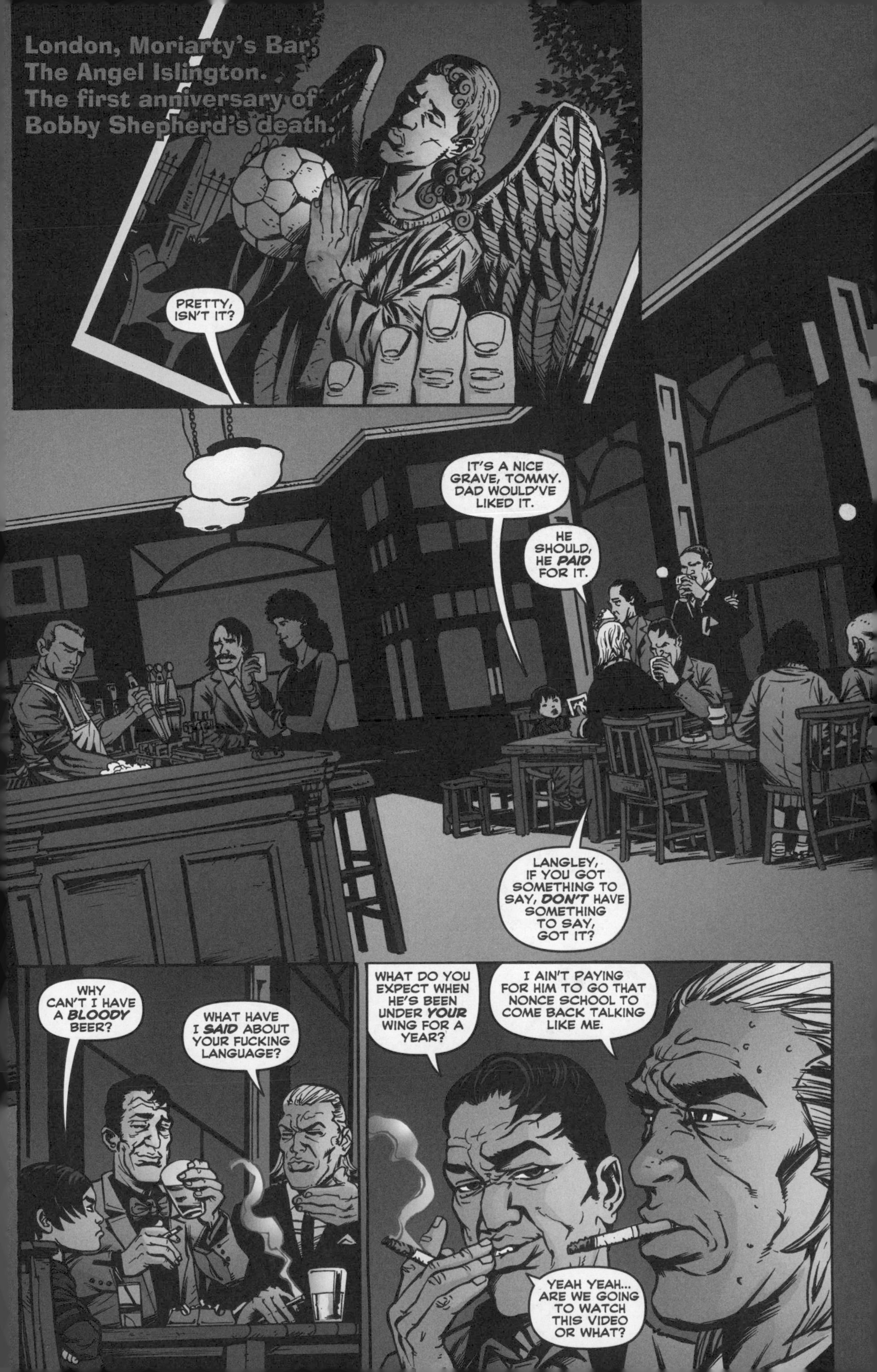
London, Moriarty's Bar, The Angel Islington.
The first anniversary of Bobby Shepherd's death.
PRETTY, ISN'T IT?
IT'S A NICE GRAVE, TOMMY. DAD WOULD'VE LIKED IT.
HE SHOULD, HE PAID FOR IT.
LANGLEY, IF YOU GOT SOMETHING TO SAY, DON'T HAVE SOMETHING TO SAY, GOT IT?
WHY CAN'T I HAVE A BLOODY BEER?
WHAT HAVE I SAID ABOUT YOUR FUCKING LANGUAGE?
WHAT DO YOU EXPECT WHEN HE'S BEEN UNDER YOUR WING FOR A YEAR?
I AIN'T PAYING FOR HIM TO GO THAT NONCE SCHOOL TO COME BACK TALKING LIKE ME.
YEAH YEAH... ARE WE GOING TO WATCH THIS VIDEO OR WHAT?

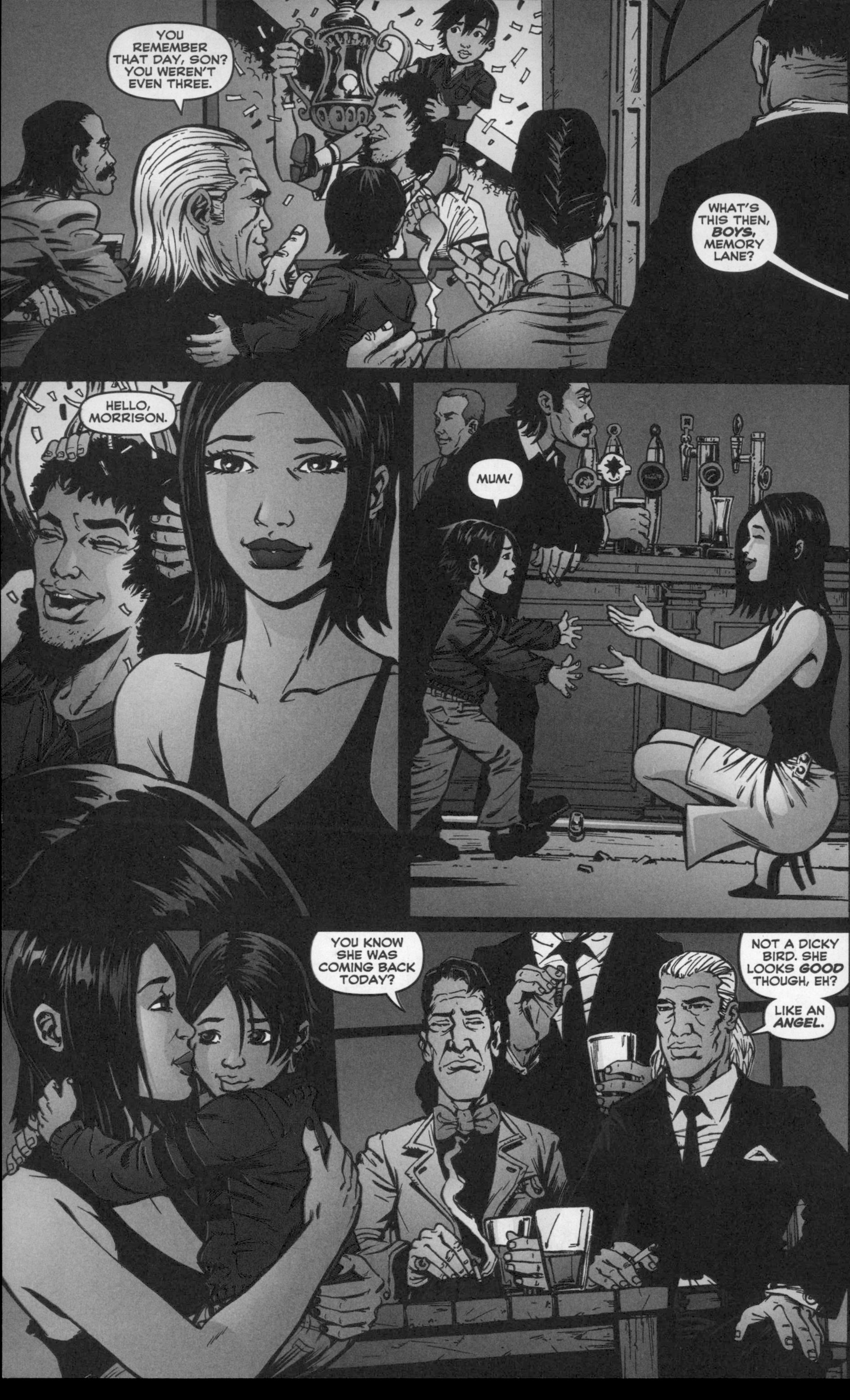

YOU REMEMBER THAT DAY, SON? YOU WEREN'T EVEN THREE.
WHAT'S THIS THEN, **BOYS,** MEMORY LANE?
HELLO, MORRISON.
MUM!
YOU KNOW SHE WAS COMING BACK TODAY?
NOT A DICKY BIRD. SHE LOOKS **GOOD** THOUGH, EH?
LIKE AN **ANGEL.**

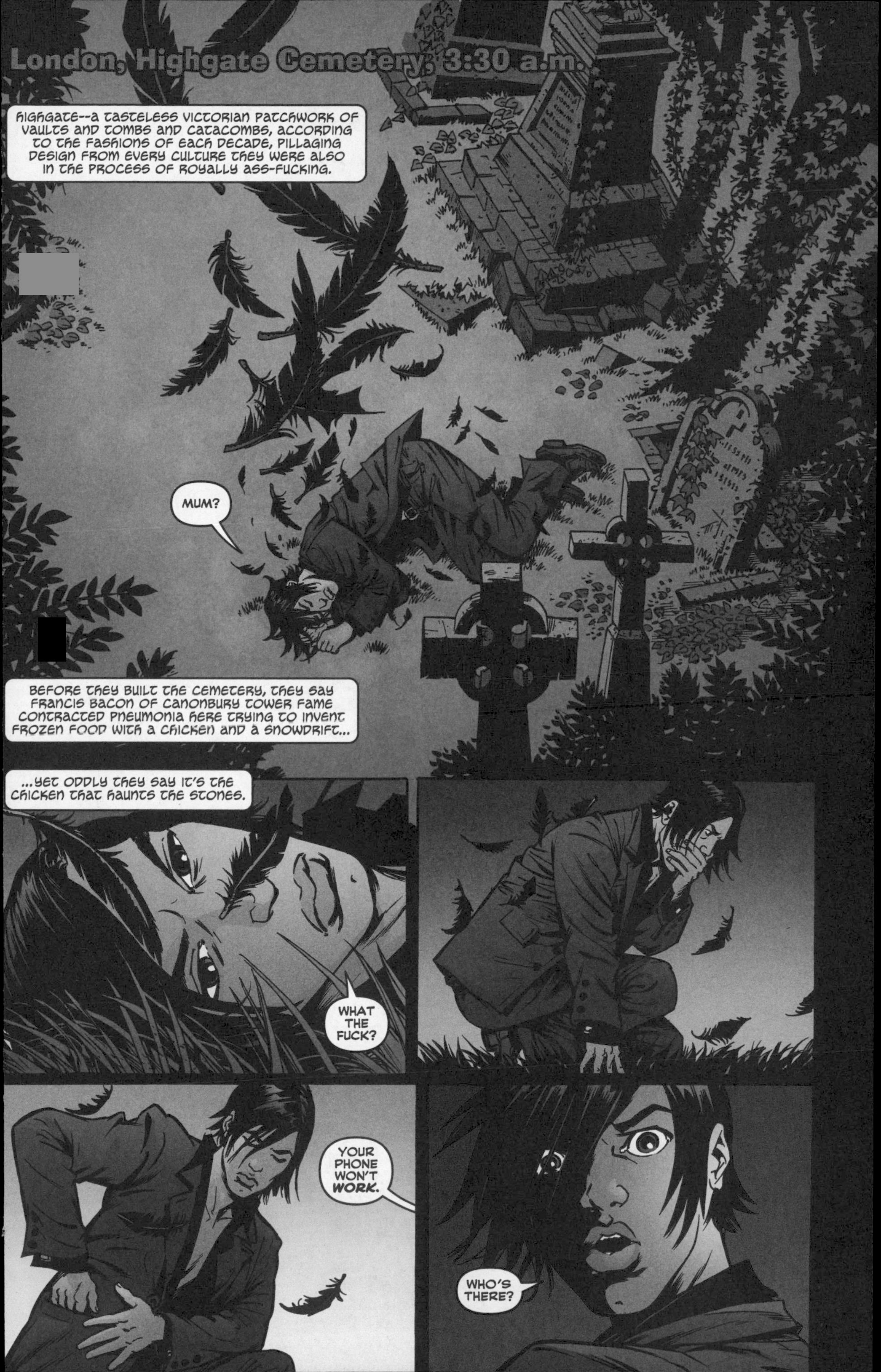
London, Highgate Cemetery, 3:30 a.m.
HIGHGATE--A TASTELESS VICTORIAN PATCHWORK OF VAULTS AND TOMBS AND CATACOMBS, ACCORDING TO THE FASHIONS OF EACH DECADE, PILLAGING DESIGN FROM EVERY CULTURE THEY WERE ALSO IN THE PROCESS OF ROYALLY ASS-FUCKING.
MUM?
BEFORE THEY BUILT THE CEMETERY, THEY SAY FRANCIS BACON OF CANONBURY TOWER FAME CONTRACTED PNEUMONIA HERE TRYING TO INVENT FROZEN FOOD WITH A CHICKEN AND A SNOWDRIFT...
...YET ODDLY THEY SAY IT'S THE CHICKEN THAT HAUNTS THE STONES.
WHAT THE FUCK?
YOUR PHONE WON'T WORK.
WHO'S THERE?

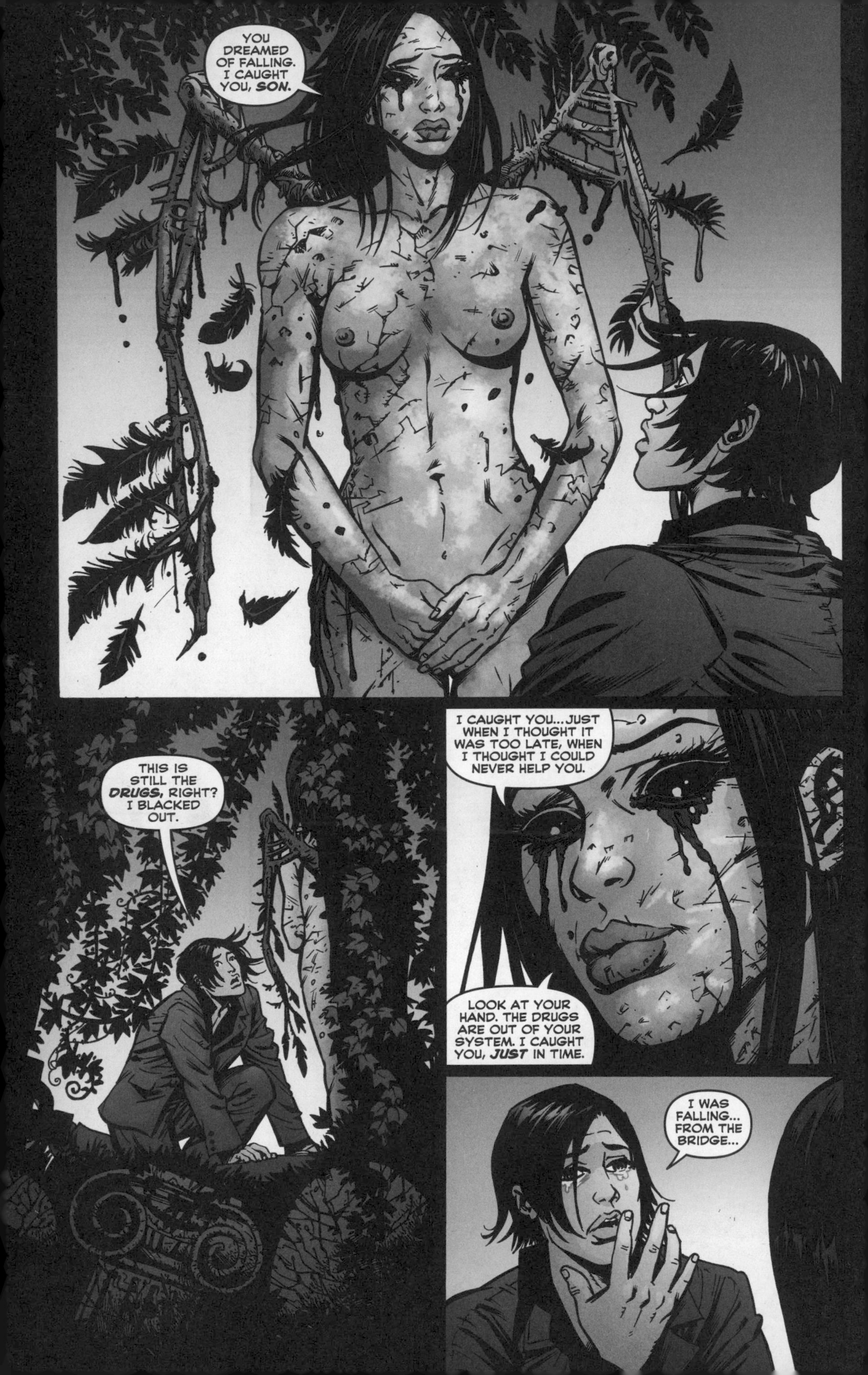
YOU DREAMED OF FALLING. I CAUGHT YOU, **SON.**
THIS IS STILL THE **DRUGS,** RIGHT? I BLACKED OUT.
I CAUGHT YOU... JUST WHEN I THOUGHT IT WAS TOO LATE, WHEN I THOUGHT I COULD NEVER HELP YOU.
LOOK AT YOUR HAND. THE DRUGS ARE OUT OF YOUR SYSTEM. I CAUGHT YOU, **JUST** IN TIME.
I WAS FALLING... FROM THE BRIDGE...

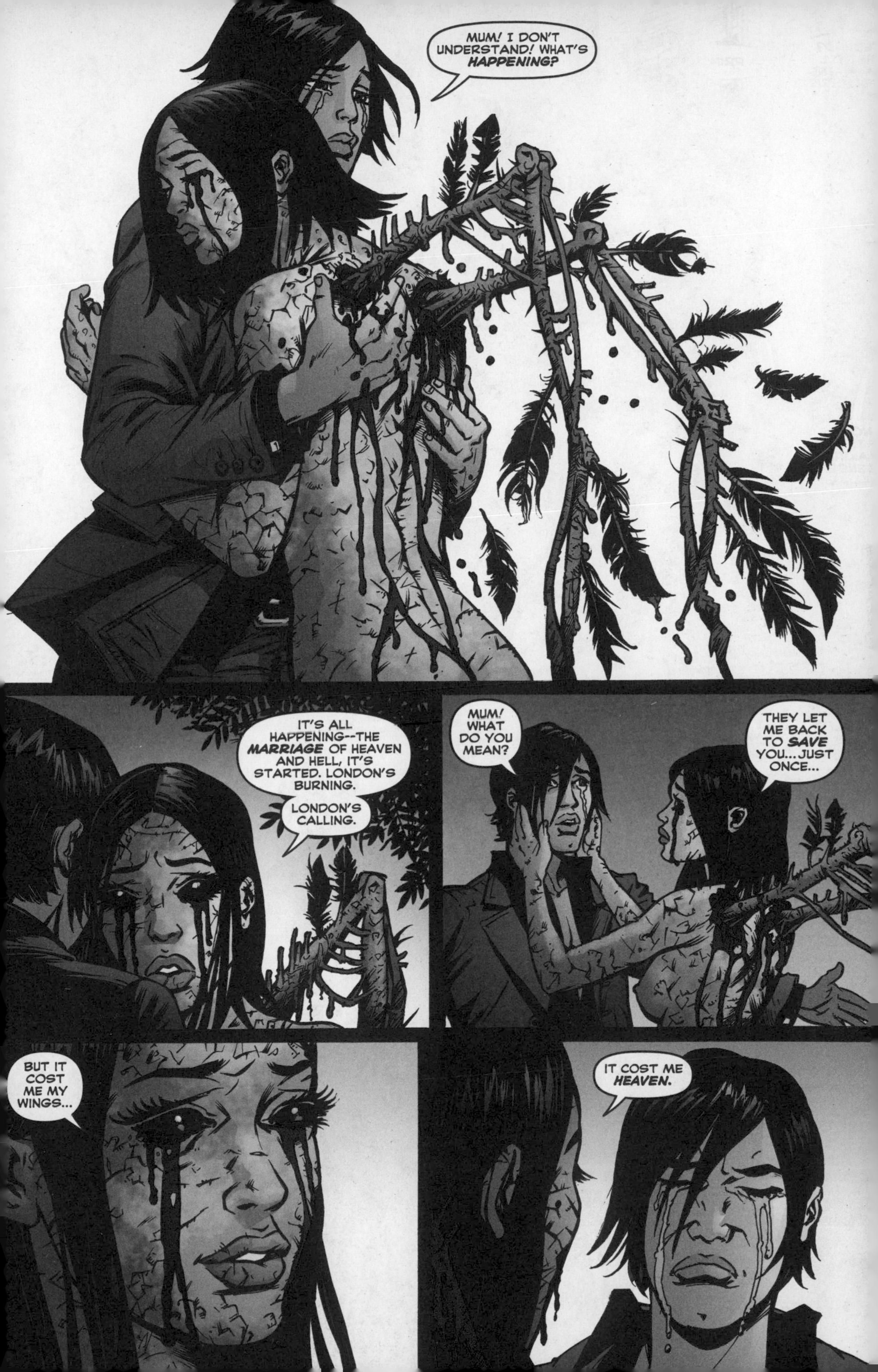
MUM! I DON'T UNDERSTAND! WHAT'S HAPPENING?
IT'S ALL HAPPENING--THE MARRIAGE OF HEAVEN AND HELL, IT'S STARTED. LONDON'S BURNING.
LONDON'S CALLING.
MUM! WHAT DO YOU MEAN?
THEY LET ME BACK TO SAVE YOU...JUST ONCE...
BUT IT COST ME MY WINGS...
IT COST ME HEAVEN.

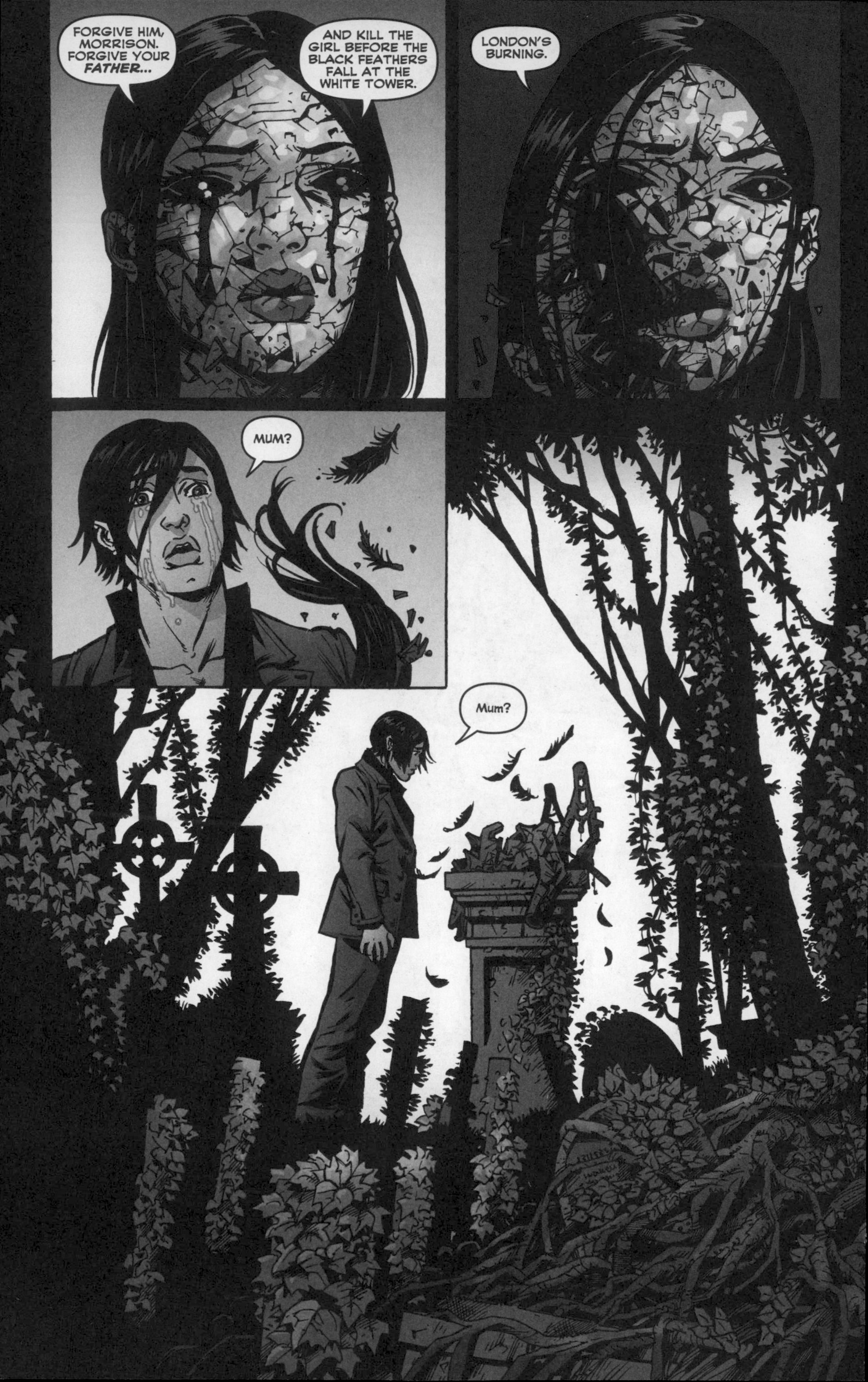

FORGIVE HIM, MORRISON. FORGIVE YOUR *FATHER*...
AND KILL THE GIRL BEFORE THE BLACK FEATHERS FALL AT THE WHITE TOWER.
LONDON'S BURNING.
MUM?
Mum?

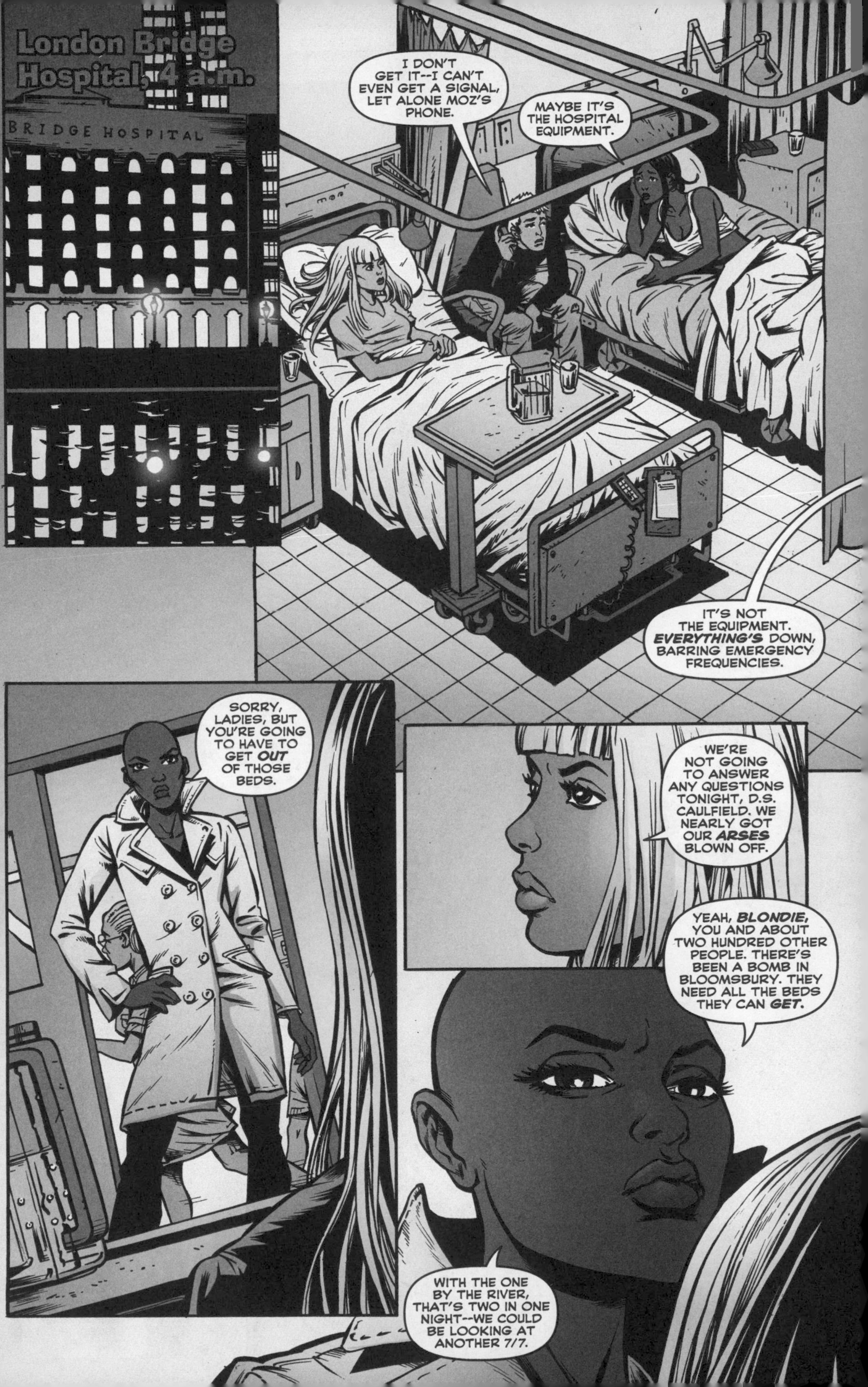
London Bridge Hospital, 4 a.m.
BRIDGE HOSPITAL
I DON'T GET IT--I CAN'T EVEN GET A SIGNAL, LET ALONE MOZ'S PHONE.
MAYBE IT'S THE HOSPITAL EQUIPMENT.
IT'S NOT THE EQUIPMENT. EVERYTHING'S DOWN, BARRING EMERGENCY FREQUENCIES.
SORRY, LADIES, BUT YOU'RE GOING TO HAVE TO GET OUT OF THOSE BEDS.
WE'RE NOT GOING TO ANSWER ANY QUESTIONS TONIGHT, D.S. CAULFIELD. WE NEARLY GOT OUR ARSES BLOWN OFF.
YEAH, BLONDIE, YOU AND ABOUT TWO HUNDRED OTHER PEOPLE. THERE'S BEEN A BOMB IN BLOOMSBURY. THEY NEED ALL THE BEDS THEY CAN GET.
WITH THE ONE BY THE RIVER, THAT'S TWO IN ONE NIGHT--WE COULD BE LOOKING AT ANOTHER 7/7.

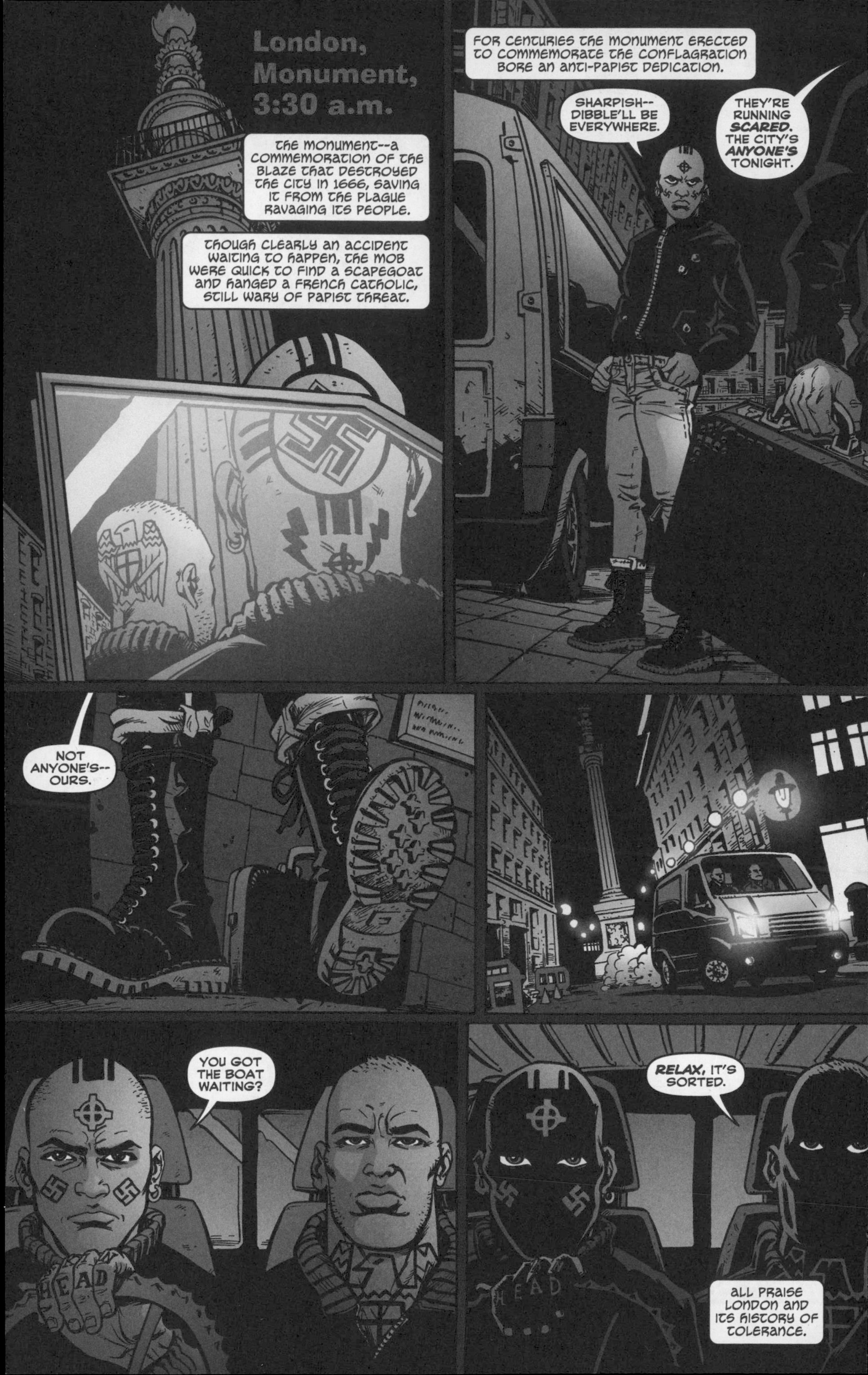
London, Monument, 3:30 a.m.
THE MONUMENT--A COMMEMORATION OF THE BLAZE THAT DESTROYED THE CITY IN 1666, SAVING IT FROM THE PLAGUE RAVAGING ITS PEOPLE.
THOUGH CLEARLY AN ACCIDENT WAITING TO HAPPEN, THE MOB WERE QUICK TO FIND A SCAPEGOAT AND HANGED A FRENCH CATHOLIC, STILL WARY OF PAPIST THREAT.
FOR CENTURIES THE MONUMENT ERECTED TO COMMEMORATE THE CONFLAGRATION BORE AN ANTI-PAPIST DEDICATION.
SHARPISH--DIBBLE'LL BE EVERYWHERE.
THEY'RE RUNNING SCARED. THE CITY'S ANYONE'S TONIGHT.
NOT ANYONE'S--OURS.
YOU GOT THE BOAT WAITING?
RELAX, IT'S SORTED.
ALL PRAISE LONDON AND ITS HISTORY OF TOLERANCE.

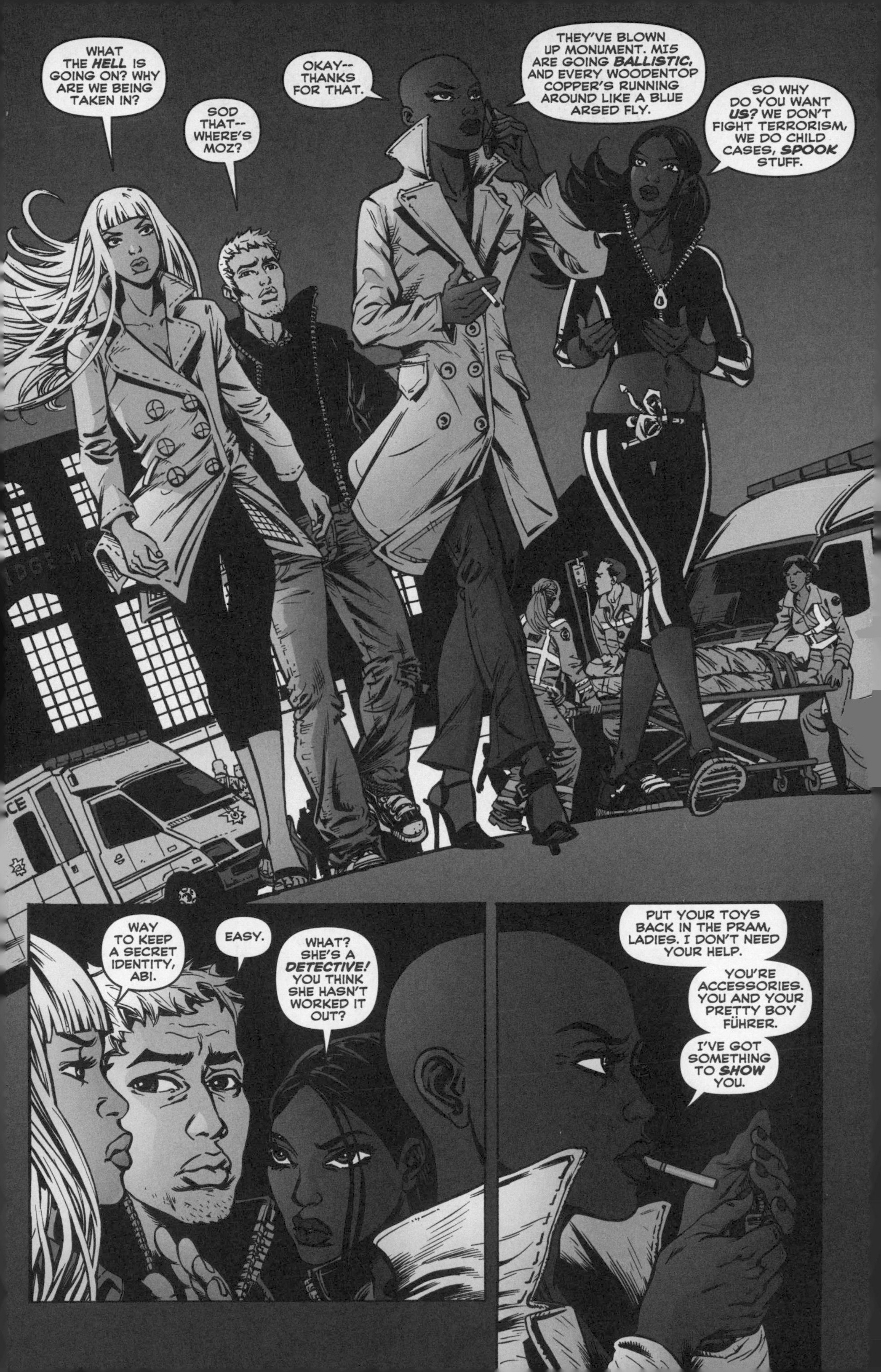
WHAT THE HELL IS GOING ON? WHY ARE WE BEING TAKEN IN?
SOD THAT-- WHERE'S MOZ?
OKAY-- THANKS FOR THAT.
THEY'VE BLOWN UP MONUMENT. MI5 ARE GOING BALLISTIC, AND EVERY WOODENTOP COPPER'S RUNNING AROUND LIKE A BLUE ARSED FLY.
SO WHY DO YOU WANT US? WE DON'T FIGHT TERRORISM, WE DO CHILD CASES, SPOOK STUFF.
WAY TO KEEP A SECRET IDENTITY, ABI.
EASY.
WHAT? SHE'S A DETECTIVE! YOU THINK SHE HASN'T WORKED IT OUT?
PUT YOUR TOYS BACK IN THE PRAM, LADIES. I DON'T NEED YOUR HELP.
YOU'RE ACCESSORIES. YOU AND YOUR PRETTY BOY FÜHRER.
I'VE GOT SOMETHING TO SHOW YOU.

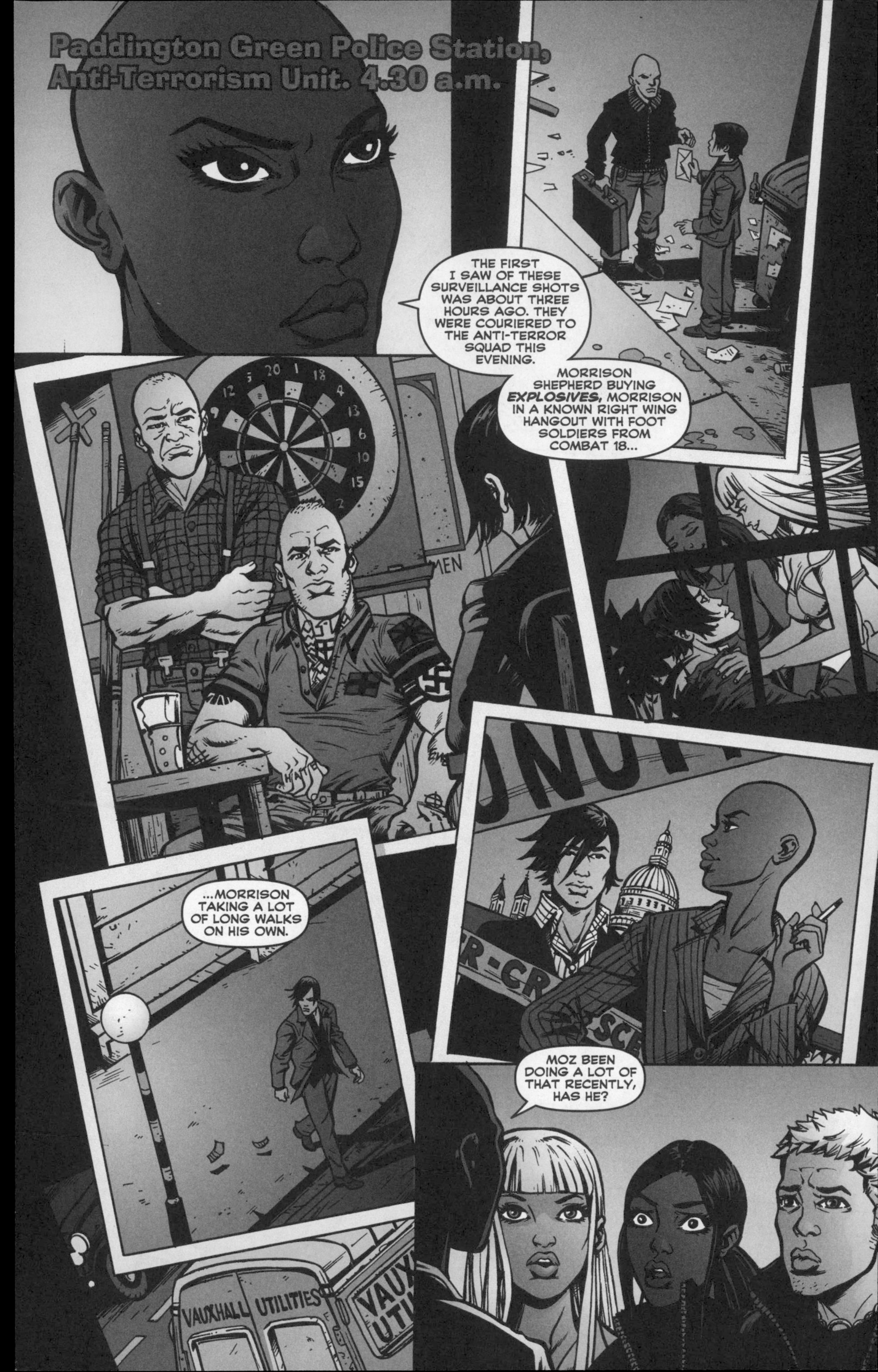
Paddington Green Police Station, Anti-Terrorism Unit. 4.30 a.m.
THE FIRST I SAW OF THESE SURVEILLANCE SHOTS WAS ABOUT THREE HOURS AGO. THEY WERE COURIERED TO THE ANTI-TERROR SQUAD THIS EVENING.
MORRISON SHEPHERD BUYING EXPLOSIVES, MORRISON IN A KNOWN RIGHT WING HANGOUT WITH FOOT SOLDIERS FROM COMBAT 18...
MEN
...MORRISON TAKING A LOT OF LONG WALKS ON HIS OWN.
MOZ BEEN DOING A LOT OF THAT RECENTLY, HAS HE?
VAUXHALL UTILITIES

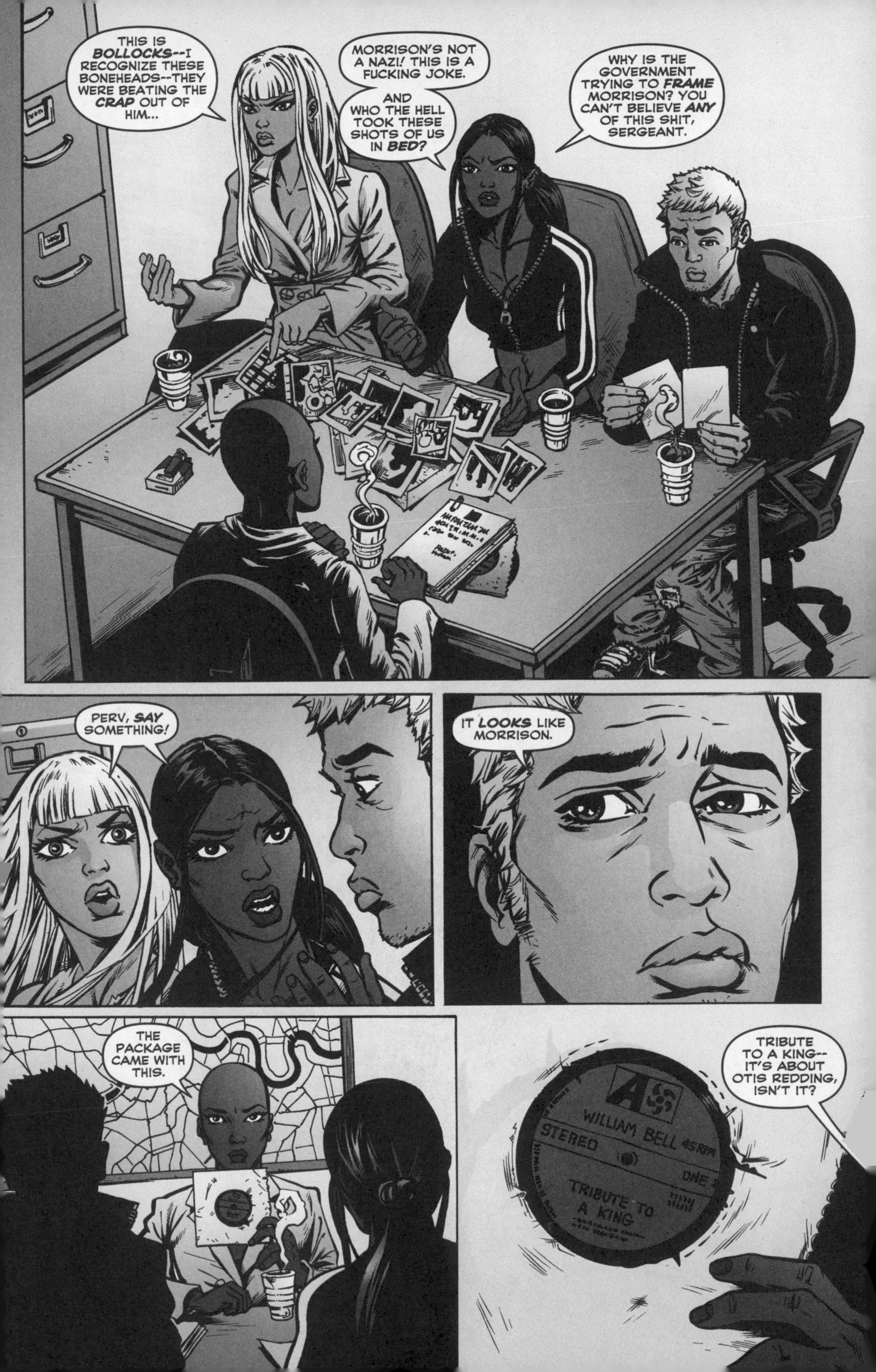
THIS IS BOLLOCKS--I RECOGNIZE THESE BONEHEADS--THEY WERE BEATING THE CRAP OUT OF HIM...
MORRISON'S NOT A NAZI! THIS IS A FUCKING JOKE.
AND WHO THE HELL TOOK THESE SHOTS OF US IN BED?
WHY IS THE GOVERNMENT TRYING TO FRAME MORRISON? YOU CAN'T BELIEVE ANY OF THIS SHIT, SERGEANT.
PERV, SAY SOMETHING!
IT LOOKS LIKE MORRISON.
THE PACKAGE CAME WITH THIS.
TRIBUTE TO A KING--IT'S ABOUT OTIS REDDING, ISN'T IT?
WILLIAM BELL
STEREO
45 RPM
ONE
TRIBUTE TO A KING

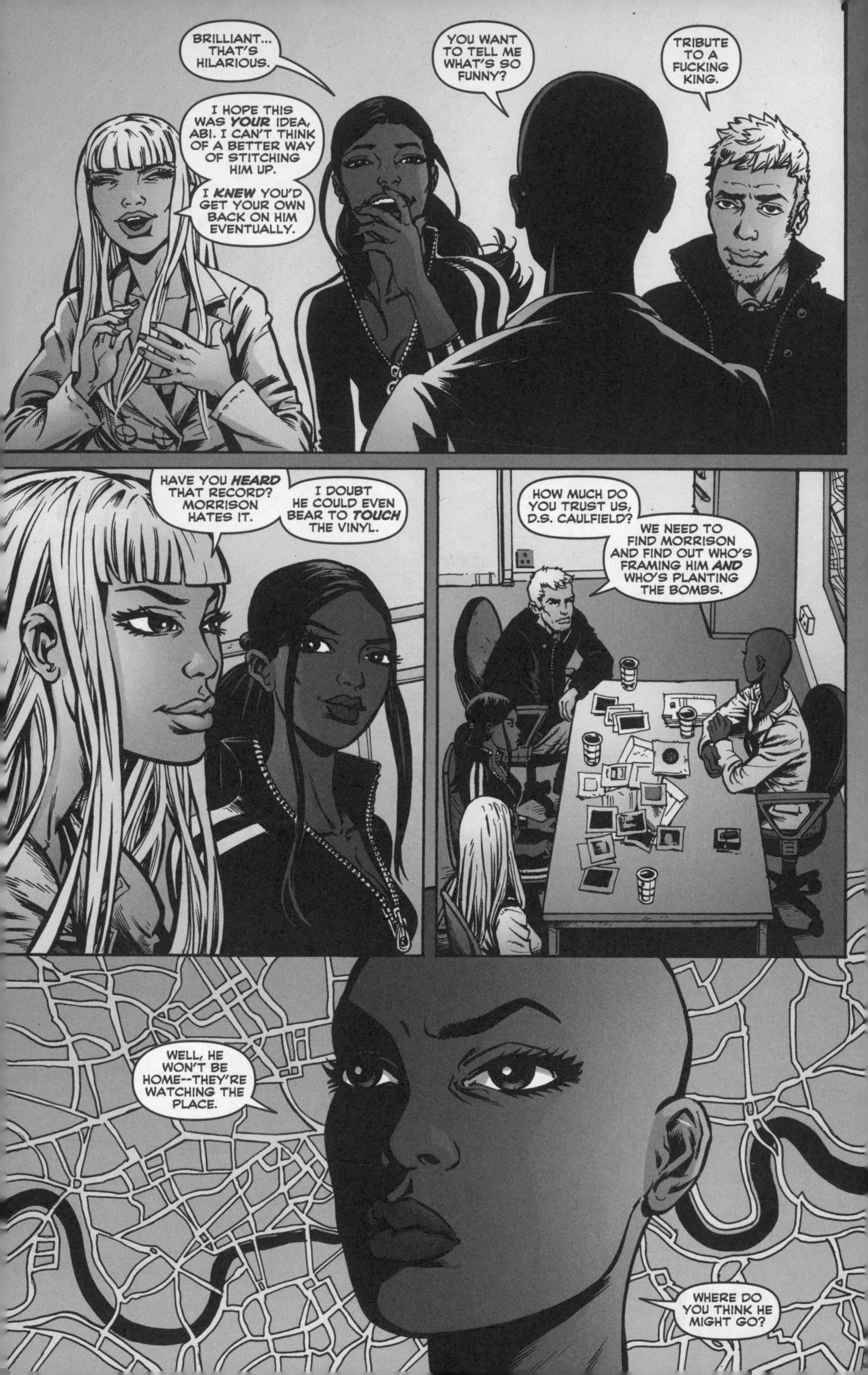
BRILLIANT... THAT'S HILARIOUS.
I HOPE THIS WAS YOUR IDEA, ABI. I CAN'T THINK OF A BETTER WAY OF STITCHING HIM UP.
I KNEW YOU'D GET YOUR OWN BACK ON HIM EVENTUALLY.
YOU WANT TO TELL ME WHAT'S SO FUNNY?
TRIBUTE TO A FUCKING KING.
HAVE YOU HEARD THAT RECORD? MORRISON HATES IT.
I DOUBT HE COULD EVEN BEAR TO TOUCH THE VINYL.
HOW MUCH DO YOU TRUST US, D.S. CAULFIELD?
WE NEED TO FIND MORRISON AND FIND OUT WHO'S FRAMING HIM AND WHO'S PLANTING THE BOMBS.
WELL, HE WON'T BE HOME--THEY'RE WATCHING THE PLACE.
WHERE DO YOU THINK HE MIGHT GO?

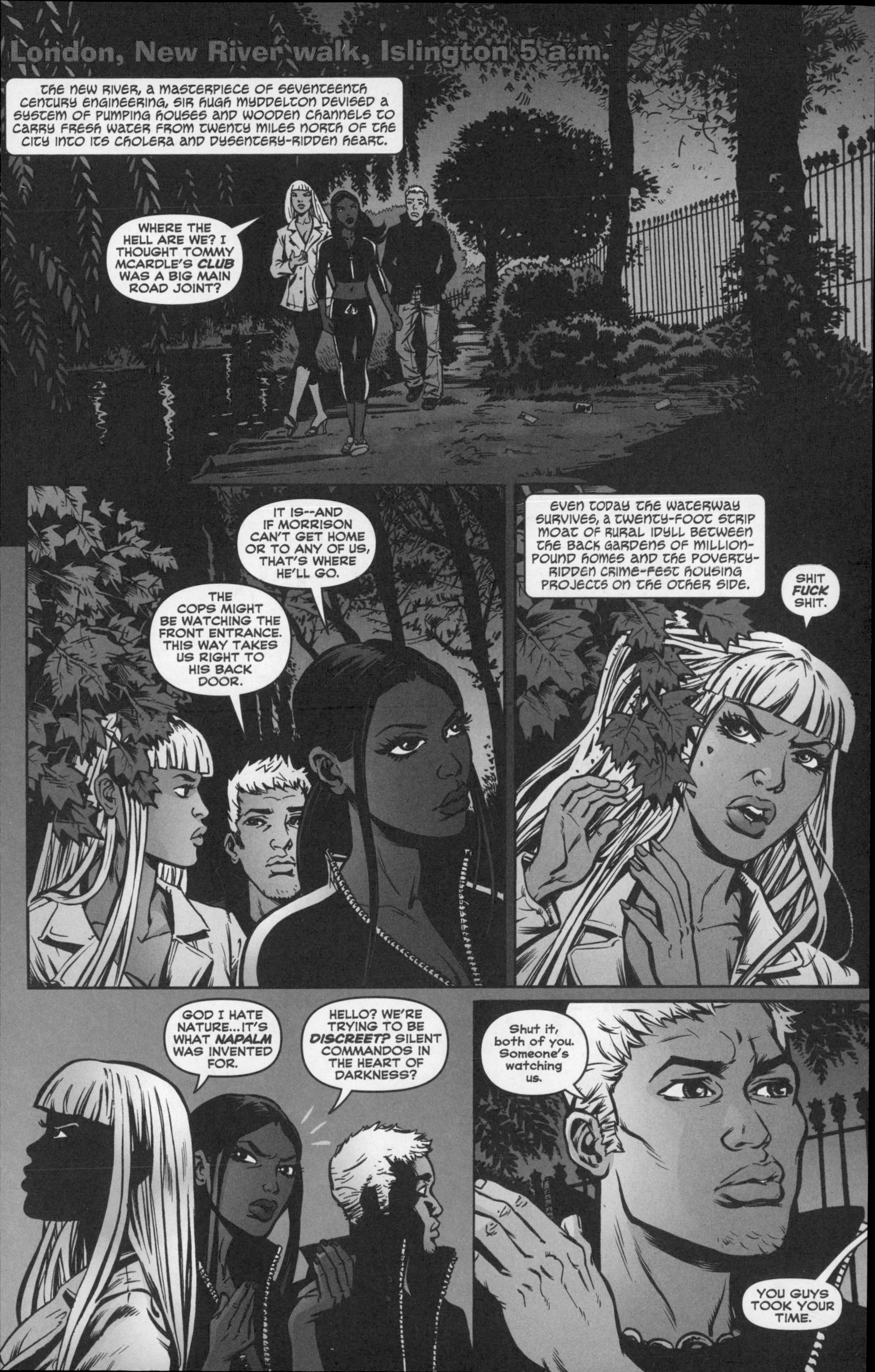
London, New River walk, Islington 5 a.m.
The New River, a masterpiece of seventeenth century engineering, Sir Hugh Myddelton devised a system of pumping houses and wooden channels to carry fresh water from twenty miles north of the city into its cholera and dysentery-ridden heart.
WHERE THE HELL ARE WE? I THOUGHT TOMMY MCARDLE'S CLUB WAS A BIG MAIN ROAD JOINT?
IT IS--AND IF MORRISON CAN'T GET HOME OR TO ANY OF US, THAT'S WHERE HE'LL GO.
THE COPS MIGHT BE WATCHING THE FRONT ENTRANCE. THIS WAY TAKES US RIGHT TO HIS BACK DOOR.
Even today the waterway survives, a twenty-foot strip moat of rural idyll between the back gardens of million-pound homes and the poverty-ridden crime-fest housing projects on the other side.
SHIT FUCK SHIT.
GOD I HATE NATURE...IT'S WHAT NAPALM WAS INVENTED FOR.
HELLO? WE'RE TRYING TO BE DISCREET? SILENT COMMANDOS IN THE HEART OF DARKNESS?
Shut it, both of you. Someone's watching us.
YOU GUYS TOOK YOUR TIME.

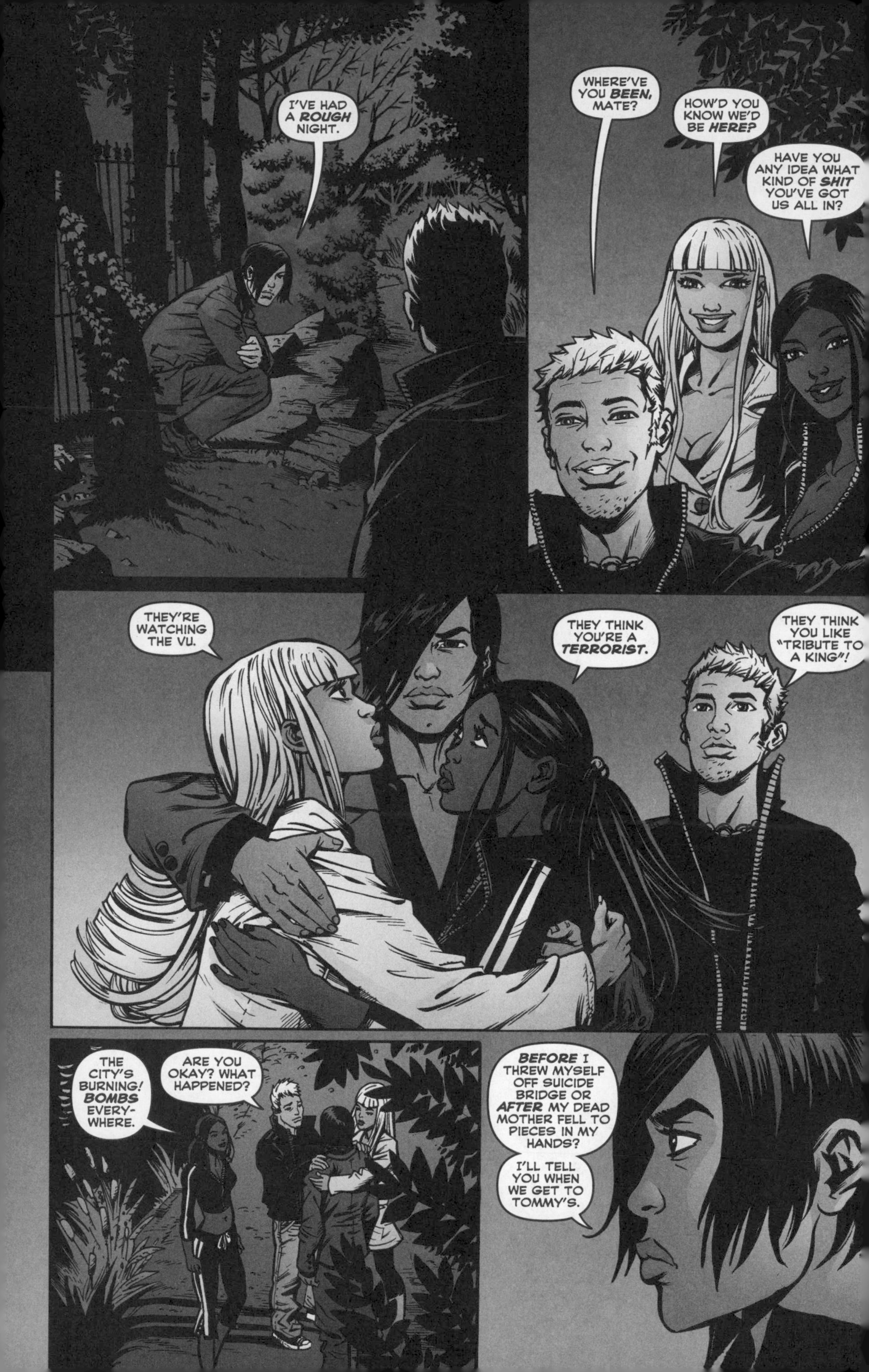
I'VE HAD A *ROUGH* NIGHT.
WHERE'VE YOU *BEEN,* MATE?
HOW'D YOU KNOW WE'D BE *HERE?*
HAVE YOU ANY IDEA WHAT KIND OF *SHIT* YOU'VE GOT US ALL IN?
THEY'RE WATCHING THE VU.
THEY THINK YOU'RE A *TERRORIST.*
THEY THINK YOU LIKE "TRIBUTE TO A KING"!
THE CITY'S BURNING! *BOMBS* EVERY-WHERE.
ARE YOU OKAY? WHAT HAPPENED?
BEFORE I THREW MYSELF OFF SUICIDE BRIDGE OR *AFTER* MY DEAD MOTHER FELL TO PIECES IN MY HANDS?
I'LL TELL YOU WHEN WE GET TO TOMMY'S.

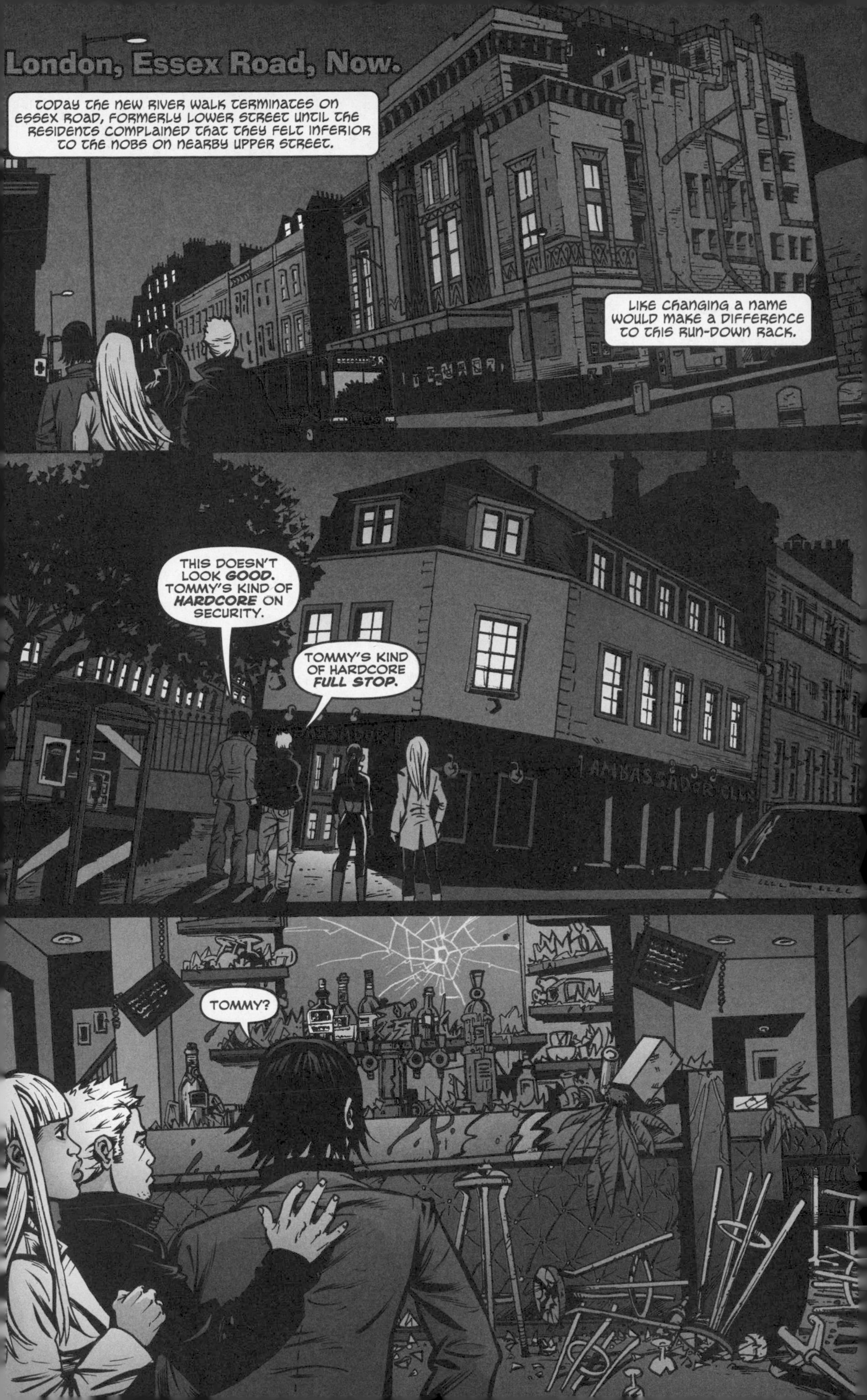
London, Essex Road, Now.
TODAY THE NEW RIVER WALK TERMINATES ON ESSEX ROAD, FORMERLY LOWER STREET UNTIL THE RESIDENTS COMPLAINED THAT THEY FELT INFERIOR TO THE NOBS ON NEARBY UPPER STREET.
LIKE CHANGING A NAME WOULD MAKE A DIFFERENCE TO THIS RUN-DOWN RACK.
THIS DOESN'T LOOK GOOD. TOMMY'S KIND OF HARDCORE ON SECURITY.
TOMMY'S KIND OF HARDCORE FULL STOP.
TOMMY?

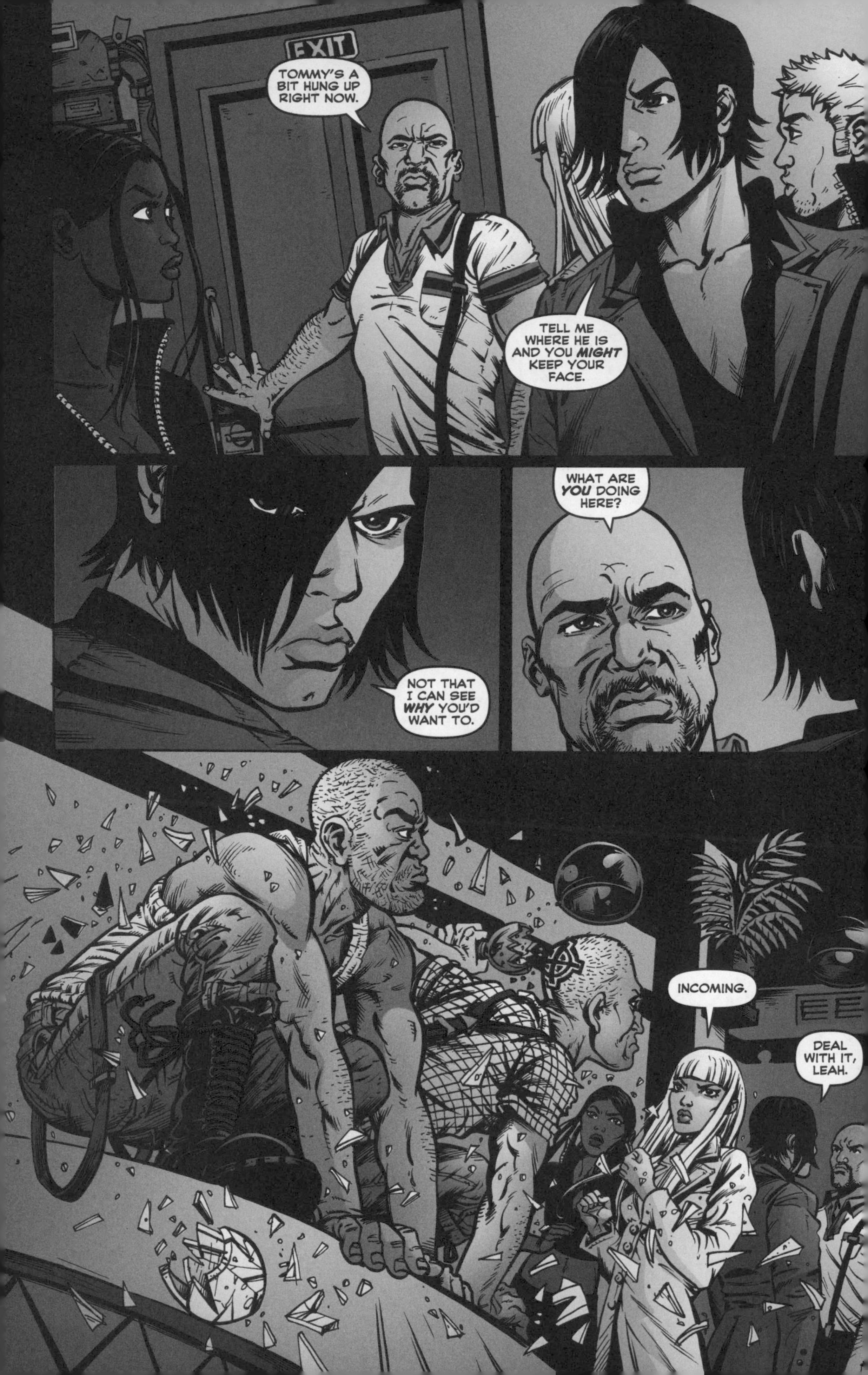
EXIT
TOMMY'S A BIT HUNG UP RIGHT NOW.
TELL ME WHERE HE IS AND YOU *MIGHT* KEEP YOUR FACE.
WHAT ARE *YOU* DOING HERE?
NOT THAT I CAN SEE *WHY* YOU'D WANT TO.
INCOMING.
DEAL WITH IT, LEAH.

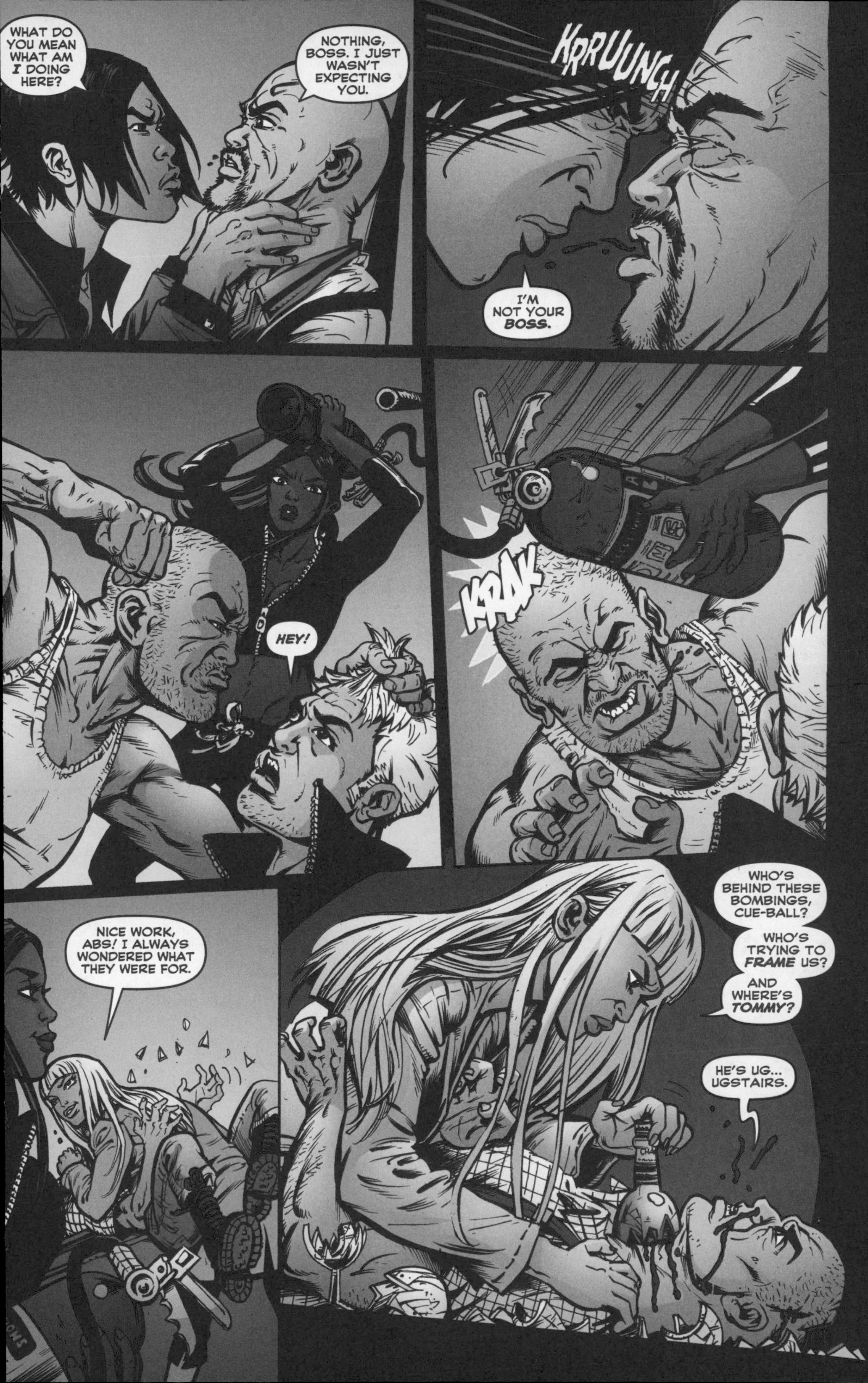
WHAT DO YOU MEAN WHAT AM I DOING HERE?
NOTHING, BOSS. I JUST WASN'T EXPECTING YOU.
KRRUUNCH
I'M NOT YOUR BOSS.
HEY!
KRAK
NICE WORK, ABS! I ALWAYS WONDERED WHAT THEY WERE FOR.
WHO'S BEHIND THESE BOMBINGS, CUE-BALL?
WHO'S TRYING TO FRAME US?
AND WHERE'S TOMMY?
HE'S UG... UGSTAIRS.

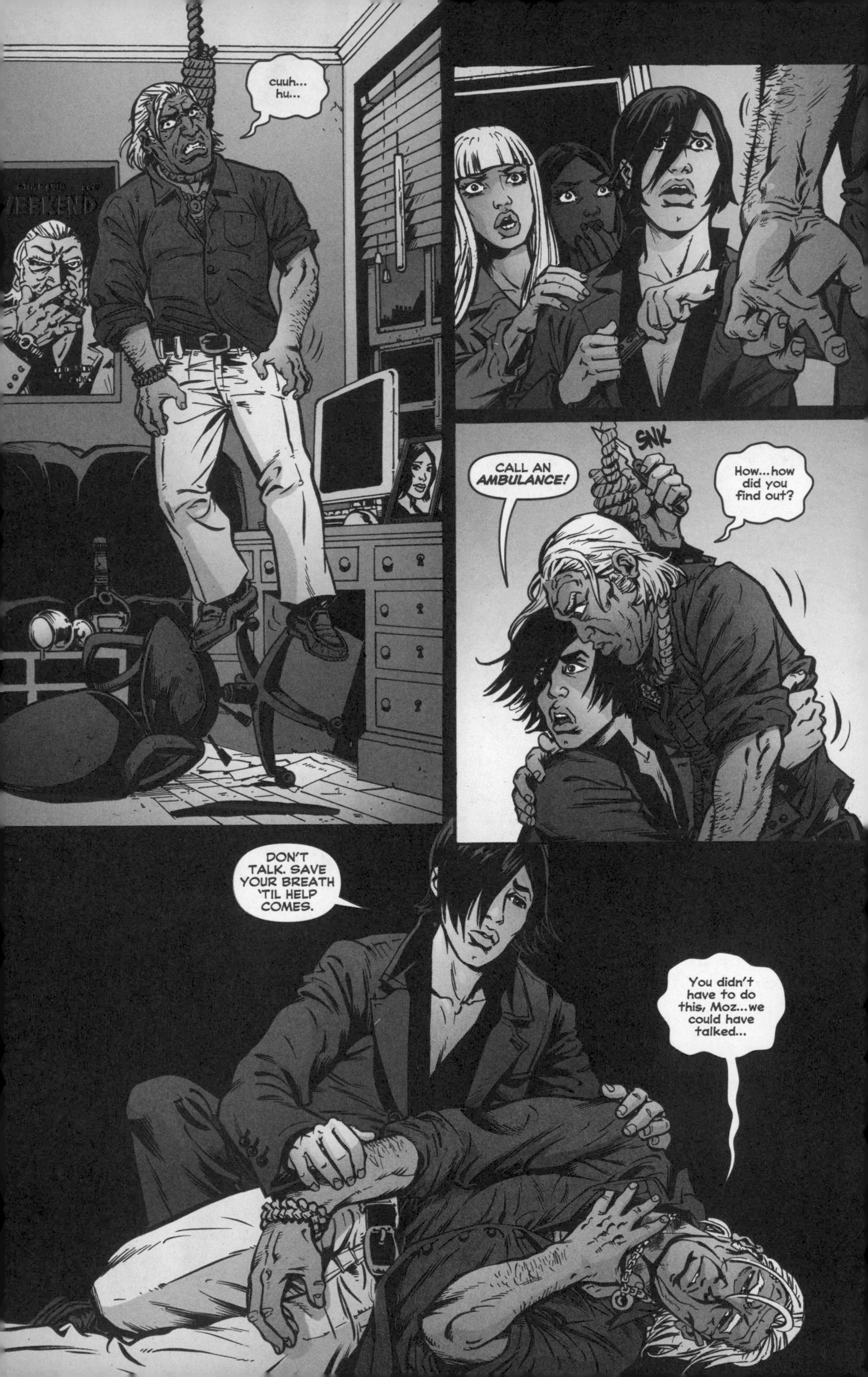
cuuh... hu...
CALL AN *AMBULANCE!*
SNK
How...how did you find out?
DON'T TALK. SAVE YOUR BREATH 'TIL HELP COMES.
You didn't have to do this, Moz...we could have talked...

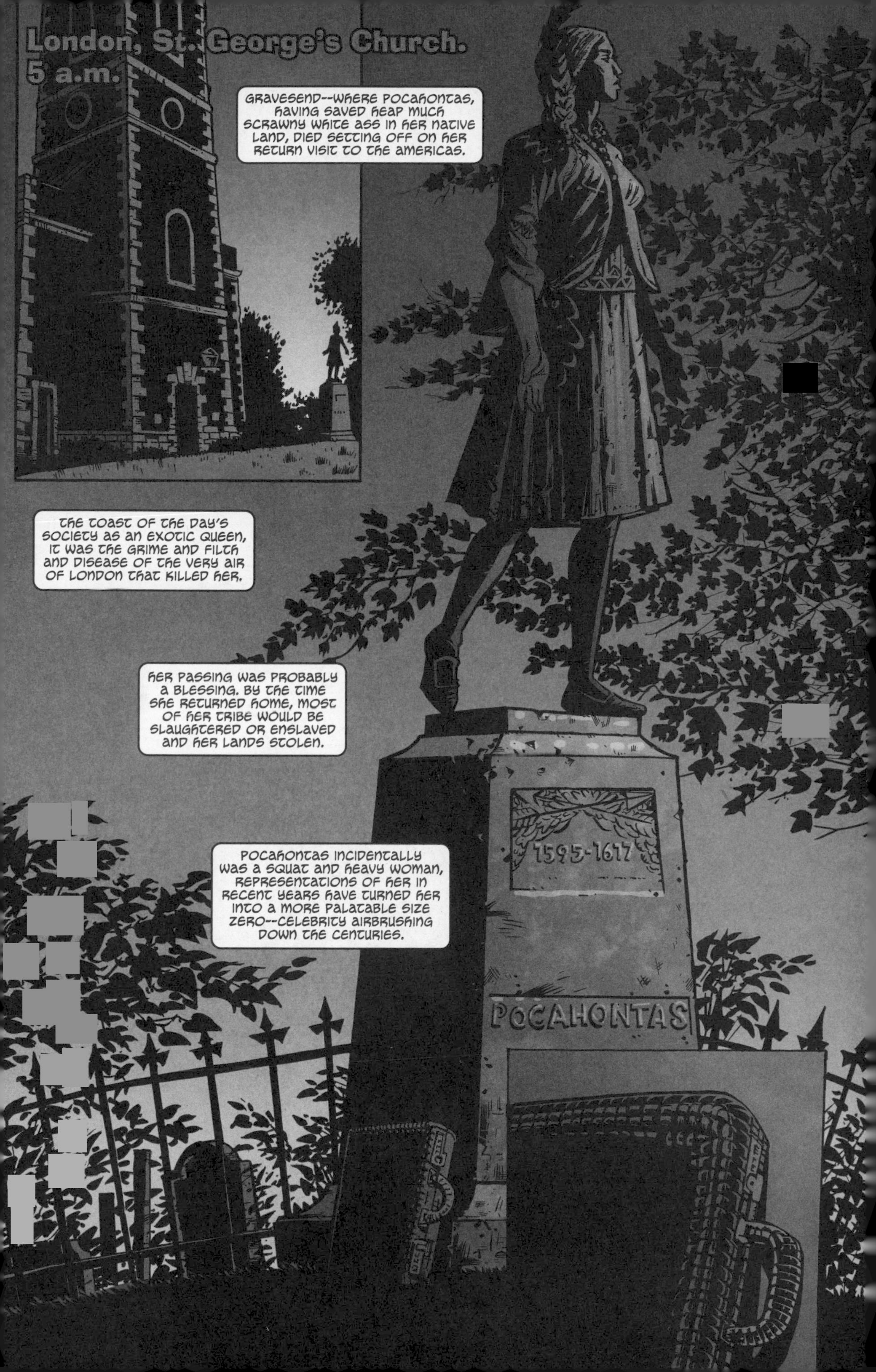
London, St. George's Church.
5 a.m.
GRAVESEND--WHERE POCAHONTAS, HAVING SAVED HEAP MUCH SCRAWNY WHITE ASS IN HER NATIVE LAND, DIED SETTING OFF ON HER RETURN VISIT TO THE AMERICAS.
THE TOAST OF THE DAY'S SOCIETY AS AN EXOTIC QUEEN, IT WAS THE GRIME AND FILTH AND DISEASE OF THE VERY AIR OF LONDON THAT KILLED HER.
HER PASSING WAS PROBABLY A BLESSING. BY THE TIME SHE RETURNED HOME, MOST OF HER TRIBE WOULD BE SLAUGHTERED OR ENSLAVED AND HER LANDS STOLEN.
POCAHONTAS INCIDENTALLY WAS A SQUAT AND HEAVY WOMAN, REPRESENTATIONS OF HER IN RECENT YEARS HAVE TURNED HER INTO A MORE PALATABLE SIZE ZERO--CELEBRITY AIRBRUSHING DOWN THE CENTURIES.
1595-1617
POCAHONTAS

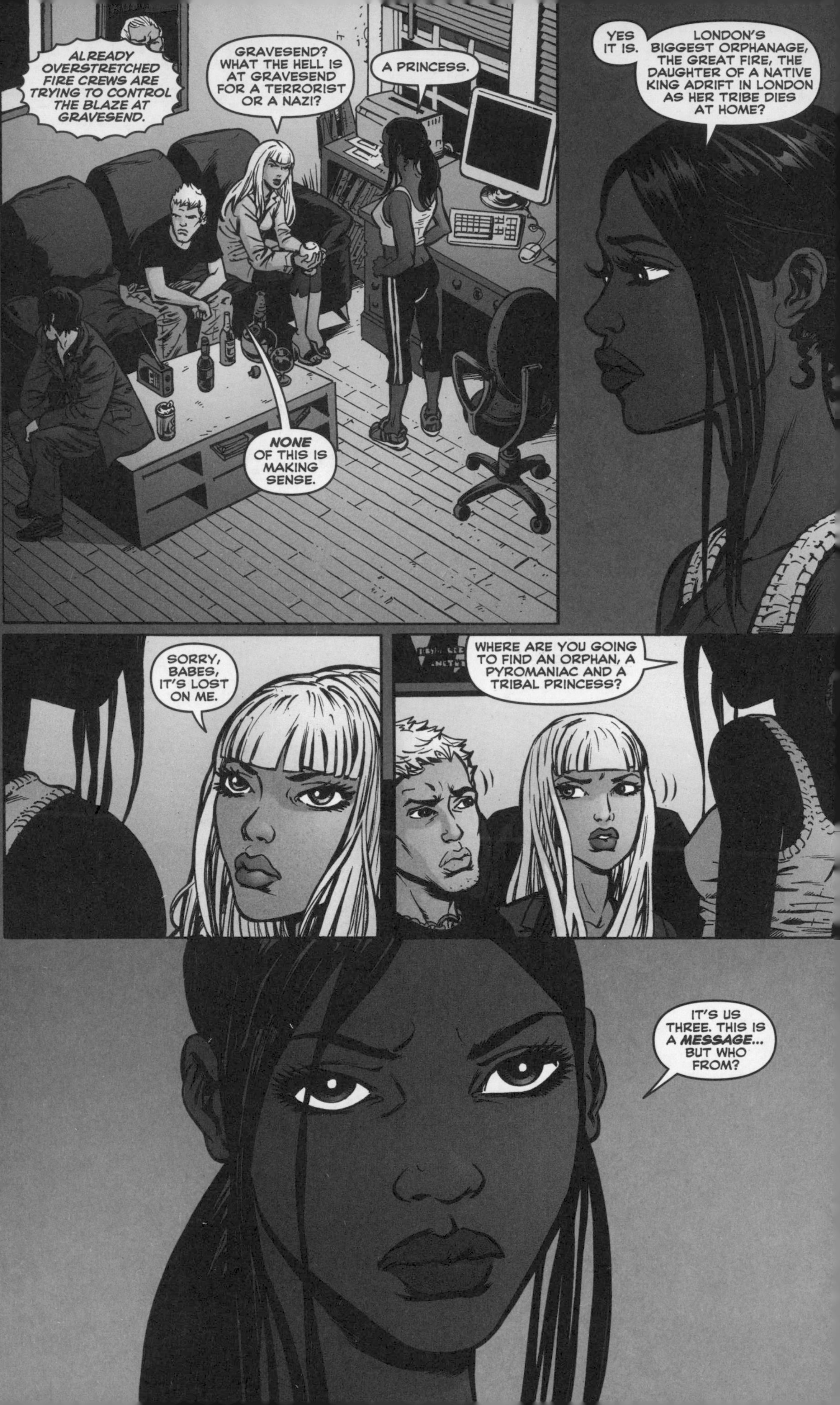

ALREADY OVERSTRETCHED FIRE CREWS ARE TRYING TO CONTROL THE BLAZE AT GRAVESEND.
GRAVESEND? WHAT THE HELL IS AT GRAVESEND FOR A TERRORIST OR A NAZI?
A PRINCESS.
NONE OF THIS IS MAKING SENSE.
YES IT IS.
LONDON'S BIGGEST ORPHANAGE, THE GREAT FIRE, THE DAUGHTER OF A NATIVE KING ADRIFT IN LONDON AS HER TRIBE DIES AT HOME?
SORRY, BABES, IT'S LOST ON ME.
WHERE ARE YOU GOING TO FIND AN ORPHAN, A PYROMANIAC AND A TRIBAL PRINCESS?
IT'S US THREE. THIS IS A MESSAGE... BUT WHO FROM?

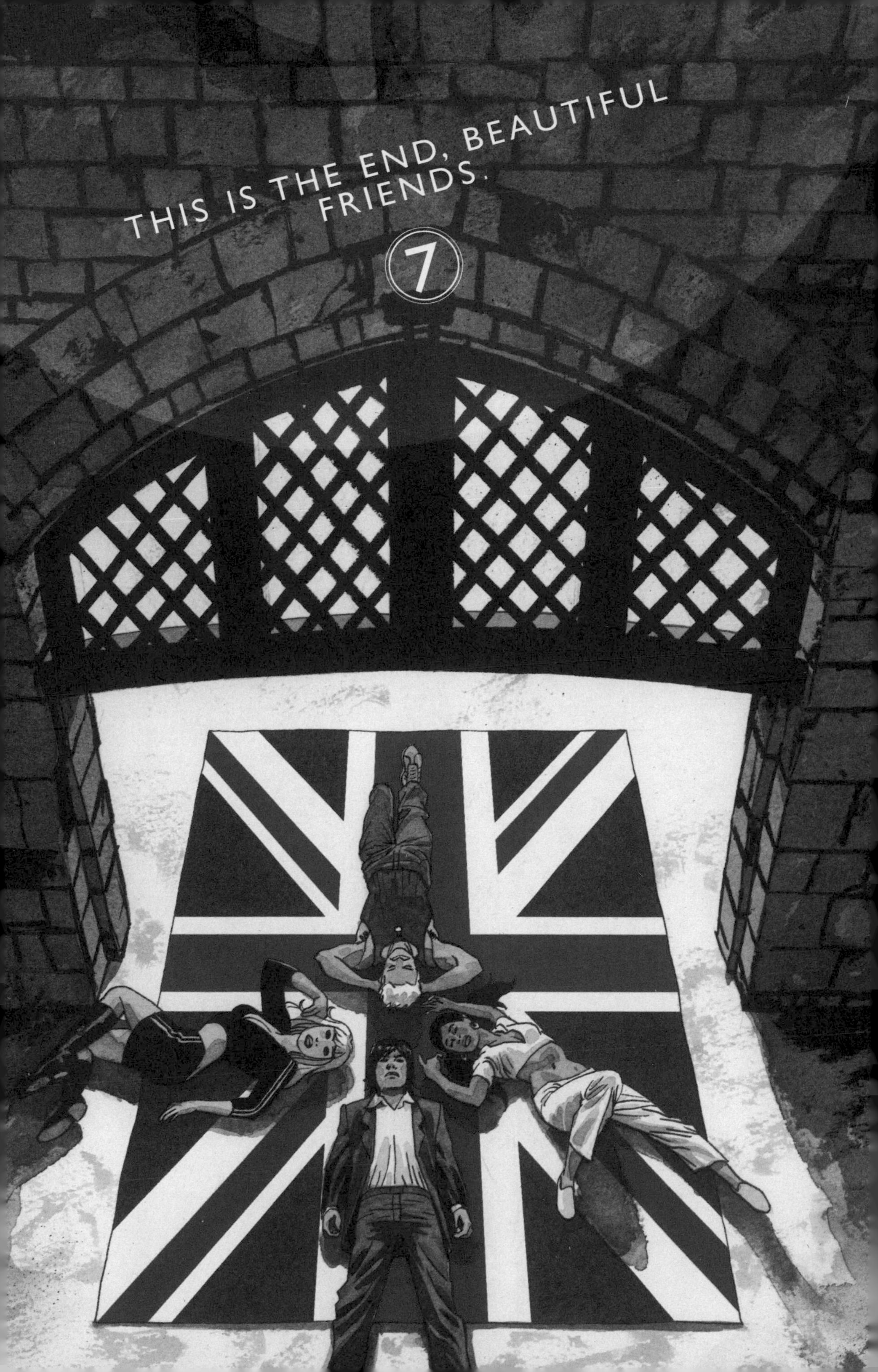
THIS IS THE END, BEAUTIFUL FRIENDS.
7

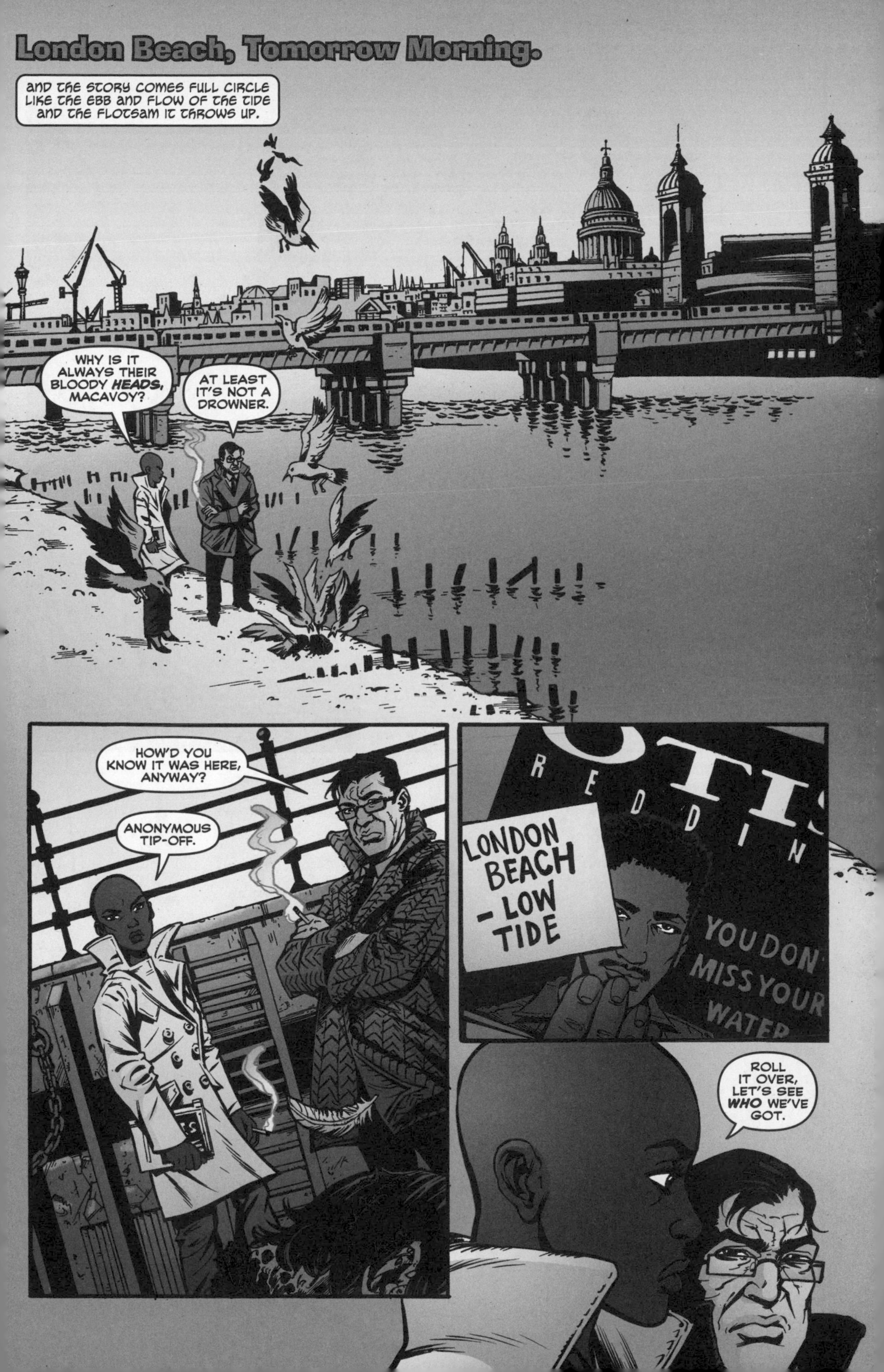
London Beach, Tomorrow Morning.
AND THE STORY COMES FULL CIRCLE LIKE THE EBB AND FLOW OF THE TIDE AND THE FLOTSAM IT THROWS UP.
WHY IS IT ALWAYS THEIR BLOODY HEADS, MACAVOY?
AT LEAST IT'S NOT A DROWNER.
HOW'D YOU KNOW IT WAS HERE, ANYWAY?
ANONYMOUS TIP-OFF.
OTIS REDDIN
LONDON BEACH - LOW TIDE
YOU DON' MISS YOUR WATER
ROLL IT OVER, LET'S SEE WHO WE'VE GOT.

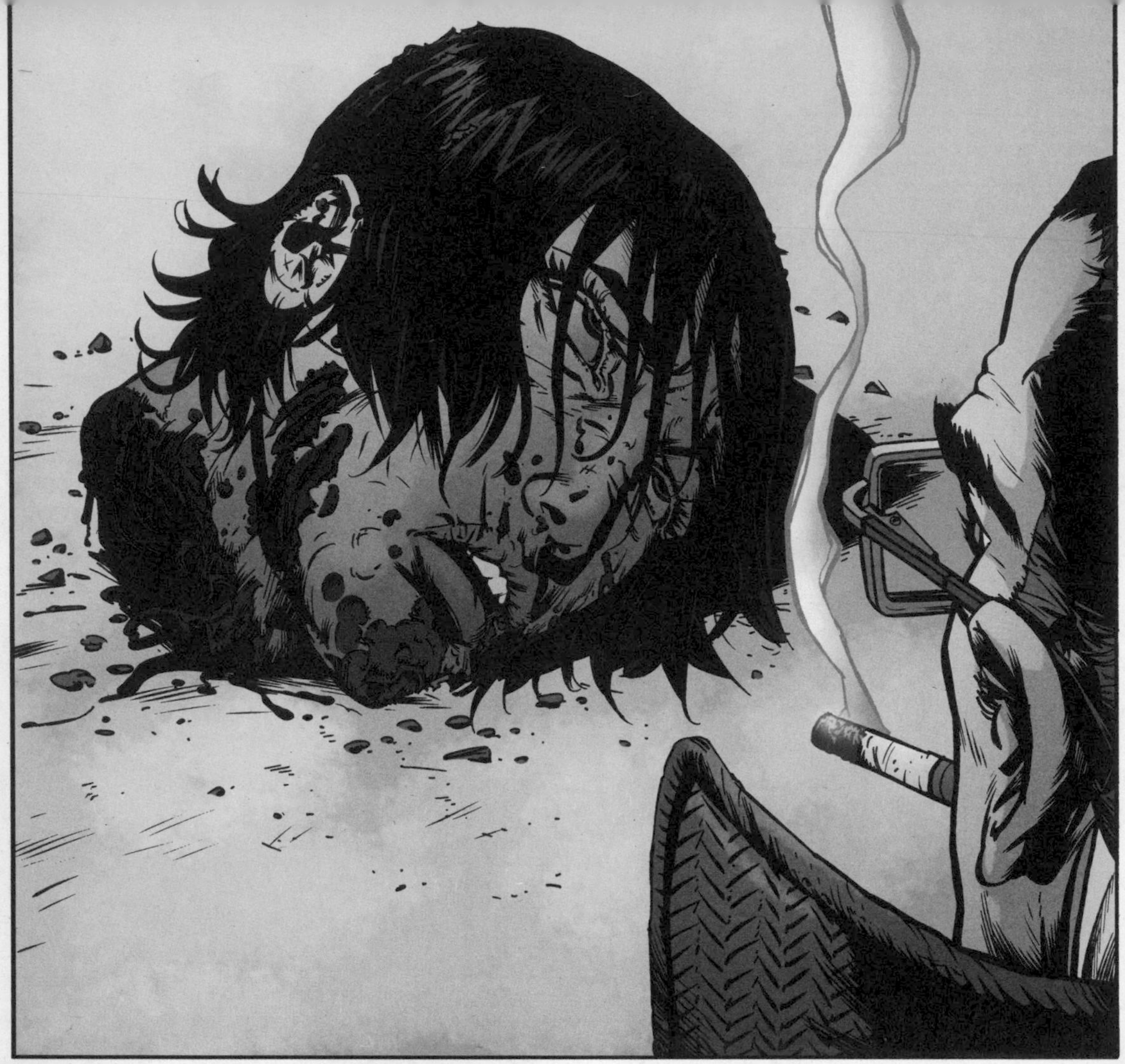

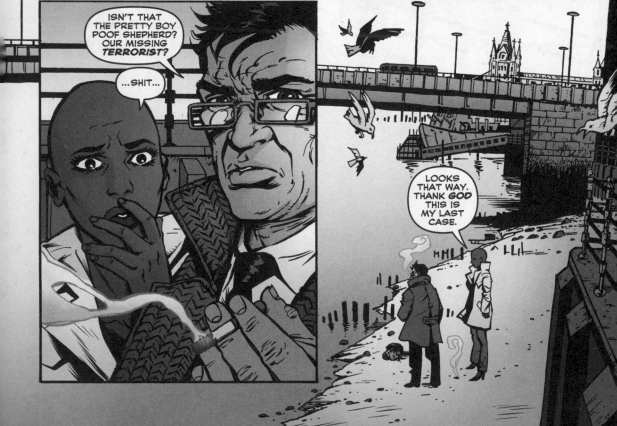

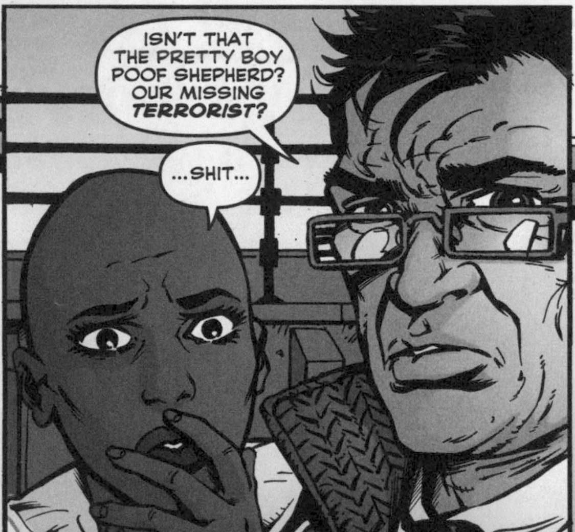
ISN'T THAT THE PRETTY BOY POOF SHEPHERD? OUR MISSING TERRORIST?
...SHIT...

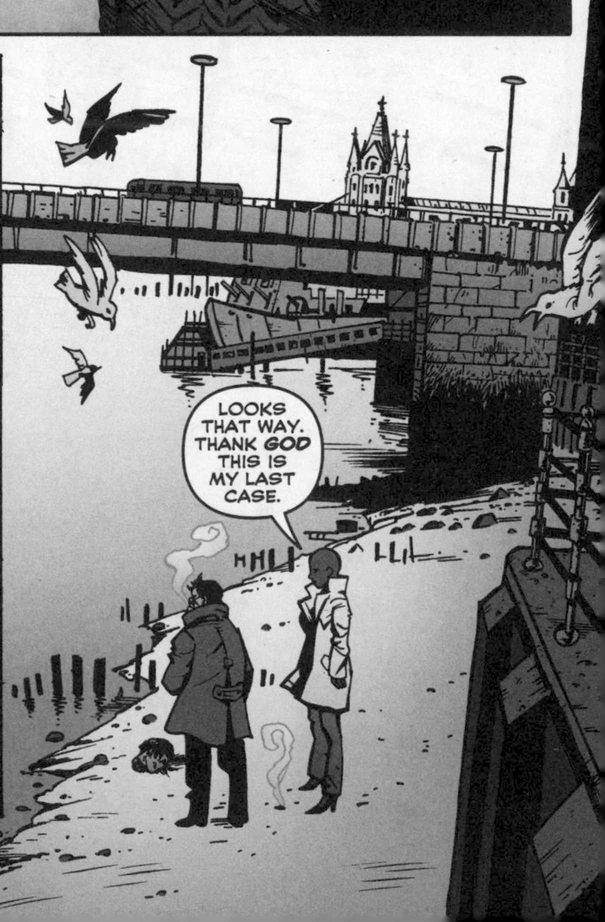
LOOKS THAT WAY. THANK GOD THIS IS MY LAST CASE.

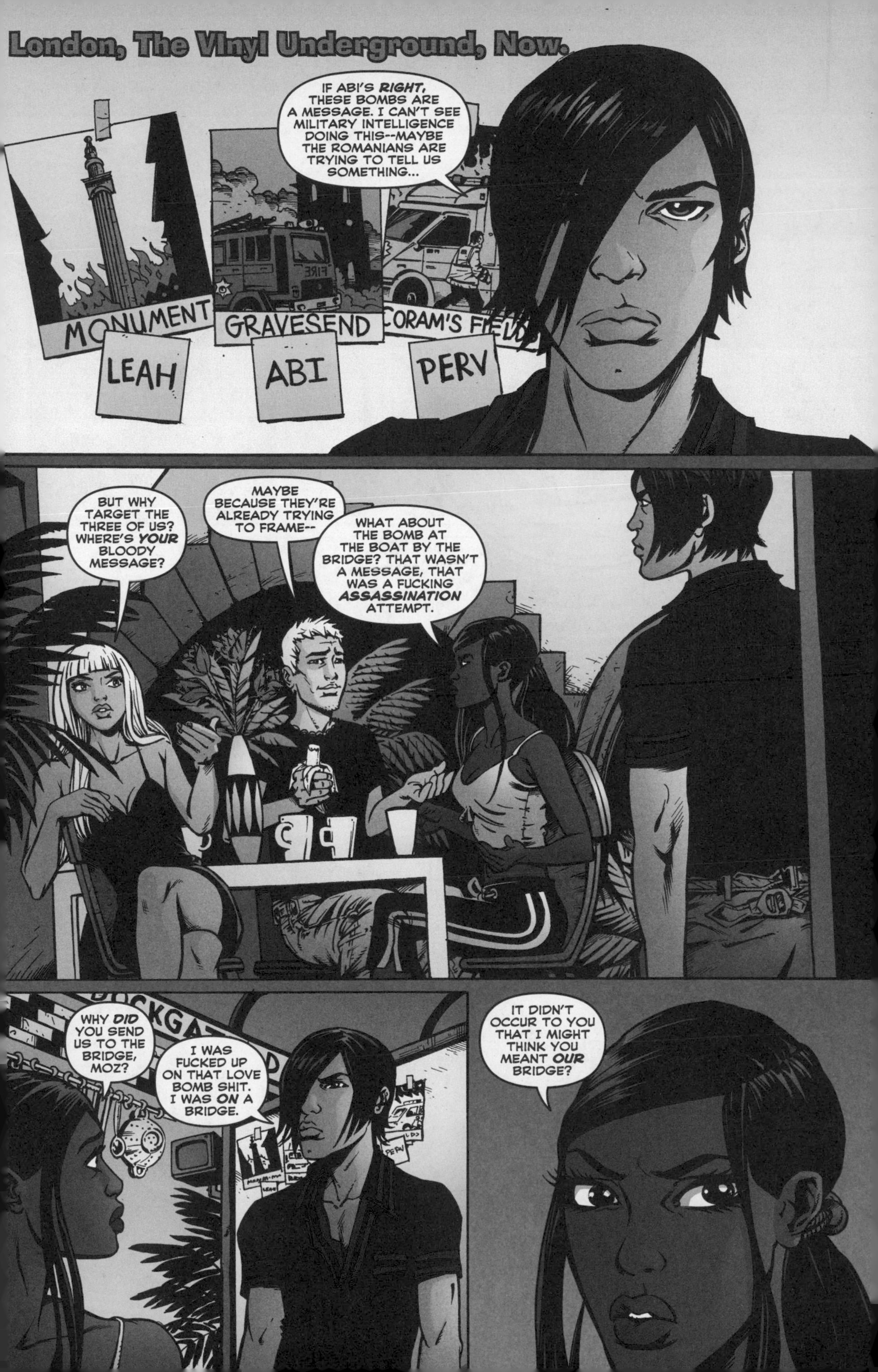
London, The Vinyl Underground, Now.
IF ABI'S RIGHT, THESE BOMBS ARE A MESSAGE. I CAN'T SEE MILITARY INTELLIGENCE DOING THIS--MAYBE THE ROMANIANS ARE TRYING TO TELL US SOMETHING...
MONUMENT
GRAVESEND
CORAM'S FIELD
LEAH
ABI
PERV
BUT WHY TARGET THE THREE OF US? WHERE'S YOUR BLOODY MESSAGE?
MAYBE BECAUSE THEY'RE ALREADY TRYING TO FRAME--
WHAT ABOUT THE BOMB AT THE BOAT BY THE BRIDGE? THAT WASN'T A MESSAGE, THAT WAS A FUCKING ASSASSINATION ATTEMPT.
WHY DID YOU SEND US TO THE BRIDGE, MOZ?
I WAS FUCKED UP ON THAT LOVE BOMB SHIT. I WAS ON A BRIDGE.
IT DIDN'T OCCUR TO YOU THAT I MIGHT THINK YOU MEANT OUR BRIDGE?

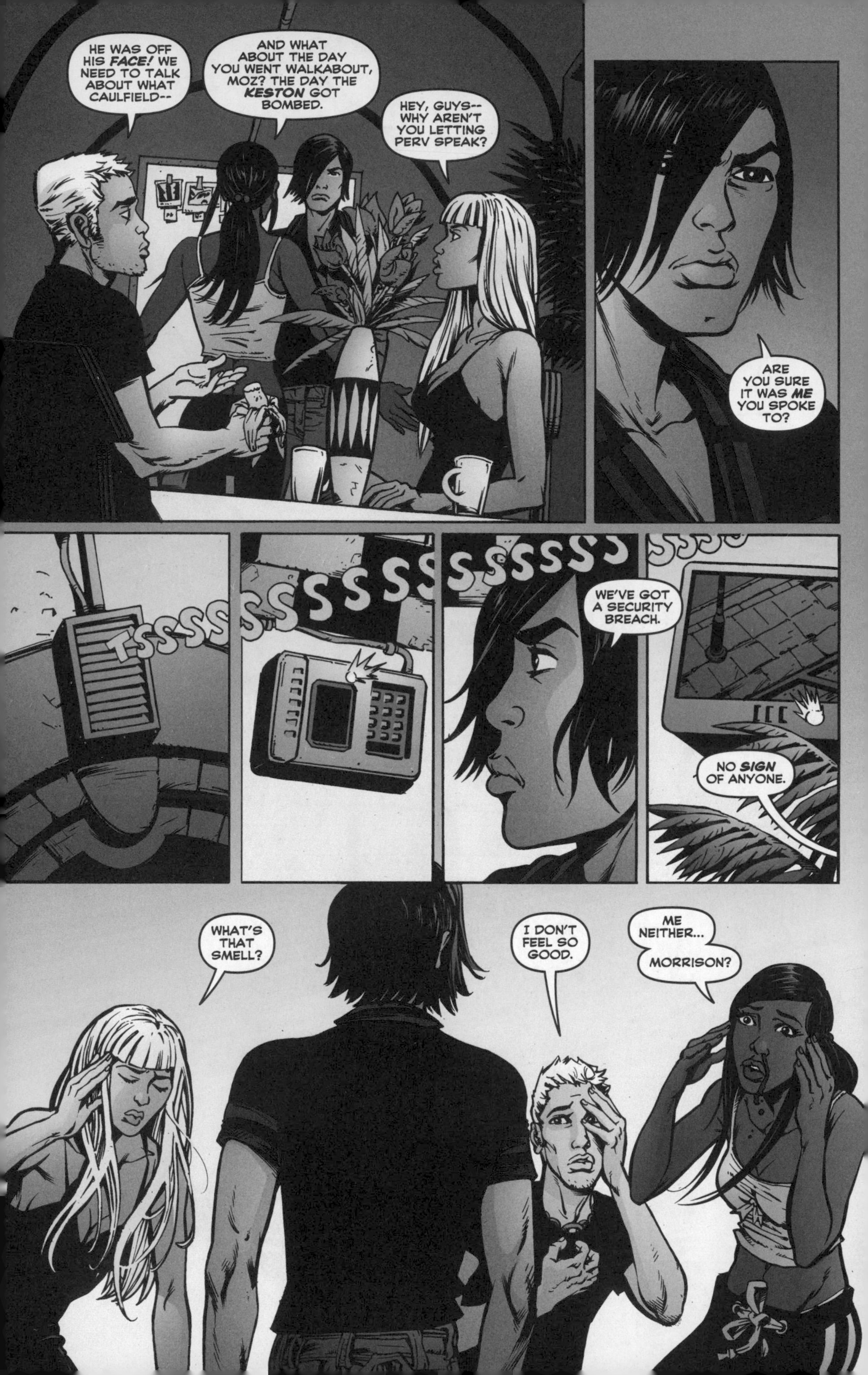
HE WAS OFF HIS FACE! WE NEED TO TALK ABOUT WHAT CAULFIELD--
AND WHAT ABOUT THE DAY YOU WENT WALKABOUT, MOZ? THE DAY THE KESTON GOT BOMBED.
HEY, GUYS-- WHY AREN'T YOU LETTING PERV SPEAK?
ARE YOU SURE IT WAS ME YOU SPOKE TO?
TSSSSSSSSSSSSSSSSSS
WE'VE GOT A SECURITY BREACH.
NO SIGN OF ANYONE.
WHAT'S THAT SMELL?
I DON'T FEEL SO GOOD.
ME NEITHER...
MORRISON?

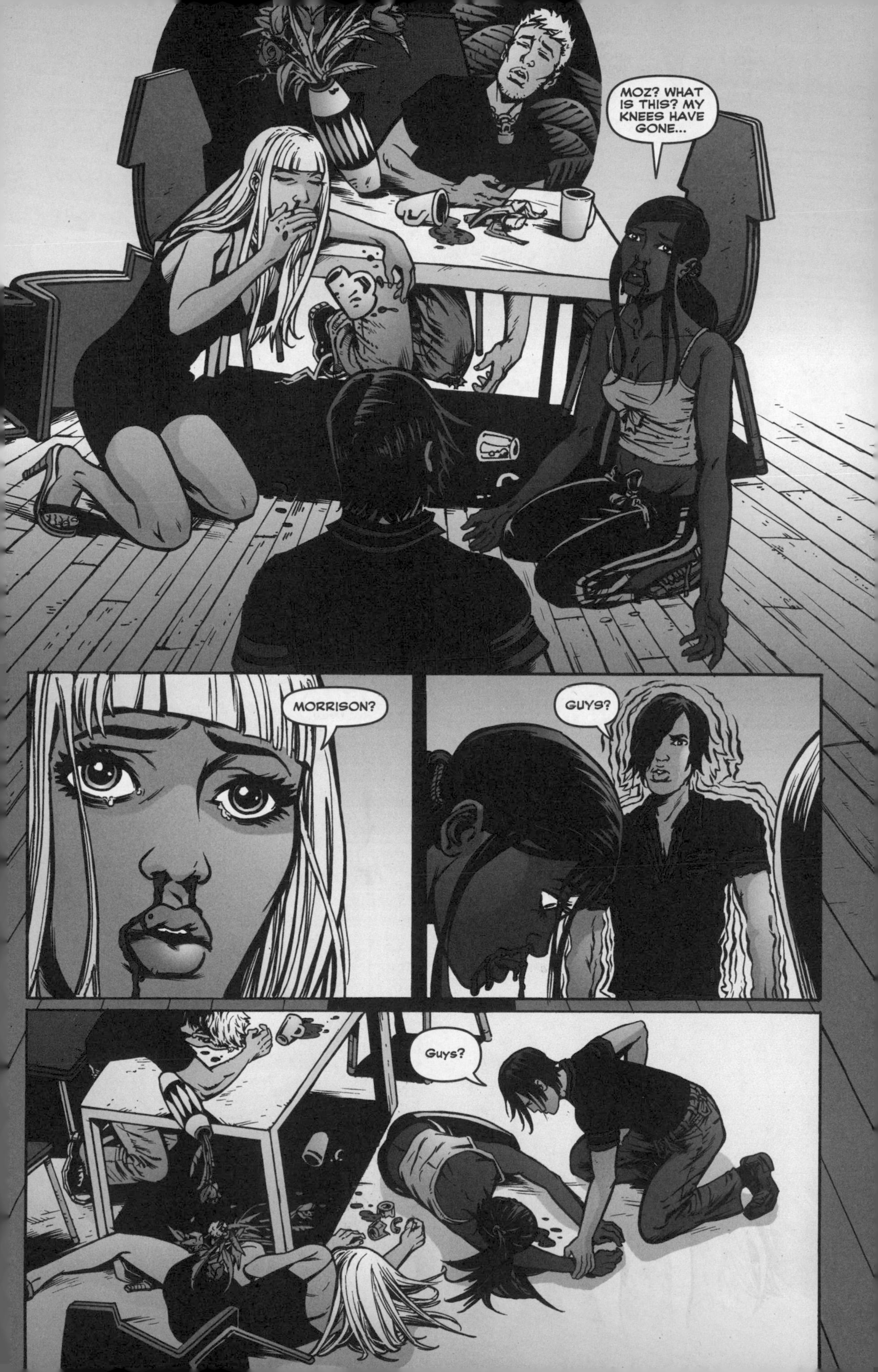
MOZ? WHAT IS THIS? MY KNEES HAVE GONE...
MORRISON?
GUYS?
Guys?

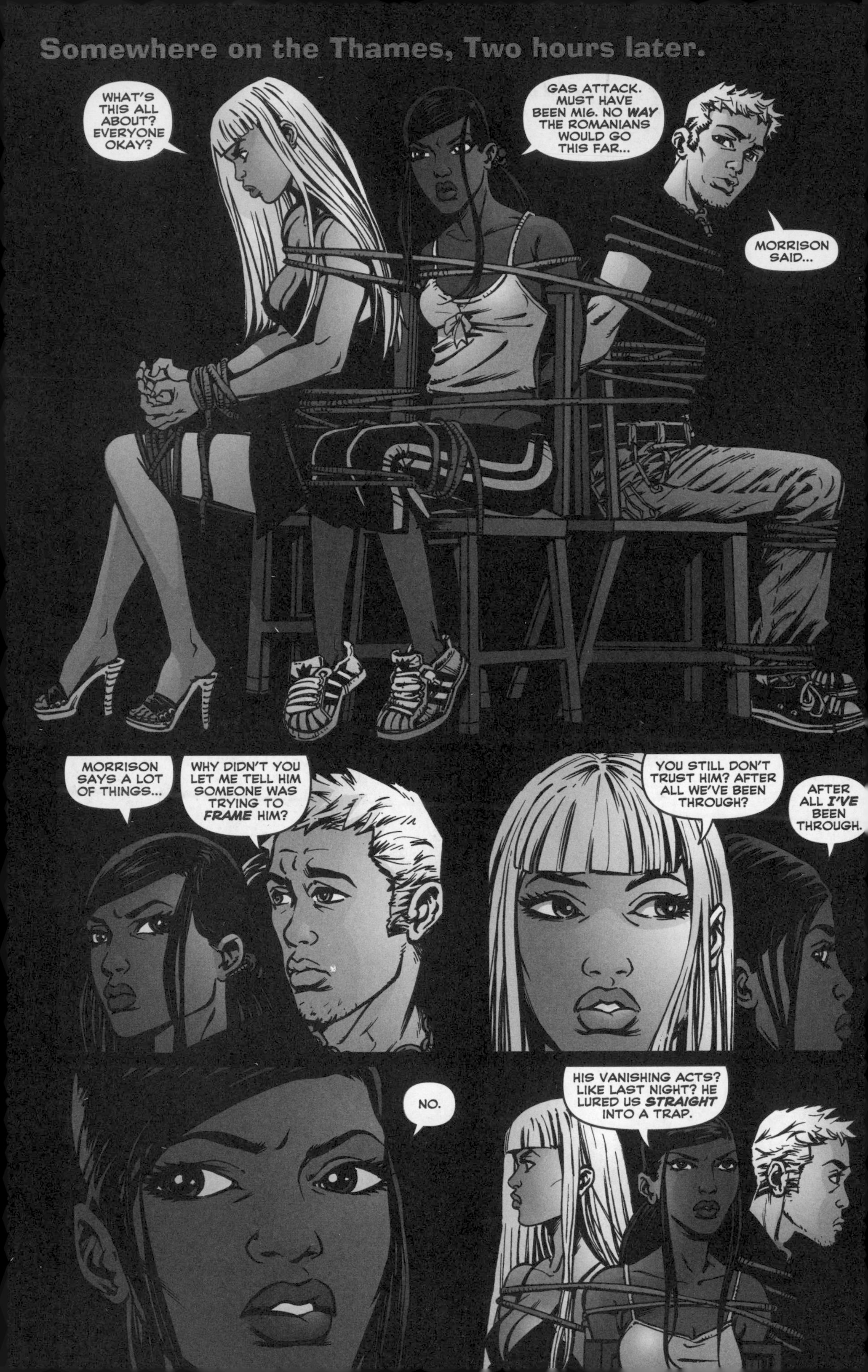
Somewhere on the Thames, Two hours later.
WHAT'S THIS ALL ABOUT? EVERYONE OKAY?
GAS ATTACK. MUST HAVE BEEN MI6. NO WAY THE ROMANIANS WOULD GO THIS FAR...
MORRISON SAID...
MORRISON SAYS A LOT OF THINGS...
WHY DIDN'T YOU LET ME TELL HIM SOMEONE WAS TRYING TO FRAME HIM?
YOU STILL DON'T TRUST HIM? AFTER ALL WE'VE BEEN THROUGH?
AFTER ALL I'VE BEEN THROUGH.
NO.
HIS VANISHING ACTS? LIKE LAST NIGHT? HE LURED US STRAIGHT INTO A TRAP.

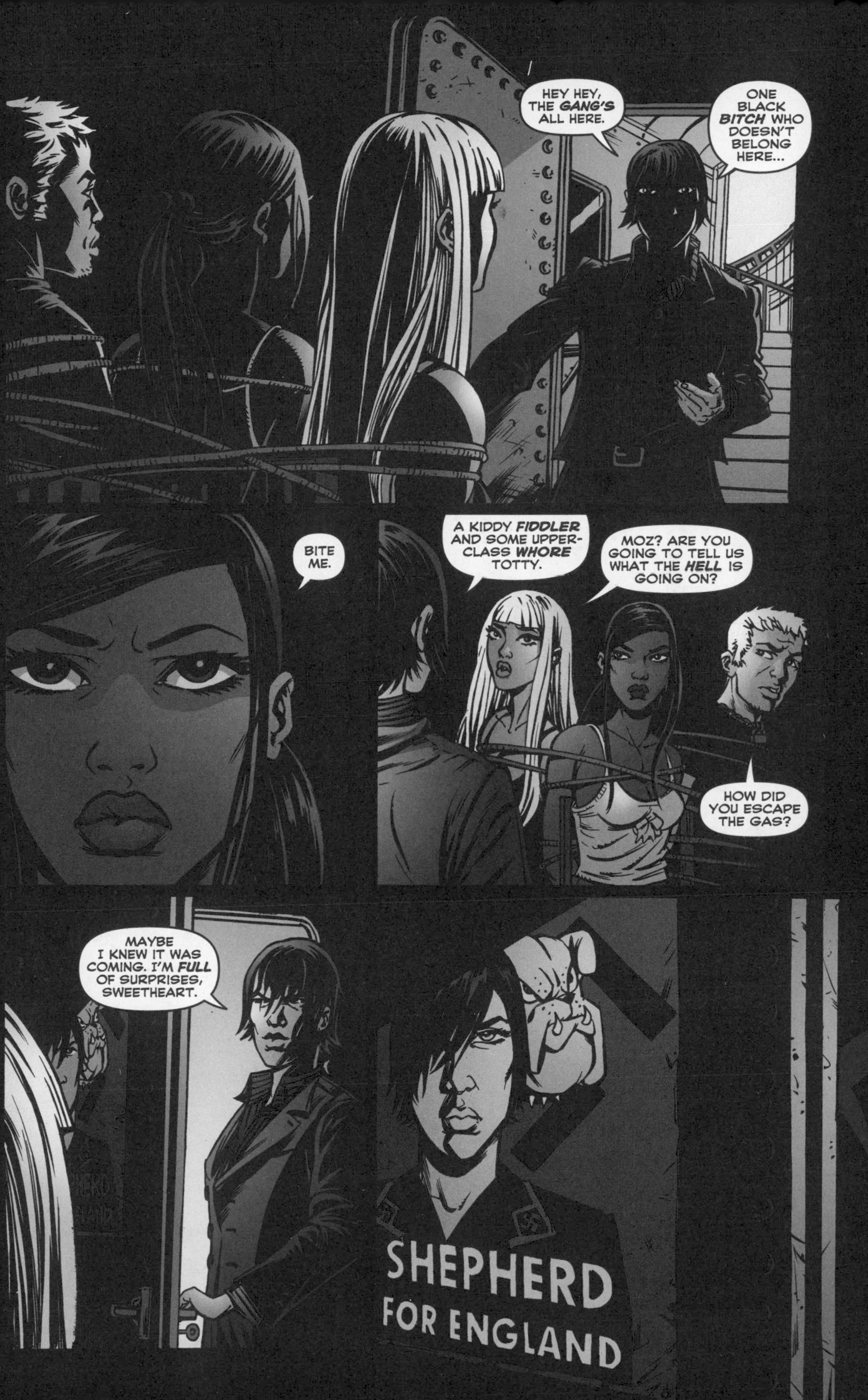
HEY HEY, THE GANG'S ALL HERE.
ONE BLACK BITCH WHO DOESN'T BELONG HERE...
BITE ME.
A KIDDY FIDDLER AND SOME UPPER-CLASS WHORE TOTTY.
MOZ? ARE YOU GOING TO TELL US WHAT THE HELL IS GOING ON?
HOW DID YOU ESCAPE THE GAS?
MAYBE I KNEW IT WAS COMING. I'M FULL OF SURPRISES, SWEETHEART.
SHEPHERD
FOR ENGLAND

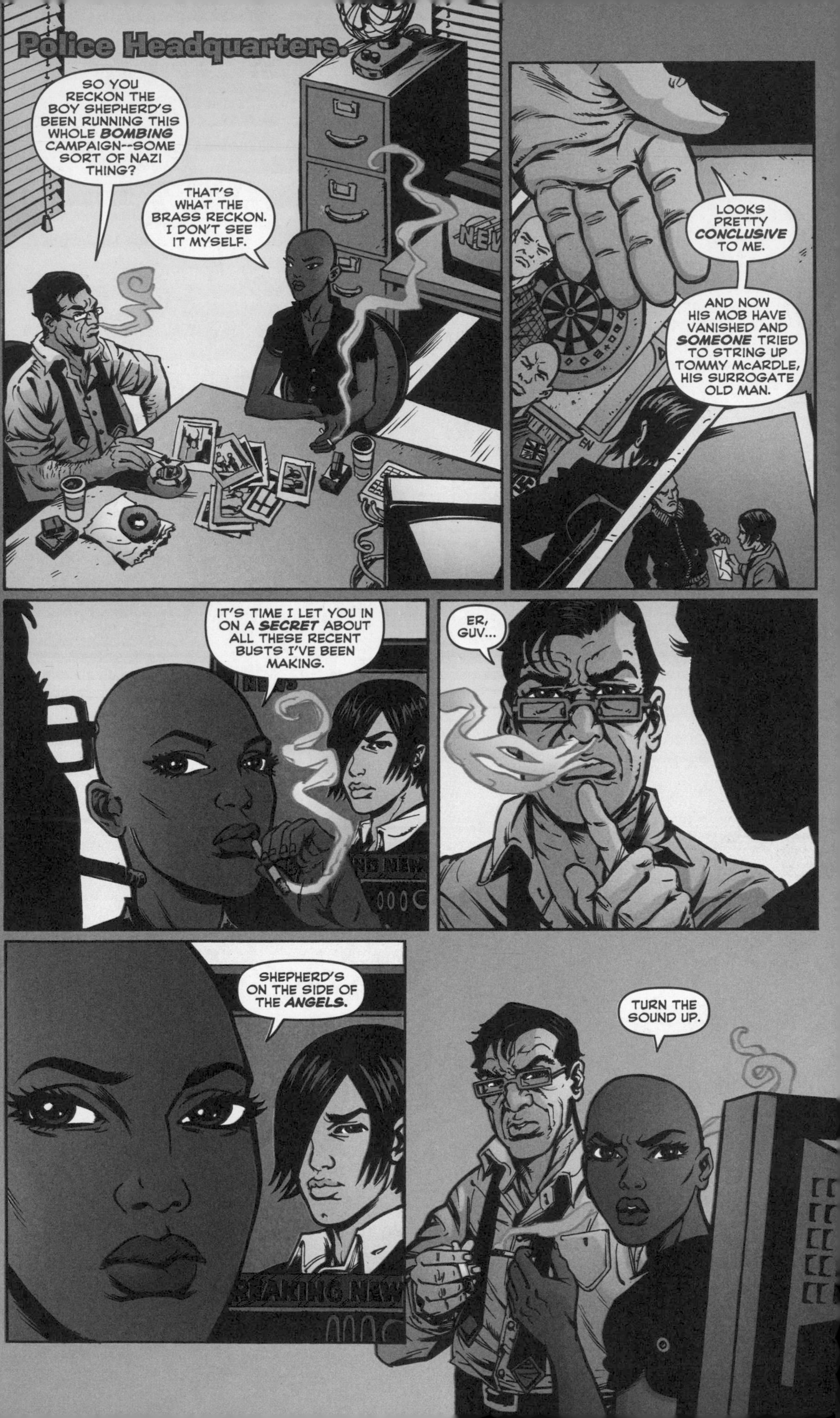
Police Headquarters.
SO YOU RECKON THE BOY SHEPHERD'S BEEN RUNNING THIS WHOLE BOMBING CAMPAIGN--SOME SORT OF NAZI THING?
THAT'S WHAT THE BRASS RECKON. I DON'T SEE IT MYSELF.
LOOKS PRETTY CONCLUSIVE TO ME.
AND NOW HIS MOB HAVE VANISHED AND SOMEONE TRIED TO STRING UP TOMMY McARDLE, HIS SURROGATE OLD MAN.
IT'S TIME I LET YOU IN ON A SECRET ABOUT ALL THESE RECENT BUSTS I'VE BEEN MAKING.
ER, GUV...
SHEPHERD'S ON THE SIDE OF THE ANGELS.
TURN THE SOUND UP.

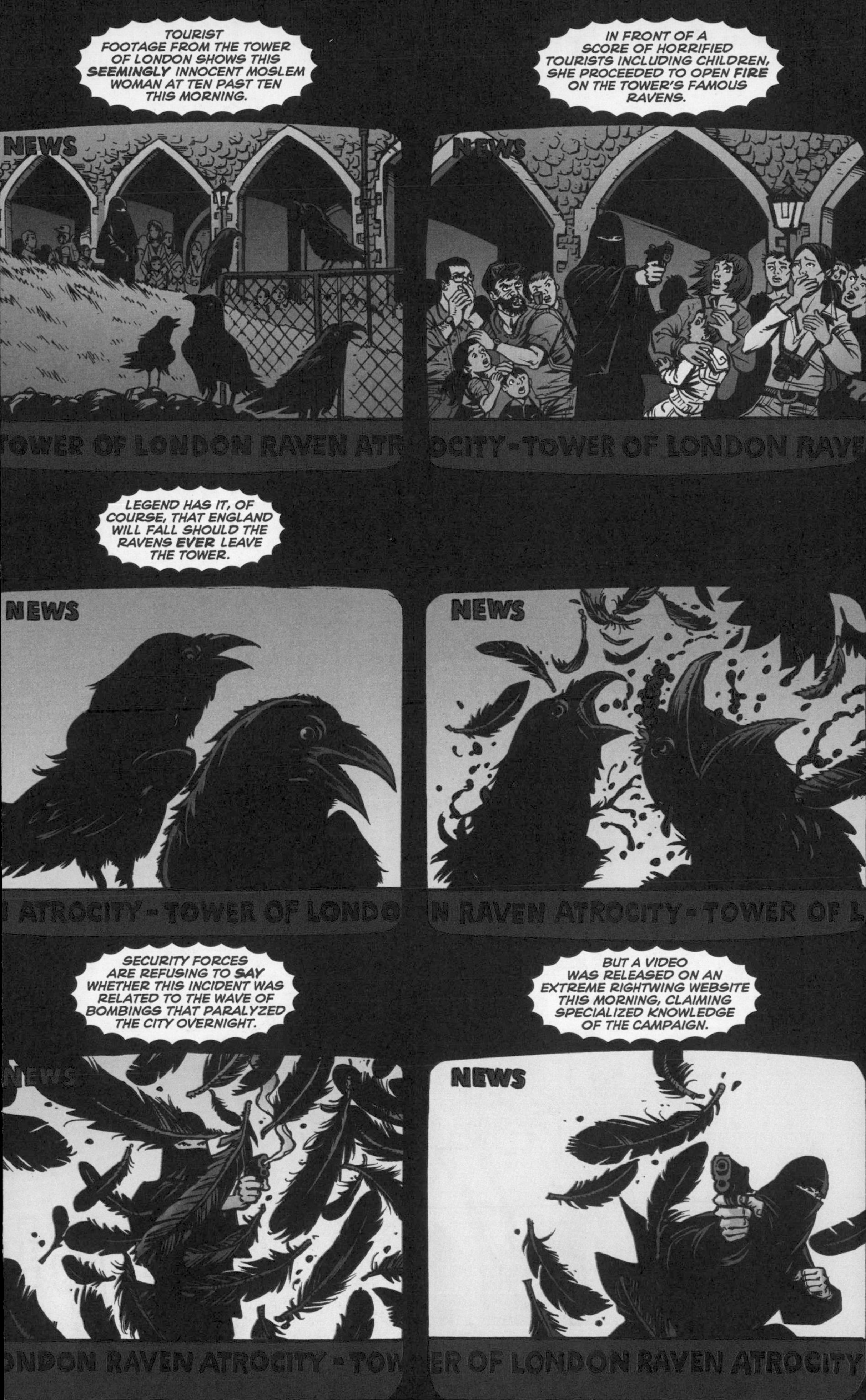
TOURIST FOOTAGE FROM THE TOWER OF LONDON SHOWS THIS SEEMINGLY INNOCENT MOSLEM WOMAN AT TEN PAST TEN THIS MORNING.
NEWS
TOWER OF LONDON RAVEN ATR
IN FRONT OF A SCORE OF HORRIFIED TOURISTS INCLUDING CHILDREN, SHE PROCEEDED TO OPEN FIRE ON THE TOWER'S FAMOUS RAVENS.
NEWS
OCITY - TOWER OF LONDON RAVE
LEGEND HAS IT, OF COURSE, THAT ENGLAND WILL FALL SHOULD THE RAVENS EVER LEAVE THE TOWER.
NEWS
N ATROCITY - TOWER OF LONDO
NEWS
N RAVEN ATROCITY - TOWER OF
SECURITY FORCES ARE REFUSING TO SAY WHETHER THIS INCIDENT WAS RELATED TO THE WAVE OF BOMBINGS THAT PARALYZED THE CITY OVERNIGHT.
NDON RAVEN ATROCITY - TOW
BUT A VIDEO WAS RELEASED ON AN EXTREME RIGHTWING WEBSITE THIS MORNING, CLAIMING SPECIALIZED KNOWLEDGE OF THE CAMPAIGN.
NEWS
ER OF LONDON RAVEN ATROCITY

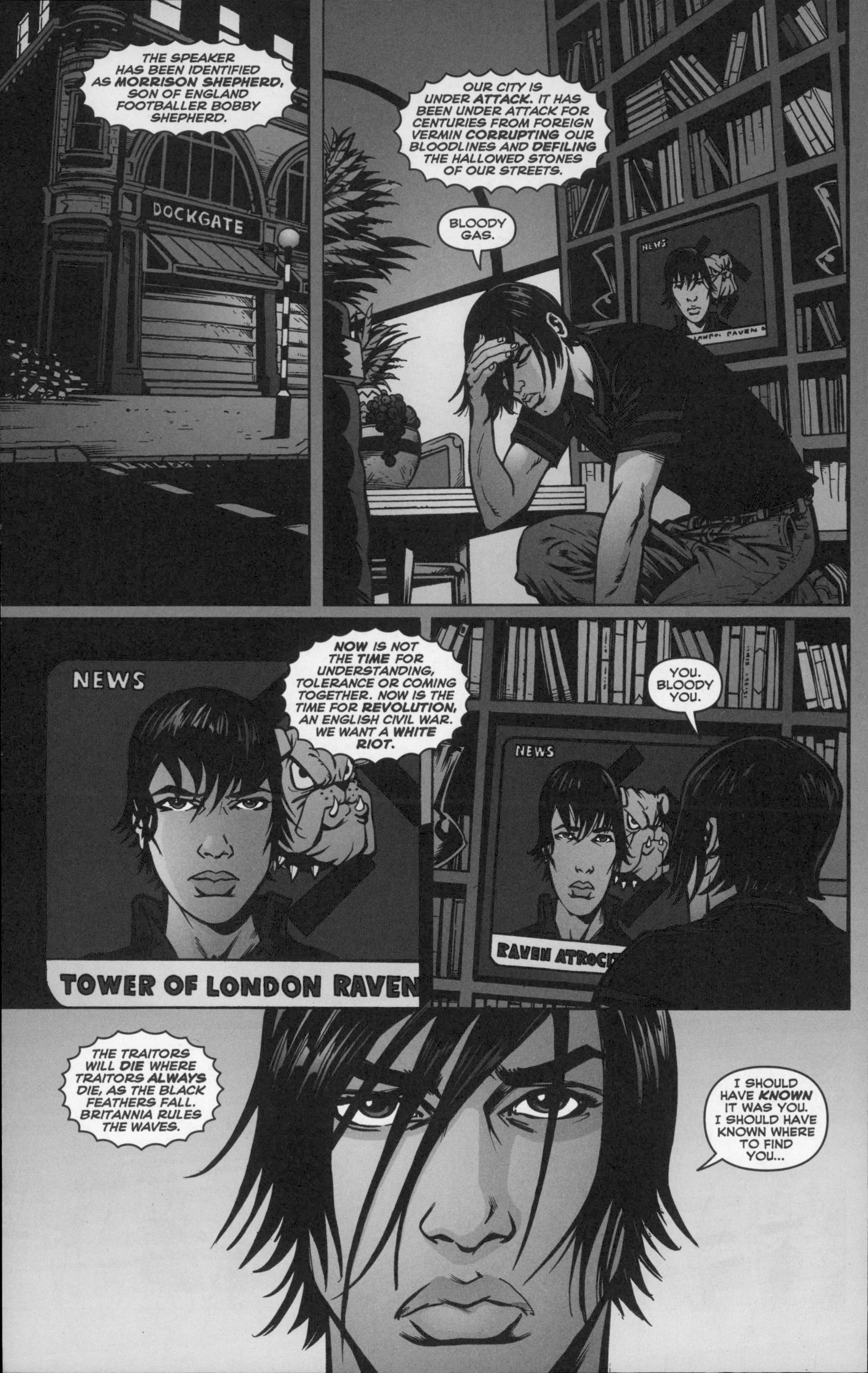

THE SPEAKER HAS BEEN IDENTIFIED AS MORRISON SHEPHERD, SON OF ENGLAND FOOTBALLER BOBBY SHEPHERD.
DOCKGATE
OUR CITY IS UNDER ATTACK. IT HAS BEEN UNDER ATTACK FOR CENTURIES FROM FOREIGN VERMIN CORRUPTING OUR BLOODLINES AND DEFILING THE HALLOWED STONES OF OUR STREETS.
BLOODY GAS.
NEWS
NOW IS NOT THE TIME FOR UNDERSTANDING, TOLERANCE OR COMING TOGETHER. NOW IS THE TIME FOR REVOLUTION, AN ENGLISH CIVIL WAR. WE WANT A WHITE RIOT.
NEWS
TOWER OF LONDON RAVEN
YOU. BLOODY YOU.
NEWS
RAVEN ATROCI
THE TRAITORS WILL DIE WHERE TRAITORS ALWAYS DIE, AS THE BLACK FEATHERS FALL. BRITANNIA RULES THE WAVES.
I SHOULD HAVE KNOWN IT WAS YOU. I SHOULD HAVE KNOWN WHERE TO FIND YOU...

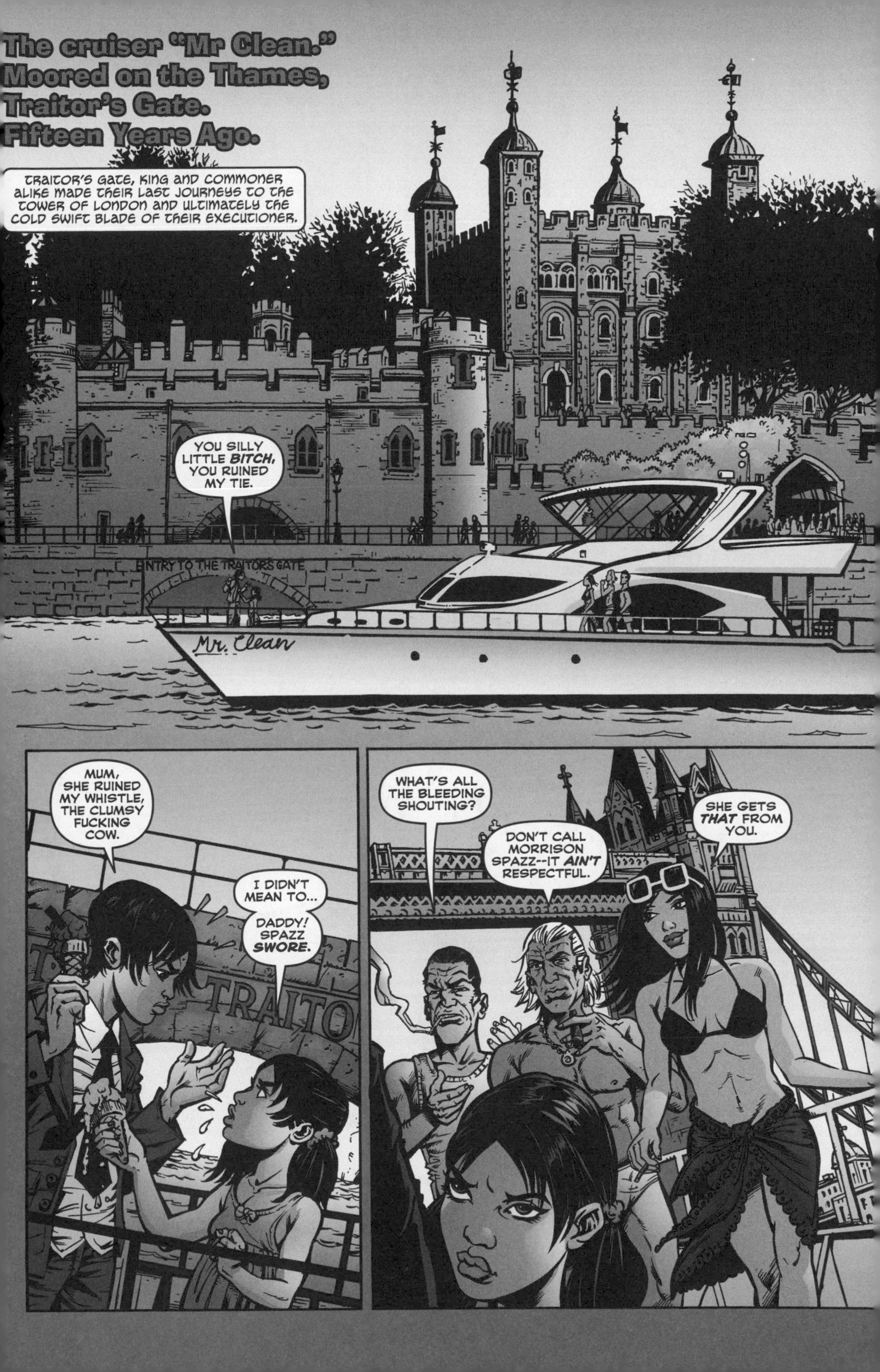
The cruiser "Mr Clean." Moored on the Thames, Traitor's Gate. Fifteen Years Ago.
TRAITOR'S GATE, KING AND COMMONER ALIKE MADE THEIR LAST JOURNEYS TO THE TOWER OF LONDON AND ULTIMATELY THE COLD SWIFT BLADE OF THEIR EXECUTIONER.
YOU SILLY LITTLE BITCH, YOU RUINED MY TIE.
ENTRY TO THE TRAITORS GATE
Mr. Clean
MUM, SHE RUINED MY WHISTLE, THE CLUMSY FUCKING COW.
I DIDN'T MEAN TO...
DADDY! SPAZZ SWORE.
TRAITO
WHAT'S ALL THE BLEEDING SHOUTING?
DON'T CALL MORRISON SPAZZ--IT AIN'T RESPECTFUL.
SHE GETS THAT FROM YOU.

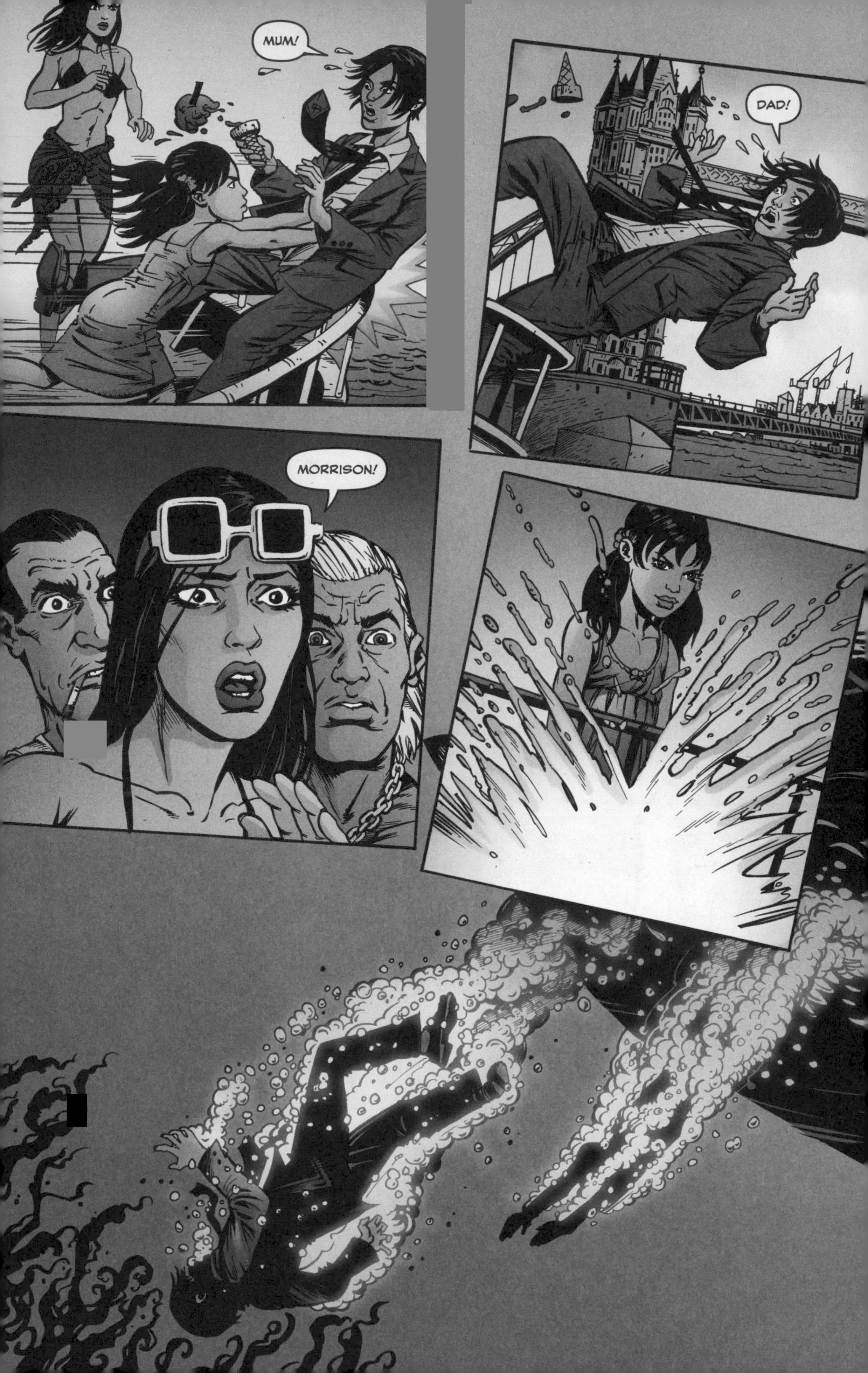
MUM!
DAD!
MORRISON!

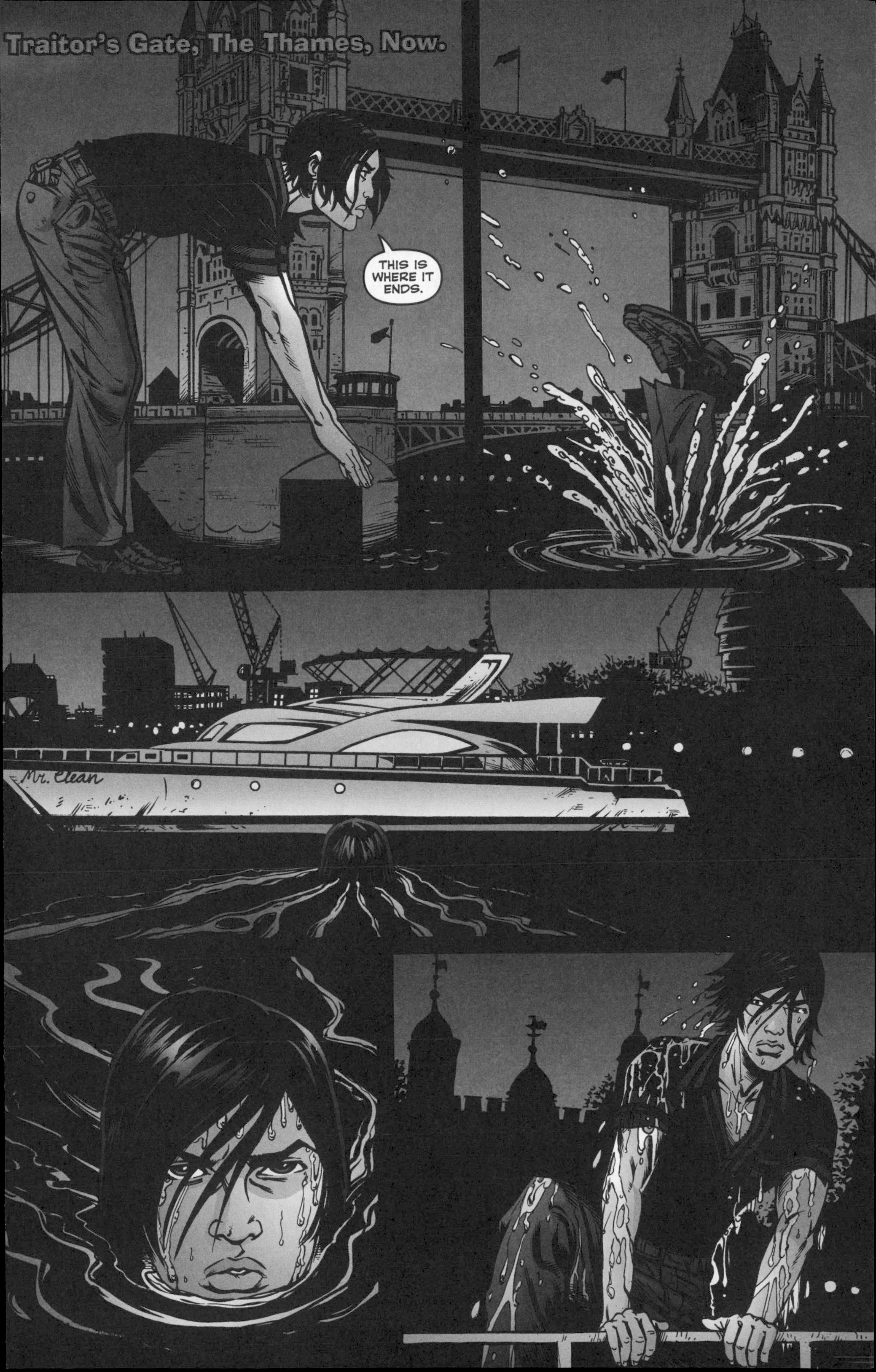
Traitor's Gate, The Thames, Now.
THIS IS WHERE IT ENDS.
Mr. Clean

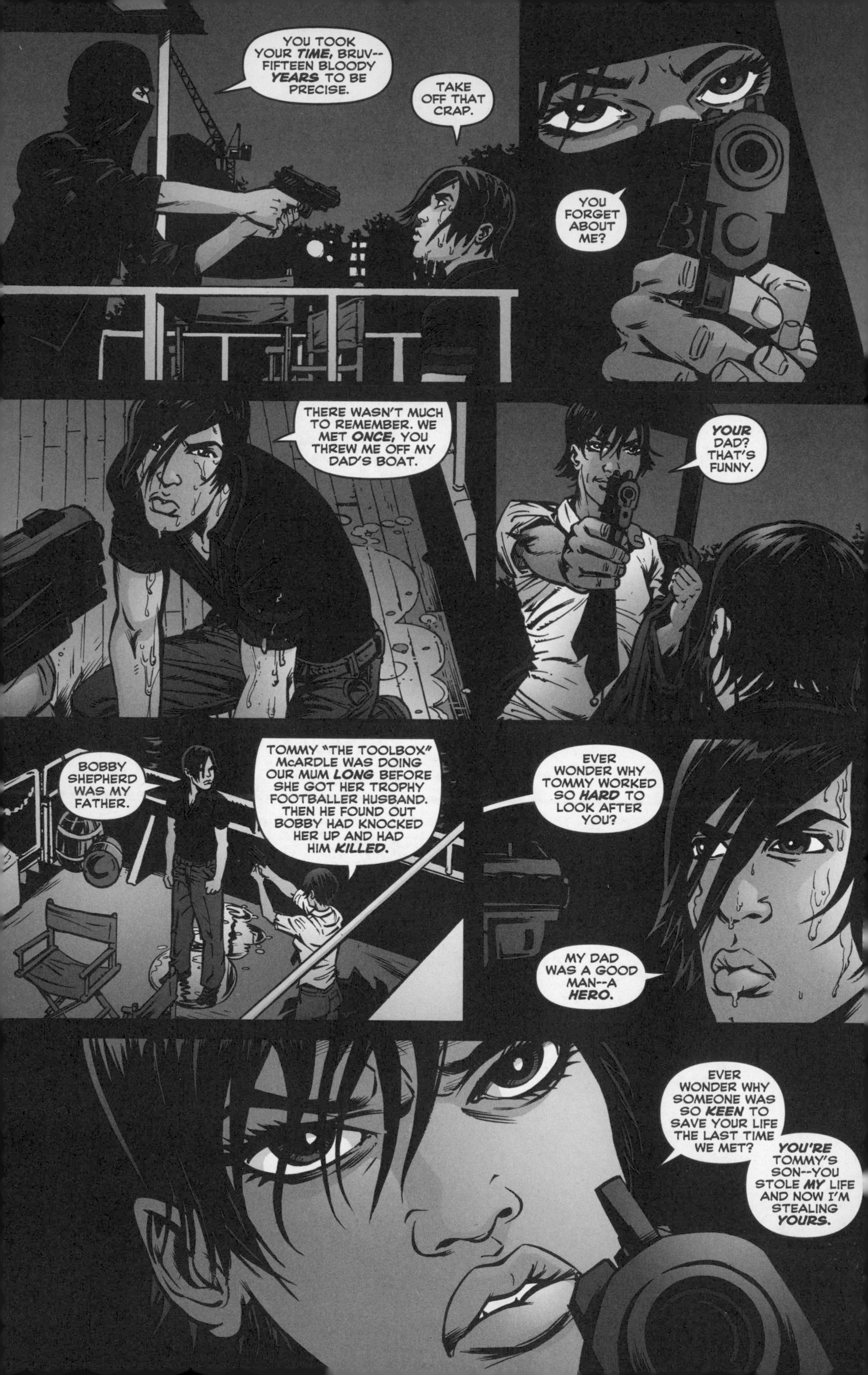
YOU TOOK YOUR TIME, BRUV-- FIFTEEN BLOODY YEARS TO BE PRECISE.
TAKE OFF THAT CRAP.
YOU FORGET ABOUT ME?
THERE WASN'T MUCH TO REMEMBER. WE MET ONCE, YOU THREW ME OFF MY DAD'S BOAT.
YOUR DAD? THAT'S FUNNY.
BOBBY SHEPHERD WAS MY FATHER.
TOMMY "THE TOOLBOX" McARDLE WAS DOING OUR MUM LONG BEFORE SHE GOT HER TROPHY FOOTBALLER HUSBAND. THEN HE FOUND OUT BOBBY HAD KNOCKED HER UP AND HAD HIM KILLED.
EVER WONDER WHY TOMMY WORKED SO HARD TO LOOK AFTER YOU?
MY DAD WAS A GOOD MAN--A HERO.
EVER WONDER WHY SOMEONE WAS SO KEEN TO SAVE YOUR LIFE THE LAST TIME WE MET?
YOU'RE TOMMY'S SON--YOU STOLE MY LIFE AND NOW I'M STEALING YOURS.

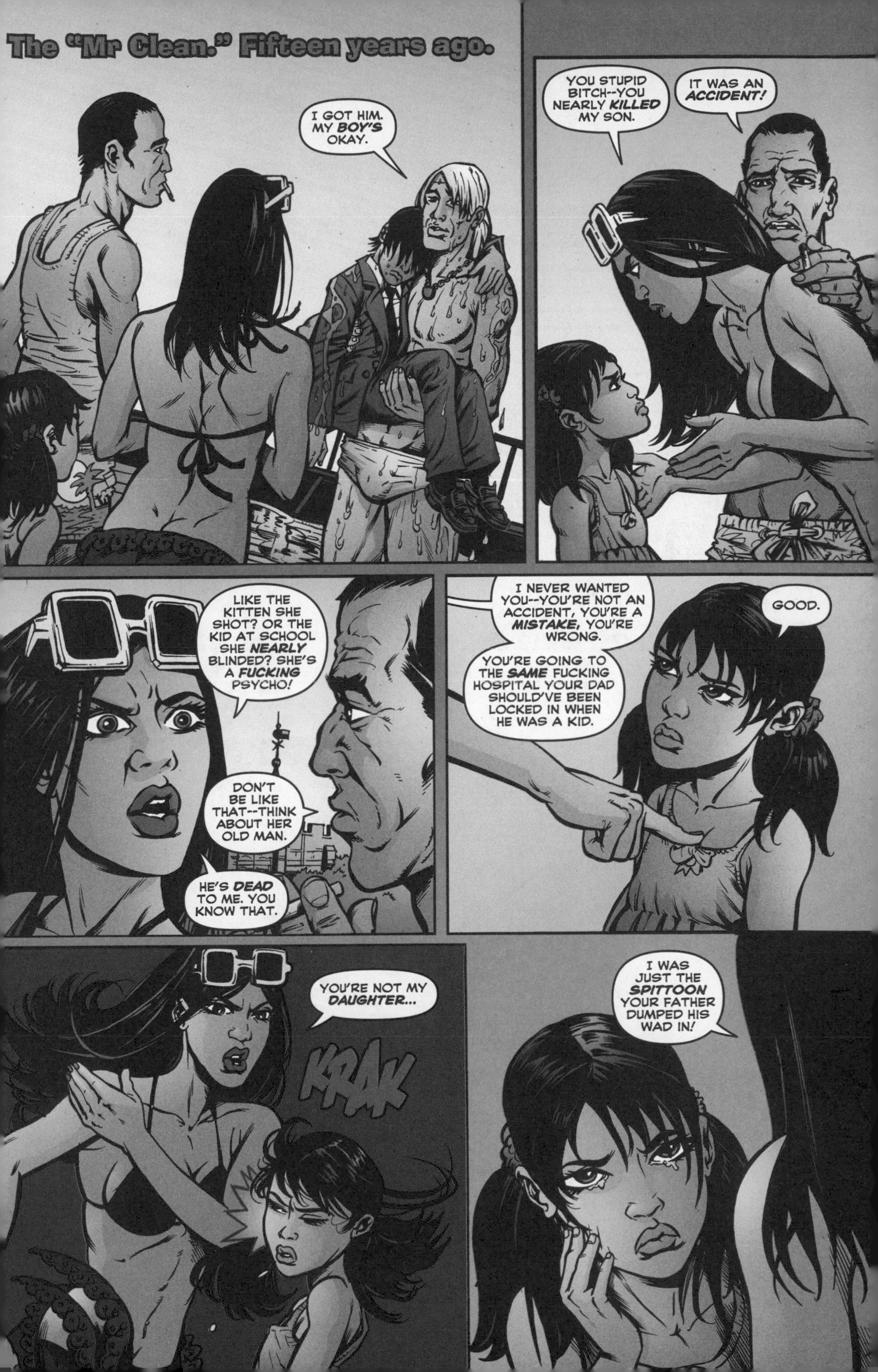
The "Mr Clean." Fifteen years ago.
I GOT HIM. MY BOY'S OKAY.
YOU STUPID BITCH--YOU NEARLY KILLED MY SON.
IT WAS AN ACCIDENT!
LIKE THE KITTEN SHE SHOT? OR THE KID AT SCHOOL SHE NEARLY BLINDED? SHE'S A FUCKING PSYCHO!
DON'T BE LIKE THAT--THINK ABOUT HER OLD MAN.
HE'S DEAD TO ME. YOU KNOW THAT.
I NEVER WANTED YOU--YOU'RE NOT AN ACCIDENT, YOU'RE A MISTAKE, YOU'RE WRONG.
YOU'RE GOING TO THE SAME FUCKING HOSPITAL YOUR DAD SHOULD'VE BEEN LOCKED IN WHEN HE WAS A KID.
GOOD.
YOU'RE NOT MY DAUGHTER...
KRAK
I WAS JUST THE SPITTOON YOUR FATHER DUMPED HIS WAD IN!

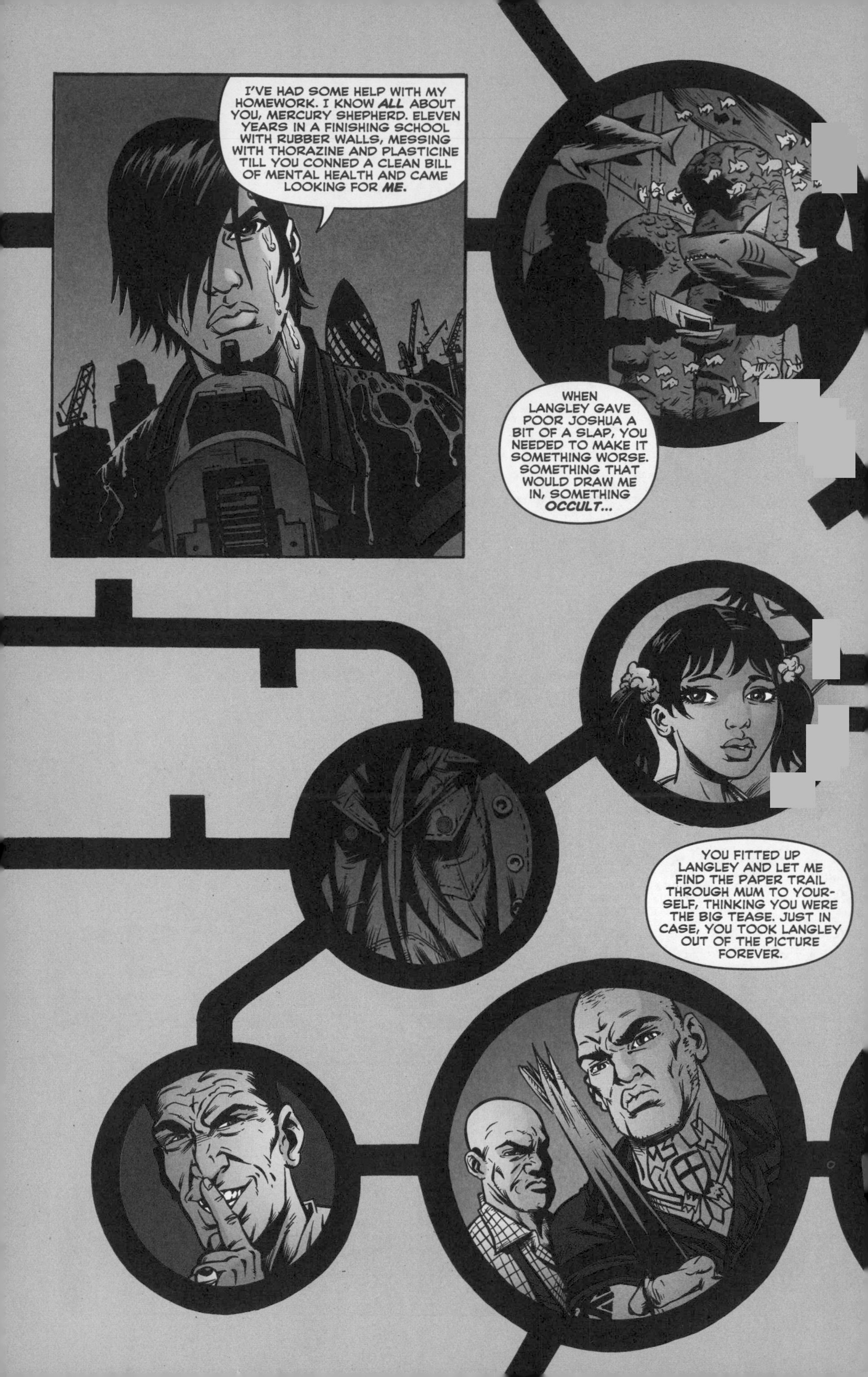
I'VE HAD SOME HELP WITH MY HOMEWORK. I KNOW ALL ABOUT YOU, MERCURY SHEPHERD. ELEVEN YEARS IN A FINISHING SCHOOL WITH RUBBER WALLS, MESSING WITH THORAZINE AND PLASTICINE TILL YOU CONNED A CLEAN BILL OF MENTAL HEALTH AND CAME LOOKING FOR ME.
WHEN LANGLEY GAVE POOR JOSHUA A BIT OF A SLAP, YOU NEEDED TO MAKE IT SOMETHING WORSE. SOMETHING THAT WOULD DRAW ME IN, SOMETHING OCCULT...
YOU FITTED UP LANGLEY AND LET ME FIND THE PAPER TRAIL THROUGH MUM TO YOURSELF, THINKING YOU WERE THE BIG TEASE. JUST IN CASE, YOU TOOK LANGLEY OUT OF THE PICTURE FOREVER.

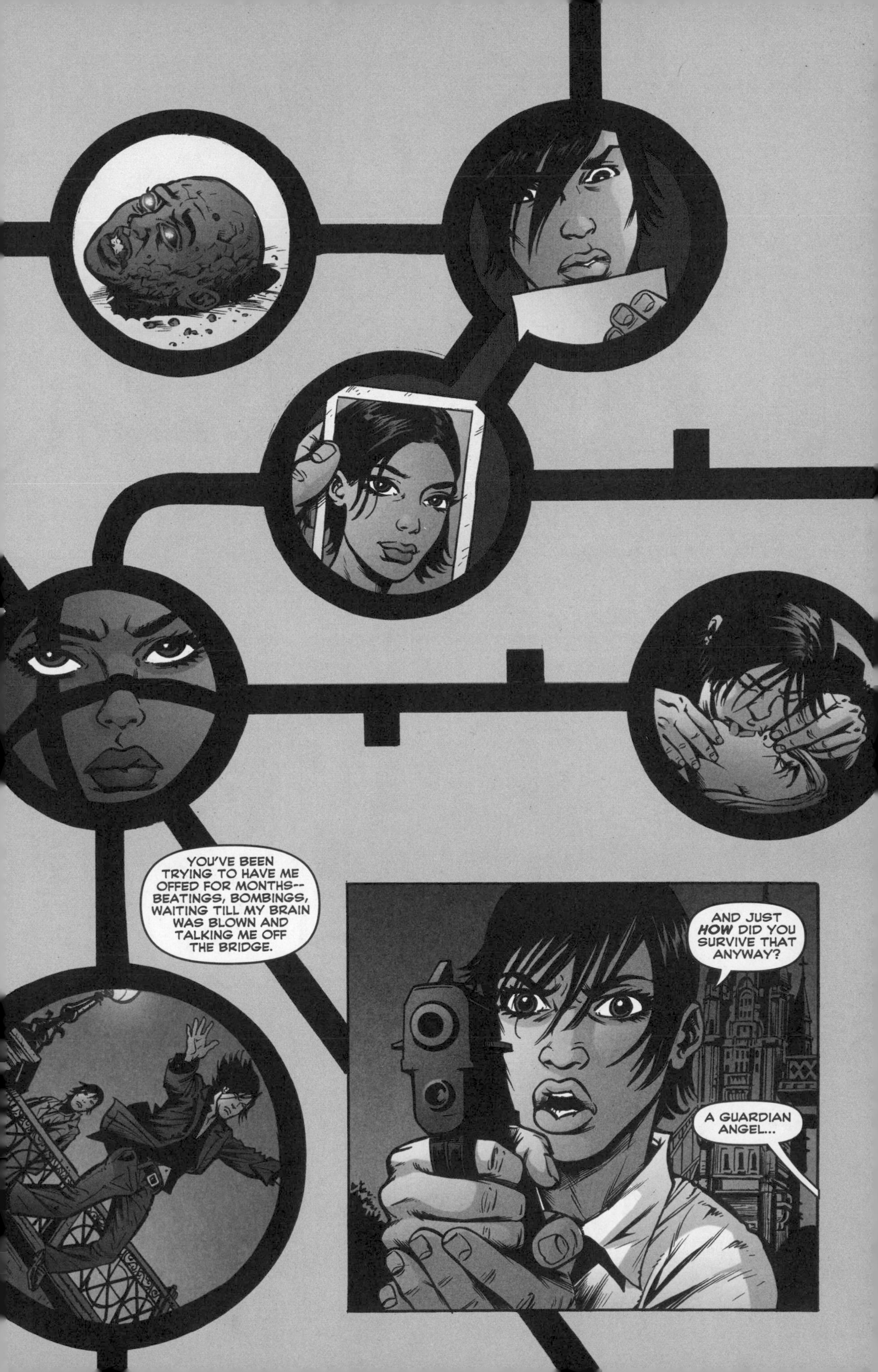
YOU'VE BEEN TRYING TO HAVE ME OFFED FOR MONTHS-- BEATINGS, BOMBINGS, WAITING TILL MY BRAIN WAS BLOWN AND TALKING ME OFF THE BRIDGE.
AND JUST *HOW* DID YOU SURVIVE THAT ANYWAY?
A GUARDIAN ANGEL...

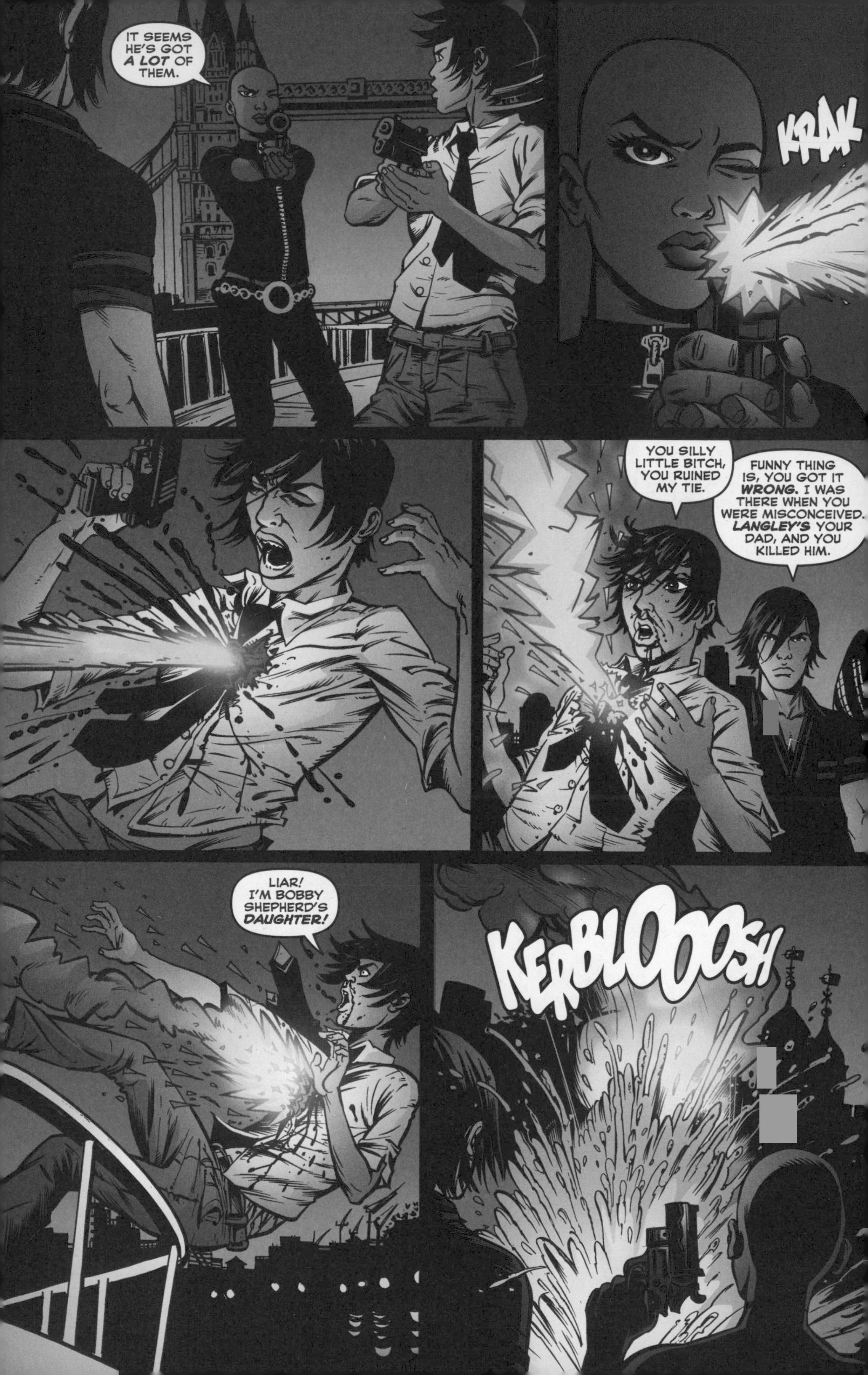
IT SEEMS HE'S GOT A LOT OF THEM.
KRAK
YOU SILLY LITTLE BITCH, YOU RUINED MY TIE.
FUNNY THING IS, YOU GOT IT WRONG. I WAS THERE WHEN YOU WERE MISCONCEIVED. LANGLEY'S YOUR DAD, AND YOU KILLED HIM.
LIAR! I'M BOBBY SHEPHERD'S DAUGHTER!
KERBLOOOSH

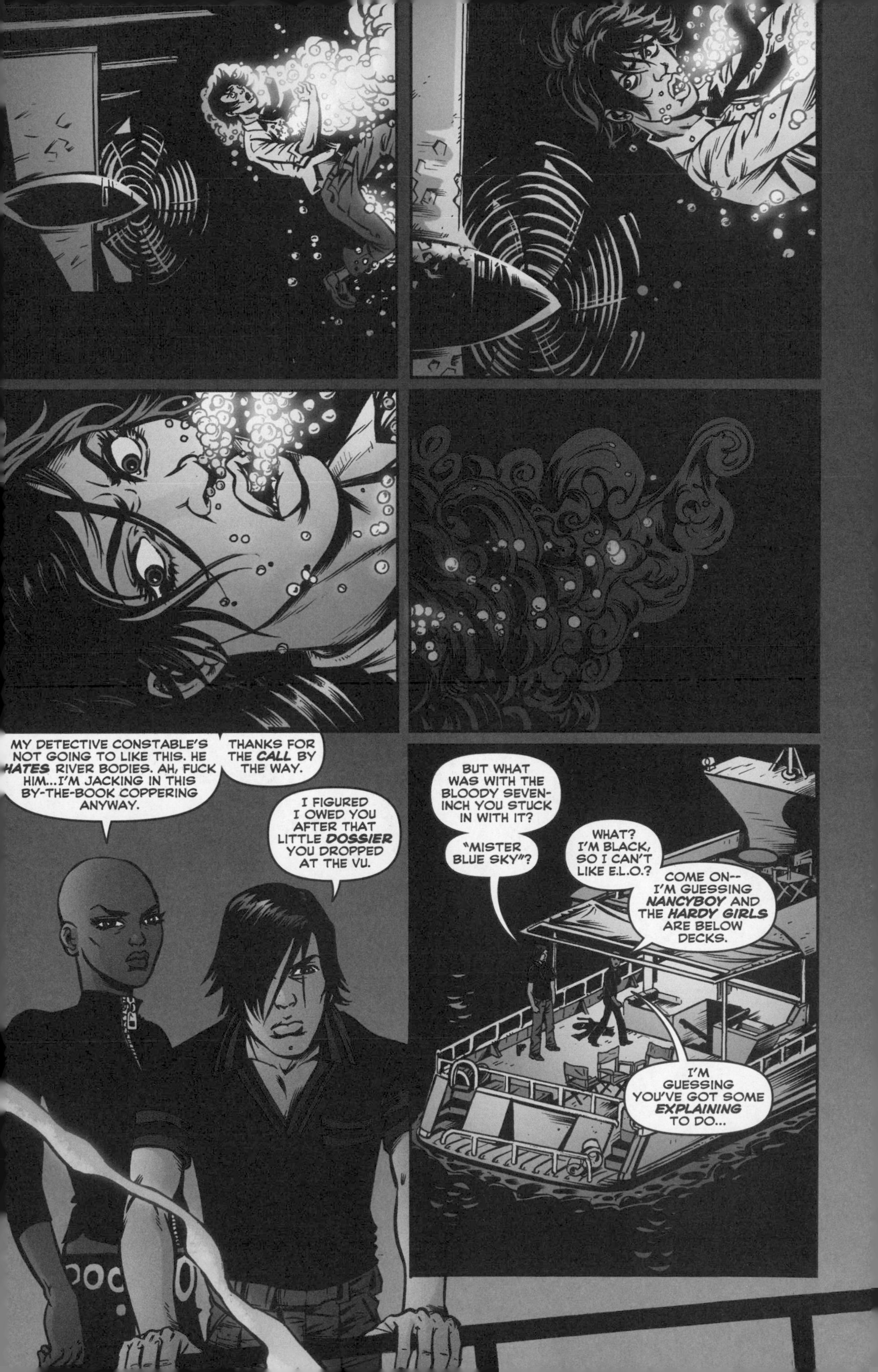
MY DETECTIVE CONSTABLE'S NOT GOING TO LIKE THIS. HE HATES RIVER BODIES. AH, FUCK HIM...I'M JACKING IN THIS BY-THE-BOOK COPPERING ANYWAY.
THANKS FOR THE CALL BY THE WAY.
I FIGURED I OWED YOU AFTER THAT LITTLE DOSSIER YOU DROPPED AT THE VU.
BUT WHAT WAS WITH THE BLOODY SEVEN-INCH YOU STUCK IN WITH IT?
"MISTER BLUE SKY"?
WHAT? I'M BLACK, SO I CAN'T LIKE E.L.O.?
COME ON-- I'M GUESSING NANCYBOY AND THE HARDY GIRLS ARE BELOW DECKS.
I'M GUESSING YOU'VE GOT SOME EXPLAINING TO DO...

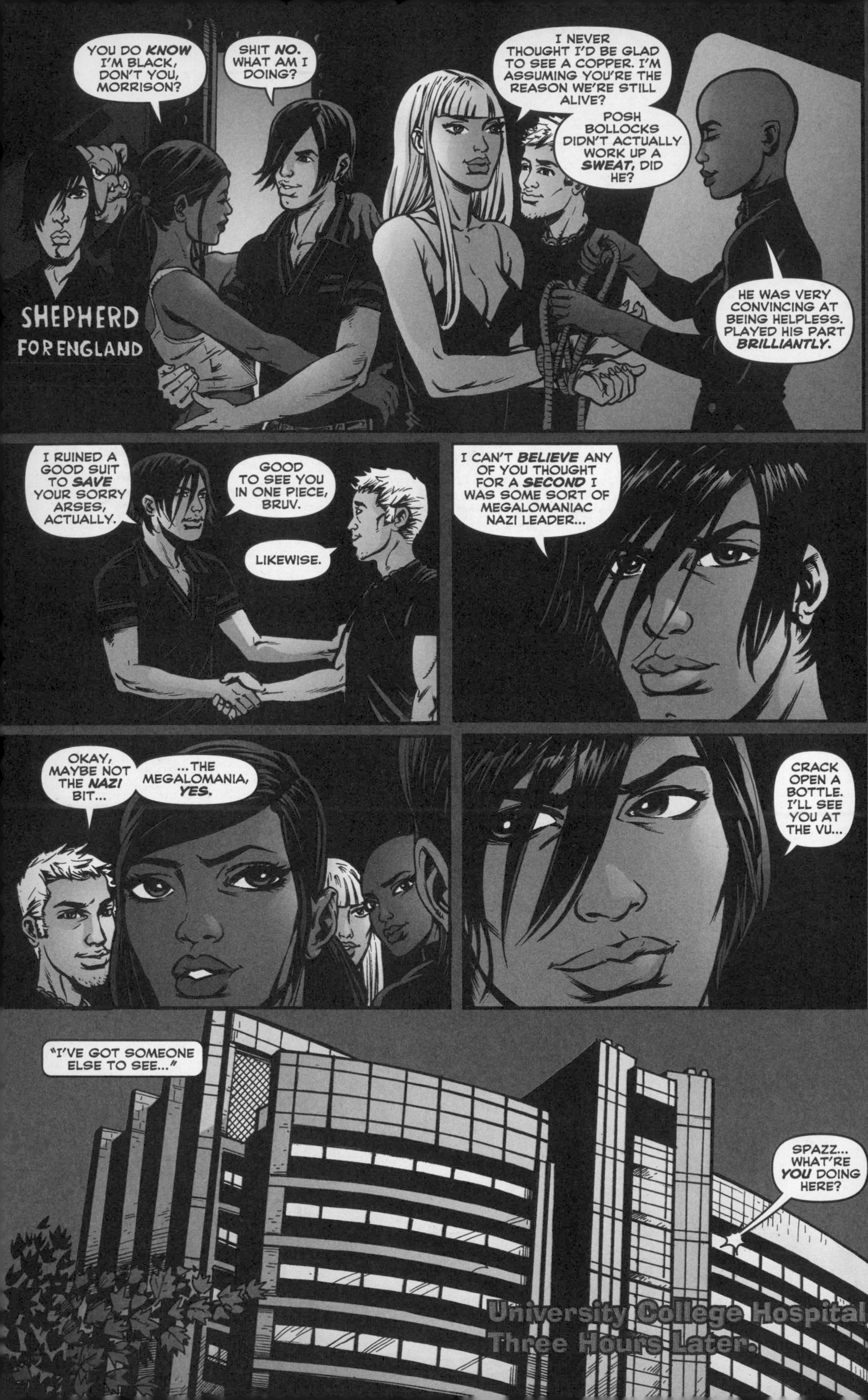

YOU DO KNOW I'M BLACK, DON'T YOU, MORRISON?
SHIT NO. WHAT AM I DOING?
SHEPHERD FORENGLAND
I NEVER THOUGHT I'D BE GLAD TO SEE A COPPER. I'M ASSUMING YOU'RE THE REASON WE'RE STILL ALIVE?
POSH BOLLOCKS DIDN'T ACTUALLY WORK UP A SWEAT, DID HE?
HE WAS VERY CONVINCING AT BEING HELPLESS. PLAYED HIS PART BRILLIANTLY.
I RUINED A GOOD SUIT TO SAVE YOUR SORRY ARSES, ACTUALLY.
GOOD TO SEE YOU IN ONE PIECE, BRUV.
LIKEWISE.
I CAN'T BELIEVE ANY OF YOU THOUGHT FOR A SECOND I WAS SOME SORT OF MEGALOMANIAC NAZI LEADER...
OKAY, MAYBE NOT THE NAZI BIT...
...THE MEGALOMANIA, YES.
CRACK OPEN A BOTTLE. I'LL SEE YOU AT THE VU...
"I'VE GOT SOMEONE ELSE TO SEE..."
SPAZZ... WHAT'RE YOU DOING HERE?
University College Hospital. Three Hours Later.

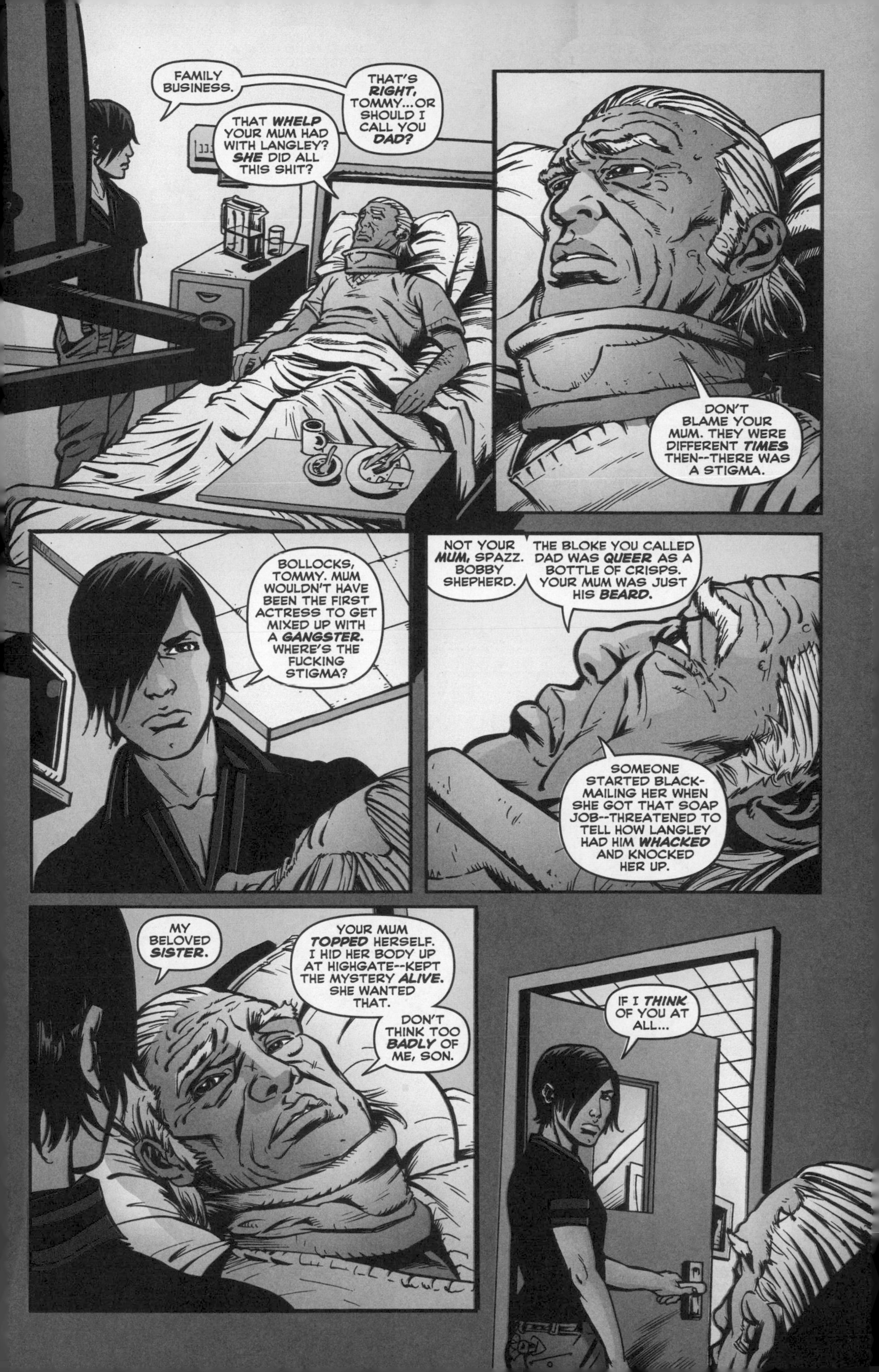
FAMILY BUSINESS.
THAT WHELP YOUR MUM HAD WITH LANGLEY? SHE DID ALL THIS SHIT?
THAT'S RIGHT, TOMMY...OR SHOULD I CALL YOU DAD?
DON'T BLAME YOUR MUM. THEY WERE DIFFERENT TIMES THEN--THERE WAS A STIGMA.
BOLLOCKS, TOMMY. MUM WOULDN'T HAVE BEEN THE FIRST ACTRESS TO GET MIXED UP WITH A GANGSTER. WHERE'S THE FUCKING STIGMA?
NOT YOUR MUM, SPAZZ. BOBBY SHEPHERD.
THE BLOKE YOU CALLED DAD WAS QUEER AS A BOTTLE OF CRISPS. YOUR MUM WAS JUST HIS BEARD.
SOMEONE STARTED BLACK-MAILING HER WHEN SHE GOT THAT SOAP JOB--THREATENED TO TELL HOW LANGLEY HAD HIM WHACKED AND KNOCKED HER UP.
MY BELOVED SISTER.
YOUR MUM TOPPED HERSELF. I HID HER BODY UP AT HIGHGATE--KEPT THE MYSTERY ALIVE. SHE WANTED THAT.
DON'T THINK TOO BADLY OF ME, SON.
IF I THINK OF YOU AT ALL...

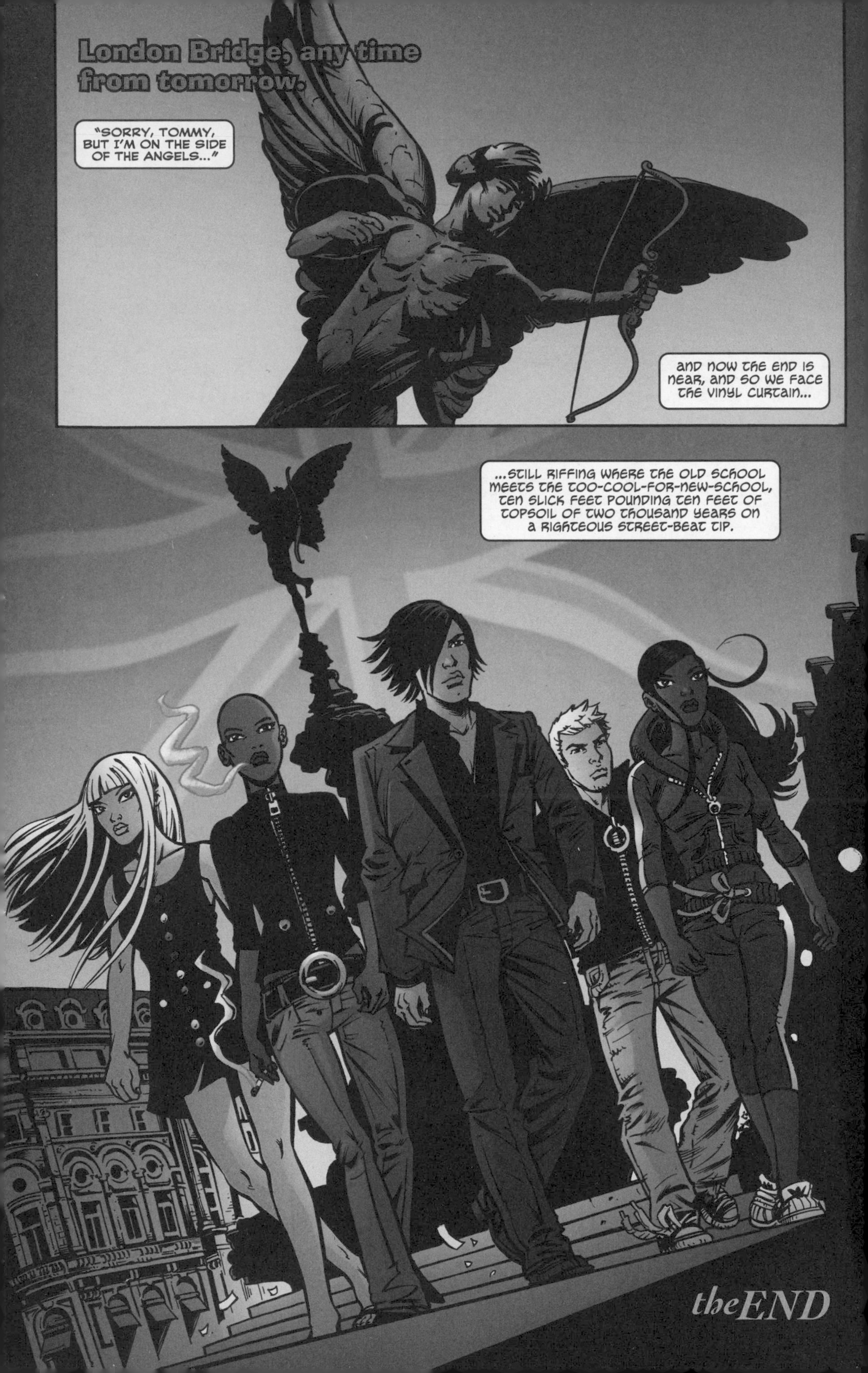
London Bridge, any time from tomorrow.
"SORRY, TOMMY, BUT I'M ON THE SIDE OF THE ANGELS..."
AND NOW THE END IS NEAR, AND SO WE FACE THE VINYL CURTAIN...
...STILL RIFFING WHERE THE OLD SCHOOL MEETS THE TOO-COOL-FOR-NEW-SCHOOL, TEN SLICK FEET POUNDING TEN FEET OF TOPSOIL OF TWO THOUSAND YEARS ON A RIGHTEOUS STREET-BEAT TIP.
theEND